Alternative Dispute Resolution
A Conflict Diagnosis Approach

Laurie S. Coltri

Department of Legal Studies

University of Maryland, University College

Prentice Hall

Boston   Columbus   Indianapolis   New York   San Francisco   Upper Saddle River   Amsterdam
Cape Town   Dubai   London   Madrid   Milan   Munich   Paris   Montreal   Toronto   Delhi
Mexico City   Sao Paulo   Sydney   Hong Kong   Seoul   Singapore   Taipei   Tokyo

Editor in Chief: Vernon Anthony
Acquisitions Editor: Gary Bauer
Editorial Assistant: Megan Heinz
Editorial Project Manager: Christina Taylor
Director of Marketing: David Gesell
Senior Marketing Manager: Leigh Ann Sims
Marketing Assistant: Les Roberts
Operations Specialist: Renata Butera
Creative Art Director: Jayne Conte
Cover Designer: Bruce Kenselaar
Manager, Visual Research: Beth Brenzel
Manager, Rights and Permissions:
  Zina Arabia

Senior Image Permission Coordinator:
  Cynthia Vincenti
**Manager, Cover Visual Research
  & Permissions:** Karen Sanatar
Cover Art: Getty Images, Inc.
Full-Service Project Management:
  Nitin Agarwal/Aptara®, Inc.
Composition: Aptara®, Inc.
Printer/Binder: Hamilton Printing Co.
Cover Printer: Lehigh-Phoenix
  Color/Hagerstown
Text Font: AGaramond

Credits and acknowledgments borrowed from other sources and reproduced, with permission, in this textbook appear on appropriate page within the text.

Many of the designations by manufacturers and seller to distinguish their products are claimed as trademarks. Where those designations appear in this book, and the publisher was aware of a trademark claim, the designations have been printed in initial caps or all caps.

Library of Congress Cataloging-in-Publication Data
Coltri, Laurie S.
   Alternative dispute resolution : a conflict diagnosis approach / Laurie S. Coltri.—2nd ed.
      p. cm.
   Includes bibliographical references and index.
   ISBN-13: 978-0-13-506406-1
   ISBN-10: 0-13-506406-6
   1. Dispute resolution (Law)   2. Mediation.   3. Conflict management.
   4. Arbitration and award.   5. Compromise (Law)   I. Title.
   K2390.C655 20XX
   303.6'9—dc22   2009002669

10 9 8 7 6 5 4 3 2 1

Prentice Hall
is an imprint of

PEARSON

www.pearsonhighered.com

ISBN-10:   0-13-506406-6
ISBN-13: 978-0-13-506406-1

To my father, who taught me to love learning

Contents

3   Mediation: An Introduction   57

4   The Law and Ethics of Mediation   106

5 Arbitration   154

6   Nonbinding Evaluation, Mixed (Hybrid), and Multimodal Dispute Resolution Processes   193

7   Putting It All Together: Selecting Optimal ADR Processes for Clients and Disputes   233

---

[1] Appendix B, which is taken from an earlier edition of the book, is located entirely online at *http://www. pearsonhighered.com/coltri*. Page references provided here are to the printed page numbers and are designated by the prefix B.

Preface

This readable, engaging book is your window into the exciting and explosively expanding field of alternative dispute resolution (ADR). Whether you plan to attend law school, look to a future career as a paralegal, or are considering becoming a professional mediator or arbitrator, this book will give you simply the best, most comprehensive introduction to these innovative and increasingly popular processes, as well as the facts about how and why they work.

Had you used one of the earliest undergraduate textbooks on ADR, you would have read descriptions of common ADR processes, but you would likely not have been given a clear and comprehensive explanation for the distinctions among these processes or for why, and when, some work better than others. The previous edition of this text was a departure from those early trends in focusing attention on how to choose an ADR process and how to predict what processes will work best in any given situation. It did so by introducing an effective and exciting method of learning about ADR. Called conflict diagnosis, this method is a series of hands-on skills you can use to become a masterful conflict manager and to select optimal strategies for resolving conflicts, whether your clients' or your own. In discovering and using these techniques, you gain an understanding of how each ADR process works, why they work, when each process is most effective, and the strengths and weaknesses of each.

The field of ADR is changing rapidly. Since the first edition of this book (*Conflict Diagnosis and Alternative Dispute Resolution*) was published in 2003, many of the trends it anticipated have played out in the legal field: Lawyers and judges are becoming increasingly aware of the benefits of many specific ADR processes and have become more and more sophisticated in their understanding of the strengths, weaknesses, and applications of these processes. By using this book to learn about ADR, you'll be ahead of the curve, situated in the crest of the market for ADR-sophisticated legal professionals.

WHAT'S NEW IN THE SECOND EDITION

This edition has been substantially restructured to make the textbook even more readable and useful, without sacrificing the first edition's successful formula for learning. Chapters 3 through 14 of the first edition, which described conflict diagnosis principles in great detail, have been moved online into this book's companion Web site at www.prenhall.com/coltri. They form an online reference accessible to all textbook users. In this edition, the highlights from these chapters have been updated, improved, and summarized in a single chapter—now Chapter 2. You have the opportunity to use the more comprehensive Web-based materials if you want to delve into components of conflict diagnosis that intrigue or seem especially pertinent to you, if the conflict diagnosis approach suits your learning process, or if something in the text seems to require further explanation. This reorganization results in a textbook that is more convenient, concise, and easy to handle in a single semester. The move to efficiency and economy is further promoted by the replacement of the first-edition appendices, all of which are readily available from stable online sources, with a single appendix referring the reader to the relevant Web links.

The other major changes involve a substantial updating of content throughout the text. ADR is one of the most rapidly evolving of all legal fields. Since the first edition of this textbook was published, a number of must-know developments in the field have taken place. For example, important elements of mediation and arbitration law have been settled, and there has been an enormous shake out in the domain of online dispute resolution (ODR). One important change is that so-called "nonadversarial," "facilitative" forms of dispute resolution (those that seek to promote empathy, mutual understanding, empowerment, and effective negotiation, rather than to pressure or coerce outcomes) have become much more accepted in mainstream legal work. It has been truly exciting to have been a mediator during mediation's early years in the 1980s and to be present in the twenty-first century to see its promise begin to come to fruition. At the same time, the issues that have churned around the move of ADR into the mainstream in the 1990s—whether it would become so much like the litigation it was replacing that it would lose its uniquely beneficial qualities—are not yet settled. So the first decade of the twenty-first century is still an exciting time to be an ADR professional. This new edition seeks to capture these developments.

FEATURES OF THE TEXTBOOK

As the reader, you'll find that the following features help you to learn about ADR in an atmosphere of fun and fascination:

- **Conflict diagnosis.** Key principles are now summarized in Chapter 2 with detailed material available online that provides the tools needed to understand ADR and manage and resolve conflicts effectively.
- **Definition boxes** throughout the text provide simple explanations for professional terminology.

- **Text box examples and illustrations of concepts** in the book will enrich your understanding.
- **End-of-chapter exercises** include thought-provoking projects designed to give you hands-on experience managing conflicts in your own life and work.
- **Numerous anecdotes** help make concepts and issues introduced in the text "come alive."
- **Role-play exercises** that illustrate the field and build skills are available in the Instructor's Manual.
- **Graphics, photos, and cartoon humor** are peppered throughout the book to help you stay focused and engaged.

A brief note about ADR terminology. ADR is a relatively new field, and, perhaps because of its rapid growth, it is marked by confusion over terminology. An effort has been made to identify and rigorously define ADR-related terms. To make for easier understanding, definitions provided in the chapters are accompanied by graphical icons that identify the field from which each term is taken:

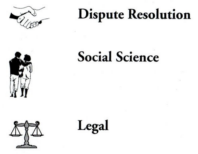

Dispute Resolution

Social Science

Legal

Technology

SUPPLEMENTS

Guidance and support for classroom and CLE courses include:

- An Instructor's Manual with lecture notes, tests, and additional cases
- PowerPoint Presentation aligned with each chapter

- Companion Web site with chapter objectives and quiz questions at *www. prenhall.com/coltri*.
- Online Appendix B, at the Companion Web site, *www.prenhall.com/ coltri* contains the entire, in-depth coverage of conflict diagnosis originally present in the first edition. The referencing and indexing of this online matter is included here, and designated by the prefix B in the table of contents and the index, and by italics in the reference lists.

ACKNOWLEDGMENTS

I feel honored and proud to have been a part of an interconnected web of dedicated, talented, and caring individuals, without whom this book, and its predecessor edition, would never have come into being.

Adelaide Lagnese, who was Director of Legal Studies at the University of Maryland, University College, when the idea for the first edition was conceived, believed in my vision and put me in touch with the editors of several publishers who could make it a reality. Without her, this book would have remained a vision unrealized.

Diane Bridge, co-creator of the alternative dispute resolution course that formed the basis for the book, is a woman of incredible energy, talent, intellect, assertiveness, and warmth. She has given me unwavering support that made it possible for me to juggle the demands of work, writing, and family life. Her voice wafts through this volume.

I am profoundly indebted to two groups of people and wish to salute them while respecting their privacy. The first are those who have been my mediation clients. Some of their stories are the basis for ideas and anecdotes that appear in this textbook. In the face of seemingly intractable situations, these courageous people have shown a creative genius and a tenacity that should be honored as heroic. The other group consists of my students, current and former. As with my former clients, some of my students' stories are adapted for use here, and like my clients, a great many of my students have struggled against, and overcome, challenges that I, a person of relative privilege, cannot imagine. Both my clients and my students have been my most important teachers. They constantly remind me of the messy diversity of real life, of the need to get and be real, of the extraordinary courage of ordinary people, and of the constant need to transcend egocentrism. Those who see the outlines of their own experiences in these pages are witness to the profound influence they have on me: Their experiences have been my guides and have become part of me.

One group provided pointed feedback on every topic in this book. This group brought focus to the content of this work, particularly the first edition. These people include, but are not limited to, Linda Cabral Marrero, Mercy College; Otis Grant, Indiana University-South Bend; and David J. White, Southern

Missouri State University-West Plains. Ellen Kandell of Catholic University has also provided invaluable feedback, which is reflected in the second edition.

I wish to especially pay tribute to my two mentors in the alternative dispute resolution field: Elizabeth Koopman and Joan Hunt. Elizabeth Koopman is a true visionary of incredible strength, creativity, and intellectual prowess. Her unwavering sense of right and wrong is a model for everyone whose lives she has touched. I aspire to be even a shadow of the positive force she exerts on Earth; and even now, after time and distance have separated us, her good works touch me every day in the work I do and the thoughts I think. Elizabeth deserves a place in the pantheon of leading lights of the dispute resolution field. Fiercely principled, Elizabeth is willing to sacrifice everything to do what is right. She has paid dearly for her integrity, and I profoundly hope that this book stands as a tribute to her.

Joan Hunt, who passed away in the spring of 2003, was my academic advisor and my guide throughout graduate school. She was a person of such astounding fidelity, integrity, intellectual prowess, warmth, and iron resolve that everyone around her inevitably became a better person. She, above all others, taught me how to take the perspective of others, which is perhaps the single most important conflict-management skill one can acquire.

I also wish to express my gratitude to Pat Martin, a colleague at University of Maryland, who has also become like family to me, and I would like to honor her; her husband, John Caughey; and their daughter, Ananda. In addition, I would like to honor Guy Williams and Edith Thompson for their important contributions to this book.

In addition, I express my gratitude to four people who have been especially important to me during the development of the second edition. Paige Getty possesses incredible wisdom about human interaction, which has amazed me since we became acquainted in 2004; she has challenged me to live and test the ideas in this textbook, and my work with her has led to refinement of many of the ideas presented here, especially in Chapter 2. Tom Benjamin, while known to the larger world as a composer and choral music director, is a conflict manager of tremendous virtuosity and the best pedagogue I've ever known; he has given me wonderful music to enjoy and help sing, generous friendship, and incredible emotional support; his energy in the service of love and generosity is a goal to which all would do well to aspire. Marjorie Seidman has generously stepped in as a friend, inexhaustible fellow volunteer, and occasional "substitute mommy" to my inner child; she is also an amazing diplomat and models many of the ideas in this book; I can't imagine life without her. And April Lee, a metaphorical warrior in the service of love and justice, serves as a constant reminder of what work in conflict resolution is all about; she challenges my assumptions, helps me to remember the real people hidden in theories and ideas, and simply gives endlessly of herself. The friendship of each of these four people has become very dear to me, and without their caring support I could not have produced this new edition.

The members of my family have made many sacrifices to allow me the time and space to complete this textbook's first edition, and then they had to go through it all again when the second edition was developed. My mother, Ruth Schalit, and my brother, Mark, are a well of daily love and support that I feel even when we don't speak. Ruth, in particular, is my tireless cheering section. Julia and Robin, my two wonderful (and no longer little) children, have had to put up with a lot—a mom absent from school activities, inconsistent guidance and supervision, mom's bad moods and writer's blocks, and incomprehensible dinner conversation, just to name some of the discomforts of living with an author. Julia has been a source of constant and quiet love, wisdom, and sophisticated insight greatly beyond her years; she has grown into a young woman of tremendous empathy, courage, and eloquence. Robin has always been there for me with a smile, a hug, and a compliment when I most needed it. Julia and Robin have taught me many things, and they continue to teach me how to love and be loved. I also wish to thank my late father, Mike Schalit, to whom this book is dedicated. Mike lived long enough to see the publication of the first edition of this book but died before he had a chance to read it. His joy in teaching and learning, his gentle and peaceful nature, and his quiet support and love, have been an inspiration to me throughout my life.

My loving husband, Alan, has been perhaps the most indispensable to me of all. He has been mother and father to our children, fearless driving instructor to Julia, cook and housekeeper, technical advisor, sounding board, list keeper, vignette source, and emotional support person. All of it has been done in his spare time after his increasingly demanding workday—and not for financial gain but simply because he knew that spreading the word about effective conflict management is my life aspiration. He has had to endure the development of both editions of this textbook, with all the unavailability of time and emotion that such projects entail. As if that weren't enough, he has also had to endure my recent foray into organizational conflict management, as well as my new obsession with choral singing. A greater demonstration of love, strength, and determination cannot be imagined. When I was twenty and single, waiting to take the elevator to work, I used to imagine that my dream-husband-to-be was waiting for me on the other side of the door. But in my wildest and most romantic dreams, I could not have cooked up Alan, nor the magical path we have taken together.

About the Author

Laurie S. Coltri was born and raised in Los Angeles, California. She received her bachelor's degree in English from the California Institute of Technology, in Pasadena, California, in 1974. Thereafter, she attended law school at the University of Southern California, graduating with a J.D. in 1979.

After several years of general law practice specializing in complex case trial work and legal research and writing, Coltri and her legal advocacy career came to a parting of the ways. In the early 1980s, after moving to Maryland, she began taking courses in divorce mediation, receiving a graduate concentration in the field from the University of Maryland at College Park in 1984. Coltri was one of the first private mediators practicing in the state. She mediated virtually the first court-referred child custody case in the Maryland trial courts in the mid-1980s and directed a telephone-based visitation mediation service for the Prince George's County Department of Child Support Enforcement in 1989–1990.

Returning to graduate school, Coltri received her doctorate in Human Development from the University of Maryland, College Park, in 1995. Her graduate work focused on the resolution of conflict and the impact of dispute resolution processes on individual development. Since 1996, Dr. Coltri, a Professor of Legal Studies, has taught at the highly regarded program offered by the University of Maryland, University College. She has received the university's Teaching Recognition Award for her work and has published several articles and book chapters in the field of Alternative Dispute Resolution.

Dr. Coltri shares a home in Columbia, Maryland, with her husband, Alan; their daughters, Julia and Robin, born in 1990 and 1994; and an assortment of slightly offbeat animal companions. In her spare time, she enjoys choral singing and cooking.

Photo Credits

1

Defining Terms

All men are caught in an inescapable network of mutuality.

—Martin Luther King, Jr.

In this chapter, you will learn . . .

- ◆ what an interpersonal conflict, a dispute, and a transaction are.
- ◆ who the participants in a conflict are.
- ◆ what the basic varieties of dispute resolution are.

Interpersonal conflict
a state of interrelationship between persons or groups in which one or more of one participant's goals are actually or apparently in opposition to those of another participant.

Dispute resolution
the methods that people use in an effort to resolve interpersonal conflicts. In this book, dispute resolution will not include physical violence, war, or extralegal approaches such as assault, bribery, and extortion.

Alternative dispute resolution (ADR)
methods of dispute resolution other than negotiation and litigation.

This book is about processes used to manage and resolve conflict. The term *conflict* conjures up many images, ranging all the way from an individual's private indecision about trivial matters to world wars. When legal professionals (lawyers, paralegals and legal assistants, judges, mediators, arbitrators, evaluators, etc.) use the term, they generally mean one of three things: that another attorney in the office has a conflict of interest in a case, that there is a controversy over which jurisdiction's law will apply, or that a client has a disagreement with another party. It is this third meaning—**interpersonal conflict**—dealt with by the processes described in this book.

Legal professionals spend their careers dealing with interpersonal conflict: They negotiate contracts (to avoid future disputes), assist clients with transactions, and act as their advocates when disputes arise. Thus, in a sense, legal professionals are *conflict experts.* In the recent past, the expertise required of legal professionals to deal with interpersonal conflict has expanded considerably. A generation ago, the typical lawyer would have said that it was her job to know the law and to know how to litigate effectively (and, perhaps, how to win at negotiation). However, today increasing numbers of legal professionals would add that they also need to be able to pick from, and effectively represent a client during, a dizzying array of alternative processes for **dispute resolution**, or resolving conflict. These processes, commonly known as **alternative dispute resolution (ADR)**, include mediation, arbitration, summary jury trial, neutral evaluation and many others.

DEFINITIONS

The field of alternative dispute resolution is characterized by widespread confusion about terminology. This confusion impedes our exploration of how conflict resolution can best occur. For this reason, it is important to begin by defining some essential terms that describe the kinds of interpersonal conflict, the participants in conflict, and the main varieties of processes used to deal with conflict.

WHAT IS INTERPERSONAL CONFLICT?

We adopt the definition of leading conflict scholar Stella Ting-Toomey:

> [interpersonal conflict is defined as] the perceived and/or actual incompatibilities of needs, interests, and/or goals between two [or more] interdependent parties *(Trubisky, Ting-Toomey, and Lin 1991, 66)*

Interpersonal conflict is ubiquitous to everyday life. Pearson Education/PH College.

What does Ting-Toomey mean by "incompatibilities of needs, interests, and/or goals" in this definition? She probably means something like the following examples:

Linda wants to buy a computer for no more than $600; the seller wants to sell for no less than $800. Here the price goals are incompatible: Since there is a disagreement over who will eventually have the $200 in dispute, there is a conflict here over the *allocation of resources.*

Pat Patient believes he was harmed by the negligence of Doreen Delacourt, M.D., and wants money damages for the injuries. Dr. Delacourt believes she was not negligent and does not want to pay Pat. Here, there are two readily identifiable sources of conflict: Pat wants Delacourt adjudged negligent, and Delacourt does not (thus, there is a *dispute over the application of law,* and, perhaps, a *dispute about facts*), and Pat wants monetary damages from Delacourt, which Delacourt doesn't want to pay (a *resource conflict*).

ABC Company leaders want the corporation to merge with XYZ Company and receive $1 million in the bargain. XYZ leaders do not feel ABC should receive monetary compensation. Here both entities' leaders want to complete a merger, but there is a goals incompatibility: whether ABC should receive monetary compensation (again, a *conflict over resources*).

Several elements of Ting-Toomey's definition bear closer scrutiny. First, the incompatibilities creating conflict need not be known by all parties who have them. Thus, an interpersonal conflict may be **latent conflict** (a situation in which incompatibilities exist, but are not recognized) or **partially latent conflict** (a situation in which some, but not all, parties to the conflict recognize that they have incompatible goals, interests, or needs). We'll call a conflict where all the participants are aware of compatibilities an **active conflict**. Here's an example of a latent conflict:

Dave and Dora have decided to go out to dinner together. Unbeknownst to either one of them, Dave prefers to go to a Chinese restaurant, and Dora prefers to go to an Indian restaurant.

Conflicts may even be simultaneously active and latent—here's how: A **displaced conflict** is one in which participants focus on one set of incompatibilities, but a different set of incompatibilities are hidden and impede resolution of the perceived conflict. (An example would be romantic partners who are arguing over some apparently trivial matter, such as which saucepan to use to cook soup, when the underlying issue is something more crucial, such as the spouses being unsatisfied with role allocations within the marriage.) In a variant of displaced conflict, called **misattributed conflict**, the driving-force incompatibilities involve some person or group who has not been consciously identified as being involved in the conflict. Misattributed conflicts often occur when a person has a conflict with a more powerful other and unconsciously misdirects his or her ire against a less powerful bystander—for example, a poorly managed employee might pick fights with other low-level employees rather than taking on his supervisor.

Latent conflict

an interpersonal conflict of which no disputing party in the conflict is aware.

Partially latent conflict

an interpersonal conflict of which some, but not all, of the disputing parties are aware.

Active conflict

an interpersonal conflict in which disputing parties are all aware of incompatibilities of interests, needs, and goals that exist between one another.

Displaced conflict

an interpersonal conflict in which there are actual incompatibilities of goals, interests, and/or needs, but the participants do not perceive them; instead, they perceive a different and minimally relevant or erroneous set of incompatible goals, needs, or interests.

Misattributed conflict

a variant of displaced conflict in which one or more of the disputing parties is, in reality, in a latent conflict with a third party, and this latent conflict is being masked by the conflict among the disputing parties.

False conflict

an interpersonal conflict in which there is an erroneous perception on the part of one or both disputing parties that their goals and/or needs are incompatible and in opposition. Sometimes referred to as *unrealistic conflict.*

True conflict

an interpersonal conflict in which there are actual incompatibilities of goals, values, and/or needs. Sometimes referred to as *realistic conflict.*

Conflict escalation

a situation in which an interpersonal conflict becomes successively more competitive and marked by impasse, spreading, intensification, and heightened animosity among participants against members of "the other side."

Second, there may appear to be incompatibilities, but this appearance may be illusory, creating a **false conflict** (also known as an **unrealistic conflict**, Zuzofski 2000). The opposite of a false conflict is a **true conflict** or **realistic conflict**—a situation in which the incompatibilities are real.

The following is an example of a false conflict:

Dean and Debbie are also planning to go out to dinner together. Dean and Debbie both want to have Japanese food. However, Dean mistakenly believes Debbie wants to go out for Italian food, and Debbie mistakenly believes Dean wants to go out for Mexican food.

This false conflict example seems silly—after all, the parties have only to talk to each other to clear up the problem—but in real-life legal conflicts, serious communication gaps attributable to the damaging effects of **conflict escalation** (a topic discussed in Chapter 2) can prevent the clarification of goals.

Transactions, such as this one in which Admiral Perry sought to negotiate a trade agreement with the Japanese, are interpersonal conflicts because of the presence of incompatible goals of their participants. Gessan Ogata, Courtesy United States Naval Marine Museum.

Third, the presence of incompatibilities among conflict participants does not preclude the existence of complimentary, compatible goals, values, and needs. For example, in the preceding merger example, leadership at both corporations want a corporate merger. Even in the medical malpractice example, it is likely that both disputants want to resolve the conflict without expending unnecessary time and money on a protracted lawsuit. Indeed, virtually all relationships between persons and organizations have both complimentary, mutually compatible goals and incompatible goals. A conflict in which the primary focus of the parties is to address a perceived incompatibility, or to repair or seek

Dispute

non-latent interpersonal conflict, characterized by the disputants' emphasis and concentration on incompatible needs, goals, and interests.

Transaction

a situation in which parties wish to create gains by creating a new relationship or alter an existing relationship.

Disputant

a person, corporation, or other entity who has the actual or perceived incompatibilities of goals, needs, and/or interests with another participant that define an interpersonal conflict.

Agent

an individual or entity that stands in the shoes of a disputant during an interpersonal conflict. For example, if a corporate entity is involved in a conflict, and its executive vice president is sent to participate in a negotiation session, the latter is acting as an agent.

Advocate

a special form of agent who is required to adhere to ethical standards mandating that he or she vigorously and competently represents and advances the interests of the disputants he or she represents. For example, attorneys are advocates when they act on behalf of their clients.

redress for harm coming from such an incompatibility, is called a **dispute**. (The malpractice anecdote is an example.) But when the primary objective of the participants is to seek gain by creating a relationship or modifying an existing one, it is known as a **transaction**. For example, potential business partners engage in a transaction when they wish to create a partnership, allocate responsibilities and revenues between partners, choose a form of business ownership, decide on a primary location for the business, and so on. The basic thrust of the relationship is to create mutual gain; yet such parties nearly always have incompatible goals, such as the share of the profits that will be allocated to each, making such transactions interpersonal conflicts. Legal professionals who focus on trial work mainly see disputes, whereas those who handle business clients and do not do trial work mainly see transactions.

It should be noted that a dispute may be a true conflict or a false conflict, but it cannot be latent (depending as it does on disputant perception that there are incompatibilities). A transaction may be a true or a false conflict (and even, though very rarely, a nonconflict), and it may also be latent if some or all participants are unaware of incompatibilities of goals, interests, or needs that are present.

Figure 1-1 shows the conceptual relationships between interpersonal conflict and nonconflict; latent, active, displaced and misattributed conflict; true/realistic and false conflict; and disputes and transactions.

PARTICIPANTS IN CONFLICTS

Every conflict involves two or more persons or organizations with incompatible goals, interests, or needs. They are called **disputants**. However, conflicts may involve others, including agents, advocates, neutrals, and constituents or stakeholders. Persons who act for a disputant—who stand in their shoes—are called **agents**. For example, if you are negotiating a deal with Nancy, and you send your brother Bob to negotiate in your place, Bob is your agent. **Advocates** are agents who have a special ethical obligation to zealously advance the interests of the disputant they represent. For most people, lawyers are the most familiar of all advocates. Some conflicts also involve neutrals. A **neutral** in this context is a person who is not affiliated with either disputant and who has a hand in managing or resolving the conflict. Neutrals can include judges, governmental hearing examiners (who act like judges in agency hearings), and many ADR practitioners. Finally, most conflicts affect bystanders; and bystanders, in turn, will affect the course and outcome of many conflicts. A person who is not a disputant, agent, or neutral, and who is affected by or who may affect the course and outcome of a conflict, is called a **constituent or stakeholder**. The term *constituent* is also sometimes used to refer to individuals who, taken collectively, form an organizational disputant for whom an agent is acting. For example, the public is comprised of the constituents for whom a legislator acts when transacting the business of representative government.

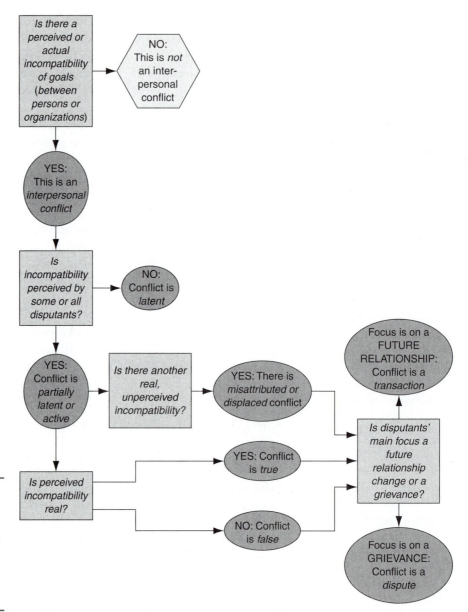

◆ **FIGURE 1-1**

Forms of Interpersonal Conflict: A Conceptual Diagram

Neutral

a third party who adjudicates a dispute or assists the disputants and/or their agents and advocates in resolving an interpersonal conflict.

Constituent or stakeholder

a person, other than a disputant, agent, or advocate, whose interests, goals, or needs, are, or might be, affected by an interpersonal conflict. The term *constituent* is also sometimes used to refer to a member of a group of disputants represented by an agent or advocate, and it is often used in a political context.

A conflict map or sociogram, showing a typical complex conflict, is shown in Figure 1-2.

Conflicts, particularly those that have become heated and difficult to resolve, often have multiple loci, much as a large thunderstorm may consist of numerous smaller thunderstorm cells aggregated into one large mass. In these super-

◆ **FIGURE 1-2**

A Conflict Map, or Sociogram

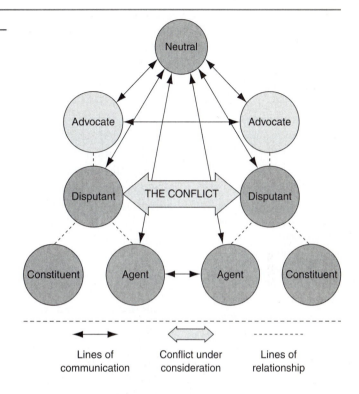

conflicts, parties playing one role in one conflict will often play another role in another related conflict. For example, consider Ed's comments to his lawyer:

> I've come to you because I'm being evicted from my property, where I have operated a printing business for fifteen years. The landlord gave me written notice two days ago that he's terminating the lease. He says it's because he needs the space for other purposes, but I'm sure it's because of the ruckus the local environmental advocacy group is putting up on the sidewalk, trying to get me to change my inks to a more expensive, nonpolluting type.

Clearly in this conflict, Ed has a conflict with the landlord—who has given him an eviction notice. If Ed's lawyer decides that Ed needs to sue to retain his lease, he'll have to sue the landlord. So in that dispute, Ed and the landlord are disputants. However, Ed also has a conflict with the environmental advocacy group, and in the latter conflict, the landlord is a constituent or stakeholder.

A TYPOLOGY OF DISPUTE RESOLUTION

The ways that people deal with conflict are known broadly as *dispute resolution.* There are a virtual rainbow of possible ways to address conflicts and disputes. Conflicts and disputes can be dealt with in virtually limitless ways, but in this book we will limit ourselves to those forms of dispute resolution that are commonly used to address disputes and transactions in legal, business, and other

Negotiation
a process in which disputants seek to resolve an interpersonal conflict through some form of dialogue or communication. In negotiation, the disputants themselves decide mutually whether, and on what terms, the conflict should be resolved.

Adjudication
any form of dispute resolution in which the disputants submit their interpersonal conflict to a third party, and in which the third party has the power to issue a decision binding on the disputants.

Unassisted or simple negotiation
negotiation in which the only participants are the disputants.

Facilitated or assisted negotiation
any form of negotiation in which the disputants are assisted by nondisputants.

Agent- or advocate-assisted negotiation
negotiation in which one or more disputants are represented by individuals who act on the disputants' behalf. The disputants retain the ultimate authority to accept or reject a settlement.

civil interpersonal settings. We will exclude from discussion physically violent, extralegal and illegal forms of dispute resolution, such as war, assault, extortion, and similar processes.

We begin by dividing the universe of dispute resolution processes according to who has control of the outcome of the dispute. In **negotiation**, disputants (or their representatives) engage in a dialogue aimed at settling or resolving the conflict. The dialogue may be verbal and face-to-face or telephone-based, written, or conducted while using one of the many modern technologies available for communication purposes, such as e-mail, instant messaging, or videoconferencing. The disputants are in control of the outcome of the conflict: *It is their decision whether to settle.* The other broad type of dispute resolution process is **adjudication**, which is distinguished from negotiation in that a neutral third party, rather than the disputants, determines the outcome, which is binding on the disputants.

Let's return to negotiation to examine its subtypes. Negotiation may be assisted or unassisted. In **unassisted negotiation**, also referred to as **simple negotiation**, the disputants are the only participants. Negotiation may also be **facilitated** or **assisted**, with three principal variations. The most common form of assisted negotiation, at least in the United States, is **agent-** or **advocate-assisted negotiation**, in which one or more of the disputants is represented by one or more persons (such as his or her lawyer) who "stand in the shoes" of the disputant and negotiate on his or her behalf. **Mediation**, the second variety of assisted negotiation, is an ADR process in which the disputants' negotiation is facilitated by a neutral called a **mediator**. The mediator's role is to help the disputants in their negotiation; the latter retain all control over whether to settle their conflict and over the details of their settlement. The disputants may attend mediation on their own, they may attend with their agents or advocates, or their representatives may mediate in their place. Mediation itself is a highly diverse process, with each variation having important uses, strengths, and weaknesses. These variations will be considered in detail in Chapter 3. The third variety of facilitated or assisted negotiation is **nonbinding evaluation**. The disputants (either on their own or, more commonly, represented by advocates or other agents) present their side of the dispute to a third party or panel of third parties. The third party is usually neutral, but in some variants of nonbinding evaluation, the neutral is a panel comprised of groups of persons who are directly interested in the outcome (such as directors or executive officers for corporate disputants). In a proceeding that often resembles a court hearing or trial, the third party renders a decision or opinion about the appropriate or expected outcome of the conflict, or an opinion about the strengths and weaknesses of each disputant's legal case, but this decision or opinion is not binding on the disputants as it is in a lawsuit. In some subtypes of this form of negotiation, the evaluation is followed by attempts to settle the dispute. Disputants use the outcome of nonbinding evaluation as information to assist them in their continuing negotiations. ADR includes several subtypes of nonbinding evaluation, the most popular of which are described in detail in Chapter 6.

Mediation

a form of facilitated or assisted negotiation in which the disputants, either alone or assisted by agents or advocates, negotiate in the presence of a neutral professional (or panel of professionals) called a *mediator* (or mediation panel). The role of the mediator is to assist the disputants in their negotiation.

Nonbinding evaluation

a form of assisted negotiation in which the disputants present their interpersonal conflict to a third party or a panel of third parties. The role of the third party is to render a nonbinding opinion, evaluation, or decision about the conflict. Sometimes considered a *mixed* or *hybrid* dispute resolution process.

Litigation

an adjudication process that proceeds under the auspices of state or federal law in a court.

Agency adjudication

an adjudication process that proceeds under the auspices of agency law or regulation and features an adjudicator and adjudicatory procedures specific to that agency.

Administrative hearing

hearing presided over by a neutral hearing examiner and attended by disputants and/or their advocates in which a dispute within the jurisdiction of a governmental agency is adjudicated.

In contrast to negotiation processes, adjudication processes feature a neutral third party who determines outcome. The most widely recognized form of adjudication is **litigation**. Litigation is the adjudication of an interpersonal conflict under the auspices of a court system and is characterized, in many Western countries, by a formalized and ritualized adversarial procedure, including carefully prescribed rules of evidence and procedure designed to ensure fairness. The law also creates adjudicatory processes for agencies. **Agency adjudication** is generally, though not always, somewhat less formal and complex than litigation. For example, laws in many states provide that drivers who accumulate too many traffic tickets may have their licenses suspended or revoked, and this process of suspension or revocation is usually done through an **administrative hearing** process performed by the state agency charged with regulating motor vehicles. The third type of adjudication is an ADR process called **arbitration**. It fits the classic definition of adjudication, in that the disputants present their cases to a neutral, called an *arbitrator,* who issues a binding decision in the matter. Unlike governmentally mandated adjudication, though, arbitration occurs because disputants have entered into a legally binding contract that it take place, either in advance of a dispute, in an effort to manage future conflicts (known as *executory arbitration*), or after the dispute has arisen (known as *ad-hoc arbitration*). (Arbitration, including executory arbitration and ad-hoc arbitration, is discussed in

Arbitration

a form of adjudication in which the decision to adjudicate is made by contract between the disputants. The agreement to arbitrate may be made either in advance of any dispute arising (see *executory arbitration* in Chapter 5) or after the dispute arises (see *ad hoc arbitration* in Chapter 5).

Mixed or hybrid dispute resolution process

any one of a number of ADR processes that feature a combination of two or more basic dispute resolution processes.

Multimodal dispute resolution

a system of dispute resolution employing more than one ADR process.

Cause of action

a group of operative facts giving rise to one or more bases for suing; a factual situation that entitles one person to obtain a remedy in court from another person (*Black's Law Dictionary*, 7th ed, s.v. "Cause of action").

Legal remedy

an outcome that, by law, a court can provide to a party in litigation, such as a legal pronouncement, money damages, and so forth.

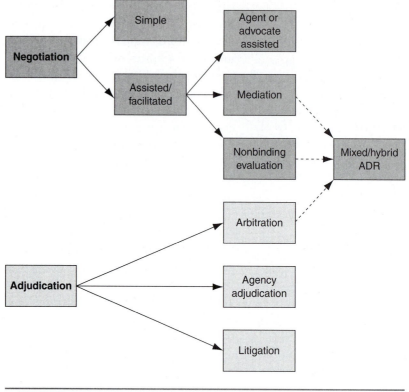

◆ **FIGURE 1-3**

A Typology of Dispute Resolution

Chapter 5.) A diagram of the varieties of dispute resolution, showing their conceptual interrelationships, is shown in Figure 1-3.

In addition to the major varieties of dispute resolution processes, some others combine features of negotiation and adjudication. ADR processes that combine elements of negotiation with elements of adjudication are called **mixed** or **hybrid ADR processes** in this book. Nonbinding evaluation is often considered a kind of mixed or hybrid ADR because in some ways it resembles adjudication, but in this book it is categorized as a form of facilitated negotiation because the disputants are solely responsible for deciding whether to settle or resolve the conflict. **Multimodal ADR** processes are entire programs or systems that employ multiple forms of ADR.

CONFLICT MAPPING

It often helps to map complicated situations involving multiple conflict and many participants. For a description of conflict mapping, see Online Appendix B, Chapter 6.

The Limits of Litigation and Agency Adjudication

The types of disputes that may be submitted to litigation (or agency adjudication), as well as the sorts of outcomes that a judge or jury (or hearing examiner) may prescribe, are defined strictly by law. A dispute that a court is empowered to pass upon in litigation is called a **cause of action**, and an outcome that a court can provide to an applicant to a court is called a **legal remedy**. The same goes for agency adjudication—the kinds of claims that can be heard, and the range of remedies that can be awarded, are restrictive. Many interpersonal conflicts either cannot be expressed as causes of action, do not have effective solutions that courts are empowered to provide as remedies, or both, and this limitation of governmentally provided adjudication processes is one reason for the growing popularity of ADR processes.

EXERCISES, PROJECTS, AND "THOUGHT EXPERIMENTS"

1. Keep a log of the television programs you watch for one week. For each program, keep track of the interpersonal conflicts shown and how they are resolved. In your log, describe each conflict, identifying what makes the situation an interpersonal conflict. Is the conflict resolved? If so, how?

2. Do you have interpersonal conflicts in your own life in which you are a disputant, an agent or advocate, or a constituent? (Careful: Even a well-functioning relationship that includes incompatible goals is technically an interpersonal conflict!) For each interpersonal conflict, do the following:

   a. Describe the conflict.

   b. State whether it is active or (until you realized the presence of incompatible goals made it an interpersonal conflict) latent.

   c. List the disputants, agents and advocates (if any), and constituents (if any), along with an explanation of what makes each of these persons a disputant, agent, advocate, or constituent.

   d. List the incompatibilities of goals that render this situation an interpersonal conflict.

   e. List any compatible, complementary goals the disputants have.

   f. List any incompatibilities of goals the disputants have with their agents, advocates, and constituents, and discuss how these incompatibilities might complicate resolution of the conflict.

3. Attend a civil trial. Keep a log of the trial. See if you can determine what interpersonal conflicts are at play in the litigation. Do you think a better alternative than litigation might do a better job of resolving this conflict? Why or why not? What, if anything, about the litigation process limits your ability to consider what alternatives might be preferable?

2

Understanding the Foundations of ADR

99 percent of the game is half mental.

—Yogi Berra

In this chapter, you will learn . . .

- some concepts for defining "good" dispute resolution.
- that what is most important in driving a conflict is often hidden from view.
- that perception and judgment about conflicts are distorted by general perceptual processes, conflict escalation, and culture, compromising the ability of disputants and their allies to plan and act effectively.
- that focusing on interests, seeking cooperation, and using power wisely are associated with optimized dispute resolution.
- that tailoring conflict resolution to the causes of a conflict and the reasons for its persistence can produce optimized dispute resolution

In Chapter 1, we learned about some of the processes legal professionals use to resolve interpersonal conflict, including ADR. It was explained that ADR stands for "alternative dispute resolution"—the processes alternative to traditional methods of litigation and lawyer-assisted negotiation that can be used to manage conflict. However, increasingly ADR is being used to stand for something else: "*appropriate* dispute resolution." For example, as of the year 2007 the District of Columbia's renowned Multidoor Courthouse, a court-based ADR system, had dropped the term *alternative* in favor of the word *appropriate* in its promotional and explanatory literature (District of Columbia Courts, 2009).

Something is important about this terminology shift. Legal professionals in the twenty-first century have responsibilities that go beyond conducting litigation: They also must be effective dispute resolution managers and good conflict resolvers. This responsibility includes the following:

- Developing a dispute resolution strategy of maximum benefit to the client (see "Are Lawyers Obligated to Advise Clients of ADR Options?")

Are Lawyers Obligated to Advise Clients of ADR Options?

Until quite recently, Doris had a successful career as a genetics counselor with a medical practice that she adored. Her job, which she had held for five years, was everything to her: She was very close to her colleagues in the office, and she felt fulfilled by her contact with patients (who she was able to help during periods of great vulnerability, as they contemplated the possibility of bearing children with serious genetic problems). Until the day her employment ended, Doris also had what she considered an excellent relationship with her supervisor, Bernadette.

Unfortunately, one day, for reasons that remain a mystery to Doris, she and Bernadette had a serious falling out, ending with the two in a very loud shouting match in the hallway. Bernadette impulsively fired Doris on the spot. Deeply hurt, depressed over the loss of her beloved job and colleagues, and with her dignity in shambles, Doris retained attorney Rachel Dornberg to "sock it to" her former employer. Rachel interviewed Doris, got the facts behind the firing, performed legal research, and informed Doris that she has a reasonably good case for damages due to unlawful discharge, though a failure-to-mitigate defense caused by Doris' high marketability with other firms might foreclose a significant recovery. Rachel further went over with Doris the likely cost and time that litigation will entail. Has Rachel fulfilled her professional obligation to advise Rachel?

Today's lawyers often take a more holistic approach to law practice than that taken by Rachel. For example, the June 2001 issue of the ABA Journal reported a business lawyer, Arnie Herz, whose practice involves helping clients unblock fearful or angry feelings that are impeding their rational judgment; assisting clients in recognizing long-term interests, values, and needs; and empowering them to select the best way to attain these goals (Keeva 2001). For example, a client might enter Herz's office wanting to litigate with a former business partner, and this might be the ultimate decision the client makes, but not until he has explored with Herz the reasons he has come into the office wanting to sue. Or the client might, after the meeting with the lawyer, decide that reconciliation with the partner, and a better-drawn contract, would better serve his long-term interests. The article reports several clients who made choices other than the one they entered the law office with, and their sense that the experience transformed their lives for the better. And Herz himself reports considerable monetary success using this approach, because it is quite popular with clients.

Not every lawyer would be comfortable with Arnie Herz's heavily psychological approach to lawyering, but an evolving body of legal ethics is beginning to move lawyering in this direction. Law practice is increasingly client-centered, with clients taking on increased control over strategic decisionmaking (Cochran, 1999). Moreover, in many jurisdictions, lawyers may have an ethical obligation to advise clients of the panoply of dispute resolution options at the client's disposal, including Alternative Dispute Resolution processes. It can be argued that Doris, who lost a treasured employment position as the result of an isolated breakdown in relationships, is precisely the sort of client for whom ADR (specifically, mediation) is ideal: Obtaining damages through litigation will not make her whole, but an apology, reconciliation with her supervisor and a return to work may well do so.

The ethical obligation of lawyers to advise their clients of ADR options is detailed in Chapter 4, at pages 137–138.

- Selecting appropriate dispute resolution processes and providers, and helping clients with this selection process
- Coaching clients to make effective use of dispute resolution processes
- Conducting themselves in ADR sessions to yield maximum benefit to the client
- Knowing the law of ADR
- Knowing when to object to the use of an ADR process and/or provider, and how to do so

These professional objectives suggest an overall goal of achieving "good" dispute resolution, but what criteria make a dispute resolution process "good"? Let's assume for the moment that, for a legal professional, the goals of "good" dispute resolution are to meet the objectives of a client, which is the stance ethically required of lawyers (however, see "Lawyer–Client Conflicts of Interest"). The client's objectives for dispute resolution will likely include the following:

- Maximizing his or her interests, goals, and needs
- Being satisfied with the outcome
- Being satisfied with the process used to address the conflict, particularly if the client has not achieved all of his or her outcome goals
- Minimizing the likelihood of a recurrence of the conflict and of new conflicts cropping up
- Saving time and money, if possible (Here it is important to clarify the perspective from which time and resource efficiency are considered: short-term savings may lead to long-term waste, as when a hurriedly negotiated settlement containing careless omissions leads to disputes down the line.)
- Preserving or improving any ongoing relationships the client has with other participants in the conflict

Lawyer–Client Conflicts of Interest

One might think that a competent lawyer would be one who never has a conflict of interest with his or her client. In practice, it is very hard to avoid conflicts of interest between lawyers and their clients. Of relevance to the field of ADR, the following are some conflicts that may prevent lawyers from providing "good dispute resolution" to their clients:

- Lawyer who has built his reputation on cooperative settlement, representing client who could benefit if lawyer surprises opposing counsel with a very adversarial strategy
- Lawyer whose financial well-being relies on fees from lengthy and intensive litigation, representing client who would benefit from early settlement
- Lawyer whose career satisfaction derives from the excitement of litigation, representing client who would benefit from avoiding litigation

Can you think of other examples?

How can these goals be addressed most effectively? In answering this question, it's important to avoid one-size-fits-all thinking: What might be good for one client and one situation might be terrible for another client and another situation. In general, however, these goals can best be addressed with approaches to conflict resolution that feature the following:

- *Minimizing perceptual error and judgmental biases:* These problems undermine effective strategic planning and implementation. All conflict participants, including disputants and legal professionals, are vulnerable to such errors.

- *Focusing on underlying interests and other concerns of the disputants, rather than on positions* (Fisher, Ury, and Patton, 1991): To promote optimal results and avoid impasse and other problems, the process should promote a focus on underlying interests, values, and needs of the participants and should steer clear of bargaining based on the stating of positions.

- *Tailoring the process to the specific causes of conflict and the forces preventing its resolution:* The process should be tailored to respond effectively to the underlying causes of the conflict and the causes of impasse.

- *Promoting psychological ownership:* To maximize satisfaction and durability of the outcome, the participants in the conflict should, to the maximum extent possible, buy into the chosen process and outcome.

- *Promoting cooperation:* To maximize both efficiency and efficacy, the process should promote cooperation among the disputants to the extent feasible.

- *Using power effectively:* The process should promote participants' effective uses of power while minimizing power's negative side effects.

This chapter discusses each of these criteria and briefly summarizes the theoretical and empirical bases for understanding the strengths and weaknesses of the panoply of dispute resolution processes, including ADR.

Knowing *why* and *how* ADR processes work will show you which particular processes work best in which circumstances, enabling you to better serve a client. This same grounding in theory and research underlies **conflict diagnosis,** a skill set that can be used to understand a conflict in depth so that strategic action can be developed to resolve the conflict optimally and select processes best tailored to optimal resolution. The theory, empirical information, and the conflict diagnosis skill set are presented in more extensive detail in Online Appendix B.

The skills of conflict diagnosis are now receiving recognition as a crucial component of competence for legal professionals. As noted by Robert C. Bordone of Harvard Law School:

> [Law] Schools . . . need to teach their students how to diagnose the quality and nature of their clients' disputes in order to train them to prescribe the appropriate dispute resolution process. In short, lawyers are increasingly aware that they need to be equipped with tools of diagnosis, not just tools to perform surgery. Demonstrating that not all disputes are alike and that

Conflict diagnosis
a set of skills, based on the ideas presented in this chapter, designed to enable the user to better understand a conflict and the situations and motivations of its participants, and that enables the user to plan and execute an optimal approach to its resolution.

litigation is not the only, the best, or even, at times, an appropriate, process for the management of many disputes, has been one of the most important contributions of the modern ADR movement to the legal profession. *(Bordone 2005, 8)*

MINIMIZING PERCEPTUAL ERROR AND JUDGMENTAL BIAS

Perceptual distortion
error, typically unconscious, in recognizing or interpreting information received using the senses.

The typical interpersonal conflict is a complex, multidimensional situation, and thus successful conflict management usually requires a high degree of strategic planning and analysis. It goes almost without saying that anything that creates errors in understanding the situation will undermine the ability of the participants to plan strategically. Three major sources of conflict—*individual, interpersonal (arising from the dynamics of escalated conflict),* and *cultural*—are responsible for a great deal of bad decision making by disputing parties and their advocates and support persons.

Unfortunately, **perceptual distortion** is a natural side effect of being in a conflict and a major force preventing effective conflict resolution. It blinds disputants and their advocates from reality and prevents them from selecting optimal strategies and processes for resolving conflict. Perceptual distortion during disputing is completely predictable but is pernicious because it occurs unconsciously in most people and in most situations. Some forms of ADR feature special methods of counteracting such perceptual distortions to create more rational and, hence, strategically more effective conflict resolution.

INDIVIDUAL SOURCES OF PERCEPTUAL DISTORTION

Individual sources of perceptual distortion derive merely from being involved in social interaction. *Human social behavior is inherently ambiguous* (which is probably why farce based on mutual misunderstanding has been a mainstay of comic literature from Shakespeare to Seinfeld). The reason is simple: We can't read minds. To respond efficaciously in frequent and often rapid-fire social interaction requires us to understand and predict the thoughts, feelings, attitudes, and behaviors of others. In the absence of time and adequate data, we make (more or less) educated guesses. We incorporate and even interject bits that come from ourselves—our understanding of the world, our values, and our frames of reference.

In this process, perceivers make characteristic, predictable errors:

- *People mistake interpretation for sense impression.* They often fail to distinguish direct observation from interpretation. This interpretational error creates problems because it is completely unconscious, thus setting the stage for unnecessary misunderstanding.

Jane, exhausted after a long day in class, sees her boyfriend's facial expression and speech inflection and thinks, "He is angry at me," when in fact he has a toothache. She begins to act defensively, setting the stage for an argument.

◆ *The Fundamental Attribution Error.* People characteristically overattribute what they observe in a situation to innate and permanent traits, rather than to the demands of the situation (see Gawronski 2003).

Rosalyn, plaintiff's attorney in a highly contentious lawsuit, aggressively cross-examines a witness, and is regarded by jurors as "an aggressive person," rather than as doing what her job demands.

◆ *Egocentric beliefs about others' backgrounds and experiences.* Perceivers often fail to realize that their interpretation of reality is colored by their personal context—their background experiences, values, and world view. Therefore, they will tend to believe that their own view of reality is "objectively correct" (Ehrlinger, Gilovich, and Ross 2005; Pronin, Gilovich, and Ross, 2004; Marks and Miller, 1987) and that others who disagree are biased or prejudiced, as when opponents on both sides of a political issue debate honestly but regard one another as biased or dishonest.

Trina is kissed on the cheek by Andrew, a seventy-five-year-old retired laboratory assistant. Trina, who was victimized by sexual abuse, interprets the action as motivated by a need to dominate women. Andrew, however, was raised in a culture in which kissing is an accepted method of greeting friends.

◆ *Egocentric beliefs about intent of others.* Perceivers have a tendency to believe, egocentrically, that actions of others are directed at them, more often than is actually the case.

Greg, going home at rush hour, hears a honk behind him and swears at Cindy, the other driver, for rudeness. In fact, Cindy had been honking at a different driver.

◆ *The fallacy of oversimplification.* People generally overestimate the extent to which behavior of others is generated by simple and consistent motivation (Lord, Ross, and Lepper, 1979). They also misjudge that what others do is always what they intended.

Studies show that observers interpret disputants as having simple motivations to either cooperate or compete, but attribute far more nuanced and complex motivation to their own behavior during interpersonal conflict (see van de Vliert and Prein, 1989).

These five sources of error are exacerbated by certain attributes of the situation, such as situational complexity, illness, fatigue, hunger, distraction, and emotional arousal (we can call these "attention robbers"; Gilbert, Pelham, and Krell 1988), by limiting our ability to correctly take in and process information. That is, these factors compromise our ability to make our guesses truly well informed. Moreover, a person having little information about the situation in which he or she finds himself or herself is more likely to fill the void with his or her own (possibly mistaken) inferences, assumptions, and stereotypes. Since interpersonal conflict is an inherently stressful and complex event, perceptual error is common and creates much misunderstanding and unnecessary discord. Here's an example of how these forces can operate to derail effective decision making during conflict:

George, an African American[1] and the father of two teenage boys, knows several friends and family who have been abused by police and, consequently, has developed a stereotypical belief that police are bigots and dangerous to young Black men and boys. Jim, his neighbor, a European (White) American who grew up in an all-White town in the Midwest, has no similar experiences and has a stereotypical belief that police are heroes. Jim is new to the neighborhood, and although he has never before been neighbors with a Black family, he prides himself in being unprejudiced.

In trying to halt a series of minor thefts in the neighborhood, Jim proposes asking the police to patrol more often, believing unconsciously that all law-abiding neighbors would be comfortable with the idea. George, unconsciously assuming "everyone knows" police are bigots, concludes that Jim is a racist—otherwise why would he intentionally inflict a police presence on a neighborhood where young Black men live? Jim, on the other hand, "necessarily" (given his world view) concludes that George or a member of his family must be responsible for the crime wave. (Otherwise, why would he object to an increased police presence?)

Meanwhile, in an unrelated development, George's youngest son, Al, comes home with terrible grades. George's own father had been too caught up in his career to be very involved in the lives of his children, and George is determined to be different. Coincidentally, George has strained his back and finds that stretching his legs gives him some relief. Thus, George begins strolling about the neighborhood to relieve his back pain and to keep an eye on Al. Jim, believing this action is directed at him and has a simple motive related to the thefts in the neighborhood, which is Jim's personal concern, "infers" that the motivation for George's sojourns is to "case out" Jim's house to steal from him.

Both of the men in this example have made errors of perception and interpretation that create unnecessary and potentially destructive conflict. Some

[1] Throughout this book, the terms "African-American," "European-American," etc. will be used when clearly referring to an individual's self-identified cultural, racial, or ethnic group, whereas the terms *Black, White,* and such will be used when clearly referring to an individual's racial group as perceived by others. Where the reference is mixed, the other-referential term (Black, White, and such) will generally be used.

Communication and Conflict Resolution

As noted in this chapter, when people encounter the behavior of others, their observations are fraught with errors of perception and interpretation. It is crucial to bear in mind that communication is subject to these very same vulnerabilities.

Two equally important behavioral acts are found in any communication: the sending and the receiving of the messages. These two acts are almost never performed perfectly. Bernard Mayer (2000, 119) reminds us of the flawed nature of communication: Senders virtually never couch their communications in ideal terms, and recipients virtually never receive the communication precisely as it was intended. Mayer wisely counsels:

> People do not become better communicators by setting up a new orthodoxy about human interaction and then judging each other in accordance with it. *(Mayer 2000, 122)*

Thus, one can identify four crucial elements to effective conflict communication: being able to send messages that are clear, precise, and nonescalating; anticipating and compensating for the errors of perception and interpretation likely to occur as one receives a communication; tolerance of imperfection in the communication behavior of others; and persistence in trying to make successful communication occur despite early failures.

Facilitative
a quality of an approach to dispute resolution characterized by the dispute resolution neutral helping the disputants to reach their own resolution, rather than imposing, advocating, pressuring, or recommending an outcome on or to the disputants.

Promotive interdependence
a state of relationship in which, predominantly, what one disputant does to benefit the self will also help another disputant.

Contrient interdependence
a state of relationship in which, predominantly, what one disputant does to benefit the self will impede or undermine the interests and goals of another disputant.

forms of ADR, most notably **facilitative** forms of mediation (Chapter 3), directly deal with and ameliorate these sorts of errors.

DISTORTED PERCEPTION ARISING FROM ESCALATED CONFLICT

We have looked at mechanisms of cognition that produce biases and distortions in people when they interact with other people. Some special biases and distortions are typically created during interpersonal conflict that has become heated and contentious, according to social and organizational psychologist Morton Deutsch (1973). As you may recall from Chapter 1, this kind of situation is an escalated conflict. Deutsch pointed out that all human relationships have both **promotive interdependence** and **contrient interdependence** aspects (see "Contrient and Promotive Interdependence"; in plain English, this means that some actions that a disputant can take will help both disputants (promotive interdependence), but other actions will help one person at the expense of the other (contrient interdependence).[2]

Deutsch thought that a good way to organize one's beliefs about a conflict is to say that a person sees a conflict as either **cooperative** (in which a perception of promotive interdependence predominates) or **competitive** (in which a perception of contrient interdependence predominates). Virtually all interpersonal

---

[2] A common way to refer to a contrient orientation in a relationship is to say that the relationship is **zero-sum**. The idea of this term is that the resources available to the disputants always sum up to zero, so the more one disputant gets, the more the other loses.

Cooperative

a conflict that is characterized by a belief on the part of disputants that interests are promotive—that what one does to benefit oneself will benefit the other. Accordingly, disputants act to promote one another's goals.

Competitive

a conflict which is characterized by a belief on the part of disputants that interests are contrient—that what one does to benefit oneself will undermine the other. Accordingly, disputants *compete*—they act to impede one another's goals and to "do better" than the other.

Mixed-motive

a conflict that is characterized by a combination of promotive and contrient elements. Virtually all interpersonal conflicts are, in reality, this type.

conflicts can be thought of in both promotive and contrient terms (we call a situation containing contrient and promotive interdependence a **mixed-motive** situation).

Deutsch has demonstrated that *just mentally focusing* on the contriently interdependent aspects of a relationship—in other words, seeing a relationship in win-lose, **zero-sum** terms, and approaching it competitively—sets in motion a dynamic that distorts the perceptions of those in the relationship. This process is known as *conflict escalation* and is diagrammed in Figure 2-1.

How Conflict Escalation Leads to Perceptual Error. To understand conflict escalation and its relationship to perceptual error, we begin with a disputant's focus on contriently interdependent aspects of a relationship with another disputant. For this analysis it is not necessary for disputants to be contriently interdependent *in fact,* only that they *believe* they are contriently interdependent. Let's suppose Disputant A, for whatever reason, believes that, if he helps himself, it will, on the whole, hurt Disputant B, and vice versa. This belief will tend to lead Disputant A, in an effort to protect and improve his own situation, to try to undermine Disputant B's goals. *In other words, Disputant A will compete.*

These actions will likely create or intensify the perception of contrient interdependence on the part of Disputant B (who will see Disputant A acting in a threatening way). Anger and hostility on the part of Disputant B are likely to result, and Disputant B is likely to obstruct Disputant A to protect his or her interests. Disputant A will egocentrically tend to see Disputant B's actions as intentionally designed to harm Disputant A rather than primarily as efforts of self-help, and this distorted perception will deepen the hostility between them. Thus, the first major thought distortion produced by escalated conflict is an *overestimate of contrient interdependence, relative to promotive interdependence.*

Contrient and Promotive Interdependence

To take a conflict and make it more promotive, all that's required is to restate the conflict as a joint problem to be solved. Table 2-1 shows some examples of how conflicts can be restated.

◆ **TABLE 2-1** Contrient and Promotive Versions of Conflict Statements

CONTRIENT STATEMENT OF CONFLICT	PROMOTIVE STATEMENT OF CONFLICT
In our partnership, I want 60 percent of the profits and John wants 70 percent of the profits.	We want a partnership agreement that seems fair to us both in terms of the profit allocations and that gives us each fair compensation for our contributions.
I want $60,000 in property damage and pain and suffering for the accident, and Smith refuses to pay.	We want to resolve our dispute in a way that is fair, conforms to applicable law, and gives due compensation for any torts, without going to court.
I want custody of Janie, and so does he.	We want to create a parenting plan that is healthy for Janie and is fair and workable for both parents.
I demand restitution for his unethical behavior.	We need to determine what is fair compensation in this situation.

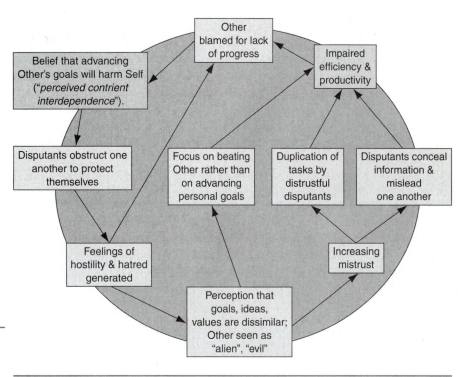

◆ **FIGURE 2-1**

Conflict Escalation

Zero-Sum

describes interpersonal conflict situations that predominantly feature incompatible interests, without any significant countervailing complementary interests. In a zero-sum situation, the more one person gets, the less the other has.

Cognitive dissonance

a social psychological theory which holds that individuals will take action (such as selective attention, thought distortion, and biased interpretation) to avoid the holding of apparently inconsistent thoughts, beliefs, and emotions.

Demonization

the attribution of deeply negative qualities to another person; in extreme cases, this results in seeing the other as subhuman.

As disputants' anger and dislike of one another grow, the theory of **cognitive dissonance** (which holds that people can't tolerate holding thoughts and ideas that are inconsistent with one another; see Barker, 2003) predicts that it will become increasingly uncomfortable for either to think of himself or herself as having any important similarity to the other. They can avoid this dissonant state by focusing on and emphasizing areas of dissimilarity with one another, by ignoring or devaluing similarities between themselves, and by interpreting ambiguous behavior as evidence of more dissimilarity. Thus, the second predictable thought distortion produced by escalated conflict is an *intensified belief in dissimilarity between disputants.* Because every person wishes to think of himself as being morally upstanding, this perception of dissimilarity typically leads each disputant to believe that the other disputant in a conflict has inferior moral values. In a highly escalated conflict, a disputant may conclude that the other disputant is "inherently evil" or even "subhuman"—a process known as **demonization.** Some examples of dissimilarity beliefs common in escalated conflicts are set forth in Table 2-2.

A by-product of the increasing enmity and perceived alienation between disputants is the *erosion of trust,* and consequently the disputants will refuse to rely on one another (e.g., if Disputant A wants to get some piece of information, he or she will not take Disputant B at his or her word but instead will seek independent

◆ TABLE 2-2	Common Dissimilarity Beliefs During Interpersonal Conflict
I AM . . .	THE OTHER DISPUTANT IS . . .
Good	Evil
Moral	Immoral
Right about the law (or facts)	Wrong about the law (or facts)
Rational and reasonable	Irrational and unreasonable
Objective and unbiased	Biased
Honest	Dishonest
Acting appropriately given the circumstances	Acting unreasonably, given my reasonableness

confirmation). This refusal to combine forces leads to duplication of effort, which lessens efficiency. Another by-product of trust erosion is the *refusal to share accurate information:* In an escalated conflict little information is shared, and misinformation runs rampant. Both duplication of effort and the refusal to share information make dispute management more time consuming and expensive, and hence productivity is undermined. Disputants do not wish to blame themselves for the poor results, and a convenient target is available: the other disputant, who is already disliked. The third perceptual distortion created by escalated conflict is that *the other disputant is seen as overly blameworthy for things going wrong in the situation.* The process of blaming the other disputant for the shortcomings in the process of resolving the conflict creates additional perceived contrient interdependence; thus, the process is self-perpetuating and self-intensifying. As conflict continues to escalate and hostility deepens, each disputant will develop a motive to seek vengeance against the other, creating or adding to real contrient interdependence and prompting further escalation of the conflict. The *exacerbation of real contrient interdependence* results, creating a self-fulfilling prophecy.

These false or distorted beliefs lead inevitably to a fourth predictable distortion: disputants caught in escalated conflict tend to *underestimate how well cooperative approaches might work* in resolving the conflict. Any competitive process used to resolve a conflict will set these processes in motion by focusing the participants on the contrient elements of their relationship, leaving them at heightened vulnerability to these perceptual distortions.

In short, the process of conflict escalation creates four predictable distortions of perception:

- ◆ An overemphasis on the contrient elements of the relationship
- ◆ An exaggerated belief in the dissimilarity and moral deficiency of the other disputant
- ◆ An unwarranted blaming of the other disputant for impasses and other impediments to resolving the conflict
- ◆ An underestimate of the likely effectiveness of cooperative processes in resolving or managing the conflict

Epistemic freezing
a premature turning away from, and failing or refusing to consider, plausible alternative explanations for a given situation.

Invisible veil
unrecognized, culturally induced overestimate of the superiority of competitive methods to resolve disputes.

Adversarial system
a dispute resolution process characterized by a competitive process in which the clash of adversaries is believed to result in justice and equity.

Conflict escalation thus promotes a kind of blinding of the participants to possible alternative interpretations of the situation in which they find themselves. The longer the conflict persists, the more escalated it is likely to become, and with conflict escalation comes a narrowing of explanations that seem plausible to the conflict participants. This foreclosure of the ability to consider all potentially relevant explanations for a situation is known to psychologists as **epistemic freezing** and is regarded as responsible for much strategic error during conflict and negotiation. (See, for example, de Dreu, Koole, and Oldersma, 1999).

CULTURAL SOURCES OF DISTORTED PERCEPTION: THE "INVISIBLE VEIL"

Biased perception also results from the overall cultural system, which in the United States perpetuates an overestimate of the superiority of competitive methods resolving legal disputes. In this book, we'll call this cultural source of distorted perception the **invisible veil**.

The United States legal system is an **adversarial system**—that is, it is based on an idea that truth, and hence justice, is best revealed through competition between legal advocates presenting their cases to an impartial judge (Fuller and Randall 1958). In other words, an adversarial system is inherently competitive. This adversarial legal system is embedded in a larger cultural system that is recognized as the most individualistic and rights based in the world (Leung and Lind 1986). Indeed, dictionary definitions of the English term *conflict* heavily feature war and battle. Law Professor Roberta K. Flowers notes that the adversarial system has historical roots in actual battle:

> The trial process in America has been referred to as "a battle of adversaries" or "legal combat." The adversarial system assumes that truth emerges from the confrontation of opposing views. In its earliest form, brought to England by William the Conqueror, the accused would physically battle with his accuser. The underlying belief was that "heaven would give the victory to him who was in the right." *(Flowers 1996, 923)*

This cultural belief system has been translated into a sort of mental blueprint that legal professionals use to deal with their clients' legal needs. The blueprint is so important and so pervasive that it has even been given a name. Leonard Riskin coined the phrase "lawyer's standard philosophical map" to describe the two basic assumptions that he believes lawyers make when dealing with disputes:

> (1) that disputants are adversaries—*i.e.,* if one wins, the other must lose—and (2) that disputes may be resolved through applications, by a third party, of some general rule of law. *(Riskin 1982, 44–45)*

The values inherent in any culture are transmitted to individuals who interact with the systems embedded in the culture, who then act to reinforce the cultural values, according to developmental ecologists such as Uri Bronfenbrenner

A common presumption holds that, in legal disputing, the truth is best determined through the vigorous clash of legal adversaries. Michael Herron, Pearson Education/PH College.

(1979), as well as "structuration" theorists Anthony Giddens, Arthur McEvoy, and Geert Hofstede (Riskin and Welsh 2008, fn. 154). Here is how this self-perpetuating process, the invisible veil, works.

In a culture dominated by adversarial approaches to legal disputing, those who deal with legal disputes and legal transactions—clients, their lawyers, and those who help to resolve them—are likely to receive only limited exposure to nonadversarial, cooperative approaches to conflict resolution because the overarching social structures built to handle conflict are predominantly adversarial. Moreover, to the extent that policy makers experiment with incorporating nonadversarial dispute resolution processes into adversarial cultures, they often incorporate adversarial features (e.g., as mediation has been adopted by courts and the legal profession, it frequently features a rather adversarial hearing, consisting of opening statements and summaries of the evidence for each side, followed by a nonbinding evaluation, opinion, or award issued by the so-called mediator). Such processes are optimized neither as adversarial processes nor as nonadversarial processes, and thus they are likely to reap the benefits of neither.[3]

Thus, legal professionals and their clients are likely to get plenty of practice honing their competitive, adversarial approaches to conflict management and virtually no practice perfecting truly nonadversarial strategies and practices. To the extent that legal professionals experience "adversarialized" ADR, they will not experience the benefits of actual nonadversarial dispute resolution.

---

[3] For discussions of the prevalence of *adversarialization* of ADR processes and the problems caused by this trend, see Lande 1997, McAdoo and Welsh 2005, and Menkel-Meadow 1991 and 1996.

On the other hand, if exposed to a truly nonadversarial dispute resolution process, it will seem alien; and if an effort is made to use nonadversarial methods of conflict resolution, the effort is vulnerable to failure due to lack of proficiency in using nonadversarial tools or because the participants use skills and techniques more suited to adversarial processes such as litigation. The people having these experiences, however, are likely to see them through the distorted lens of the fundamental attribution error and will interpret the outcomes as proving the inferiority of nonadversarial processes, rather than attributing the failure to a lack of practice and proficiency or to a failure of a specific implementation of ADR.

By this dynamic, a preference for using adversarial processes to resolve conflict can be expected to be perpetuated and transmitted to individuals who encounter the system. These individuals, in turn, will ultimately find themselves in a position to make policy and are likely to perpetuate the existing system out of an honest belief that it is superior. Hence, the fact that we have an adversarial legal system is likely to perpetuate a distorted belief in the inherent superiority of adversarial, competitive processes to resolve "the most important" conflicts. This process of confirmation of cultural values blinds individuals to the opportunities presented by nonadversarial dispute resolution. A sense of the dynamics of this process is suggested in Figure 2-2.

It is not being suggested that adversarial processes are never the best option. Rather, the perceptual distortion lies in the propensity to see adversarial processes as the best alternative in an *unwarrantedly broad range* of situations—that an epistemic freezing takes place that rules out other possibilities. When evaluating dispute resolution processes for suitability to a client's situation, it is important to take this invisible-veil cultural bias into account and to take steps to overcome it. Lifting the invisible veil can lead a legal professional to better evaluate options for the client, as well as to select a better and more appropriate dispute resolution process to meet client needs.

PERCEPTUAL DISTORTION AND CONFLICT RESOLUTION: CONCLUSION

The three major sources of distorted perception during interpersonal conflict emanate from the challenges of all social interaction, involvement in escalated conflict, and cultural belief systems. It follows that dispute resolution processes that address these sources of distortion will enable disputants and their agents and advocates to make better decisions about how to handle their conflict. Providing participants with information, lowering stress, lessening emotional arousal, and simplifying the situation will lessen the likelihood of drawing erroneous inferences due to lack of cognitive and emotional resources. Processes that lessen the likelihood of conflict escalation and promote cooperative approaches are effective in reducing the perceptual distortions that come from a competitive and defensive orientation. Simply knowing that the culture predisposes one to overdepend on

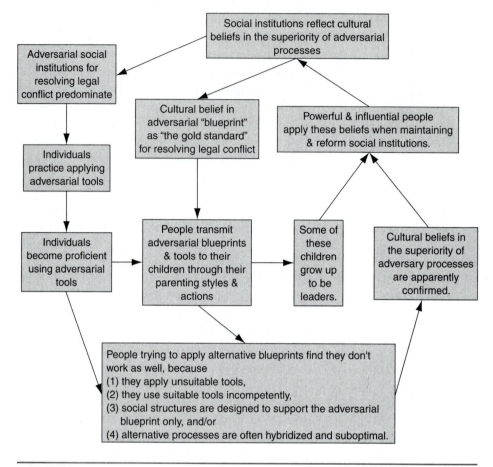

◆ **FIGURE 2-2**

Perpetuation of Cultural Beliefs About Dispute Resolution

adversarial approaches to legal disputing can free a disputant and his or her team to scrutinize dispute resolution processes from a more objective frame of reference and to reserve adversarial processes for when they will be most effective.

FOCUSING ON INTERESTS, RATHER THAN ON POSITIONS

Thus far, the discussion has focused primarily on the need to prevent perceptual distortion in conflict participants, and we have seen that avoiding processes that create contentiousness, if possible, can reduce the likelihood of proliferating perceptual distortion. We now turn to a closely related topic: how to characterize and articulate the goals of the participants.

In the previous section we've seen reasons for avoiding adversarial processes such as litigation if you can otherwise protect the client: Involvement in an adversarial process can exacerbate perceptual distortions that impair strategic planning and implementation. If you've worked in a law office, you've probably been exposed to the traditional alternative: legal negotiation. In traditional legal negotiation, disputants negotiate through a series of demands and counterdemands, resulting, if the negotiation is successful, in a compromise. This process is called **positional bargaining.** Here is an example of positional bargaining:

Positional bargaining
a kind of negotiation characterized by the trading of initially extreme and successively more moderate demands and counterdemands, until, ideally, a compromise results.

> Drake, a paralegal in a law office, received information concerning a slip-and-fall accident suffered by a client, Claire, in a grocery store. Drake believed that if the case went to litigation and Claire prevailed she would receive in the neighborhood of $60,000 in damages. However, there were uncertainties in liability, so he decided, with the concurrence of the client, that he would accept as little as $30,000. Drake telephoned Ernie, a claims adjuster for the liability insurer, presented the situation in the light most favorable to Claire, and demanded $130,000. Ernie laughed, said that he couldn't believe Drake was claiming that Claire deserved any recovery at all, presented a (weak) argument that in fact Claire was liable for property damage to an expensive freezer case, and demanded that Claire pay $20,000. A series of gradually moderating demands and counterdemands followed. Ultimately, Ernie committed his insurer to pay $31,000 to settle Claire's claim.

Reservation price
the worst deal a negotiator would be willing to settle for (often also referred to as a *bottom line*).

The typical positional bargainer has two principal goals. The first is to try to pinpoint the other negotiator's *bottom line* (also referred to as the **reservation price**—i.e., what the other would be barely willing to accept). The second is to make the other believe that one's reservation price is more extreme than it is (to persuade the other to make the best possible offers). For example, in the preceding anecdote, Drake had two motives: to learn what Ernie would actually be willing to pay to settle the claim and to try to get Ernie to think that he, Drake, would require much more than $30,000 to settle the claim.

Positional bargaining has three principal negative consequences, as discussed in the famous negotiation text *Getting to YES* (Fisher, Ury and Patton, 1991). First, one tends to become "locked into position" psychologically. Once a bargainer draws a line in the sand, it becomes an independent psychological necessity to get the other to cross the line—otherwise one loses face (and, as we will see, preserving face is an extremely important human motivator). This feature of positional bargaining increases the likelihood of impasse. Second, because of the line-in-the-sand quality, using positional bargaining promotes a tendency to see the other disputant as the enemy. Such enmity promotes the dynamics that lead to conflict escalation. Third, taking a position causes one to become blinded to issues unrelated to the position. Settlements reached through positional bargaining tend for this reason to be unidimensional, uncreative, and less well tailored to the participants' situations and needs. Thus, such settlements tend to use resources suboptimally.

A mediator tells this story of separated spouses, both professionals, who entered mediation after a long period of trying to negotiate a settlement of

Positional bargaining, though the norm in many circumstances, has many disadvantages. Tony Souter, Dorling Kindersley Media Library.

their property. They had bargained to what they both agreed was economic parity. However, although the children lived primarily with their mother, the husband refused to bargain away furniture that would have been useful in a family game room. The wife, on the other hand, had possession of the lovely family piano, which had been used during marriage solely by the husband. A long period of demand and counterdemand had led to impasse, with both feeling they would lose face if they gave in to the other's desires for the property in question. As a result, both spouses were unable to have what they most wanted. The spouses were able to trade the furniture for the piano only after the mediator effusively praised past clients (not by name, of course, since mediators are careful to preserve privacy) who had been able to complete difficult trades of similar household items.

INTERESTS, VALUES, AND NEEDS

The bottom line, or reservation price, held by a disputant is one way to think about disputant goals and underlying concerns. A different and more inclusive way for disputants and their advocates to think about goals and concerns—and one that opens greater opportunities for collaboration, cooperation, and optimization—is to focus instead on underlying interests, values, and needs. Keeping the focus on underlying interests, values, and needs while discouraging any emphasis on stating positions and demands avoids the disadvantages of positional bargaining and creates an opportunity to reach better outcomes.

Briefly, an **interest** (using the term in a broad, categorical sense) is the motivation for *why* a conflict participant makes a **demand** or has a concrete

Interest
broadly, one's motivations in an interpersonal conflict. See *underlying interest.*

Demand
a disputant's assertion to the other disputant as to what would be required to resolve a conflict.

Aspiration
a disputant's concrete, specific, material goals for resolving a conflict.

Underlying interests
those goals that underlie a disputant's aspirations, not including values or basic human needs.

Values
held beliefs about the importance or moral rectitude of a goal, underlying a disputant's positions, aspirations, and underlying interests.

Basic human needs
those elements that underlie positions, aspirations, underlying interests, and values and that are considered by psychologists to be essential to healthy human existence and not subject to compromise.

aspiration (Riskin and Welsh 2008). For example, if a claimant with a reservation price of $20,000 *demands* $50,000 for a breach of contract:

- her *aspiration* might be to get at least $35,000,
- she might have this aspiration because she wants full compensation for lost profits (an **underlying interest**),
- she might believe that people who intentionally breach a contract should not be allowed to profit from their misdeeds (a **value**), and
- she might have a strong desire not to be taken advantage of (at the heart of this underlying interest would be a **basic human need** for self-esteem).

Deep interests underlie shallower interests, and basic human needs are the driving force underlying all other motivations. Thus, conflict participants' individual motivations can be thought of as being organized into a sort of layered relationship, which we'll call the *conflict onion* (Figure 2-3).

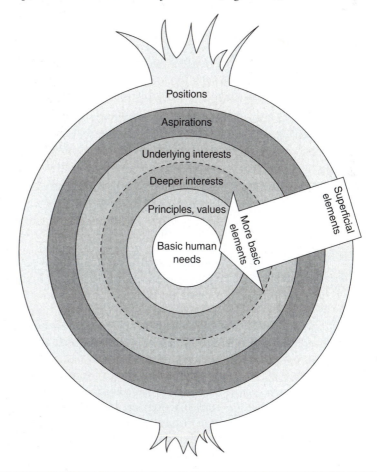

◆ **FIGURE 2-3**

The Conflict Onion

"Issues"

Riskin and Welch (2008) define an *issue* as "a question that could be included as part of the subject matter or problem definition in a dispute resolution procedure." The authors identify the following "problem definition continuum" of issues, in order of narrow to broad scope: litigation issues (that deal with law and evidence), business/economic issues (that deal with monetary and resource allocation considerations), core issues (psychological dimensions of autonomy, affiliation, appreciation, status, and role), and community issues (effects on those outside the group who are disputing). According to the authors, to ensure that no important interests, values, or needs are forgotten, disputants and their legal teams should explore issues across this continuum. Using a medical malpractice mediation example, the authors demonstrate how a focus on legal issues to the exclusion of other issues can lead to dissatisfaction on the part of the disputants with both process and outcome. In the example, an important concern felt by plaintiffs was to understand exactly what had happened to their child, who had become profoundly disabled during medical intervention—but their core need to have this topic addressed was never acknowledged by other participants in mediation. This lack of attention led to dissatisfaction of the plaintiffs with the proposed settlement. This example illustrates that if disputants or their advocates fail to consider the range of issues that define their concerns in a conflict, they may fail to consider potentially important interests and concerns, leading to suboptimal resolution of conflict and, possibly, to dissatisfaction, impasse, and conflict escalation.

Discovering and articulating interests, values, and needs—and understanding how they create the motivation to seek particular concrete goals in a conflict—are probably the most important steps a disputant or his or her advocate can take in creating the conditions for an optimal outcome.

Why is this step so crucial? First, a disputant who fails to understand his or her own motivations is in danger of missing out on opportunities for optimum results. Interpersonal conflict is a complex situation, and participants do best when they are clear about what they really want and need. Here's an example:

Polly, a therapist formerly partnered with Rebecca, sued Rebecca for allegedly stealing her client base after their partnership broke up. Rebecca offered a settlement, which Polly refused. With the help of her lawyer, Polly came to realize that her refusal to settle for the amount offered by Rebecca was due to a motivation to seek vengeance—Polly's self-esteem had been wounded when Rebecca dissolved the partnership to become affiliated with a different counseling group. Polly came to realize, looking at the strengths and weaknesses of her legal case, that if her self-esteem needed rehabilitation, it was very costly and counterproductive to use the dispute with Rebecca for this purpose. Moreover, she admitted to herself that even a large court award would not really change the reality of the fact that Rebecca had chosen to work with another group. Polly settled the dispute, gritting her teeth, and used part of the money she saved by settling outside of litigation to send herself on a very emotionally healing Caribbean cruise.

It's also often the case that when one focuses on underlying interests, values, and needs, one can attain a level of flexibility not possible when focusing on positions and concrete aspirations. This flexibility can break impasse and lead to more optimal, win-win outcomes.

> Patient, age fifty, suffered a heart attack during a procedure performed by Doctor at Hospital. Patient suffered some permanent long-term disability. Both Doctor and Patient consulted lawyers. Negotiation began, and ended, with Patient demanding $5 million for pain and suffering, loss of prospective income, and disability, and Doctor refusing to pay because liability was not clear.
>
> Both disputants, frustrated by the outcome of the first session, introspected, asking themselves what was really important. Patient came to the realization that all the money in the world would not buy him the ability to turn back the clock on his heart attack. He further realized that what was most important to him at this point was an acknowledgment from Doctor of the suffering he had caused, and a degree of certainty that similar errors would not happen to anyone else. Patient's extreme demand had felt good to him because of his sense that "anything less would belittle what I've been through," and Patient realized that behind this feeling was a need to save face and dignity. Doctor realized that his most important needs were to be able to continue to be a respected practitioner in his field—financial ruin would come from being adjudged negligent. Indeed, Doctor realized that his strongest motive was to be a respected physician at the top of his specialty—a desire for self-actualization. These deep-seated needs would not be served by litigating, nor would they be served by Doctor bankrupting himself at the negotiation table.
>
> In their next negotiation session, Doctor began by apologizing to Patient, something Doctor had longed to do anyway, given his strong motive to set high professional standards for himself. Patient accepted the apology but expressed his desire to ensure that no other patient suffer the same fate. This exchange revealed to Doctor and Patient their common desire to eliminate similar errors in future medical care, and they agreed to spearhead a task force to reduce such errors at the hospital where the incident had occurred. This settlement met the needs of Doctor, to enhance his professionalism, and of Patient, to prevent similar errors happening to other patients, far better than any of the monetary proposals that had been floated during their prior negotiation. Doctor also offered to reimburse Patient for his expenses and loss of prospective income, totaling about $125,000, according to actuarial analysis, plus an additional $100,000 for pain and suffering. Despite the fact that the proposal was less than 10 percent of his original monetary demand, Patient gladly accepted.

Knowing underlying interests, values, and needs—one's own and those of other conflict participants—also reduces the tendency to make strategic errors. Having a degree of certainty about what motivates each participant in a conflict lessens the attention-robbing effect of confusion and uncertainty, thus reducing the likelihood of perceptual distortion.

Conflicts of interest among members of a negotiating team can ruin settlement efforts.
Eye Wire Collection, Getty Images—Eye Wire, Inc.

INTERESTS, VALUES, AND NEEDS OF CONSTITUENTS, AGENTS, ADVOCATES, AND OTHERS

Thus far, we have considered the benefits of knowing one's own interests, values, and needs. It also helps to know about the interests, values, and needs of other members of one's "team," as well as those of the "other" disputants and members of that disputant's team. Divergent and incompatible interests, values, and needs in one's own team will complicate and obstruct efforts to optimally resolve conflict. Knowing the interests of those "on the other side" of a conflict allows one to creatively tailor proposals to address them (thus getting one's own proposals adopted), to anticipate and develop strategy to get around conflicts of interest among members of the other team, and, if necessary, to know what form of pressure and coercion will be most effective.

GENERALIZING THE SIGNIFICANCE OF INTERESTS, VALUES, AND NEEDS

Given the many advantages of understanding and focusing on underlying interests, values, and needs, it follows that dispute resolution processes that promote or facilitate negotiation having this focus will have advantages over those that promote positional bargaining or that do not help participants to clarify interests, values, or needs. However, in contexts where negotiators bargain repetitively with one another, where the prevailing culture is to expect positional bargaining, and where outcome optimization is less important than simply disposing of disputes quickly, positional bargaining is often a quicker, more efficient process.

(See Online Appendix B, Chapter 8, for further information and resources concerning the analysis of interests.)

TAILORING THE PROCESS TO THE CONFLICT'S CAUSES

Just as good medical practice takes account of the causes of a patient's illness and the factors preventing recovery, the best conflict resolution processes take into account the causes of the conflict and the causes of impasse and lack of progress in conflict resolution. Processes that work effectively in resolving certain kinds of conflicts may work very poorly in others.

There are many ways of thinking about what causes conflict to develop and reach impasse. Mediator Bernard Mayer (2000) provides a helpful overarching conceptual organizer he calls the "Wheel of Conflict." At the center of his wheel, Mayer places basic human needs, in recognition that, as stated, these critical drives underlie *all* conflicts. Between the spokes of the wheel, Mayer locates five crucial forces that interact with the multiplicity of human needs to create (or exacerbate) conflict. These forces are communication (which is inevitably flawed and drives misunderstanding), emotion (which keeps participants in a conflict from acting rationally), values (differences in which can create intractable conflict), structure (by which he means the procedural structure in which a dispute is managed or processed—e.g., our invisible veil dispute resolution system), and history (or the context in which people interact). Mayer wisely reminds us that these forces interact to create and heighten conflict. When characterizing the origins and persistence of an interpersonal conflict, evaluating the situation in the context of each of these five forces can be a valuable tool, ensuring that evaluation of the causes of the conflict has been thorough.

MAYER'S WHEEL OF CONFLICT

You can see a discussion of Mayer's Wheel of Conflict, by the author, at *http://media.wiley.com/product_data/ excerpt/9X/07879501/078795019X.pdf.*

Interpersonal sources of conflict causes of interpersonal conflict that emanate from the interrelationships of disputants, as distinguished from positions, aspirations, interests, values, and needs, which are intrapersonal causes of interpersonal conflict.

SOURCES OF CONFLICT

One helpful way to organize and understand the causes of a conflict is to ask oneself which goals, needs, and interests of the disputants are incompatible. Commonly occurring incompatibilities can be thought of as falling into groups or categories, and it's useful to think of them categorically because it suggests ways to address entire groups of conflicts effectively. We will call these categories of incompatible goals, needs, and interests **interpersonal sources of conflict** (Table 2-3). (For more detailed information, see Online Appendix B, Chapter 7.)

◆ **TABLE 2-3**   Interpersonal Sources of Conflict

CONFLICT TYPE	EXAMPLES	USEFUL APPROACHES
<u>Control Over Resources</u> Struggle over control of valued items or ownership of scarce commodities	Dispute between neighbors over property boundaries	Uncover and and deal with any "deeper" sources of conflict. Integrative tactics (tactics aimed at "expanding the pie") can also be useful, followed by compromise.
<u>Data-Type Conflicts:</u> *Conflicts Over Facts:* A conflict over what is happening or has happened *Conflicts over law:* A disagreement over how the law impacts the relationship between the disputants	*Facts:* Two drivers disagree over who drifted into whose traffic lane. *Law:* A disagreement between divorcing spouses over the appropriate appraisal and allocation of pension rights	Generally, data-type conflicts are relevant only because people are in conflict about resources, values, identity, or power. So, uncover these other, deeper sources of conflict. Encourage or guide disputants to focus on deeper interests, concerns, values, and needs. Use reality testing techniques, nonbinding evaluation, and other tactics designed to help disputants self-discover the reality of the data.
<u>Values</u> Disputant's actions antithetical to the deeply held values and principles of other disputant.	A storefront church sues to evict a new neighbor, an adult bookstore.	Sometimes can be resolved if the disputants can "agree to disagree" about the underlying values, as when a disputant agrees to go along with a settlement without admitting liability. Difficult to resolve peacefully if the values are central to self-concepts or world views of the disputants or if coupled with many other sources of conflict, such as disputes over limited resources.
<u>Attributional Disagreement</u> Given an agreement upon set of facts, difference in beliefs about what has produced a given state of affairs	In medical malpractice case, parents contend that failure to perform emergency caesarean section was responsible for child's brain injury, while doctor contends that a cord wrapped around the baby's head caused the injury.	An attributional disagreement is actually a values conflict and should be handled as such. Often laws control the attribution to be made in a given set of facts.
<u>Identity</u> One disputant's actions seem to threaten the self-esteem and face of another.	An employee's allegation of racism on the part of a supervisor threatens the supervisor's self-concept as racially tolerant and his concept of U.S. society as color-blind and fair.	Identity conflict tends to be intractable. Use tactics that affirm and protect the dignity of each participant. Narrative mediation and transformative mediation, which encourage each disputant to become familiar with the life story of the other, can be useful. Sometimes these conflicts can be handled through the use of negotiating agents. Conflicts based on the negative stereotypes held by one social group about another social group are often coupled with power imbalance situations (see following) and will often require legislative or judicial activism.

◆ **TABLE 2-3** Interpersonal Sources of Conflict *(continued)*

CONFLICT TYPE	EXAMPLES	USEFUL APPROACHES
Perceived unjust power imbalance A disputant perceives an unjust balance of power and struggles to rectify it. Often coupled with world view conflicts, with the oppressor honestly denying the existence of an imbalance.	School integration, affirmative action disputes, international ethnic conflict	The more powerful disputant is generally unwilling to give up power and may honestly fail to see that a power imbalance exists. Power imbalance is typically conflated with value and identity conflict, making it highly intractable. Use power of moral authority and reality testing to convince powerful disputant to give up power to preserve long-term social structure, avoid violent struggle, or make his/her/its/their actions consistent with own deeply held values. Frequently, appeal to a more powerful authority (e.g., litigation) is necessary. In some very intractable situations, the disputants disagree about whose is the disempowered one (e.g., Israeli–Palestinian conflict).
Displaced and Misattributed Conflict There is an unacknowledged, often hidden conflict; disputants are disputing over something else (displaced conflict) or with the wrong people (misattributed conflict).	Business partners who have an unacknowledged conflict over the allocation of rights and responsibilities dispute about minor aspect of the business.	The real conflict should be uncovered and diagnosed. Often, the underlying conflict is a structural/power issue that the disputant feels powerless to change. Unfortunately, the underlying conflict is typically deep rooted and difficult to resolve (otherwise, it would not have stayed hidden). Mediation can often produce clarity about the real conflict.

These are sometimes obvious and sometimes not so obvious—and like icebergs, what is most important is usually hidden from view.

Nearly every legal dispute can be characterized as a *dispute over resources* (such as a disagreement over whether a litigant should receive damages) or a *dispute over facts* (Did the driver change lanes into the other driver's car) or law (Who had the right of way, Driver A or Driver B?). Resource conflicts, disputes over facts, and *disputes over law* are the meat and potatoes of the legal profession. Indeed, lawyers and paralegals are conditioned to look for these elements in every situation: Facts and law determine whether a litigant can establish a cause of action, and determining **legal remedies** involves looking for resource conflicts.

However, these obvious causes are almost never the whole story—or even the most important reason for conflict. If a conflict seems difficult to resolve, it's a good bet that other sources of conflict lie beneath the surface. These need

Legal remedy
the rights that, by law, a litigant can or does receive as a result of establishing a cause of action in court.

to be recognized and dealt with to resolve the conflict optimally. Consider the following example:

> Dartmouth and Dartmouth have been hired to represent a developer in its quest to redevelop an urban block. To complete the development, the developer must buy out the interests of a number of flat owners in some high-rise buildings that will be razed. The developer had been careful to lay a foundation for popular support by going door to door to sell its idea of an innovative shopping-parkland-apartment-condominium complex, and it met with a lot of apparent enthusiasm from the flat owners. Management believed it was sailing along until caught off guard by a well-organized parade of protesters who railed against the proposal at a town meeting. Speakers complained that the process of adopting the developer's plan had been illegal and underhanded. Other speakers complained that residents were being heavy-handedly pressured to leave their homes.
>
> Dartmouth recommended hiring a **facilitator** to research the problem. The facilitator discovered that leaders of a local resident's rights group had been responsible for inciting most of the protest. The group had formed some years ago to ameliorate substandard conditions in the flats now being bought up to create the development. The developer had hired former occupants to assist with the development plan but had failed to formally consult the rights group and had not spoken to its leadership. The replacement housing units proposed in the development would represent a complete achievement of all the goals sought by the group. This success would render the group obsolete, and the group responded by nitpicking the proposal to pieces. Thus, the developer, by being so careful to accommodate the needs of residents for better housing, had created an **identity conflict**, a particularly intractable variety of conflict, with the resident's rights organization, by eliminating its relevance in the community. Moreover, by not seating the organization at the negotiating table, the developer had created a loss of face, deepening the identity conflict.

Facilitator
a dispute resolution professional whose practice often consists of developing an environment and process in which complicated, large-group conflicts can be better managed or resolved. A facilitator often researches a conflict, determines who the true disputants and de facto stakeholders are, and recommends a process, agenda, and attendance list.

Identity conflict
conflict produced when the actions of one disputant threaten the self-esteem or self-concept of the other or produce loss of face.

Any effort to resolve a conflict without dealing with its deep sources is likely to lead to a suboptimum result or to complete impasse. For example, unless the identity conflict with the resident's group can be resolved, the pressure of the protests are unlikely to lessen. This continued protest may result in the developer being unable to buy out the flats, in which case the project may have to be abandoned, or at best it may have to pay a much higher price for the flats. Yet there may be relatively inexpensive, simple ways to handle the situation based on understanding the hidden source of the conflict: Future negotiations could feature the formal participation of the resident's group, the group could be publicly recognized as the reason for various housing-friendly development features, the new development could be named for the resident's group, the group itself could be transformed into a watchdog organization for the welfare of the tenants in the new building, and so forth.

Identity conflict deserves special emphasis for two reasons. First, it tends to be unusually intractable and pernicious, as it is usually hidden and is often disguised beneath a resource conflict (Rothman, 1997). Identity conflict often produces conflict escalation because of the intense enmity created by the threat or fact of humiliation and loss of face. In addition, identity conflict is needlessly widespread because it can occur as a by-product of positional bargaining. Once a disputant articulates a concrete position in a conflict, being forced to move off the position can create loss of face. Thus, seemingly garden-variety conflicts can be converted into intractable, escalating identity conflicts. Relatedly, values conflicts tend to be fierce and difficult to resolve because they often produce identity conflicts. Often, one's values are so closely tied to one's identity that an attack on values can feel like existential threat (Mayer 2000, 12).

A conflict participant who invests the time and attention to determine the underlying sources of a conflict will gain insights into the best ways to resolve the conflict. Table 2-3 lists some typical approaches to dealing with conflicts having the listed sources. Failing to attend to underlying sources of conflict will often lead to impasse or to poor resolution. Here's an example:

> Dereck and Fran, both CPAs, formed a general practice accounting partnership in 1985. The following year they bought a small building in which to house their practice. The building contained four offices (two of which they rented to others) and a large conference room, as well as a lobby, restroom, storage area, and kitchen.
>
> In 1996, Fran, having become interested in accounting for nonprofits, asked to dissolve the partnership, to which Dereck acceded. The two former partners formed a corporation that co-owned the building, and they continued to share common space and expenses. Gradually over the next ten years, Fran's practice grew more and more profitable, while Dereck's practice remained flat. The building co-ownership agreement was rendered less and less useful for Fran, given her increasing need for additional staff and space. Fran now would like to take over the building entirely, remodel to add office space, or sell out her interest to Dereck or another owner so she can move into another larger building. Dereck flatly refuses all proposals on Fran's part, stating simply that he has no interest in changing the existing arrangements. This impasse leaves Fran hamstrung and her professional practice in jeopardy. Leaving would be terribly costly to her and to the goodwill she has gained in her practice; moreover, Dereck refuses to cooperate in modifying the deed to allow Fran to sell her interest.

This situation easily can be characterized as a conflict over resources, since the office space is a resource. It can also be characterized as a conflict over law: over the meaning of the contractual relationship between the two former partners and the options Fran has in unilaterally altering the mutual business relationship. If this were all there is to the situation, then negotiating an accommodation of the disputants' mutual resource interests should resolve the conflict. However, Dereck's flat refusal to negotiate, even to his monetary bene-fit, signals that more is going on. Consider the following additional facts:

> Fran comes from a poor immigrant family and is the first of her family to have gone to college. She graduated from a topflight accounting school and has an MBA from Duke, whereas Dereck barely got through trade school. Dereck's father is a dean of the business administration department at a renowned university, and his mother is the chief executive officer of a best-selling magazine. Dereck is a brilliant accountant, and frequently, in interacting with Fran during their partnership days, has made sure he repeated stories to her that suggested his superiority. However, Dereck is a poor entrepreneur, and he is now barely breaking even, a fact he hasn't ad-mitted to Fran, though it's obvious to her. Dereck has a contentious rela-tionship with his father, who never lets Dereck forget how disappointed he is with him. When Fran suggested to Dereck that a profitable deal could be struck to give her the additional office space she needs, Dereck became snide and arrogant and more than once alluded to her poor background and his aristocratic one.

These additional facts add to our knowledge of the sources of this conflict. Both Fran, who has been belittled by Dereck, and Dereck, whose lack of success in his practice are deeply wounding to him, are undermined in their self-esteem by the conflict. An identity conflict is the result. In addition, there may be a misattributed conflict here, in that the conflict Dereck has with Fran may be a reflection of a more intractable identity conflict Dereck has with his own father. In these circumstances, direct efforts to create a situation in which the dis-putants try to adjust property and business interests in negotiation are likely to fail. Given the identity conflicts, the disputants are more likely to have luck with **transformative mediation, narrative mediation,** or another process that directly supports the self-esteem of the participants (though it may be a challenge to in-duce one or both to participate). The important lesson to take from the discus-sion is that there are typically multiple sources of conflict, that the most important sources (from the perspective of determining the best way to resolve conflict) are often hidden, and that knowing the sources can guide a participant in choosing the best approaches to managing the situation.

IMPEDIMENTS TO CONSTRUCTIVE RESOLUTION

Frequently the forces keeping a conflict from ending are just as important to consider as the forces that produced the conflict in the first place. Table 2-4 shows the kinds of impediments that commonly keep a conflict from resolving well. These impediments fall into three basic categories: forces that create inde-pendent motives against resolving the conflict; forces that complicate the situa-tion and make it harder to find a solution; and forces that reflect, or produce, perceptual distortions. (For a more detailed discussion of impediments to con-structive conflict resolution, consult Online Appendix B, Chapter 11.)

Transformative mediation
a form of highly facilitative mediation in which the goals are to empower each disputant and encourage each disputant to recognize and acknowledge the point of view of the other.

Narrative mediation
a form of highly facilitative mediation in which the goal is to promote peacemaking through encouraging the participants to tell their versions of the conflictual situation, subsequently supporting the disputants in recasting elements of these versions into less polarized narratives.

◆ **TABLE 2-4**   Impediments to Resolving Interpersonal Conflicts

IMPEDIMENT	SUBTYPES	EXAMPLE
Motive inconsistent with resolution of the conflict (*Solution: Discharge inconsistent motive or strengthen motive to resolve the conflict*)	Motivation to Seek Vengeance: A disputant wants retribution against another participant more than he/she wants settlement.	Knowing she will lose in court, a plaintiff pursues a lawsuit because of the inconvenience she knows it will cause the defendant.
	Unpleasant Disputant: A disputant, or a member of disputant's team, is so unpleasant that settling with her leaves a bad feeling.	A defendant can't bring herself to settle with plaintiff: The latter has made defendant's life so miserable that defendant finds giving her any sort of satisfaction to be intolerable.
	Overcommitment and Entrapment: Disputant commits so much to a competitive position that settlement seems to be wasteful or humiliating.	After committing $50,000 to preparing for trial, plaintiff refuses an eleventh hour offer to settle for an amount the plaintiff originally felt would be in his best interests.
	Excluded Stakeholder: An important stakeholder in the conflict is left out of the negotiations and, therefore, sabotages efforts to complete a settlement.	During negotiations over custodial arrangements for a teenager, parental efforts to institute visitation arrangements fall apart when the child refuses to go to the mother's house as specified in the agreement.
	Competitive Culture or Subculture: Disputant or negotiator comes from a culture or subculture in which competition is the primary blueprint for conflict management.	In a dispute over baseball salaries, both owners and players believe that it is inappropriate to cooperate with the opposition.
Forces that complicate the conflict (*Solution: Simplify the conflict or help the participants handle the complexity*)	Meta-Conflicts: Conflicts and disputes over how the main conflict is or has been handled.	During a labor dispute, one side accuses the other of unfair practices.
	Linkages: Settling this case will affect other situations in unpredictable or damaging ways.	A prosecutor refuses to accept a plea bargain offer in an accounting fraud case—even though the evidence in the case is weak—because of the slap-on-the-wrist message that might be sent to others.
	Conflicts of Interest Among Team Members: Addressing the interests of one team member undermines the interests of another team member.	A mother refuses to settle a pending child custody case with her child's father because civility with this man enrages her present husband.
Forces that involve, or create, perceptual distortions (*Solution: Use processes that prevent or deal with perceptual distortion; empower disputants with knowledge that increases the propensity to act rationally*)	Disempowered Disputant: Disputant feels overmatched during a conflict and is fearful that agreeing to a settlement will harm him.	A major corporation can't convince a frightened consumer to settle a warranty claim despite the corporate counsel's honest belief that the consumer would be getting an extremely good deal.

(Continued)

◆ **TABLE 2-4** Impediments to Resolving Interpersonal Conflicts *(continued)*

IMPEDIMENT	SUBTYPES	EXAMPLE
	<u>Mistrust:</u> Belief that the other disputant is likely to use a settlement process as an opportunity for exploitation.	During Israeli–Palestinian conflict, Israeli government was unwilling to take word of Yasser Arafat that he would take care of anti-Semitic terrorists; as a result, the Israeli government took military action against Palestinian militants.
	<u>Lack of "Ripeness":</u> One or both disputants have not yet come to believe that there is an urgent need to settle.	A defense lawyer in a case scheduled for trial in 15 months refuses plaintiff's requests for settlement discussions, hoping that playing hard to get will sweeten the eventual outcome.
	<u>Jackpot Syndrome:</u> Disputant is willing to trade a huge risk that he or she will lose for the opportunity to obtain a huge recovery.	The plaintiff sues for $10 million and refuses to settle despite her attorney's warning that she's highly unlikely to beat the defendant's latest offer of $30,000.
	<u>Loss Aversion:</u> Disputant would rather gamble on a likely huge loss than pay out a smaller but certain loss now.	Defendant, faced with an offer of settlement if he pays $25,000, prefers to try the case even though his lawyer warns that he's very likely to lose ten times that much.

An experienced mediator tells the following story:

Today I had the unusual experience of seeing three different sets of clients, all with similar disputes on their hands. In all three cases, there was a piece of jointly held property, worth around $500,000, which the disputants had decided to transfer to one of them in exchange for cash compensation to the other. The problem in each case was the inability to decide on the amount of the payoff. In group A, the disputant who is to give up title and receive cash is an impoverished young man with a grade school education and is negotiating with a middle-aged chief financial officer at a large holding company. In my opinion the settlement being proposed is fair, but the proposed cash recipient does not trust the proposal because he doesn't have the knowledge to evaluate it and, out of fear, has said "no." I referred him to a legal services corporation to get legal advice. In group B, the two disputants have a history of tremendous animosity, and it is extremely difficult for either disputant to agree to anything the other proposes, no matter how advantageous. So I met with each of them out of sight of the other. They're both very grateful because they know the deal is good, but they can't say "yes" when they see the whites of each other's eyes. In group C, the problem is that the settlement of this case will be seen as precedent for a number of similar cases involving one of the disputants. This last mediation is perhaps the hardest to resolve. I referred the disputant with the linked cases problem to a financial advisor to work out the details of how this deal will affect all the others in the pipeline, and to his lawyer to clarify whether he has other options that are better.

This example illustrates the limitations of one-size-fits-all thinking. Each conflict, though identical on the surface, was impeded by something different, and therefore it was important to break each impasse with a different approach. This is the point that was made by Frank E. A. Sander and Stephen Goldberg, two of the most notable pioneers in the ADR movement when they wrote "Fitting the Forum to the Fuss," a seminal scholarly article proposing that one can select an ADR process to fit a given case based, in part, on the impediments to settlement presented by the situation (Sander and Goldberg 1994).

PROMOTING PSYCHOLOGICAL OWNERSHIP

Psychological ownership
the extent to which a participant in a dispute resolution process and outcome feels that the process and/or outcome were freely chosen by him or her and is what he or she would have wanted.

The term **psychological ownership** refers to a sense of having freely chosen a given option. Often, this phenomenon occurs when a person expresses a preference for a particular choice—in doing so he or she stakes his or her ego on the choice. For example, a litigant who announces to the other side "I think we should arbitrate this case" develops psychological ownership of the arbitration option by articulating the preference. Psychological ownership of process and outcome by conflict participants increases that person's satisfaction with the outcome and creates a commitment to preserving the integrity of the result. On the other hand, lack of psychological ownership can derail even the best settlement and make the lives of successful litigants miserable.

A successful business executive describes the reason for his success in negotiation using psychological ownership ideas:

> I get my way by sitting more or less quietly in the room and finding a way to make others in the room think they want what I privately hope will be the outcome. If possible, I let someone else propose the ideas I'm hoping for, and I participate just enough to encourage others to voice the strengths of the proposal. After my proposal is adopted, they leave the room thinking they've won the negotiation. The greater my outward role in the decision-making process, the less bound to the outcome the others in the negotiation are and the less likely it is that the decision will "stick." So it's in my interests to stay in the background if I can.

Quality of consent
the extent to which the consent of a participant to a dispute resolution process and outcome is "owned psychologically" by the disputant and is based on voluntary and well-informed consent to the process and/or outcome.

A concept closely related to psychological ownership is **quality of consent** (Lande 1997), which refers to the willingness of a disputant to accede to a dispute resolution process and outcome after being well informed of the issues. Regardless of whether the outcome itself is exactly what a disputant initially sought, he or she is more likely to "buy into" the outcome and "own" it psychologically if he or she is a willing participant in the process. The concept of quality of consent in ADR is conceptually related to **procedural justice***, that the process being used to resolve a conflict is just, fair, and equitable, regardless of ultimate outcome. High-quality consent in a dispute resolution process, which is crucial to the durability of outcomes, requires that the disputants readily

Procedural justice
the extent to which a dispute resolution process is considered fair, equitable, and protective of the rights of the participants. In contrast, *substantive justice* refers to the same qualities in the *outcome* of a dispute resolution process.

consent to the dispute resolution process being used and that they do so from an informed and empowered position. Lande (1997) lists the following seven attributes of high-quality consent in ADR:

- Explicit identification of the principals' goals and interests
- Explicit identification of plausible options for satisfying these interests
- Disputants' generation of options for achieving their interests
- Disputants' careful consideration of these options
- If a dispute resolution process involving an adjudicator or other third-party neutral is being used, the neutral's restraint in pressuring principals to accept particular substantive options
- Limitation on the neutral's use of time pressure
- Neutral's confirmation of principals' consent to selected options

By this definition, the best quality of consent (and hence the greatest psychological ownership) occurs in conflict resolution processes that are entered into freely and voluntarily, and which feature purely facilitative (and not coercive, directive, or adjudicatory) efforts on the part of agents, advocates, and neutrals. (This point and the subject of how quality of consent impacts the selection of dispute resolution processes are discussed in more detail in Chapter 7.)

Whether produced by some or all of the quality-of-consent factors articulated by Lande (1997), psychological ownership of a dispute resolution process is likely to promote willingness to abide by the terms of an outcome and to reduce the likelihood of future disputes. For example, a litigant who proposes arbitration of a dispute will be predisposed to like the process and the outcome and will be more eager to abide by such an outcome and protect it—even if it's not quite the process or the outcome he had hoped for—as he would have been had he not favored its use in the first place. Indeed, psychological ownership can sometimes be used in escalated conflict to create a sort of reverse psychology: A disputant who wants a particular process to occur can speak out against it, and often this tactic will make the process more palatable to the other disputant.

The flip side of a process and outcome owned psychologically by disputants is a process and/or outcome imposed on a disputant against his or her will. Even if a given process or outcome would have been otherwise acceptable to a disputant, it will become less desirable if imposed involuntarily, particularly by the other disputant. A disputant who has little psychological ownership of a given process or outcome will frequently derail the process or sabotage the outcome. For example, suppose a litigant proposes arbitration. If the court then requires the parties to engage in arbitration,[4] the other litigant, who has had the option imposed on him, is likely to find reasons to object, "forget" to appear for hearings or come late, find legal grounds for attacking the arbitration process, or, if the outcome of arbitration requires acts of responsibility on his part, fail to comply.

---

[4] In fact, court-ordered arbitration raises constitutional problems, as is discussed in Chapter 5.

For these reasons, it is helpful for a conflict resolution process to be as purely voluntary as possible—to allow the disputants to select by consensus both the outcome and the specifics of the process used. If the process being used is an ADR process, it helps for the neutral in the process not to be in charge of making the decision, and it's optimal for the neutral to help the disputants articulate their underlying interests, needs, and goals but to refrain from expressing opinions about the conflict or expressing an evaluation or a preference for an outcome. This hands-off policy extends to important, but less obvious, elements of the dispute resolution process, such as how the conflict is framed, what standards are used to guide the decision-making process, and so on. The importance of disputant autonomy in creating psychological ownership extends to what standards of fairness and equity are applied to the situation:

> A divorce mediator tells of two sets of clients with similar financial situations— grown children, a pension from the husband's employment worth several hundred thousand dollars, a pension from the wife's employment worth about one hundred thousand dollars, two used vehicles worth relatively little, and four-bedroom homes in equivalently middle-class suburban neighborhoods. Both sets of clients had decided that the spouses would own their respective pensions and vehicles, that title to the house would be transferred to the wife, and that personal property would be divided equally. In such situations, family law often specifies that the spouses tally up how much monetary value each is receiving, and negotiate a transfer of money to compensate the spouse receiving less value.
>
> Couple A, the Johnstones, immediately set about negotiating to hire an appraiser to determine the value of the house so that the monetary compensation could be calculated. However, couple B, the Smiths, both said that no money needed to change hands. Mr. and Mrs. Smith stated that they mutually believed the house equity to be worth about $350,000, which would create a relatively even division of the property. However, to avoid buyer's remorse, the mediator decided to do some reality testing: He asked Mrs. Smith how she would feel if she later learned that the house was only worth half that amount and asked Mr. Smith how he would feel if the house turned out to be worth double that amount. Both said, "We don't care—we think this is a fair division anyway." In other words, the traditional manner in which the law addressed equitable division of property was not chosen by the Smiths as a criterion they wished to use to distribute their marital property. For the Johnstones, the need to follow the law's approach to equitable distribution was a given.

THE BENEFITS OF PROMOTING COOPERATION

The preceding discussion suggests a number of advantages to resolving interpersonal conflict cooperatively, if possible. We have seen previously in this chapter ("How Conflict Escalation Leads to Perceptual Error") how cooperation can avoid some of the perceptual biases and distortions that occur when a conflict becomes competitive and starts to escalate, and we have seen how voluntary resolution of a conflict promotes psychological ownership of its outcome, and, hence durability of the outcome. Mutual disputant cooperation serves both of these ends. But cooperation confers additional advantages to effective resolution, according to Deutsch (1973): efficiency, optimality, and relationship preservation.

EFFICIENCY

First, cooperation is more efficient than competition. Because disputants are motivated to help one another, they direct more effort to resolving the conflict. In contrast, in a competition, disputants are motivated to keep one another from reaching their goals, so they spend additional time and resources trying to impede and undermine one another. The motivation to do harm is exacerbated by the enmity each disputant comes to feel toward the other. Thus, in a competition, time and resources otherwise available to resolve the conflict are diverted to the purpose of undermining the other disputant. There is also greater duplication of effort, resulting from the refusal of each disputant to trust the statements and actions of the other. Instead of coordinating their efforts, time and money are spent attacking the findings of the other disputant and his or her experts. Because of the mistrust, each disputant has a tendency to **reactively devalue** suggestions made by the other. For example, if disputant A in an escalated conflict wants to receive $30,000 to settle the case, and disputant B offers $30,000, disputant A is likely to reconsider his aspiration, suspicious that the offer of $30,000 is based on an ulterior motive. Reactive devaluation also prevents disputants from agreeing to dispute resolution strategies, processes, and providers if favored by their "opposition." Thus, reactive devaluation can further undermine efficient dispute management. If the matter is litigated, the inefficiencies of formalized structure, designed to prevent unfairness in a process in which each side is trying to exploit the other, result in a cumbersome, time-consuming, and extremely expensive process.

Indeed, cooperation makes dispute resolution more efficient even if resolution is not attained. The process of working for amicable interaction and the open sharing of information can provide benefits to clients and their legal team as they prepare for court. When cooperating litigants must go to court, the process can be streamlined and the outcome can be attained more quickly and more cheaply.

RESOURCE OPTIMIZATION

Cooperation also tends to promote the more effective utilization of resources—in other words, cooperating disputants have more to divide. The reasons go beyond efficiency considerations. In cooperation, because of the more open sharing of underlying goals, interests, and needs, outcomes can be better tailored to the disputants. This is particularly true of disputants who utilize a **collaborating** *or* **integrating**

Reactive devaluation
the devaluing of a choice, option, or recommendation merely because it is seen to be favored by an opposing party in an escalated conflict.

Collaborating (Integrating)
a negotiation style or strategy characterized by the seeking of solutions that maximize the interests, values, and needs of all disputants.

Learning to Negotiate

For the classic text on how to perform interest-based, collaborative negotiation, pick up the enormously popular 1991 text by Roger Fisher, William Ury, and Bruce Patton: *Getting to YES: Negotiating Agreement Without Giving In.* An account of adversarial legal negotiation is presented in Harry Edwards and James White's 1977 book *The Lawyer as a Negotiator.*

negotiation style in resolving their dispute. (See Online Appendix B, Chapter 12.) Collaborating is a strategy based on placing a high priority on addressing the underlying interests, values, and needs of *all* disputants in the conflict (see "Learning to Negotiate"). In addition to sharing information, collaborating disputants have mutual benefit as an explicit goal toward which they work. And co-operators of all stripes are less likely to be mentally sidetracked by playing blame games and finding ways to undermine one another. Competition, on the other hand, promotes a sort of "binary thinking" (Menkel-Meadow 1996) by framing the conflict as a contest: Disputants tend to characterize the conflict as "Either my position wins out or his position wins out," without any thoughts of alternative options other than perhaps the possibility of splitting the difference. This win-lose orientation focuses disputants on the clear indicia of victory and defeat in the conflict (such as who gets more money), while sidetracking them from the important detail work that they must do to optimize the outcome. Because of this binary thinking, competition has a tendency to produce less creative, less optimal, and less appropriately detailed outcomes.

CONFLICT CONTAINMENT

Cooperation is also less likely than competition to lead to *escalation and spreading of the conflict.* We have already seen that competitive conflict leads to exacerbation of disputant hostility. As it escalates, competitive conflict also pressures bystanders to form alliances with disputants, thus increasing the number of partisans. In addition, because of the barriers to resolution created in competitive conflict and the misunderstandings that arise from interruptions of communication, the situation tends to spin off conflicts (and disputes) over how the main conflict is being resolved (**meta-conflicts** and **meta-disputes**). For example, a dispute during litigation over whether one side has responded adequately to requests for discovery from the other side is a common example of a meta-dispute. Thus, cooperation avoids the proliferation and expansion that often occur in a competitive conflict.

Meta-conflicts (Meta-disputes) interpersonal conflicts (disputes) about the manner in which a main conflict (dispute) is being handled.

RELATIONSHIP PRESERVATION

Cooperative approaches to conflict also tend to preserve personal relationships more effectively than competitive approaches. The forces that lead to feelings of animosity and hostility in competitions do not operate in a cooperative conflict;

The Dispute Resolution Relationship: Worth Caring For?

It is frequently said in ADR texts and training programs that some forms of ADR are preferential *if* the disputants expect to have a continuing relationship with one another. However, an amicable and cooperative relationship sets the stage for extremely beneficial conflict outcomes for disputants—better congruity with disputant needs and interests, more optimal utilization of resources, less likelihood of violation of agreements, and greater efficiency. It is therefore helpful to think of the dispute experience as *itself* a relationship worthy of nurturing, even if the disputants will never interact after settlement.

on the contrary, cooperative conflict is marked by feelings of friendliness and closeness on the part of the disputants. If the disputants have an ongoing relationship to protect, this aspect of cooperation can be extremely important. Examples of disputants who need to protect ongoing relationships include divorcing parents of minor children; business partners; those attempting to establish or maintain a business relationship (such as repeat buyers and sellers); employers and employees; schools, parents, teachers, and students; landlords and tenants; and others. The positive regard promoted by cooperation can improve relationships on multiple fronts; thus, the advantages go beyond the immediate conflict itself to improving the relationship altogether (see "The Dispute Resolution Relationship: Worth Caring For?").

COOPERATION AND ADR

Many ADR processes and providers set cooperation as a goal, for many of the reasons advanced above. Since escalated conflict tends to create a perception that cooperation is not possible, some of the tactics used in some ADR processes, particularly those that are facilitative, are designed to reduce competition, temper animosity, overcome the natural fear of conflict participants to engage in cooperation, and structure a cooperative process that participants are able to use.

Beyond simple cooperation, advanced ADR processes frequently promote collaborative variants of cooperative negotiation processes such as "principled negotiation" (Fisher, Ury, and Patton 1991). The following are the hallmarks of these processes:

- ◆ Discouragement of the disputants from stating positions
- ◆ Careful analysis and articulation of underlying interests, principles, values, and basic human needs
- ◆ The use of a collaborative negotiation approach

Pareto-efficiency
an economic term meaning that a particular allocation of resources is efficient in the sense of allocating each resource to the person who most values it.

This sort of negotiation process is thought to have a number of advantages. First, by promoting fulsome interests analysis and the sharing of information underlying interests, this form of negotiation is thought to be the best for allocating resources to those who value them most. Economists refer to this form of efficiency as **Pareto-efficiency.**

Second, because this form of negotiation combines a high degree of both cooperativeness and self-assertion, it is thought to capture the benefits of cooperation without requiring personal sacrifice or the opening of oneself to exploitation. Thus, the use of principled, collaborative negotiation is the goal for many ADR providers and their clients.

COMPETITION'S ROLE

So when is competition a better option to use? First, it is necessary where there is no other option—as when the one or the other disputant refuses to cooperate, or when the other party cannot be trusted and there is no way to structure a settlement to protect one's interests. However, a caution is in order: One of the known perceptual biases that results from escalated conflict is for disputants to see a conflict as less amenable to cooperative settlement than it really is. Most disputants in an escalated conflict will tend to see themselves as more cooperative than the other disputant—that's part of the blame game of competition. Thus, it's important to diagnose the conflict carefully to avoid unnecessary use of competitive processes.

Competition will also be necessary when structural power imbalances prevent a disempowered disputant from getting a fair shake. Of course, in those situations competition must be used carefully. If, for example, a disempowered disputant takes a dispute to court, the result may well be a court order that further entrenches the power imbalance.

Another situation in which competition may be useful is where the other disputant obligingly allows your side to impose itself. Game theory research indicates that cooperators often suffer large losses when encountering an opponent who uses competitive tactics. However, since the losing party can often find a way to sabotage the outcome and make life miserable for the "winner," this tactic can backfire when the disputants will be involved in a continuing relationship.

A fourth situation in which competition may be useful is in situations in which not much is at stake and the parties will not have an ongoing relationship (minor auto accident claims, barter of goods): A quick resolution through a brief round of positional bargaining may be worth more than the optimality of outcome that comes from a cooperative negotiation. A fifth situation is one in which the participants are used to a culture of competition and value intrinsically the competitive process.

USING POWER EFFECTIVELY

Power
deliberate or purposive influence over a person or one's surroundings (Deutsch 1973, 87).

It is evident that clients and other disputants get the best results when **power** is used effectively on their behalf. However, like chemotherapeutic drugs, many kinds of power have highly destructive side effects. The best conflict resolution makes careful and considered use of power in a manner that does not undermine the client's interests in the long run. (For a detailed look at power issues in the context of conflict diagnosis, see Online Appendix B, Chapter 13.)

Relationship power is the ability to intentionally influence others. Dorling Kindersley Media Library

Relationship power
power to influence other persons.

Environmental power
power to alter one's surroundings or one's location.

Alienation
a quality of a person feeling disconnected from, or actively adverse to, the goals, motivations, aspirations, and so on of some other person.

Illegitimate
in the analysis of power, the belief and feeling, on the part of someone, that the use of power by someone else is not appropriate or not morally right.

Relationship power can be defined as the power to exert influence over others with whom one interacts (e.g., the power to serve as a positive role model or the power to threaten litigation), whereas **environmental power** can be defined as the power to control one's surroundings (e.g., the power to leave a location or situation). Numerous scholars have created typologies of power. Many of them include sources of power based on coercion, fear, threat or aggression, money, the power to confer rewards, charisma, moral rectitude, and power based on expertise. One such typology is presented in Table 2-5.

One of the major negative side effects of using power is that it can alienate the person on whom it is imposed. **Alienation** here is defined as an undermining of a sense of positive regard for the power wielder, what he or she stands for, and what he or she is striving to accomplish. It is believed that alienation is most likely to occur with the imposition of coercive power and least likely with the employment of expert power (Deutsch 1973). Moreover, the likelihood of alienation is exacerbated if the person on whom power is imposed sees the imposition as **illegitimate.**

Alienation disempowers the wielder of power, so avoiding alienation if possible is a good idea. Consider why wielding an alienating form of power is so damaging to the user: Imagine that Mr. Power is attempting to influence Mr. Money during a negotiation. In doing so, Mr. Power alienates Mr. Money. Alienation directly impairs both Mr. Power's *referent power* (his ability to use charisma to influence Mr. Money) and his *normative power* and *reward/exchange power,* by causing Mr. Money to dislike him and anything he does. Moreover, by creating distrust in anything Mr. Power says and does, alienation also undermines his *expert power* with Mr. Money.

◆ **TABLE 2-5** Sources of Relationship Power

Type of Power	Definition	Example	Sources of Power: Examples	Likelihood of Alienation from Use
Coercive	The ability to influence others by coercing, threatening, harming, irritating, etc.	A disputant tries to get the other disputant to agree to his terms by threatening litigation.	Physical strength, weaponry, ability to file lawsuit, ability to write threatening letters, having law on your side	Very high
Reward/Exchange	The ability to influence others by rewarding or withdrawing threats of coercion	A disputant offers to dismiss a lawsuit if other disputant agrees to terms.	Wealth, possession of something the other disputant wants, ability to inflict coercion	High
Referent	The ability to influence others based on charisma, attractiveness	To improve a client's chances at trial, a lawyer trains her witnesses in appropriate dress and demeanor.	Improvement of physical appearance, improvement of deportment (charm school), hiring of charismatic spokesperson	Moderate
Normative	The ability to influence others based on high moral standing	A large corporation polishes its image by embarking on a highly publicized campaign to support a charitable organization.	Association with a "good cause," hiring of influential spokesperson, "image management"	Moderate
Expert	The ability to influence others based on superiority of knowledge	A lawyer wins a negotiation by demonstrating a superior knowledge of the law.	Research, investigation, formal learning, hiring of experts	Low

This leaves Mr. Power with only *coercive power*. As Mr. Power continues to wield the only power he has left—the power to hurt Mr. Money—Mr. Money will become increasingly hostile and vengeful. The ultimate result will be that even Mr. Power's coercive power will eventually be exhausted, and even if Mr. Power imposes a solution on Mr. Money, it is likely to be costly and inconvenient to enforce.

In short, it's helpful to choose forms of dispute resolution that allow a disputant or the disputant's legal team to apply the least alienating form of power that accomplishes the task of attaining the disputant's goals. Often some amount of coercive power is needed to get the attention of a disputant, but the trick is not to apply so much coercive power that the disputant is alienated. For example, it is often necessary to order litigants into mediation, but heavy-handed tactics used to enforce such an order will often derail mediation and create a sense in the disputants that mediation was nothing but an exercise in futility.

Best Alternative to a Negotiated Agreement (BATNA)
considering one's aspirations, interests, values, and needs, the best option that one has *other than* the ones possible in a given negotiation.

Worst Alternative to a Negotiated Agreement (WATNA)
considering one's aspirations, interests, values, and needs, the worst possible outcome of a specific option, where the outcome of choosing the option is uncertain.

BATNA AND WATNA AS ELEMENTS OF EXPERT POWER

To know one's **Best Alternative to a Negotiated Agreement (BATNA)** means that one knows the best one can do if a negotiation fails to produce an agreement. The **Worst Alternative to a Negotiated Agreement (WATNA)** is the worst possible outcome that could come out of a failure to negotiate an agreement. Together, these constitute crucial elements of expert power for disputants and their representatives. For this reason, several ADR processes are designed to inform participants of BATNA and WATNA.

Here's an example of BATNA:

> Jeffrey wants to buy a car and is negotiating with Dan Dealer. Jeffrey has his heart set on a particular make and model of car, believes that spending $18,500 is a fair price, but hopes to get one for $18,000. He researches terms for this particular make and model in depth and finds several offers that range from $18,750 to $20,500, plus a price of $18,400 in another state, but that sale will cost $400 in additional delivery charges. Dan Dealer has offered $18,650.

In this situation, Jeffrey's BATNA—his best alternative to making a deal with Dan—is $18,750: It's the best price he can get outside of negotiating with Dan. If Jeffrey holds out for a price of $18,000 rather than making a deal with Dan, he is not likely to get it. Dan's offer of $18,650 is better than Jeffrey's best alternative to accepting the offer, which is $18,750, so if Dan does not seem to be receptive to continuing to bargain down the price, Jeffrey should take the deal. On the other hand, if Jeffrey has found an equivalent car at another dealer for a firm price of $17,950, he'd be foolish to spend $18,650—his BATNA, $17,950, is better. Thus, the BATNA tells a negotiator when to consider settlement and when to continue to hold out for a better result. This knowledge gives a disputant a tremendous amount of power, control, and a sense of peace during periods when it is unclear how to deal with a conflict. (For guidance in how to assess a BATNA, see Online Appendix B, Chapter 13, pages 246–248.)

Whereas the BATNA represents the best certain alternative to negotiation, the WATNA represents the doomsday scenario in a situation where outcome is uncertain. For example, lawyers generally estimate the value of a litigated case as the probabilities of the likely outcomes multiplied by the probabilities of each outcome. Suppose a defendant in an accident case has a 95 percent chance of prevailing in litigation, but because the plaintiff was seriously injured, a 5 percent chance of losing $2,000,000. Court costs and attorney's fees are anticipated to be $25,000. To determine the value of the case, one multiplies the probabilities of each option times their cost, and adds the total—in this case, the value would be 95 percent times $25,000, plus 5 percent times $2,025,000, or a cost of $125,000. If litigation were the only alternative to negotiation (and leaving out nonmonetary costs such as time lost from work and relationship damage), $125,000 would be the defendant's BATNA—he or she should seriously consider any proposal that has him paying out less, and look with skepticism on higher demands from the plaintiff. The WATNA, however, would be $2,025,000. The WATNA is important to know if the disputant is risk-averse. In some cases a disputant might not want to risk a WATNA regardless of how likely a good outcome might be. If out disputant does not want to risk a loss he might take a settlement of higher than $125,000, even though the BATNA is lower, so that he can avoid the possibility of the doomsday scenario if he loses in court.

For most legal disputes, litigation is an alternative to negotiating an agreement, so disputants and their teams generally want to estimate the most likely outcome of litigation, as well as the possibility of a disastrous outcome. Thus, many ADR processes, most notably nonbinding evaluation, are meant primarily to clarify a disputant's BATNA and WATNA by simulating or estimating what would be likely to occur in litigation (and what might go wrong). Knowing this information increases the disputant or his/her team's expert power, allowing more optimized decisions about whether to settle, negotiate, choose another ADR form, or litigate.

UNDERSTANDING THE FOUNDATIONS OF ADR: PUTTING IT TOGETHER

In this chapter, we explored the factors that affect the course and outcome of dispute resolution. We saw that many of the crucial factors that can make or break a dispute resolution process are perceptual, psychological, and typically hidden from view. We also considered the many possible benefits of a nonadversarial, voluntary, facilitative approach to conflict resolution in some instances: the ability to engage in better strategic planning, lessened likelihood of conflict escalation, more optimal outcomes, more satisfied disputants, lessened likelihood of conflict recurrence, and better relationships among disputants who must continue to deal with one another. We learned some of the reasons why such helpful approaches are underused today.

In the chapters to come, we'll learn about ADR processes in detail. As you encounter each process, think back to the concepts you've learned in this chapter. And if you are able to use these fundamentals of ADR in your professional practice, you will find that you reap professional benefits for your client as well as your own career.

EXERCISES, PROJECTS, AND "THOUGHT EXPERIMENTS"

1. In real-world international conflicts, policy makers conclude, often erroneously, that punitive sanctions will be effective in getting other nations to change their behaviors and policies. Researchers Myron Rothbart and William Hallmark (1988) tested this effect in a research study. They asked undergraduates to imagine that they were citizens of one of two imaginary countries. The undergraduate subjects were given a description of a conflict over military buildups between the countries. The subjects were asked to

consider five possible disarmament strategies. Some were asked which strategy would be most effective for their own country to use to limit military expansion by the other, whereas others were asked which strategies the other country could use most effectively to limit its own country's buildup. The strategies ranged from coercive, as in "increase military buildup and threaten to use weapons unless country disarms," to conciliatory, as in "unilaterally stop production of weapons with the expectation that the other country would act in kind." The subjects who were asked what techniques would be most effective for their own country to use to disarm the other rated coercive strategies as more effective, but the subjects who were asked what techniques would be most effective for the other country to use in disarming their own country rated conciliatory strategies as more effective. This effect held true regardless of to which imaginary country the subjects were assigned. What mechanism do you think is responsible for this difference in beliefs about the effect of coercion on one's own "in-group," as contrasted with beliefs about its effects on the "out-group"?

2. Debate and discuss the following proposition: *Undergraduate college courses should be graded on the curve*. There should be two groups in this discussion: One group should defend the proposition, and one should attack the proposition. One individual should moderate the discussion, and one or two people should keep a list of the interests, principles, and values that underlie each position statement.

    a. Post these interests, principles, and values on large sheets of paper around the room or on the chalkboard.

    b. After the debate, brainstorm some possible grading methods that meet all the expressed interests, principles, and values.

3. Think back on the last interpersonal conflict in which you were involved personally. This may be a conflict that is currently active.

    a. How did it feel when you first realized a conflict was occurring?

    b. What steps did you take, or are you taking, to handle the conflict?

    c. What does this information tell you about your overall attitude toward conflict? Do you welcome conflicts or try to avoid them?

    d. Think hard about what the advantages are of your overall approach to conflict. What are the disadvantages? What can you do to minimize these disadvantages while retaining the advantages?

4. Which of the following statements are you in more agreement with? Discuss your decision with your classmates.

    a. "As a society, we need to realize that litigation is not a very good way of dealing with most disputes. We need to develop other ways of handling legal disputes, so that these disputes can be resolved more effectively."

    b. "Our judicial system is seriously underfunded and understaffed, but it remains the best way to resolve legal disputes, and we should do a better job of providing it with resources."

5. Using the Internet, research an international peace movement or organization devoted to resolving a hot conflict, such as the Israeli-Palestinian conflict. An example of such an organization is Americans for Peace Now (*http://www.peacenow.org*). Examine the programs undertaken by the organization you choose. Do you see instances in which the activities of this organization could be viewed as attempts to counteract biases and errors of perception and interpretation discussed in this chapter? For example, an organization that sponsors ongoing dialogue between groups in conflict might be seen as making an effort to counteract errors of interpretation of behaviors that occur during a conflict. Find as many such instances as you can, and describe how they address these biases and errors.

6. *Part A.* Imagine yourself in the following situation:

> *You are driving north on the highway. You enter an intersection at a green light to turn left. You wait, since there are oncoming cars. The light turns yellow, then red, and you start your left turn to clear the intersection, but the oncoming car fails to stop at the red light. It comes right for you, and only quick reflexes on your part keep you from colliding.*

Before going on to read Part B of this question, put the book aside and write down your attitudes and feelings about the other driver. Are you making any assumptions about what this person is like?

Part B. Now read the following paragraph. It describes what is going on in the mind of the driver of the other car.

> *I am driving home from the hospital. Three days ago, my fiancé of five years and I were coming back from our wedding rehearsal dinner with our families. We are devout Christians who do not drink. On the way home, our car was struck by a drunk driver. The car hit us on the driver's side. I was shaken but not seriously hurt. My fiancé was hit on the side and was thrown against the windshield. In the hospital, the doctors have been trying everything. They have operated to set his broken tibia. They have performed a number of scans in an attempt to figure out why he hasn't regained consciousness. They have put in a tube so he can breathe. They have fed him through an IV. I have stayed by his side every moment. I've heard that if you talk to the person and tell him you love him there is a better chance of his waking up. But this morning they said the latest MRI looked very bad. They say he really doesn't have any chance of ever waking up. I am just in shock. They won't let me stay with him anymore; they say I should go home and get some rest. My whole life is over. He was my whole life.*

Does this new information cause you to consider revising your assumptions about what caused this driver to nearly hit you? Does the new information change the way you think about this person? If so, how?

7. Do you agree or disagree with the following statement? "To serve a client adequately, a lawyer should consider all sources of the client's dispute, not just

those legal issues that may be relevant to a cause of action." In an essay discuss both sides of this issue—reasons in support and reasons in opposition.

8. In an effort to maintain control over potentially damaging admissions by clients, lawyers often ask their clients to stop communicating directly with the other disputants or their legal representatives: For the duration of legal representation, communication generally is performed only by the lawyers. Do the ideas presented in this chapter suggest that this practice will reduce, or exacerbate, interpersonal conflict? Explain your answer.

9. Consider the following ethical dilemma: Pearl is a paralegal working in a small law firm. She attended the initial client interview conducted by her supervisor, attorney Arlene, with potential divorce plaintiff Pam. Pam, a fairly wealthy woman, made it clear that she wanted the case to settle with a minimum of expense paid to legal fees. Pearl has since had the impression that Arlene is fanning the flames of the conflict. Arlene has filed numerous motions in the case, some of which seem unnecessary, and she seems to be inflaming passions in her letters and phone calls. Arlene charges by the hour, which is typical in divorces. Might Arlene be violating any ethical obligations? What should Pearl do, and why?

10. What are the risks to the client for attorneys to attempt cooperative approaches to resolving conflict? What are the risks to the client for attorneys *not* to make a diligent effort to cooperate in settling the client's dispute? Use the ideas of Morton Deutsch in considering this question. Where should attorneys draw the line between protecting the client from exploitation and protecting the client from escalating and destructive conflict?

11. Consider the Smiths' decisions (page 43) not to use the criterion set in the law to decide how best to divide and distribute their joint property. Should disputants using an ADR process, such as mediation, to settle legal disputes be allowed to ignore such legal criteria in their settlements? If you are part of the legal team for either of these spouses, and he or she came to you for legal advice prior to the described mediation session, what advice would you give him or her about how to deal with the property distribution, and why? How strongly would you push the spouse to adopt the criteria specified by the applicable law, and why? Discuss these questions in an essay.

RECOMMENDED READINGS

Auerbach, J. S. 1983. *Justice without law: Resolving disputes without lawyers.* New York: Oxford University Press.

Bandura, A. 1977. *Social learning theory.* Englewood Cliffs, NJ: Prentice-Hall.

Blake, R. R., and J. S. Mouton. 1964. *The managerial grid.* Houston, TX: Gulf.

Brazil, W. D. 2000. Symposium: Continuing the conversation about the current status and the future of ADR: A view from the courts. *Journal of Dispute Resolution* 2000:11–39.

Bronfenbrenner, U. 1979. *The ecology of human development.* Cambridge, MA: Harvard University Press.

Bunker, B. B., J. Z. Rubin, et al. (eds). 1995. *Conflict, cooperation and justice: Essays inspired by the work of Morton Deutsch.* San Francisco: Jossey-Bass.

Burger, W. W. 1982. *Isn't there a better way?* Annual Report on the State of the Judiciary, presented at the 1982 midyear meeting of the American Bar Association, Chicago, January 24 . Reprinted as Burger, W. W. 1982. Isn't there a better way? *ABA Journal* 68 (March):274.

Deutsch, M. 1973. *The resolution of conflict: Constructive and destructive processes.* New Haven, CT: Yale University Press.

Deutsch, M., and P. T. Coleman (eds.) 2000. *The handbook of conflict resolution.* San Francisco: Jossey-Bass.

deWaal, F. 1989. *Peacemaking among primates.* Cambridge, MA: Harvard University Press.

Edwards, H., and J. White. *The lawyer as negotiator.* St. Paul, MN: West.

Eisler, R. 1988. *The chalice and the blade: Our history, our future.* San Francisco: Harper & Row.

Epstein, S. 1973. The self-concept revisited or a theory of a theory. *American Psychologist* 28:405–16.

Erikson, E. 1950. *Childhood and society.* New York: W. W. Norton.

Fisher, R., W. Ury, and B. Patton. 1991. *Getting to yes: Negotiating agreement without giving in,* 2nd ed. New York: Penguin Books.

Fiske, S. T., and S. L. Neuberg. 1990. A continuum model of impression formation from category based to individuating processes: Influences of information and motivation on attention and interpretation. In *Advances in experimental social psychology,* Vol. 23, edited by M. P. Zanna (pp. 1–74). San Diego: Academic Press.

Fiss, O. 1984. Against settlement. *Yale Law Journal* 93:1073–90.

Fuller, L. L., and J. D. Randall. 1958. Professional responsibility: Report of the Joint Conference. *ABA Journal* 44:1159–61.

Gilligan, C. 1982. *In a different voice: Psychological theory and women's development.* Cambridge, MA: Harvard University Press.

Goble, F. G. 1970. *The third force: The psychology of Abraham Maslow.* New York: Pocket Books.

Goodpastor, G. 1996. A primer on competitive bargaining. *Journal of Dispute Resolution* 1996:325–77.

Keeva, S. 2001. What clients want. *ABA Journal* 87 (June):48–52.

Kim, S. H., and R. H. Smith. 1993. Revenge and conflict escalation. *Negotiation Journal* 9(1):37–43.

Kritek, P. B. 1994. *Negotiating at an uneven table: Developing moral courage in resolving our conflicts.* San Francisco: Jossey-Bass.

Menkel-Meadow, C. 2000. Mothers and fathers of invention: The intellectual founders of ADR. *Ohio State Journal on Dispute Resolution* 16(1):1–37.

Mnookin, R. E. 1993. Why negotiations fail: An exploration of the barriers to the resolution of conflict. *Ohio State Journal on Dispute Resolution* 8(2):235–49.

Mnookin, R., and L. Kornhauser. 1979. Bargaining in the shadow of the law: The case of divorce. *Yale Law Journal* 88:950–97.

Riskin, L. 1982. Mediation and lawyers. *Ohio State Law Journal* 43:29–60.

Rothman, J. 1997. *Resolving identity-based conflict.* San Francisco: Jossey-Bass.

Rubin, J. Z., D. G. Pruitt, and S. H. Kim. 1994. *Social conflict: Escalation, stalemate, and settlement.* New York: McGraw-Hill.

Sander, F. E. A. 1976. *Varieties of dispute processing.* 70 *Federal Rules Decision* 111.

Sander, F. E. A., and S. Goldberg. 1994. Fitting the forum to the fuss: A user-friendly guide to selecting an ADR process. *Negotiation Journal 10* (January):49–68.

Schneider, A. K. 2000. Building a pedagogy of problem-solving: Learning to choose among ADR processes. *Harvard Negotiation Law Review* 5(Spring):113–35.

Shapiro, D. L., B. H. Sheppard, and L. Cheraskin. 1992. In theory: Business on a handshake. *Negotiation Journal* 8(4):365–77.

Strick, A. 1978. *Injustice for all: How our adversary system of law victimizes us and subverts justice.* New York: Penguin.

Wade, J. 2001. Don't waste my time on negotiation and mediation: This dispute needs a judge. *Mediation Quarterly* 18(Spring):259–280.

Williams, G. R. 1996. Negotiation as a healing process. *Journal of Dispute Resolution,* 1–66.

3

Mediation:
An Introduction

A pessimist sees the difficulty in every opportunity; an optimist sees the opportunity in every difficulty.

—Winston Churchill

In this chapter, you will learn . . .

- ◆ what mediation is and how it differs from other ADR processes.
- ◆ the uses of mediation today.
- ◆ the varieties of mediation and their goals, characteristics, advantages, and disadvantages.
- ◆ the roles played in mediation by mediators, disputants, disputants' lawyers, paralegals, constituents and stakeholders, and experts/consultants.
- ◆ the stages and phases of a typical mediation.
- ◆ some of the techniques used by mediators.

When interpersonal conflict occurs, the most common approach to resolving it is negotiation—a dialogue among the disputants and their representatives aimed at resolving the conflict. If negotiation does not resolve the conflict, and if the conflict involves legal issues, litigation is the only option many disputants see as recourse.

Negotiation offers many benefits over litigation. Negotiation is a process offering complete control on the part of disputants over both the process and outcome. Done optimally, in a cooperative and collaborative manner, negotiation can offer all the advantages of the best dispute resolution: relationship preservation, creative problem solving, economy, time saving, and a greater likelihood that the settlement will not unravel over time. From the societal perspective, negotiation offers a more effective use of resources, relief of overcrowded court dockets, the likelihood of lowered relitigation rates, and the reduced need for increases in court infrastructure and personnel. Thus, negotiation is frequently the best option for addressing conflicts.

A principal drawback to negotiation is that sometimes it fails to produce a settlement. Is there any way to preserve the advantages of negotiated settlement—particularly those of collaborating—when negotiation leads to impasse or when it is anticipated that negotiation is not likely to settle the dispute? One approach is to support negotiation with other processes to increase the likelihood that effective settlement will be the result—that is, to provide *negotiation-plus.* Many of the ADR processes described in this text have been developed to achieve just this end. The ADR process most capable of capturing the benefits of cooperative and collaborative negotiation is the technique we will turn to next. This technique, often considered the "Cadillac" of ADR processes, is mediation.

BASIC DEFINITIONS

Mediation
a form of assisted negotiation, in which a disinterested or neutral third party (called a **mediator**) assists the disputants, with or without their agents and/or advocates, in negotiating a resolution of their interpersonal conflict. In mediation, the neutral is not empowered to make a decision and does not typically press for a particular alternative.

MEDIATION

Mediation is a type of assisted negotiation that uses a third party (or panel of third parties) to help disputants negotiate their settlement. This third party, who is called the *mediator,* is typically impartial with respect to the disputants and neutral as to the settlement reached.[1]

Mediation is distinguished from other ADR processes in two principal ways:

1. In other forms of ADR, such as arbitration and nonbinding evaluation, the process ends with the neutral issuing a decision, whereas in mediation a decision or evaluation either does not occur at all or is simply part of the overall assisted negotiation process.
2. In mediation, the disputants retain the power to settle, or not (unlike adjudicatory processes, such as arbitration).

In mediation, participants meet with a mediator to attempt to negotiate a settlement of their dispute. If the parties to mediation settle their dispute, the settlement is usually written down. Even if the disputants are unable to settle all

---

What Is Mediation?
◆ It is an ADR process.
◆ It is a type of assisted negotiation.
◆ It uses a neutral.
◆ The neutral does not issue a decision.
◆ The disputants retain the power to settle (or not).

---

[1] This is true, at least, for mediation as practiced in most Western nations. In many non-Western cultures, mediation is conducted by a prominent and powerful community elder or another appointee with explicit preferences and biases. Enlightening research on this topic is collected in Shapiro (1981).

Primatologist Franz de Waal has discovered that our closest nonhuman ancestors are capable of mediator-like interventions, in which group leaders help to de-escalate conflict and promote reconciliation. Digital Vision Ltd.

the elements of their dispute, frequently they are able to settle some of their issues or come to a temporary agreement. In mediation, even these interim or partial agreements are valued for their ability to advance the goals of the disputants, to reduce levels of conflict, and to build trust, so that future, more comprehensive settlements can be constructed later.

If disputants reach an agreement of some sort in mediation, some mediators provide the parties with a written **memorandum of settlement, memorandum of agreement,** or **memorandum of understanding (MOU).** This document is not intended to be binding but, instead, is "translated" by the parties' legal advocates into a contract of settlement, or stipulation; or, if the mediation is of a case filed in court, by the judge into an order or judgment. Other mediators draft a document intended for legal enforceability without rewriting. In any event, in general an agreement reached in mediation has the status of a **contract,** no more and no less. However, the fact that an agreement is reached through a process of mediation may create special complexities (see Chapter 4).

The Facilitative-Evaluative Distinction. Beyond this very general definition of mediation as negotiation facilitated by a third party, the process of mediation varies widely: It is not one size fits all. The variations in mediation practice profoundly affect the sorts of situations mediation is suitable for handling. To help us understand the nature of these differences, it is useful to define two other terms denoting a basic quality of mediation practice: the so-called *facilitative-evaluative distinction,* a concept first set forth by eminent legal scholar Leonard L. Riskin in his article "Understanding Mediators' Orientations, Strategies, and Techniques: A Grid for the Perplexed" (Riskin 1996). This conceptual distinction has become "part of the standard mediation nomenclature" for those seeking to understand mediation and how it functions (Goldfien and Robbennol 2007, 280).

Memorandum of settlement, memorandum of agreement, or memorandum of understanding (MOU)
a document memorializing an agreement worked out in mediation; generally, not considered legally binding. Occasionally, it is called a *stipulation.*

Contract (settlement, stipulation, agreement, settlement agreement)
a document, produced by a mediator, by a disputant's attorney, or occasionally by a disputant, memorializing an agreement reached in mediation or other negotiation process, and intended to be legally binding.

Facilitative mediation
mediation in which the mediator focuses on facilitating effective negotiation among the disputants and their teams.

Evaluative mediation
mediation featuring an evaluation of the merits of each disputant's case by the mediator.

Facilitative Mediation. In **facilitative mediation,** the mediator's primary function is to promote effective negotiation. Facilitative mediators use techniques designed to, in their expert opinion, optimize negotiation: They lay ground rules for effective communication, help participants discover their interests and those of their counterparts, guide the disputants in the steps of cooperative negotiation, and intervene at all stages of the conflict cycle to keep the conflict as noncompetitive as possible. The strictly facilitative mediator assiduously avoids any evaluation of the merits or strengths of either disputant's case.

Evaluative Mediation. In **evaluative mediation,** the mediator works to narrow the gap between the demands of each disputant by expressly evaluating the merits, strengths, and weaknesses of each disputant's position and by strategically communicating these evaluations to the disputants (Goldfien and Robbennol 2007, citing Riskin 1996, 24, fn. 8). In a sense, then, evaluative mediation is an intervention based on the notion that negotiation is a process of positional bargaining. The evaluative mediator attempts to minimize the effective distances between the disputants' positions and to create overlap if possible. Another way of understanding evaluative mediation is that it is a process of reducing the optimism of each disputant's BATNA assessment. With each disputant's confidence in his or her alternatives to negotiated settlement reduced, each is more likely to accept compromise settlement terms.[2]

As with the semantic confusion that characterizes many other aspects of the ADR field, the terminology *evaluative mediation* is the subject of some confusion. Many, if not most, scholars (e.g., Schwartz 1999) presume that *evaluative mediation* means that the mediator conducts, and issues to the parties, some sort of evaluation of the merits of the disputants' legal case. Others use the term *evaluation* in a far broader sense, to mean *any* evaluation by the mediator, including making judgments about the information given by the clients (Lowry 2000). This sense of the term seems so broad as to be useless as a practical distinction. However, other commentators note that many techniques used by highly facilitative mediators could be seen as "evaluative" (McDermott and Obar 2004). For instance, many mediators "reality test" what disputants are proposing (e.g., "Do you think your expectation of winning a million dollars in court is realistic"?).

Nevertheless, the important issue hidden within the facilitative-evaluative construct is the impact of the mediator's approach on the process of dispute resolution. Does the mediator's tactic take away party autonomy and quality of consent, by advocating a specific outcome? Does the tactic unduly narrow the scope of discussion, damaging optimization, by forcing the discussion into a one-dimensional, either–or view of what outcomes are possible? Does the tactic,

---

[2] A case can be made for the proposition that a mediator who evaluates the disputants' case may be engaging in the provision of legal advice, which arguably constitutes the unauthorized practice of law (for nonlawyer-mediators) and the representation of parties with conflicting interests (for lawyer-mediators). You will see more about this issue in Chapter 4.

by focusing disputants on what might happen in court, allow the interaction to tilt toward positional bargaining and conflict escalation?

In extreme forms of evaluative mediation, the centerpiece of the process may be a single evaluation of the likely outcome if the dispute is taken to court. At its extremes, evaluative mediation closely resembles nonbinding evaluation (see Chapter 6): The neutral hears all sides of the issue and then issues an opinion regarding how the case might be decided if it were litigated. This opinion may be virtually indistinguishable from the nonbinding decision issued by a neutral in a minitrial or another nonbinding evaluation process. The primary difference between evaluative mediation and nonbinding evaluation is that a neutral performing nonbinding evaluation generally stops with the evaluation, whereas an evaluative mediator proceeds to work with the disputants to reach a settlement. Nonetheless, even this distinction sometimes vanishes. For example, the so-called **Michigan Mediation** process is nothing more than court-connected nonbinding arbitration (Federal Judicial Center and CPR Institute for Dispute Resolution 1996). In short, as with any form of ADR, it obviously pays to get the details before signing on to any proposed mediation plan.

There is also much blurring in practice between facilitative and evaluative mediation. Many mediators practice midway along this continuum, and many jump from facilitative to evaluative approaches based on what they think will promote the goals of the disputants.[3] Most evaluative mediators also use facilitative mediation tactics (we will learn about some of these tactics later in this chapter) to promote cooperation and a speedy conclusion to the process. Even Riskin himself has partially disavowed facilitation and evaluation as crucial to understanding mediation's diversity, in favor of "elicitive" and "directive" dimensions (Riskin 2003). Nonetheless, the facilitative-evaluative distinction effectively explains many of the important differences among mediation programs, processes, and providers and how particular forms of mediation will respond to the unique characteristics of a particular conflict, and the distinction has spurred much scholarly discourse and important advances in mediation theory (see, e.g., Lande 2000; Stempel 2000; Zumeta 2000a). Thus, the distinction will be used in this chapter as we explore the many varieties of mediation and the implications of these varieties for dispute resolution.

PROCESSES RELATED TO MEDIATION

It is also helpful at this juncture to define what is *not* mediation. Four dispute resolution processes have characteristics in common with mediation but are not mediation as strictly defined in this section: settlement conference, facilitation, conciliation, and Collaborative Law.

Michigan Mediation
a form of nonbinding evaluation provided by the Michigan State Courts for certain cases filed in the court system.

---

[3] Note that different forms of mediation are associated with different goals. This issue is addressed later in this chapter.

Practical Implications of the Facilitative-Evaluative Distinction

In one of the very few empirical studies to compare facilitative and evaluative mediation, E. Patrick McDermott and Ruth Obar studied Equal Employment Opportunity mediation clients and mediators to study the effects of facilitative and evaluative mediation tactics on outcomes and disputant satisfaction.

Mediators were asked to report the kinds of tactics they had used in mediation. These self-reported tactics were correlated with disputant satisfaction and monetary award sizes. Whether the disputants were represented by counsel was also considered. It was found that the clients (both employer representatives and employees) of mediators using more facilitative mediation tactics tended to be more satisfied with both the process and outcome of mediation than those whose mediators used evaluative mediation tactics. Paradoxically given the disputant satisfaction results, the use of evaluative tactics was associated with higher monetary recovery among employee claimants than the use of facilitative tactics. The factor most strongly associated with high monetary recovery by employee-claimants was representation by legal counsel. It cannot be determined, however, whether the presence of legal counsel was due to the likelihood of a high monetary recovery or whether the presence of counsel more effectively promoted claimant monetary wins. In the absence of legal counsel, evaluative mediation was actually associated with low monetary recovery by employee-claimants.

These results are extremely hard to interpret because there are so many possible reasons for the results. It is not clear whether facilitative mediation tactics were a cause of high rates of satisfaction with processes and results, or whether some characteristic of the disputants promoted the mediators' use of facilitative tactics. In addition, it cannot be determined whether cases having higher monetary values tended to be routed to more evaluative mediators; whether mediators, sensing a likelihood of high monetary recovery, engaged in more evaluative tactics, such as quantifying likely monetary recoveries if the case should go to court; whether the need to compromise produced by the use of evaluative mediation produces dissatisfaction; or whether evaluative mediation is more protective of claimant monetary entitlements. If evaluative tactics actually produce higher monetary outcomes than facilitative tactics, this result may reflect a more nonmonetary emphasis in facilitative mediation. This result would be consistent with other research (discussed later in this chapter) in which it seems that some groups of disputants who recover nonmonetary settlements express a high degree of process and outcome satisfaction. The results additionally may raise a moral and ethical issue: Is it a good result to society if employees who claim discrimination on the basis of race, sex, age, and so forth are satisfied with lower monetary recovery, or should employees be encouraged to take stronger stands against employers at the expense of personal satisfaction?

McDermott and Obar, 2004.

Settlement conference
the process in which a judge meets with litigants and their attorneys prior to a scheduled trial. Settlement conferences are typically used to streamline and plan the trial process and to determine whether action is needed on pretrial matters. Many judges also use a settlement conference to attempt to settle the overall dispute.

Settlement Conference. A **settlement conference** is a judicially created process presided over by a judge (or, occasionally, a master, hearing examiner, or magistrate). Settlement conferencing is used for legal disputes filed in court and headed for trial. The function of a settlement conference is typically to reach agreement as to which legal issues will be litigated, to plan the trial so it is orderly and efficient, and to determine whether there are any extant disputes regarding witness and documentary evidence. Settlement conferences are frequently also used by the presiding court officer to attempt to settle the case in its entirety. The person presiding over the conference will sometimes apply mediation-style tactics to promote agreements. In fact, many judges who hold settlement conferences say that, in that role, they are actually mediating. In this text, however, mediation is not so defined.

Facilitation

a conflict resolution professional's efforts to design and organize a dispute resolution process for an interpersonal conflict involving large or multiple groups of people and/or complex interpersonal conflicts.

Facilitation. **Facilitation** is a term usually applied to a process in which a neutral third party, or panel of neutrals, helps prepare for a complex negotiation. Typically, facilitation is used if an interpersonal conflict involves multiple, complex parties and issues (e.g., a negotiated rulemaking to create regulations for pollution control in which various municipalities, state agencies, and advocacy groups consider themselves stakeholders). The facilitator typically takes on a number of important tasks, including identifying interested participants; assisting corporate, governmental, or advocacy-group disputants in selecting representatives for the bargaining table; helping select mediators or other ADR providers to participate in the negotiation; and planning and selecting the time, place, and available amenities for the negotiation. A competent facilitator effectively sets the stage for a negotiation in which no participant feels left out and in which principled bargaining leading to effective settlement and maximal quality of consent is likely. (The term *settlement facilitation* is sometimes also used to connote mediation in which the disputants' lawyers, but not the disputants themselves, are the participants.)

Conciliation

a poorly defined term, sometimes referring to mediation, sometimes to facilitation, and sometimes to reconciliation in a relationship.

Conciliation. **Conciliation** is another term commonly applied to numerous processes conceptually related to mediation. Sometimes the term is applied to mediation itself, sometimes it is applied to facilitation, sometimes it is applied to nonbinding evaluation, and sometimes it is given other meanings. Care should be taken to clarify meaning if the use of conciliation is raised as an option.

Collaborative law

a form of legal advocacy characterized by a contractual commitment by clients and lawyers to a collaborative negotiation process. Lawyers are contractually bound to withdraw if the dispute cannot be settled without adjudication, and clients are contractually required to assent to this withdrawal.

Collaborative Law. **Collaborative law**, a special form of lawyer-assisted negotiation, is distinguished by the special contractual relationship of the lawyers and their clients. Practitioners of collaborative law enter into retainer agreements with their clients providing that the lawyer must withdraw from representation if litigation begins. The clients also retain experts for the negotiation jointly, and these experts are similarly disqualified from participating in any subsequent litigation. The retainer agreement further provides that the lawyer will use his or her skills to seek a collaborative settlement with the other disputant and his or her team using an interest-based negotiation strategy. Collaborative lawyers are permitted—indeed, they are expected—to help the client consider his or her long-term and nonmonetary interests, values, and needs. Thus, although a traditional adversarial lawyer who foregoes an opportunity to obtain a high monetary settlement—at the cost of alienating an ex-spouse or a business partner—might be accused of failing to represent the client zealously, a collaborative lawyer who advises the client to make this choice to preserve long-term relationship interests rests on firmer ethical ground. Collaborative lawyers make extensive use of the mediators' toolbox of techniques designed to de-escalate conflict and move clients toward win-win settlements. However, because a neutral party is not involved in this process, it is not mediation.

USES OF MEDIATION TODAY

Mediation is actually an ancient form of conflict resolution, having been used in Eastern and African societies for thousands of years. Even today, mediation is practiced all over the world. Elsewhere, mediation-like styles of dispute resolution are much more predominant than they are in Western cultures, although mediation in non-Western nations is often quite different from its counterpart here (Shapiro 1981).

In the United States, mediation has been used for centuries in the commercial arena to maintain good ongoing business relationships. Some religious groups and traditional Native American societies have also relied on mediation-style interventions to resolve disputes among members. Moreover, historically the handling of conflicts in many ethnic communities by powerful elders is very similar to mediation. In general, mediation and mediation-like practices of dispute resolution tend to flourish in subcultural groups and eras in which a homogeneous value system predominates among most disputants, making it easier to reach consensus about underlying principles, values, and interests (Auerbach 1983).

The past quarter-century marks the first time that a consensual and non-adversarial dispute resolution process such as mediation has been tried on such a broad and mainstream basis in a time and society of unprecedented social diversity. Necessity has been the mother of this invention: The modern ADR movement has been precipitated by widespread frustration with the high

Mediation is not a recent development. This historic lithograph by T. H. Matteson shows a youthful George Washington mediating among his squabbling companions. Library of Congress.

expense, overwhelming investment of time, and egregious social toll taken by litigation.[4] At the time ADR began to be discussed seriously, there was concern that the court system, already slowed to a virtual crawl, would become completely paralyzed by the huge litigation backlog. Thus, the first efforts to adopt mediation as a mainstream process for resolving legal disputes were primarily efforts to divert cases from the legal system to save time and money, as well as to free up the courts, so that cases remaining to be litigated could be handled more effectively. All forms of ADR were tapped for this case-diversion goal, but the process of mediation, specifically, was also seen as a method of providing better, more appropriate dispute resolution.

The 1990s saw a dramatic expansion of mediation into the legal mainstream. It is currently seen in the following areas:

- *Labor and employment relations,* particularly in federal agencies—precipitated by a host of federal statutes and regulations
- *State civil litigation,* particularly in major urban metropolitan areas
- *Federal civil litigation:* with fifty-one federal districts offering some form of court-connected mediation as of 1996 (Gauvey 2001)
- *Private and court-connected divorce and custody cases:* as of December 2000, researchers Carrie-Anne Tondo, Rinarisa Coronel, and Bethany Drucker (2001) had found some form of court-annexed family mediation practiced in all states except Indiana, New York, and Vermont.
- *Special education disputes:* among schools, service providers and parents of special-needs children
- *Neighborhood disputes*
- *Disputes between disputants of different countries:* in which the choice-of-law problems are too expensive or difficult to sort out in court
- *Disputes involving consumer grievances against commercial entities*
- *Outside the legal arena in public and private schools:* to resolve conflicts and prevent violence by and to students (These programs use students trained to use mediation and are called peer mediation.)

The past decade has seen a significant shift of mediation's acceptance by the nation's bar. Although the bench, which has been directly burdened with the consequences of a highly litigious society, has backed ADR processes for years, the bar has been slower to accept mediation. This caution can be partially attributed to mercenary concerns (fears that mediation will take business away from

---

[4] Jerold Auerbach (1983), who tracked the use of ADR processes historically, predicted this swing away from litigation as well as the demise of ADR in diverse populations. By his judgment, a society that swings toward litigation processes to cope with the problem of diversity eventually becomes fed up with the inefficiency and costliness of the litigation alternative and swings back toward ADR. By Auerbach's assessment of the situation, modern Western nations are between a rock and a hard place, striving to preserve diversity yet seeking to streamline dispute resolution.

lawyers) but also to concerns that the mediation process would compromise the best interests of clients. The former concerns have been seen to be largely unfounded, as many lawyers have discovered that, when their clients use mediation, they tend to be more satisfied and to place less blame for poor outcomes on the lawyer (Kichaven 1997), and, because cases settle faster lawyers tend to get paid sooner for work done (Mosten 1997). The concern for the welfare of clients is still being sorted out by the bar and by ADR scholars and professionals.[5] Mediation, unless coercive or deceptive in some manner, generally does not raise due process issues for disputants for the reason that disputants may simply walk away without settling. A more difficult issue concerns the impact of mediation on disempowered disputants. (This issue is addressed in more detail later in this chapter.)

Commensurate with a growing acceptance of mediation by the bar comes a struggle over just how mediation will come to be practiced. One recent trend is for mediation to become "adversarialized" by lawyers who become involved in the process of creating legal and ADR policy. An example of such an adversarialization of mediation is a recent effort to allow clients to move for sanctions in court against a disputant who is accused of causing an impasse. Another is the current trend in civil mediation for the process to begin with opening statements by legal counsel (Maryland State Bar Association 2007). This adversarialization is reflected in increased litigiousness about mediation: Coben and Thompson (2006) note that in the years between 1999 and 2003, the number of published court opinions involving an adversarial dispute over a mediation issue skyrocketed from 172 in 1999 to 335 in 2003, with no sign of diminishment in the years since, and the authors point to signs that the increase is not due merely to an increase in the availability or use of mediation. The movement toward mediation's adversarialization is noted with dismay by prominent scholars and policy makers who view mediation as offering a way to avoid the drawbacks of the prevailing adversarial approach. People such as UCLA Law School's Carrie Menkel-Meadow (Menkel-Meadow 1991); University of Florida Law School's Len Riskin and Dickinson Law School's Nancy Welsh (Welsh 2001a and 2001b; Riskin and Welsh 2008); prominent mediator Zena Zumeta (Zumeta 2000a); and Lela Love of the Benjamin Cardozo School of Law (Love 1997) all express concerns that, in building adversarial features into mediation, policy makers are threatening to kill the most important advantages of mediation over adversarial conflict management. Kimberlee Kovach, of the University of Texas School of Law and former chair of the American Bar Association Section of Dispute Resolution, directly expresses this concern:

> The notion of mediation as a different paradigm for dispute resolution is being eroded with the lawyers now viewing the process as merely another tool within the litigation arena to be used combatively rather than for any intended purpose. Noting that mediation may be different processes when involved in the court system, the phrase "liti-mediation" is now

---

[5] The assumptions of the lawyer's standard philosophical map may predispose lawyers to suspect mediation, a nonadversarial process, of producing second-class justice. See Riskin (1982).

used. Additional evidence is the remark of one lawyer telling another that he "won" the mediation. If this trend of "adversarial mediation" continues, then any opportunity for the mediation process to effect change as a novel process will be lost. *(Kovach 1997, 593, citations omitted)*[6]

It is likely that the tension between the prevailing invisible-veil approach to conflict resolution and the push to taking advantage of nonadversarial alternatives will continue. Although the adversarialization of mediation seems to be continuing, the collaborative law movement, a distinctly nonadversarial development in legal practice, continues to explode in popularity along with mediation. Natalie Wright (2008) in 2008 reported exponential growth in the practice worldwide, with a twelvefold increase in members of the International Academy of Collaborative Practitioners over the past five years, and over ten thousand collaborative lawyers in the United States at the time of her writing. Legal scholarship continues to focus heavily on the merits of cooperative, collaborative dispute resolution that encourages the affirmation of disputant dignity and perspective in an increasingly sophisticated manner—ideas that, a generation ago, could be found principally only in social science scholarship (e.g., see Barton 2007 and articles cited therein; Lande 2006, 246). Even at the level of legal practice, a more radical version of mediation seems to be increasingly accepted by members of the mainstream bar. For example, in 2008 the website of the American Bar Association described mediation as examining "the underlying causes of the problem and looks at what solutions best suit your unique needs and satisfy your interests" and including the acknowledgment of "emotional" elements of a situation, characteristics more typical of a pure form of mediation than a "liti-mediation" hybrid (American Bar Association 2008). Thus, as might be predicted by Bronfenbrenner (1979) and his ecological theory, traditional cultural institutions have affected the innovation represented by mediation, but mediation has also altered our cultural institutions.

APPROACHES TO MEDIATION

To understand how mediation works, when it is effective, and what its advantages and disadvantages are, it is important to understand the great diversity of mediation forms. Each type of mediation has its own distinct characteristics, uses, strengths, and limitations. *Five fairly typical forms of mediation* are present in the United States today.[7] Each of these five forms has unique characteristics that suit it for particular sorts of disputes. Each has particular problems that make it unsuitable in certain situations. (The five major forms of mediation are summarized in Table 3-1.)

---

[6] Also see Coben and Thompson 2006, 45, fn. 1.

[7] Omitted from this discussion and this text as a whole is labor mediation. Although resembling bargaining-based mediation in some respects, labor mediation is so specialized that it is best treated as an element of labor law rather than alternative dispute resolution.

◆ TABLE 3-1   Forms of Mediation

FORM	TYPICAL ADHERENTS	MAJOR GOALS	TYPICAL TECHNIQUES
Triage mediation	Underfunded court systems	Getting an agreement cheaply and quickly	"Muscle mediation": very directive and structured; may include elements of coercion and pressure, particularly to the disputant with the least bargaining power. Often includes nonbinding evaluation. May include "med-arb" (see Chapter 6) and/or directive to report to court which disputant was responsible for an impasse. Usually very time limited.
Bargaining-based mediation	Lawyer-mediators, retired judges	Getting a "fair" settlement, getting a compromise	Evaluative: "instilling doubt," often in caucus format; showing each disputant that he or she has overestimated his or her chances of winning; correcting misapprehensions of the law's influence where they hamper settlement. Sometimes resembles nonbinding arbitration or judicial settlement conference.
Pure mediation	Some private mediators, particularly family law	Facilitating collaboration between the disputants to get a win-win outcome	Facilitative: active and reflective listening, encouragement of brainstorming, reframing and refocusing of communication, brief confirmation of feelings, refocusing on dispute, recasting positions into needs. Caucusing (see definition at page 70) used less often than in bargaining-based mediation.
Transformative mediation	Expanding use among private mediators, used by U.S. Postal Service REDRESS program	Extremely broad, facilitative; promote empowerment of each disputant and recognition of each disputant's perspective and situation by the other; attaining settlement considered a secondary goal	Helping each disputant understand the nature of the dispute, helping each disputant understand the other's point of view, educating the disputants in effective negotiation techniques when necessary, facilitating assertive behavior by each disputant, encouraging each disputant to acknowledge the perspective of the other. Caucusing almost never used.
Narrative mediation	Not widely used at this time in the USA.	To deconstruct and revise internal narratives or stories, influenced by cultural context, which emphasize conflict	Asking specially designed questions to reveal the possibility of other interpretations of fact underlying the conflict, examining the history of the conflict, writing down revised narratives.

TRIAGE MEDIATION

Triage mediation, a term coined by this author, is believed to be relatively uncommon today. Formerly, it was widely seen in court systems and was developed to divert large numbers of cases away from the trial system.

This sort of mediation is typically very brief and focused. The *goal* of triage mediation is to get the dispute out of the court system as quickly as possible by seeking a quick settlement. The *focus* of triage mediation is typically narrow: It is focused in the short term on *this* dispute because that's all that's needed to get the case out of court. Because of the emphasis on expediency, the process is typically evaluative, which tends to bring cases quickly to either settlement or impasse. Pressure and coercion (referred to by some as *muscle mediation*) are frequently used to push the disputants into a quick decision. For example, in some triage mediation programs, if an agreement is not reached, the mediator may be required to report to the court which disputant was responsible for the impasse.

> Arthur Jones sued Brenda Smith for visitation of their one-year-old son, Martin. The court sent Arthur and Brenda to court-connected mediation. After a brief orientation, a volunteer mediator was assigned. The mediator met with both parties together for about twenty minutes to get a flavor for the nature of their dispute. Then she met with each of them privately. She asked Arthur about whether he had been up to date on his child support payments ("No, not really") and suggested that he might not want to push too hard for visitation lest Brenda get really angry about the money. To Brenda, the mediator laid out the usual policy of the court, which was to order child visitation every other weekend and overnights once a week. "Wouldn't you rather have some say in the visitation plan?" the mediator asked. Brenda finally relented and agreed to every other Saturday and overnights once a month. Arthur had wanted more time but was reluctant to alienate the mediator and risk a child support action. The entire mediation took about ninety minutes.

The main advantage of triage mediation is that it's cheap, it's quick, and it clears court dockets. However, triage mediation presents a number of significant problems (Beck and Sales 2000). Because its principal goal is to save money and avoid court, mediators are often poorly trained and poorly paid and carry overly heavy caseloads. Often, an implicit or explicit goal is to reach as many agreements as possible as quickly as possible, so the mediators may feel compelled to pressure disputants into agreement. If so, the advantage of disputants' retaining control over the outcome of mediation is lost. Also, there is a due process problem with a mediator pushing disputants into an agreement, particularly if the mediation is court ordered: The mediation process may effectively deny one or both disputants their day in court without due process of law. Moreover, the well-being of the disputants (or, in the case of disputes involving dependent persons, such as child custody mediation, their dependent constituents) may take a backseat to getting the agreement. This form of mediation is less prevalent today because it has been so strongly discredited.

BARGAINING-BASED MEDIATION

Bargaining-based mediation (a term coined by Elizabeth Koopman and the late Joan Hunt, both formerly of the University of Maryland at College Park) is an extremely common form of mediation. Sometimes called *concession-hunting* (Young 2001), it's the predominant style used in court-connected civil dispute mediation, as well as the mediation of commercial, construction, and personal injury cases. Members of legal teams—lawyers and paralegals—are more likely to see this form of mediation than any other. The primary goal of bargaining-based mediation is to attain a fair agreement through compromise.

Lawyer-mediators and judge-mediators often use bargain-based mediation. The focus is usually *narrow* (focused on "this dispute") and the process is typically *evaluative.* Usually, the disputants' lawyers participate in the mediation and often do the negotiating in place of their clients. Since lawyer-mediators and lawyer-advocates do most of the work, the lawyer's standard philosophical map colors how the participants frame the issues and work out a solution (Guthrie 2001; Kovach and Love 1998). Typically, bargaining-based mediators give the disputants or their representatives a chance to state their cases and follow this phase with a series of **caucuses** (separate meetings with one disputant and then the other) in which interests and positions are explored. The mediator shuttles back and forth, exploring areas of agreement and, occasionally, strategically revealing information where it would lead to compromise. Often, a compromise proposal suggests itself in the shuttle diplomacy process; then the mediator may present it to each party and solicit consent to its terms. Outcomes are usually monetary and usually display a lack of creativity and innovation (Welsh 2001a). Nonetheless, litigants typically express a high degree of satisfaction when bargaining-based mediation works—and it frequently does.

> Rick Polanka, a bricklayer, sued ABC, a general contractor, over fees he alleged to be overdue on a large construction project. Both Rick's and ABC's legal counsel secretly admitted having some doubts about how the law would apply to the dispute. The court referred the dispute to court-connected mediation presided over by Lorinda Lattislaw, Esq., a volunteer attorney-mediator. She asked that each lawyer state his client's case, then scheduled separate private sessions for each disputant's team. In the private meetings, Lorinda expertly attacked the basis for each attorney's confidence in the case's "winnability"—in other words, to each side she cast doubt on the strength of the BATNA estimates they had developed. In addition, she explored the bottom lines of each side and looked for some ways to trade off some monetary concessions for other issues, such as modifying the payment date, building in some interest payments, and ensuring that the dispute stayed private. Eventually, she was able to carve out a set of terms with which both sides could live. After one initial joint session, two private sessions, and several telephone conferences, Linda was able to bring the parties back into mediation to jointly confirm a compromise settlement.

Bargaining-based mediation is particularly good for cases in which the principal source of conflict is highly divergent perceptions of fact or law, because it can provide an independent opinion that all participants can rely on. It's also good for cases involving highly complex legal issues, since lawyers tend to be closely involved in the mediation process. Bargaining-based mediation can also be helpful if there is not much time to obtain a settlement: Because it tends to be evaluative and relies on compromising, it can be speedier than some alternative processes (Baruch-Bush 1996; Hermann, Honeyman, McAdoo, and Welsh 2001; Kovach and Love 1996; Welsh 2001a, 2001b).

Caucus
a meeting between a mediator and one disputant (with or without the disputant's representatives), out of the earshot of the other disputant and his or her representatives. A caucus is different from a joint session, which all the disputants involved in mediation, and/or their representatives, attend.

Bargaining-Based Mediation:
Bronfenbrenner's Ecological Theory in Action

The latter half of the 1990s saw a remarkable rise in the dominance of bargaining-based mediation as the primary method of handling civil disputes, such as tort and commercial litigation.

Researcher Bobbi McAdoo has presented survey results that indicate a strong preference on the part of lawyers who participate in mandatory, court-connected mediation services for lawyer-mediators who have strong backgrounds as litigators. The principal quality cited by the lawyer-respondents is the ability of the mediator to value the disputants' case effectively.

Since these lawyer-respondents are the primary customers of civil mediation services offered by the courts, their preferences control the demand for mediation services and, hence, have shaped the sorts of mediation available for civil disputes. As Bronfenbrenner (see Chapter 2) would predict, the invisible veil permeating the beliefs of those who use court-connected mediation services has influenced the sorts of mediation that are made available. Thus, although mediation has become much more popular in recent years, its adversarialization has rendered it almost unrecognizable to those who would define mediation primarily as a process for facilitating collaboration and creative problem solving between disputants, such as Carrie Menkel-Meadow (1991), Kimberlee Kovach and Lela Love (1998).

A number of legal scholars have documented this evolution of court-connected mediation, with its increasing emphasis on case evaluation as the predominant mediator strategy, the reduced role of disputants, the increased dominance of legal counsel in mediation sessions, the reduction or elimination of joint mediation sessions, and the lack of creativity in the settlements produced by this sort of mediation. Deborah Hensler, a prominent researcher in the mediation field, remarks that examples of facilitative mediation are fast disappearing, leaving a process that mostly resembles judicial settlement conferences (Hensler 1999). Nancy Welsh comments that "the bargaining paradigm that dominates and delivers settlements in most civil cases is capturing the mediation process" (Welsh 2001a, 789), and prominent mediation scholar John Bickerman (1999, 3–5) laments that, if mediation is treated "as glorified settlement conferences, then the value of the process may be lost."

The reader may recall the discussion of Uri Bronfenbrenner's theory of social ecology in Chapter 2. The evolution of mediation from radical alternative to the legal mainstream—and its simultaneous transformation into an adversarial process—makes sense if we recall Bronfenbrenner's concept of bidirectionality. As he would predict, the introduction of mediation has transformed prevailing societal institutions, but these institutions have also transformed the practice of mediation.

Because the process is evaluative, bargaining-based mediation tends to cause the disputants to become increasingly position bound. In other words, the focus is on each disputant's position and how successful he or she is likely to be with it. Because of this focus, the outcome tends to be a compromise rather than an integrative solution, so the outcome tends to make less optimal use of resources than would occur if a more collaborative approach were used. If the lawyers participate *in place of* the disputants, they may also miss aspects of the dispute that are important to the disputants. This is both because of the influence of the lawyer's standard philosophical map (which causes the lawyers to focus on causes of action and money) and because the lawyers never know as much about the disputants as the disputants know about themselves. Usually, little is done to correct the aspects of the overall relationship that might cause problems in the future. This limited focus on the relationship is only a disadvantage if the disputants will be dealing with one another in the future. Another limitation of bargaining-based mediation is that, since it tends to be highly evaluative, only individuals with expertise in the subject matter of the dispute are appropriate mediators. Their authoritative pronouncements on the merits of the case will have the intended impact only if the disputants regard these pronouncements as legitimate.

Finally, the evaluative nature of bargaining-based mediation can be predicted to be more likely to escalate conflict and lead to impasse than more facilitative types of mediation. To understand this point, it is useful to return to the theory of Morton Deutsch, first introduced in Chapter 2. You may recall that conflict can start to escalate when disputants begin to think of their situation as contriently interdependent (see Figure 2-1) and that conflict escalation has a cyclical, self-intensifying quality. Referring to the elements of the cycle of conflict escalation shown in Figure 2-1, it was Deutsch's belief that intensification of any one of these elements will exacerbate the escalation process. Since many of these elements are perceptual, he further proposed that anything that promotes a perception that a conflict is competitive or escalated will produce escalation of the conflict in fact. This hypothesis is known as *Deutsch's Crude Axiom.*[8] Because evaluative mediation focuses disputants on their positions, it can be expected to create the perceptions of difference, enmity and threat that are produced by positional bargaining. Deutsch's Crude Axiom would therefore predict an increased likelihood of conflict escalation would result from such a process.

PURE FACILITATIVE MEDIATION

Pure mediation is a facilitative process whose goal is to promote collaborative, integrative, principled bargaining. (It is very important to note that the goal of pure mediation is *not* to reach agreement but, rather, to promote the sorts of negotiation behaviors that will lead to reaching agreement.)[9]

Pure mediation is often seen in community and divorce mediation, and it is being found in other contexts in increasing numbers. It is also becoming more accepted by the legal profession. It is highly facilitative, and the breadth of issues dealt with is as broad or narrow as the disputants wish it to be.

"Pure" mediators work to keep the disputants in a cooperative conflict cycle and structure the process to encourage interest-based, nonpositional negotiation.

---

[8] Deutsch's Crude Axiom applies equally to cooperation: he proposed that merely focusing disputants and their team on the cooperative elements of their situation would tend to make a conflict more cooperative in fact. For an in-depth discussion of Deutsch's Crude Axiom, see Online Appendix B, Chapter 9, pages 154–169 (Deutsch's Crude Axiom is specifically discussed at pages 167–169).

[9] The term *problem-solving mediation,* occasionally applied to this form of mediation, is avoided in this text because it is also often applied to bargaining-based mediation.

The mediator sets ground rules to improve communication and often structures the mediation sessions to track through the steps of a principled negotiation. Pure mediators also work to remove impediments to settlement, such as helping disputants understand how meta-disputes occurred and referring disputants to experts so that different perceptions of fact and law can be resolved. Caucusing is seldom used, since caucusing fosters mistrust and usually does not promote collaboration.

> Sherry and Colleen had been students at the Anytown Cooking Academy, where Sherry had majored in restaurant management and Colleen had studied to become a pastry chef. Upon graduation, the two had embarked on a joint venture: a coffee and dessert café they named Au Lait. Unfortunately, the two were at loggerheads over salaries to be paid to each employee, over the appropriate degree to which the café should be marketed, and whether to open additional branches.
>
> They had come to the brink of dissolving their partnership when a mutual friend suggested Mort Nathan, a mediator. Mort met with the two women in a series of eight ninety-minute sessions. After introducing the mediation process, Mort asked each woman to describe her goals and hopes for the future. Each had a vision of Au Lait and articulated the wish that it remain viable. From these descriptions, Mort helped the women list a series of mutually shared goals for the venture. As they had spoken, the women had also revealed their areas of dispute, which Mort also listed. Mort had a separate list for goals that one of the disputants, but not the other, found important.
>
> The next step was to list multiple options for meeting each of the goals the women had described. Several sessions were spent fine-tuning and comparing these options. At several points in the process, one or the other disputant became so frustrated that she wanted to quit. At those times, Mort often commented on how far they had come, or he reminded the women of the principal goal held by each, which was to continue to nurture their joint venture. Out of the mediation, ultimately, came a new and improved joint venture agreement, one in which salaries were more clearly stated. The women also agreed to hire a marketing agent so that neither would be responsible for a task at which neither was skilled. Their plan was to consult the marketing agent about expansion after a six-month period and to return to mediation if they were unable to agree on expansion.

There are many advantages to pure mediation, and they mirror many of the advantages we have already noted for mediation in general. Since pure mediation facilitates collaborative negotiation, the agreements reached tend to be highly creative, win-win outcomes that optimize the use of resources. Pure mediation may have long-term benefits for disputants who must continue a relationship. If the mediator is able to resist the temptation to pressure the disputants into an agreement, then this sort of mediation provides a high quality of disputant consent. As a result, the disputants will psychologically "own" any resulting agreement, with the typical benefits of psychological ownership. There are long-term benefits even if agreement is not reached:

- Pure mediation narrows the issues so that it's likely to be easier and faster if another dispute resolution process is required.
- Chances are good that the disputants will be more cooperative, so other alternatives will not be as expensive, time consuming, or traumatic.
- Pure mediation can teach effective collaborative negotiation to the disputants so that they can use it elsewhere in their lives.

Despite the advantages of pure mediation, its use in legal disputing is less widespread than the use of bargaining-based mediation. It is unclear exactly why, but the reasons may relate to one or more of the disadvantages of pure mediation. First, if time is an important consideration and if only a narrow, short-term perspective is important, bargaining-based mediation may be a better choice. This is particularly the case if disputants enter mediation with widely divergent BATNAs. Also, pure mediation may not be appropriate for disputants with limited cognitive functioning, such as children or the mentally disabled, because of the need for higher-level thought processes involved in principled bargaining, although the mediator may be able to take some actions to compensate for such problems, such as involving an advocate or referring the client to a support person for assistance. Marketing problems are also associated with pure mediation. When disputants turn to mediation, they are often desperate for a quick fix and tend to want a mediator who is pushier or more evaluative—someone who will tell the disputants what they should do. Moreover, many lawyers don't understand what pure mediation is or its advantages over bargaining-based mediation. Pure mediation also doesn't fit well into the *lawyer's standard philosophical map* of disputing, which posits conflict as a contest and outcomes as primarily about monetary allocation (Riskin 1982). Finally, pure mediation is also more difficult to practice than triage and bargaining-based mediation: It requires a great deal of knowledge and skill in facilitating client communication without coercion. If the mediator is not competent, this sort of mediation may be no better than any other type and may be worse than another form practiced well.

TRANSFORMATIVE MEDIATION

Transformative mediation resembles pure mediation, except that its goals are even more completely removed from "getting an agreement." According to Robert Baruch-Bush and Joseph P. Folger, who coined the term *transformative mediation* and introduced the concept in their seminal book *The Promise of Mediation* (Baruch-Bush and Folger 1994), this form has as its goal the improvement or transformation of those who participate in the process. Specifically, there are two primary transformative goals:

- *Empowerment:* the improvement of the personal power of each disputant
- *Recognition:* the ability of each disputant to take the perspective of the other disputant and to communicate this sense of understanding to the other disputant

Note how completely disconnected this goal is from "reaching agreement." In transformative mediation, the disputants are provided with the opportunity to become empowered and are encouraged to give the other disputant recognition. Then if the disputants want to negotiate and reach agreement, they can.

When Baruch-Bush and Folger first proposed the concept of transformative mediation, it was regarded as entirely theoretical. However, it is being adopted and used in real-world applications, most notably by the U.S. Postal Service, apparently with substantial success (Antes, Folger, and Della Noce 2001; Bingham, Baruch-Bush, Hallberlin, and Napoli 1999).

> Next-door neighbors Abel and Baker saw one another as nuisances: In Abel's mind, Baker played the stereo too loudly, and Baker thought Abel was way too nosy. Their animosity often erupted into loud arguments in the street. They were pressured by their frustrated neighbors into trying a storefront community mediation service, a program populated by transformative mediators. Lotta, a mediator with this service, met with Abel and Baker in two two-hour joint sessions. She helped each of them understand the perspective of the other and articulate to one another some degree of validation ("I think that, if I saw things from your point of view—which I don't—I would feel the same way you do"). She also helped each of the disputants become empowered, by referring them to legal advisors to learn more about the law of nuisance and by helping each of them understand the other. Eventually, each came to see that they would have to live with the other and that this process would be easier if each moderated his behavior. Finally, an agreement was made limiting the hours that Baker played his stereo (so that Abel could have rest time); in return, Abel agreed to stay off Baker's stoop and to stop peeking in his window.

The focus of transformative mediation is often extremely broad (the dispute isn't really the focus at all) and extremely facilitative (since case evaluations don't generally promote either empowerment or recognition). The process is much like pure mediation but less structured. The mediator encourages each disputant to tell his or her story and looks for opportunities to promote empowerment and recognition as the conversation continues.

Transformative mediation's advantages are similar to those of pure mediation. Agreements reached in transformative mediation are psychologically owned in full by the disputants, who are very likely to abide by them. However, no one really knows whether using transformative mediation instead of an alternative process would change the rate at which disputants reach agreement, either for better or for worse. The authors of *The Promise of Mediation* also assert that the use of transformative mediation will improve society at large by improving the moral development of disputants who use it. Critics counter by asserting that it is the height of arrogance for mediators to be in the business of improving their clients' characters.

NARRATIVE MEDIATION

Narrative mediation (Hansen 2004) is another form of highly facilitative mediation. The premises of narrative mediation are difficult to encapsulate in a brief account, but basically the technique is founded on the idea that disputants become caught up in internal narratives or stories that emphasize the conflictual elements of their relationships with one another. Generally these narratives are cast in a right/wrong dichotomy, in which the teller of the story has been victimized by the other disputant in some way. Narrative mediators consider these stories to be strongly influenced by context, particularly the cultural context of invisible-veil approaches to dispute resolution. The principal task of the narrative mediator is to guide the disputants in the creation of an alternative narrative that allows other, equally important aspects of the situation to be brought into consciousness and emphasized. This concept, of narrative being of supreme importance, is at stark variance with the standard frame of jurisprudence, in which *justice* is understood as a search for objective truth that stands outside the points of view of the disputing parties. It also differs from the premises of the lawyer's standard philosophical map, which posits that every legal dispute has a winning and a losing party.

To accomplish the goals of narrative mediation, mediators ask "deconstructing questions" that challenge the legitimacy of unexamined assumptions. This effort is thought to help the disputants discover nonconflictual elements of their shared experience and weave these together into a coherent alternative narrative.

> Grace sued Gerry for the return of the considerable purchase price of a purebred puppy she had purchased from Gerry. The dog, she said, had been ill and had died of a rare congenital illness, which she attributed to improper breeding or whelping. Gerry denied having any knowledge that the dog was ill and blamed the dispute on rumors of Grace's litigiousness. Nancy, a narrative mediator, explored the disputants' narratives, focusing attention on the attributions of causation each had made against the other. Grace and Gerry each eventually admitted that they had little hard evidence to blame the other but had done so in the absence of their own perceived responsibility for the death of the dog. With the help of Nancy, the two disputants developed an alternative narrative that better explained the tragedy, focused on the affinity both had for dogs, and blamed the sale on the absence of veterinary advances that might have given Gerry some inkling of the dog's affliction. Consequently, they agreed that Gerry would donate the price of the dog to a canine medical organization and that each disputant would kick in an additional thousand dollars in contributions. Grace would thus gain the knowledge that Gerry would receive no profit from selling a dog with a fatal congenital illness, and both, as dog lovers, would gain the satisfaction of knowing that canine health issues would be better addressed as a result of their efforts.

Narrative mediation originated in New Zealand, and it is not yet widely used in the United States but has gained some prominence in scholarly and professional discourse.

PARTICIPANT ROLES IN MEDIATION

We turn now to the question of who participates in mediation. Mediation may involve some or all of the following persons:

- The mediator (or mediators)
- The disputants (or, if a disputant is a group or corporation, the disputant's agent)
- Disputant's counsel and associated personnel, such as paralegals
- Constituents and dependents of the disputants
- Consultants and experts

MEDIATOR(S)

Of all the participants to mediation, the only party who is always present, without fail, is the mediator. Mediators, particularly in the United States and other Western countries, are generally regarded as being, of necessity, neutral and impartial, a characteristic discussed in greater detail in Chapter 4. The mediator is often one person, or multiple individuals may be serving as a *panel* of mediators. Hiring one mediator to conduct mediation is, obviously, the least expensive option. However, cost aside, having multiple mediators is generally a better option. Since mediation is complex, it helps to have more than one mediator to pay attention to what is going on (e.g., one mediator can focus on legal issues, the other on relationship building). The panel members can also role model appropriate negotiation conduct for the disputants, such as politeness, active listening, turn taking, and so forth; the mediators can even plan such interactions in advance. Mediators can also be chosen for their substantive expertise in the area of the law or a substantive subject-matter area, and multiple mediators can provide the opportunity to meet diverse needs for such expertise. Another advantage to having multiple mediators occurs in disputes between members of distinct social groups. A mediation panel consisting of representatives of the salient disputant social groups can help each disputant feel more validated, heard, and empowered. For example, in divorce mediation, having a mixed-gender mediation team is often helpful in preventing one of the disputants from feeling intimidated. Moreover, in culturally diverse conflicts, it is often helpful for a mediation panel to be representative of all the cultural groups in the conflict. This cultural diversity enables the mediators to share their understanding of the social contexts of the disputants and to interpret communication that might otherwise lead to misunderstandings.

A high school student informally takes a mediator's role in a dispute between his two friends.
David Mager, Pearson Learning Photo Studio.

Since mediation is a relatively new profession in Western nations, mediators are generally career changers or add a mediation practice to a preexisting professional practice. There is no authoritative research documenting the professional backgrounds of mediators; however, based on anecdotal information, mediators most commonly come from the legal and mental-health professions. There is no uniform educational requirement for mediators, although individual jurisdictions impose specific qualifications on mediators working in particular fields. Mediator competency issues are considered in Chapter 4.

DISPUTANTS AND THEIR LAWYERS

It is the norm in some kinds of cases and in many jurisdictions for disputants to participate actively in mediation. However, both the issues involved and regional variations affect disputant involvement. In certain sorts of legal disputes (domestic relations being one important example), disputants nearly always attend mediation sessions, whereas in other sorts of disputes (e.g., appellate mediation) they seldom do. Riskin and Welsh (2008) note a current trend in non–family law, court-connected mediation, such as medical malpractice mediation, to limit attendance to the lawyers. In settings where disputants attend mediation, there are also diverse practices with regard to whether the disputant attends on his or her own or is accompanied by legal counsel. In some practice areas, such as the mediation of commercial disputes, it is more the norm for the attorney and disputant to attend together, with the attorney doing most of the negotiation. In other practice areas, such as divorce mediation, whether the lawyer accompanies the client to mediation at all seems to vary across jurisdictions and may be a matter of local culture and the influence of respected persons in the legal or ADR communities.

It is important to appreciate the benefits of direct disputant participation from the perspective of conflict diagnosis. Disputants always know their own interests better than their lawyers do, although lawyers may be needed to explain the legal situation to disputants so the disputants understand their interests better. Moreover, unless disputants themselves can frame the problem and express their concerns, mediation is unlikely to address their most deeply seated needs and interests (Riskin and Welsh 2008). Thus, unless the mediation is a purely evaluative process focused on positional bargaining, lawyers are poor substitutes for disputants. Also, disputants who directly and actively participate in mediation more fully psychologically own the resulting agreement and are less likely to be disgruntled with its terms. Thus, direct disputant participation is more likely to have effects that fulfill the promise of mediation in dealing effectively with interpersonal conflict.

At what point in the process of mediation does legal counsel become involved? There is no one answer to this question. The work of a legal advocate for a mediating client begins *before the first contact* with a mediator. A member of the legal team can explain the mediation process and its benefits to the client and can prepare the client for the collaborative negotiation that will take place in some forms of mediation. If an evaluative mediator is used, the lawyer can also help the client place his or her case in the best possible light. An effective lawyer can also help his or her client shop for an effective mediator well suited to deal with the dispute in question.

The heart of legally representing mediation clients is empowerment and BATNA clarification through *interests analysis and case preparation.* The lawyer often helps the client clarify his or her underlying interests, values, needs, and

---

Lawyer Roles in Mediation

Vital

- Giving legal advice to prevent unexpected impact of settlement

Considered Extremely Important

- Giving legal advice and case preparation for empowerment and BATNA clarification
- Explaining how mediation works and what to expect

Sometimes Useful

- Giving support during mediation
- Helping instill doubt about the strength of the client's BATNA

To Be Avoided

- Appropriating (taking over) the mediation
- Adversarial posturing
- Using mediation for trial discovery

principles by helping him or her understand how the applicable law affects these elements. The lawyer should make it clear to the client that, although the lawyer's role is to view the conflict from a legal perspective, this emphasis in no way minimizes the nonlegal aspects of the conflict. In other words, an effective legal advisor recognizes the lure of the lawyer's standard philosophical map and makes efforts to maintain an appropriate perspective. In addition to clarifying interests, the lawyer helps the client identify and maximize the BATNA by preparing the case: reviewing the law, interviewing the witnesses, gathering and organizing documentary evidence, and so forth. An effective case valuation gives the client the information he or she needs to understand the BATNA, so that effective negotiation can occur during mediation. Effective case preparation also increases the client's expert power and, incidentally, moves the case closer to being ready for trial in case mediation does not result in a settlement. A continuing dilemma for lawyers and clients in mediated cases is how thoroughly to prepare: A very well-prepared case is best for effective mediation, but thorough case preparation is also very expensive.

Unfortunately, some lawyers, either for mercenary reasons or because of conceptual blinders created by the lawyer's standard philosophical map, may try to divert the client to a more adversarial method of resolving the dispute. Occasionally, mediation is, indeed, the wrong choice for the client, but a lawyer who systematically undermines his or her clients' efforts to choose mediation is doing a disservice and may even be violating the ethical obligation of effective representation (Breger 2000; Cochran 1999; see also American Bar Association 2008, Rule 2.1, comment 5, providing that an attorney may be required ethically to advise a client of the ADR options available).

Lawyers may also *attend mediation sessions,* either with their clients or instead of their clients. There are advantages and disadvantages to lawyer attendance. Lawyers can help clarify legal issues for their clients as they arise during mediation. This role can be particularly helpful if the conflict presents very complex legal issues. A lawyer can also help support a frightened or intimidated client or calm down a very angry client. And, if the mediator uses an evaluative style, the lawyer can work in tandem with the mediator to help to temper unreasonable client expectations during the caucus.

There are, however, several disadvantages to lawyer attendance at mediation sessions. The disputant may inappropriately lean on the lawyer instead of confronting the problem head on, leading to a situation in which the lawyer negotiates, instead of the disputant. This development compromises client self-determination, which could theoretically undermine settlement durability. Some lawyers are tempted to misappropriate the mediation; that is, regardless of the disputant's desire for autonomy, the legal professional may be enticed to take over and perform the negotiation in place of the disputant. Obviously, such an appropriation could occur if the lawyer attends mediation in the client's place. If the lawyer takes over the negotiation, the client usually does not get his or her own needs and interests out on the table and usually does not psychologically own the outcome as fully as the client would have done with active participation. A lawyer may also turn the mediation into an opportunity for adversarial posturing, which pushes the mediated negotiation toward a competitive and escalating conflict cycle. The temptation to engage in adversarial posturing can be irresistible for a lawyer steeped in the adversarial system and unfamiliar with conflict and negotiation theory. Finally, a less than ethical lawyer may even use the mediation as a discovery device—to try to obtain confidential information about the other disputant. It is also the case that some lawyers, or some clients with the participation of their lawyers, will use mediation as a delay tactic to avoid a trial and try to outlast the other side (Dunham 2007).[10]

If the lawyer does not attend the mediation sessions, he or she can play a vital role by staying in touch with the client throughout the mediation process. As we have noted elsewhere, the mediator is ethically prohibited from giving legal advice during mediation, so, if a legal issue arises, a competent mediator will frequently suggest to the client "Run the issue by your attorney." Having access to legal advice can maintain client empowerment and make settlement more likely. For example, some divorce mediators find that client misunderstandings about the nature of marital property law prompt some spouses in mediation to take extreme positions on property issues. There is a cogent argument that the mediator is ethically prohibited (see Chapter 4) from correcting the client's misapprehension of the law, except to suggest the possibility of error and referring the client to the attorney. Many a mediation has been saved by the rational advice of competent attorneys.

Following mediation, the lawyer may review, or even draft, the mediated agreement. The attorney can suggest areas the clients did not consider and can point out the possibility that agreements might have unexpected or unintended consequences. This role is important, but an effective lawyer should be sensitive to the accomplishments of the disputants and take care not to use the opportunity to criticize and undermine the decisions made by the disputants in mediation.

PARALEGALS (LEGAL ASSISTANTS)

Paralegals (sometimes known as *legal assistants*) are becoming increasingly important members of the legal team, and many of the activities for lawyers in the mediation process are appropriate paralegal functions. It is fair to say that paralegals are limited only by the proscription that they not practice law; that is, they may not give legal advice to the client and may not draft the agreement without attorney supervision. Because of the intensive involvement of the legal team with the client in preparing a case for mediation, clarifying and improving the BATNA, and speaking with the client extensively about underlying

---

[10] Dunham cites a CNN investigation of an insurer that established a mediation program in the wake of the Hurricane Katrina disaster, allegedly with no intention of settling any of the mediated cases (by making and maintaining ridiculously small offers), as a way to delay the payment of claims and to discover the level of preparation of claimants and their representatives. Dunham 2007, fn. 161.

interests, the cost savings of delegating as many of these tasks as possible to the paralegal become extremely important in a legally complex mediation. A paralegal may also have the responsibility of keeping a roster of mediators and making suggestions for referrals to the attorney and client,[11] of contacting mediators to set up initial sessions, of educating the client about the mediation process, of following and making regular contact with the mediating client, of helping create the formal settlement agreement, and even of participating in the mediation sessions to note down matters of importance.

Paralegals are also qualified to act as mediators in many instances and are becoming practitioners in increasing numbers. It is fair to say that paralegals will play an increasingly important role in the mediation profession in the years to come.

CONSTITUENTS AND DEPENDENTS

Whether constituents and dependents participate in mediation and the nature of their participation are often decided by mediation participants on a case-by-case basis. The question whether to include dependents (such as children in child custody cases) exemplifies some of the complexities of involving constituents in the mediation process. There are good reasons and bad reasons to have children participate in the mediation of custody disputes. Adolescent children whose expanding autonomy and independence are facts of life may undermine or sabotage a parenting plan unless they feel heard and recognized in the process. Younger children are sometimes brought into a session with the mediator so that the children can get a sense of the person the parents are working with and to get confirmation that their parents are working on their behalf. To foster healthy development, younger dependents should not be put in the position of feeling as if they are choosing between parents, nor should they be given the power to decide their own custody arrangements. Competent mediators sometimes use the session with the children to confirm and emphasize to the parents the need to work at keeping the children out of the middle of adult conflict.

Nondependent constituents can be important either as potential supporters or as saboteurs of agreements reached in mediation. These constituents are sometimes brought into mediation to give them a sense of greater psychological ownership of the result. Other constituents function almost as advocates: A disputant may want to bring a friend or an ally into a mediation session to reduce fear and increase comfort. Such constituents should be brought in, only with great care, to prevent the other disputant from feeling ganged up on.

---

[11] The information available in this text concerning conflict and negotiation theories and the varieties of mediation can help legal professionals, such as paralegals, evaluate specific mediation processes and providers for suitability in various conflicts and disputes. A sophisticated paralegal should consider how to parlay this knowledge into a database of mediators that enables the paralegal to suggest good matches between clients and mediators.

CONSULTANTS AND EXPERTS

In keeping with the general notion that a disputant negotiates more effectively if empowered, mediators frequently refer clients to experts to increase disputant knowledge and comfort level and to improve negotiation. In a commercial mediation, it may be appropriate to suggest an appraiser, an evaluator, or a marketing specialist. In divorce mediation, child psychologists, financial planners, accountants, and other professionals may be tapped to help disputants come to terms with issues raised by the divorce. In special education mediation, teachers, school psychologists, and others who have worked with the child may be consulted. Although these ancillary personnel usually remain on the sidelines to consult with disputants outside of mediation sessions, they may occasionally attend a mediation session to provide additional information to the mediator and the disputants.

The prevailing practice in the mediation of civil claims is to utilize a mediator who will provide a case evaluation so the parties can more precisely know their BATNAs. However, as previously noted, evaluative mediation has the potential to create impasse, undermine creativity, and escalate conflict by tending to nudge disputants into positional bargaining. One way to obtain the requisite BATNA clarification is to provide for evaluation within a mediation context. Thus, mediating parties who require clarification about the merits of a particular issue in the case can be referred to an evaluator or arbitrator for enlightenment or even a binding decision.

STAGES OF MEDIATION

What is mediation actually like? Of course, we have seen that mediation is a highly variable process, difficult to describe with specificity. However, it is reasonable to make a few overall generalizations about the mediation process and how it works.

Mediation generally takes place in a series of one or more sessions. Most mediators set the length of the sessions at between one and two hours, although some mediation sessions are much longer.[12] A typical mediation begins and ends with a joint session, at which the mediator and all the disputants (and/or their lawyers) are in attendance. The prevalent model for civil and personal injury mediation is for the initial joint session to be followed by several sessions in caucus, followed eventually by more joint sessions to secure agreements. In divorce and family mediation, there is less likelihood of caucus sessions, and much if not all of the mediation occurs in joint sessions.

Although mediation is a highly fluid process, it is possible to conceptualize mediation as occurring in a series of stages. Table 3-2 shows one such stage model.

---

[12] In labor and international mediation, so-called marathon sessions are held. These sometimes depend on fatigue factors to move the disputants closer to agreement.

◆ **TABLE 3-2**   Stages and Phases of Facilitative and Evaluative Mediation

STAGE	DETAILS: FACILITATIVE MEDIATION	DETAILS: EVALUATIVE MEDIATION
Initial client contact	Basic information taken without compromising future impartiality or appearance of impartiality. Basic marketing of process. If one disputant team has contacted mediator, development of strategy for involving other disputant.	Basic information taken without compromising future impartiality or appearance of impartiality. Basic marketing of process. If one disputant team has contacted mediator, development of strategy for involving other disputant.
Introductory stage	Describe ground rules, rights, and responsibilities; break the ice; educate about the mediation process. Review and sign any contractual documents. Begin reframing of issues from contentions to joint problems to be solved.	Describe ground rules, rights, and responsibilities; break the ice; educate about the mediation process. Sign any needed contractual documents.
Issues clarification and communication	Use active listening to obtain information about disputants' shared and divergent interests and their goals in mediation. Develop list of areas of agreement and disagreement. Develop list of disputants' interests in a working document. Reframe contentions as goals, joint problems to be solved, and deep-seated interests, values, and needs. Address "people problems." Seek understanding of meta-disputes and linkages. Seek mutual recognition on the part of each disputant ("If I saw things as you do, I'd feel the same way").	Ask parties to state cases or positions or describe the nature of the conflict. (Some facilitative techniques may also be used.) Develop lists of areas of agreement and areas of nonagreement.
Productive stage	Using list of principles, brainstorm multiple joint options for mutual gain. Develop objective standards for assessing options. Fine-tune and select options, using the objective standards. Compromise often used to select between candidate options. Write draft agreement and get feedback.	Instill doubt and provide evaluation in an effort to reduce differing perceptions of facts and law and to move disputants' aspirations closer together. Explore whether aspirations overlap using backwater techniques applied during caucus. In joint session, compromise may be used to finalize settlement. Write down agreement and get feedback.
Agreement consummation	Develop formal agreement and execute agreement; may occur within or outside of mediation.	Develop formal agreement and execute agreement; may occur within or outside of mediation.
Debriefing and referral	Assess whether tasks of mediation are complete and, if not, what else needs to be done. Refer to other professionals as necessary. Assess successes and failures of process.	Assess whether tasks of mediation are complete and, if not, what else needs to be done. Refer to other professionals as necessary. Assess successes and failures of process.

Note: These stages are not strictly chronological: Participants will repeatedly loop back through earlier stages on their way to completing mediation. Most mediations are neither purely facilitative nor purely evaluative, although it is safe to say that evaluative mediators are much more likely to incorporate facilitative techniques than facilitative mediators are likely to incorporate evaluative techniques. Transformative mediation is considered facilitative but is staged differently.

INITIAL CLIENT CONTACT

Mediation begins when one or both disputants make contact with a mediation provider. Although clients may be referred to mediation by a court or their lawyers, often one of the disputants contacts the mediator directly to inquire about services. The mediator must inform the person making contact of the nature of the services, answer relevant questions, and at the same time avoid discussing substantive details about the dispute (the mediator will appear biased if one disputant has been allowed to state his or her side of the dispute before the other disputant becomes involved). The mediator will also try to motivate the client to choose mediation, not only for marketing reasons but also because, since mediation is a consensual process, some level of trust in the process is essential to its success. The mediator will frequently send informative brochures that provide specific facts about mediation and demonstrate its advantages. During the initial client contact, the mediator will often also need to provide guidance to the disputant on how to coax the other disputant into the mediation process. This task can require much tactical skill. Although some disputants will be making contact with the mediator with the knowledge and consent of the other disputant, others will be making contact independently. Almost inevitably, if the disputants are hostile, the move to contact a mediator will be reactively devalued by the other disputant. The other disputant will, moreover, regard as a hostile invasion of privacy any effort made by the mediator to contact him or her directly. Some mediators find that offering a free initial consultation can help overcome this barrier to involvement.

INTRODUCTORY STAGE

The purposes of the introductory stage of mediation are to break the ice and get comfortable, to introduce and clarify the mediation process, to establish the ground rules and policies of mediation, to clarify and establish the legal basis of mediation, and to begin to orient the disputants toward productivity in mediation.

Assuming that both disputants decide to give mediation a try, an appointment for an initial session is scheduled. Mediators usually seat their clients around a conference table. The table may be round to eliminate symbolic power distinctions between mediator and clients, emphasizing the critical role the disputants have in fashioning the settlement. After introductions, the mediator may allow the clients to talk about what brought them to mediation, but typically this phase is very short because of the tendency for disputants to become caught up in arguments and statements of positions. A competent mediator will balance the need of each client to talk about what is upsetting him or her with the need to avoid conduct that escalates the conflict.

Once a certain comfort level is established, the mediator will typically spend a substantial amount of time talking to and at the disputants. Usually, it is at this stage of the mediation process that the mediator will appear most active to the clients. The mediator must ensure that the clients know exactly what mediation is all about. The mediator must communicate his or her style of mediation, the goals of mediation, and the typical techniques the mediator uses to help the participants strive toward these goals. The mediator will also discuss the ground rules for behavior in mediation, such as the need for turn taking, the need to curtail name calling, the need for promptness, and so forth. The mediator will typically also present contractual documents that participants must sign in order to create a mediator–client relationship, protect the confidentiality of the mediation process, and so forth. In addition, most mediators will present information on the many benefits of this ADR technique in order to further co-opt the disputants to trust the process and motivate them to negotiate in good faith.

Because disputants entering mediation have been unable to achieve a settlement of their differences on their own, it is typical for them to enter mediation caught up in a competitive conflict cycle. The mediator will often experience immediate and continuous pressure from the disputants to get swept up in mutual blame games and recriminations. For this reason, from the first moments, mediators will work actively to interrupt this cycle and replace it with a cycle of cooperation. This aspect of the art of mediation is most important in facilitative mediation and is emphasized less in evaluative mediation.

Numerous techniques are used to subtly reorient the disputants away from conceptualizing the conflict as a win-lose contest and replacing it with the idea that the disputants have a joint problem to be solved together. The mediator will choose his or her words with extreme care to reflect this noncompetitive perspective on the conflict. For example, given parents disputing over where a child will live after divorce, instead of saying "So, you have come to mediation to settle your dispute over child custody," the mediator might instead say, "So, you have come to mediation to create a parenting plan that will be healthy for your child."

Another technique used by mediators to interrupt the competition cycle is to emphasize the cooperative elements of the disputants' relationship and to deemphasize the competitive elements. For example, if during the introduction to mediation one disputant, a longtime business partner of the other disputant, says, "I have no confidence that Joe will ever stop his abusive name calling of me! Good luck with your so-called ground rules," the mediator might respond, "You are showing a lot of optimism by being willing to come into mediation, and I am impressed that you and Joe have been able to keep your business relationship so profitable for so long despite the hard feelings. You must both be very hard workers. Let's work together to get the relationship onto an easier plane." The point is that the work of the mediator in reframing the disputant's perceptions away from a competitive conflict cycle begins from the first moment of contact and is continuous throughout the mediation process.

ISSUES CLARIFICATION AND COMMUNICATION

Following the introductory stage of mediation, the mediation will move into a stage of actively *communicating and clarifying issues.* It is here that the details of the dispute, and the nature of whatever impasses are preventing settlement, become most explicit.

Facilitative and evaluative mediators generally handle the issues clarification and communication stage quite differently. An evaluative mediator's goal at this stage is to get a sense of the positions and aspirations of each disputant. The evaluative mediator is apt to begin by asking each disputant to state the case or to describe the disagreement. What follows will typically be each disputant's efforts to convince the mediator of the merits of his or her case. Although the mediator is not the person who must be persuaded (after all, the mediator does not decide the dispute), it is almost inevitable that aggrieved disputants will want to win over the sympathies of the mediator. Moreover, the persuasiveness of each side's contentions may alter the evaluations the mediator gives to each side. The mediator will sometimes use information gained during the other side's presentation in an effort to lower the expectations of each disputant. The mediator will typically become actively involved in filling in the details of the disputants' contentions and getting up to speed on important details of the dispute. The National Institute for Trial Advocacy's text *The Art of Mediation* (Bennett and Hermann 1996) contains an excellent description of the art of mediator information-gathering questioning.

Following this joint session, the evaluative mediator will typically meet each disputant separately to gain further information about the disputant's real aspirations. The disputant has been posturing in front of the other disputant, but, without him or her present, the disputant is free to reveal more about what he or she really thinks. In addition, the mediator will use the caucus sessions to determine whether there are secrets in the dispute that are impeding successful negotiation and that the disputant is unwilling to share with the other disputant.

Issues clarification and communication in a facilitative mediation usually occurs entirely in a joint session. The reason for this emphasis is that, in a facilitative mediation, the primary goal at this stage is to facilitate the disputant's clarification of issues and underlying interests *with each other*. This goal cannot be accomplished if the disputants are not communicating with each other.

A typical facilitative mediation that has reached the stage of issues clarification and communication is focused on developing an interests analysis for each disputant. Most disputants enter mediation without a carefully conceived notion of their interests but, instead, with a list of positions and aspirations. Disputants also typically have a negatively biased belief about the motivations of the other disputant. For this reason, the facilitative mediator will begin this phase with specific tactics designed to deflect the disputants away from positional bargaining and set the stage for interests analysis. For example, in a dispute between the parents of a special-needs child and the school system, a facilitative mediator is apt to ask each disputant to tell about the child, an initiating gambit that usually elicits child-centered goals from all the participants.

As each disputant speaks about the conflict, the facilitative mediator reframes and refocuses the communication to defuse personal attacks directed at the other disputant and to clarify the interests, needs, principles, and values connoted by the speakers' statements. *Active listening* is a critical skill the mediator uses at this juncture to help speakers feel they have been heard while reconstructing the message, so that it can be absorbed and accepted with less defensiveness by the other disputant.

Active Listening

Active listening is a skill vital to effective mediators. It is also a skill that proves useful to all effective negotiators.

Active listening serves several vital purposes: It helps the speaker feel heard by the listener, helps the listener understand more fully the interests that underlie the speaker's position, and helps both speaker and listener become more "legitimized" in one another's eyes. Because each feels the other is taking him or her seriously, active listening improves trust and communication. Active listening is also a powerful tool in the process of principled bargaining.

To engage in active listening, simply listen very carefully to what a speaker has said. Then repeat, in your own words, what was stated. Do not say that you either agree or disagree with what the speaker has said. A key aspect of active listening is that, when you repeat the speaker's statement, you must reframe it to remove any aspects of the comment that are designed to make the listener feel angry or hurt (some negotiators like to call these "zingers"). Following the restating, you then draw the speaker out so that he or she will say more.

For example, suppose you are having a conversation with a member of the opposite political party, and this person says the following:

> I just think that _____ is the best presidential candidate out there. He seems to be in favor of everything I think is important. Anyone who thinks otherwise is a real idiot!

You oppose this candidate vigorously, and detest him. To engage in active listening, you would say something like the following:

> So you feel that _____ would make the best president of all the candidates out there right now. Tell me more about why you hold that opinion.

The response reframes the speaker's statement, omits the aspect of the communication that functioned as a personal attack, and asks for further information. Repeat this cycle of reframing and drawing the other person out as long as he or she seems willing to share his or her opinion. The act of actively listening does not require you to engage in any dishonesty—and it does not require you to agree with the other speaker's opinion (though it may have require a degree of emotional restraint).

Active listening also helps the mediator reframe the disputant's communication from statements of position into statements about underlying principles.

Mediators of all persuasions often act as organizers of information. An evaluative mediator will often summarize the conflictual issues in a single document or will write a list on a white board or poster. Facilitative mediators will also make a list of the issues that must be resolved but will also typically list the deep-seated interests, needs, values, and principles with which the disputants agree. The agreed-upon interests are used as a sort of map, or "constitution," to guide the disputants in the next stage, the productive stage, of their negotiation.

PRODUCTIVE STAGE

As issues are clarified, communicated, and organized, the mediation enters the third stage: the productive stage. In the productive stage, issues are resolved and the agreement is written down.

In an evaluative mediation, it is in the productive stage that the evaluation occurs. During caucus, the evaluative mediator expertly probes the situation, pointing out weaknesses in the case of the disputant before him or her and suggesting strengths in the opponent's case that the disputant might have missed or discounted. Occasionally, an evaluative mediator will, instead, perform an evaluation in front of the two disputants together, indicating that "If this case were to go to court, it seems to me it would come out about this way." The evaluative mediator will tactfully probe each disputant for bottom lines, looking for integrative opportunities and mutually beneficial concession trades. If the mediator can help the two disputants get to the point at which their bottom lines overlap, the mediator will often bring the parties back together and allow them to conduct the final act of reaching agreement themselves. The mediator will gently coach the disputants in how to bring about this final agreement, avoiding telling either disputant what the other's bottom line is but suggesting appropriate directions in which to go.

In facilitative mediation, the productive stage often involves a period of brainstorming for possible options to address the list of interests that the disputants generated previously. These possible options are then examined and reality tested. At some point in this process, some amount of compromising, or haggling, is generally required to reach ultimate agreement. The mediator may suggest selecting "objective standards" to guide this final selection process if the disputants are unable to make this final decision themselves. The mediator may encourage the clients to use their list of interests, values, and needs, generated earlier, as the standard by which the options are tested. Often, the disputants will readily agree to some final minor compromising once they are very close to full settlement.

Both facilitative and evaluative mediators will write down any settlements that the disputants reach, either in an informal memorandum of agreement or in a formal contract. Mediators will typically ask disputants for feedback on this written product and make revisions as needed. If the disputants' attorneys participated in the mediation sessions, they will sometimes do the agreement drafting instead of the mediator.

A Sample List of Shared Principles for a Child Custody Mediation

We, John Jones and Mary Smith, the loving parents of Margaret Jones, agree to the following shared principles:

1. We agree to keep our daughter's needs and interests at the forefront of our negotiations.
2. We agree that our daughter should have the opportunity to spend lots of time with each of us.
3. We agree that we should find a way to structure our parenting agreement so that our daughter's present school system, after-school activities, church, and so on are not disrupted very much.
4. We agree that our daughter should have permission to love and care about both of us and that neither of us should put the other parent down in front of her.
5. We agree that our daughter should be kept safe, so neither of us should do risky things, such as drinking and driving when she is with us.
6. We agree that it is important for us to have effective and friendly communication, so we demonstrate good problem-solving techniques for our daughter.
7. We agree that our daughter needs for each of us to support the discipline of the other parent as long as it isn't damaging to her.

AGREEMENT CONSUMMATION

Agreement consummation can occur inside or outside of mediation. If the mediator has drafted a formal contract, sometimes the disputants will execute this contract at a mediation session. More commonly, a written account of the settlement is transformed into a formal written contract outside of mediation, after the disputants have had a chance to discuss the settlement with legal counsel. (See the discussion in Chapter 4 regarding the ethical issues involved in mediators' drafting the settlement agreement.)

DEBRIEFING AND REFERRAL

The last stage of mediation is *debriefing and referral.* This stage may occur before or after the agreement consummation stage. The mediator and disputants review what has been decided in mediation and what remains to be done. The mediator may provide guidance as to the appropriate next steps and as to the appropriate professional assistance needed for these next steps. If the disputants have reached a temporary agreement, plans may be made for a return to mediation in the future. The disputants and the mediator may also discuss and confirm the successes and drawbacks of the mediation process.

The process of mediation is typically nonlinear. The stages presented in this section and, indeed, in any description of mediation are not fixed in sequence. Often, mediation backtracks to an earlier stage. For example, during the agreement consummation stage, the participants may realize that they have forgotten to deal with an issue, which will require a return to the issues clarification and communication stage. Or communication in mediation may break down, necessitating a return to the ground-rules phase of the introductory stage of mediation.

WHAT DO MEDIATORS DO?

Mediation is both a science and an art. Although some sense of the mediator's toolbox of strategies and tactics can be gained, you should be aware that each mediator and each mediation is different. For a better idea of how mediators work, a number of helpful descriptions of real mediations are available. For an even better idea of what mediation is like, you should find a way to attend some actual mediation sessions.

FACILITATIVE TACTICS IN MEDIATION

Even highly evaluative mediators have as a goal the facilitation of a negotiated settlement. For this reason, nearly every mediator uses a number of facilitative tactics.

It is helpful to an understanding of mediator behavior to place facilitative mediator tactics in the following categories:

- Educating
- Structuring the negotiation
- Improving communication
- Handling emotions
- Maintaining disputant motivation

Educating. Mediators *educate* their clients in many ways. Much of this educational process occurs in the introductory stage of mediation but continues throughout the mediation process. Mediators provide information about the benefits and appropriate uses of mediation. This information allows the disputants to make informed choices about whether mediation is right for them, and it persuades disputants to make an emotional commitment to trying mediation. Mediators also educate their clients about the process of mediation. This information enables disputants to anticipate what they will experience and minimizes surprises. For example, mediators will often anticipate the likelihood that an impasse will be encountered in mediation by warning the disputants of this possibility and reassuring clients that impasse is both expected and manageable. Mediators also educate clients about the ground rules of mediation. In this fashion, the mediator begins to control and structure the mediation process in a way that promotes effective negotiation. For example, a mediator will typically begin a mediator–client relationship by distributing and discussing one or more written documents containing ground rules—such as the need to take turns without interruption, the need not to use abusive language, and the need to arrive at all sessions promptly. By this means, the mediator tells the clients how to conduct themselves in mediation, further increasing the likelihood that the mediation will meet the goals set for it. Many mediators also teach clients the value of, and the steps of, principled bargaining. This educative function helps clients buy into the premises of mediation, helps clients negotiate effectively, and, as a side benefit, may help clients in negotiations that occur outside mediation.

Mediators educate didactically: in other words, by direct lecture to the clients. They also teach indirectly in a number of ways. One of the most effective educative techniques is *role modeling.* The nonconfrontational active listening techniques and other communication tactics engaged in by mediators not only serve as a direct intervention in the conflict but also educate clients as to the behavior expected of them during the mediation. Mediators acting in panels also frequently role model cooperative behavior in front of clients. This is the reason that some mediators insist that all communication regarding the substance of mediation take place in a joint session: any communication can be of positive educational value. Mediators also role model appropriate behavior: staying calm, listening actively, avoiding name calling, staying positive, and so forth. In addition to role modeling, mediators may educate by assigning outside activities—"homework"—and by referring clients to other professionals, such as therapists, appraisers, and financial planners.

Structuring the Negotiation. The "meat" of what a mediator does is to *structure the negotiation.* The clients have presumably come to the mediator specifically to get help in negotiating effectively. Thus, the mediator's efforts to structure the negotiation are designed specifically to address this need of the clients.

The precise structure imposed or promoted by the mediator depends on the mediator's chosen style, on the preferences of the clients, and on the demands imposed by the situation. Nearly all mediators impose basic ground rules related to the number and length of sessions and the behavior required of both the clients (e.g., the use of respectful language) and the mediator (e.g., lack of bias in favor of either client). Beyond these nearly universal truths about mediation, the structure varies. Pure mediators frequently impose a structure following the principled-bargaining model: They encourage a period of interests analysis, followed by brainstorming sessions, a period of reality testing of options, and, throughout mediation in general, guidance in staying "soft on the person, tough on the problem" (Fisher, Ury and Patton 1991). Bargaining-based mediators, on the other hand, often call for an initial statement of the case in an initial session, followed by an examination of interests and aspirations in caucus, followed by an evaluation and then an exploration of opportunities for compromise. Other structuring by the mediator is determined by the specific situation in which the mediator finds the parties to be involved. For example, a facilitative mediator may conclude that a mutual acknowledgment and recognition may further settlement, and, based on this conclusion, the mediator may structure a mutual active listening session.

Improving Communication. At all times, a competent mediator *promotes more effective communication* between the disputants. Effective communication has the following goals:

- Developing a complete and accurate interests analysis (particularly for pure mediation)
- Encouraging a perception of cooperation among the disputants, thus interrupting or preventing a competitive conflict cycle
- Airing misunderstandings and meta-disputes, so that mutual trust building can begin
- Recognizing and acknowledging the perspectives of the individual disputants ("If I had seen things from your point of view, I probably would have felt the same way") if possible by one disputant to the other and, if not, by the mediator to each disputant
- Avoiding conflict escalation brought on by inflammatory communication
- Performing effective conflict diagnosis
- Engaging in effective principled bargaining and collaboration, which is built on complete, open, and honest communication

Handling Emotions. Mediation inevitably gives rise to strong emotion, and *dealing effectively with these emotions* is a vital element of the mediator's craft. One of the things that distinguishes the mediation process from what goes on in

a therapy session is the manner in which emotions are addressed. A mental-health professional, such as a psychotherapist, often works on the assumption that, by unblocking difficult emotions, the patient can make strides in healthy functioning. Thus, providing emotional catharsis for patients is frequently a direct goal of mental-health professionals. On the contrary, getting emotions out and on the table is *not* a primary goal of mediation.

The primary goals of most mediation processes typically revolve around setting the stage for effective negotiation, although, of course, this can vary depending on the form of mediation being practiced. A disputant's emotional state sometimes prevents him or her from dealing rationally with substantive issues in the negotiation, and sometimes the client's emotional state points the way to an important issue in the conflict that was buried or not acknowledged. To get past such issues, to address them appropriately, and to reach a lasting agreement acceptable to all disputants, these emotions must be explicitly acknowledged. Moreover, for a disputant to feel heard and cared for in the negotiation process and by the settlement, the emotions raised by the conflict must be validated. Ideally, the best person to validate a disputant's emotion is the other disputant, because the recognition conferred by the other disputant promotes positive feelings and cooperation. However, sometimes the hot and hurtful emotions around the conflict prevent the other disputant from conferring this element of recognition, and in such a case the mediator is often forced to provide the recognition in the disputant's place.

On the other hand, there are problems when emotional expression is unfettered in mediation. Encouraging a disputant to freely vent feelings can scare and anger the other disputant and can cause the conflict to enter a period of destructive escalation. Moreover, if the mediator validates a disputant's emotions based on a grievance aired against the other disputant, the mediator runs the risk of appearing to agree with the aggrieved disputant's version of the story. If the mediator is to validate the disputant's feelings, he or she must do so without seeming to agree with the disputant's account of the underlying facts. A mediator does not act as a fact finder: If he or she did, the process would be nonbinding evaluation, not mediation.

How are disputants' emotions validated as necessary without creating problems of conflict escalation and mediator bias? The solution is to find a way to validate feelings in a depersonalized way. Professor Elizabeth Koopman (1983, 1985), formerly of the University of Maryland, College Park, developed the *confirm-and-focus* technique to create respectful, distancing, and bias-free responses to emotionality in mediation.

Confirm-and-focus works like this: Imagine an emotion-laden comment made by a client in mediation. For example, suppose a fifty-year-old wife in a divorce case says, "My husband's a total jerk. In our entire twenty-five years of marriage, he never lifted a finger to help with the kids!" First, the mediator attempts to determine all of the feelings being expressed. To do this, the mediator has to "listen with the third ear," looking for the feelings that lie beneath the words spoken. It helps for the mediator to have expert knowledge of the typical experience of individuals in the position of the disputant. Sometimes, active listening is helpful in developing an accurate picture of the emotions being expressed. In our example, the mediator might hear anger, frustration, and possibly some underlying fear of having insufficient support in the future. Second, the mediator confirms the expressed feeling *but uses the third-person voice,* not first-person. This impersonal voice confirms that such feelings are understandable, but it does not encourage the speaker to vent more. In addition, the response does not validate the underlying factual allegation; instead, it presumes that the version of the facts is an opinion held by the speaker. This point of view avoids putting the mediator in the position of expressing agreement with the factual component of a disputant's statement. Thus, an *improper* response might be the following:

> *Wrong:* "I can see how angry, scared, and frustrated you are that he was so uncooperative and unreliable."

An *improved* response takes care not to confirm the factual underpinnings of the statement:

> *Better:* "I can understand that, if you felt you didn't get support for your parenting, you would react with anger, fear, and frustration."

Still better is a response that uses the third-person instead of the first-person voice. Using the third-person voice does not encourage further expression of emotion as much as the first-person voice:

> *Better yet:* "People who feel they didn't get support for their parenting often feel angry, scared, and frustrated."

Note how this response allows the mediator to validate the wife's feelings without agreeing with her assessment of the facts and without encouraging a lot of additional venting. Finally, to form a true confirm-and-focus response, the mediator couples the validating statement with a direction to *refocus* the speaker on the mediation issues raised by the statement:

> *Best:* "People who feel they didn't get support for their parenting often feel angry, scared, and frustrated. Let's work on setting up some clear parenting responsibilities, so that you won't be so likely to feel let down. What promises do you need from John about future parenting?"

This response validates the wife, obviates the need for the mediator to become entangled in an argument over whether the husband was a good spouse (which is irrelevant to the task at hand), and directs the couple back to the substantive task of mediation.

The gold standard in any negotiation process involves the disputants, themselves, behaving empathically toward one another. Sometimes, the mediation reaches a point at which disputants gain the capacity to say "If I had had the experiences you had, I'm sure I would feel the same way." This state of emotional openness creates a climate in which conflict resolution is welcome. Disputants who are able to communicate a sense of recognition of the other's perspective are often well on their way to leaving emotional baggage behind and achieving a rationally negotiated settlement.

Transformative Mediator Tactics—Facilitating, But with a Difference

The predominant form of facilitative mediation practiced today is *pure mediation,* but *transformative mediation* is another important form—one that is experiencing a great rise in popularity today.

Researchers Dorothy Della Noce, James R. Antes, and Judith A. Saul (Antes, Della Noce, and Saul 2002) have explored some of the differences between pure (referred to in the research as "problem-solving") mediators and transformative mediators. To do this work, the researchers selected four mediators, two of each type, all of whom were recognized as preeminent practitioners in the field. Studying mediator-client discourse during videotapes of these mediators in action, they found several important differences between the facilitative behavior of pure mediators and that of transformative mediators.

Whereas pure mediators often structure the mediation process to encourage effective negotiation, transformative mediators are careful to leave the structuring of the process to the disputants themselves. For example, a pure mediator typically sets ground rules for mediation, such as "The disputants will take turns speaking," but a transformative mediator more often asks the disputants themselves whether any ground rules would be helpful and what those rules should be. The latter approach is grounded in the transformative goal of granting the disputants the opportunity to empower themselves.

Transformative mediators "orient the parties to each other," whereas pure mediators orient the disputants toward the problem they need to solve. Moreover, transformative mediators are trained to follow the hot buttons in the conflict and encourage the disputants to expand on them. Thus, the common pure-mediation strategy of refocusing disputants away from hot emotion and back on solving the substantive problem, as is seen in the tactic *confirm and focus,* would be rejected by transformative mediators, who would be more likely to confirm a point of view and then invite further comment. This encouragement of emotional expression is an effort to give disputants opportunities to give one another recognition.

Whether the clients have attained this capacity is a judgment call for the mediator, and, if the mediator incorrectly guesses that a disputant is ready to communicate empathically with the other disputant, the results can wreak havoc on the mediation (e.g, when a disputant who, when called upon to say "I understand your feelings," responds, "No way," creating a sense of betrayal and probably escalating the conflict).

Maintaining Disputant Motivation. The final group of facilitative mediator tactics relates to *maintaining disputant motivation.* Conflict is usually an unpleasant experience, and mediation confers only limited protection from this unpleasantness. Disputants are confronting difficult issues, issues they have not been able to deal with without help. Moreover, interpersonal conflict frequently presents difficult issues of ego and identity repugnant to the disputants. When mediation hits a snag, disputant pessimism often takes over. When enthusiasm flags, a good mediator intervenes to raise the disputants' motivation to continue.

Numerous tactics are used by mediators to maintain or improve disputant motivation. Mediators frequently remind disputants of how far they have come already. If confidence seems to be flagging, many mediators will review the list of partial agreements already made. Mediators will make a practice of praising agreements as they are reached, no matter how minor they seem, mining the discussion for small victories to celebrate. For example, one mediator half-jokingly says that, if confidence seems low, the mediator can suggest an outrageous settlement and, when both disputants attack the mediator's suggestion, the mediator can point out that at least they agree on the idiocy of that option. Mediators frequently remind the disputants of the dismal alternatives to settlement, as well as, in appropriate cases, the potential benefits of being able to keep their relationship going. Mediators will frequently remind the disputants of how far they've come, demonstrating that giving up now would abandon important work they've already done.

EVALUATIVE TACTICS IN MEDIATION

Even evaluative mediators use many of the facilitative tactics we've just discussed. However, some techniques are unique to evaluative mediators, and some are used more frequently in this style of mediation:

- ◆ Instilling doubt
- ◆ Offering opinions about the case (case evaluation)
- ◆ Caucusing

Instilling doubt
a mediator tactic in which the confidence of each disputant in the strength of his or her legal case is called into question in an effort to move the disputants closer to a compromise.

Instilling Doubt. An extremely powerful tool in the evaluative mediator's arsenal is known as **instilling doubt**. This tactic consists of identifying overly optimistic BATNA assessments and providing strategic information to lower expectations.

(You may recall that BATNA stands for Best Alternative to a Negotiated Agreement, a concept discussed in Chapter 2.) This technique is used heavily in the mediation of many civil and contract legal disputes.

As an example of the technique of instilling doubt, imagine a mediated dispute over a medical malpractice case. Typically, both patient and physician will use case valuation to assess the BATNA. The mediator, to instill doubt, will attack each side's valuation of the case, trying to make each less optimistic. In our imaginary medical malpractice mediation, the mediator might take the patient, and the patient's lawyer, into a private caucus session and question the merits of their case. Perhaps there is an issue of whether the doctor's provision of care did or did not meet the "reasonable physician" standard for physicians in the community. The mediator will place the physician's version of the case in the best possible light in an effort to reduce the patient's expectations about how the litigated case will come out. Subsequently, the mediator will meet with the physician and the lawyer, also in caucus. The mediator might instill doubt with this team by emphasizing the patient's sympathetic demeanor and the horrible disability with which he was left. Emphasizing the best aspects of the plaintiff's case, the mediator might argue to the physician and her lawyer that there is a substantial chance of the plaintiff's prevailing on the law and that the typical jury would bend over backward to give this plaintiff a huge judgment to compensate him for his awful injuries.

The technique of instilling doubt makes compromising more likely by reducing the confidence of each disputant in his or her BATNA. If the disputants are bargaining positionally, reducing disputant expectations is essential to overcoming impasse. Instilling doubt can be helpful in dealing with disputants afflicted with the *jackpot syndrome*—that is, with disputants whose highly inflated idea of possible recovery is blinding them to the likelihood that they will lose in court. It is also helpful to lawyers whose clients want them to fight like gladiators on their behalf: it allows the lawyer to delegate to the mediator the task of reality testing the merits of the case. Unlike more facilitative techniques, in a case of overly optimistic BATNA evaluations the instilling doubt tactic is highly efficient at creating quick settlements.

Instilling doubt has some drawbacks as a mediation technique. Because it focuses on the disputant's case and treats the conflict as a zero-sum game, it tends to draw the disputants into a cycle of positional bargaining and competition. And, because it focuses on positions rather than on interests, it draws disputants away from the sort of introspection that creative problem solving requires. Many times, a more facilitative mediator can accomplish the same BATNA-clarification goal by reality testing, assigning homework in which the disputant gathers information about the case, or referring the disputant to experts.

Obviously, the technique of instilling doubt requires the use of caucusing. If instilling doubt is used in joint session, more often than not the reduction in one disputant's BATNA will produce more optimism on the part of the other disputant. Also, to use this technique effectively, a mediator must be able to claim substantive expertise in the subject matter of the legal dispute. For example, the mediator in our medical malpractice example would have a legitimate claim of being able to instill doubt if she were a trial judge with extensive experience trying medical malpractice cases. A nonlawyer-mediator with terrific credentials in conflict resolution, but no experience with medical malpractice litigation, would have a difficult time convincing the disputants to believe her assessment of their BATNAs.

Offering Opinions About the Case (Case Evaluation). Highly evaluative mediators may go beyond instilling doubt and actually offer an opinion about the likely outcome of the case, were it litigated. Such a mediator may listen to both sides present their cases—almost as if they were presenting opening statements at trial—and then offer an opinion. The opinion may represent a range—"I think it's likely the plaintiff would recover between twenty-five and thirty-thousand dollars"—or be more specific—"I think the case is worth around thirty thousand dollars." Specific evaluation is often followed with more facilitative tactics: the mediator might then try to help the disputants reach a compromise based on the evaluation. As with the tactic of instilling doubt, the offering of opinions is best done by a mediator who can hold himself or herself out as a substantive authority in the type of case presented by the disputants. This sort of evaluation is frequently offered by mediators who are retired judges.

The function of offering opinions is to narrow the distance between the positions of the disputants by providing a specific estimate of what the litigation alternative would yield. In some cases, the opinion would moderate both disputants' BATNAs; in others, the opinion might be very close to the demands of one of the disputants but distant from the demands of the other. In either case, the goal, similar to that of instilling doubt, is to narrow the distance between BATNAs and to prompt compromising. Unlike instilling doubt, this sort of opinion need not be given in caucus. If presented in caucus, the opinion can be combined with instilling doubt to create a stronger impetus to moderate the BATNA. Such an opinion is also quite useful if both disputants have a strong desire to settle the case and are not particular about the exact nature of the settlement but are reluctant to lose face by making voluntary concessions. Such disputants can justify their concessions by rationalizing that it was the mediator's idea.

As with instilling doubt, the offering of opinions about case value focuses the disputants on their positions and on the likelihood that their position will prevail, diverting attention away from underlying interests and integrating tactics. As such, pure, transformative, and narrative mediators argue that this tactic creates a suboptimal mediation process.

In addition, providing a specific opinion, or range of opinions, may create the appearance of bias if the opinion is substantially closer to the contentions of one disputant than the other:

Peter has filed an action for medical malpractice against Dinah, an anesthesiologist. They are involved in evaluative mediation before the Honorable

Minnie Mediator, a retired judge. Peter presents his contention that his case is worth $1,500,000, and Dinah presents her contention that the case is worthless. Minnie listens to the two statements, discusses the case with each legal team, and reviews documentary evidence prepared by both sides. Minnie comes to the conclusion that Peter's case is extremely weak. She brings the parties back together and conveys her honest opinion that Peter has a very poor case and will be lucky if he recovers anything in court. She follows her comments with an invitation to both legal teams to engage in some further compromising so that the disputants can avoid the cost and trauma of litigation.

In such a dispute, when the mediator's opinion is much more in line with the contentions of one disputant, the mediator will have difficulty avoiding the appearance of favoring that disputant, and the mediator, by expressing her opinion about the merits of the case, will appear to be pressuring the party whose contention is further from the mediator's opinion. Such pressure is inconsistent with the primary tenet that mediation be purely voluntary and free of coercion.

Another problem with issuing an opinion, according to business law professor Murray S. Levin of the University of Kansas (Levin 2001), is that such evaluations have little likelihood of accuracy. Professor Levin canvassed the rather sparse research regarding the valuation of legal disputes and found vast discrepancies in valuations even among experienced litigators with objective perspectives on the disputes in question. For example, in one study, a personal injury case that settled for $25,000 was evaluated by five experienced personal injury lawyers for values of $2,500, $3,000, $7,500, $12,000, and $25,000; another personal injury case, which settled for $2,500, was valued by the experts at $7,500, $17,500, $20,000, $22,500, and $40,000 (Levin 2001, 290). Thus, the estimate of a mediator, whose familiarity with the issues is typically less thorough than that of the disputant's legal team (Levin 2001, 295), is not likely to represent an accurate prediction of what would happen if the dispute went to court.

Caucusing. The technique of caucusing, or meeting with one side individually and out of earshot of the other side, is used by both evaluative and facilitative mediators. However, since virtually all evaluative mediators caucus and a significant number of facilitative mediators reject caucusing out of hand, it is considered an evaluative tactic in this discussion.[13]

It has already been mentioned that caucusing is typically necessary if the mediator instills doubt. The caucus can also be used to confront disputants about issues that would cause loss of face if dealt with in joint session. In addition, mediators can use the caucus to perform backroom negotiation—that is, informal exploration for information about positions that the disputants do not

---

[13] The technique is so widespread among particular subgroups of mediators that many accounts of the "stages of mediation" include the caucus as a necessary component of the mediation process, yet other mediators never caucus.

wish to share with one another or with the general public. For example, in international mediation, the mediator will often meet with world leaders, or their representatives, in caucus to discuss elements of the negotiation (such as concessions of land) that these leaders cannot articulate publicly without loss of face or authority. Caucusing is also used by both facilitative and evaluative mediators to uncover secrets clients are uncomfortable articulating in joint session with the other disputant.

Generally, to promote open communication in caucus sessions, the mediator will hold all utterances in caucus confidential unless the disputant explicitly consents to the mediator's sharing the information with the other disputant. Most mediators try to preserve as much perceived impartiality as possible by offering equal time in caucus to each of the disputants.

The reason that many facilitative mediators avoid caucusing is that caucusing does not advance the cause of principled bargaining, which requires honest and open communication between the disputants. In addition, the caucus process raises trust and mediator bias problems. There is a strong temptation for the individual disputants to try to use the caucus to convince the mediator that his or her side is "right." When trust is low between the disputants (which is typically the case with clients in mediation), disputants, who are aware of their own temptation to co-opt mediator sympathy and assume the other disputant is similarly motivated, will frequently suspect that the other disputant is telling the mediator lies, exaggerations, or half-truths in the caucus. This suspicion undermines the perception of mediator impartiality, further eroding trust between the disputants, and may create meta-disputes. Thus, if the facilitation of principled bargaining, rather than the attainment of settlement, is the principal goal of mediation (as with many pure mediators), the caucus can be counterproductive. These mediators often conclude that the risks of caucusing outweigh the benefits.

What Is Mediation Like? Some Ways to Find Out

Some descriptions that offer a taste of how mediation really works can be found in the following sources:

Riskin and Westbrook's (1997) law school text, *Dispute Resolution and Lawyers* (2nd ed.), contains a section entitled "Brief Takes on Real Mediations," which contains accounts of the use of mediation in professional malpractice disputes, personal injury claims, corporate shareholder management disputing, environmental disputing, and Native American fishing rights disputing.

On the Internet, Mediate.com Resolution Solutions, *http://www.mediate.com*, contains a number of descriptions of mediation. They include "With No Lawyers in Sight, Landlords and Tenants Talk Out Disputes," by Gustav Spohn (*http://www.mediate.com/articles/landlord.cfm*); David Gage, Dawn Martin, and John Gromala, "Mediation During Business Formation or Reorganization" (*http://www.mediate.com/articles/formation.cfm*); and Forrest Mosten, "What Happens in Mediation?" (family mediation) (*http://www.mediate.com/articles/mosch3.cfm*). In addition, Resolution Forum, Inc. (*http://www.resolutionforum.org/s_demo.html*) contains a transcript of a simulated mediation session dealing with a contracting dispute. Several videos excerpting mediation sessions can be streamed at YouTube (exercise some care—some entries entitled "mediation" are actually about "meditation").

EXERCISES, PROJECTS, AND "THOUGHT EXPERIMENTS"

1. Find the Web sites of at least three different mediators, all of whom practice in different firms, whose sites include a list of their qualifications and a description of the types of cases they accept. List the jurisdictions in which they practice, the types of cases they handle, and their qualifications. What similarities do you see in their qualifications? What differences are there? If you do this assignment as a class project, discuss the results in class. See if you can discern patterns of qualifications among mediators specializing in the handling of particular kinds of cases.

2. Imagine yourself as a lawyer. A client enters your office with a divorce matter. She is extremely shy and reserved and seems to be intimidated by everything. The client has learned about mediation from her husband, who wants to resolve the matter out of court. She asks you to suggest a mediator and represent her during the mediation process. What do you do? Be specific and detailed.

3. Interview a mediator. Some of the questions you might pose include the following:

   a. What is your professional background?

   b. What specialized mediation training or education have you completed?

   c. Are you a member of any professional mediation or ADR associations? Which ones, and what benefits do you obtain from membership?

   d. What sorts of disputes do you mediate?

   e. How long have you been practicing mediation? How many cases have you mediated?

   f. What is your mediation style? Can you give some specific examples (while maintaining your clients' confidentiality, of course) of how you apply your style in mediating disputes?

   g. What is the most difficult aspect of the mediation profession, and what do you do to deal with it?

   h. What is the most rewarding aspect of mediation practice?

   i. Do you have any advice for people considering a career as a mediator?

4. Identify each of the following descriptions of mediation processes as one of the five varieties of mediation:

   a. Erica Sloane, a former marketing analyst turned mediator, offers disputants a chance to sit down and air out what has led them into conflict. She works to ensure that each disputant has a very clear picture of what the other's perspective on the conflict is. She also works to ensure that each disputant has enough knowledge, assistance, and strength to negotiate effectively. She tells her clients in her initial mediation session that these goals—empowerment and recognition—are the essential goals of mediation but that the most effective and lasting agreements often come from this style of mediation.

b. Josh Bluefield is a retired hearing officer for the workers' compensation commission of his state. He has now volunteered for a new program in his state aimed at settling workers' compensation claims out of the adversarial system. The disputants and their attorneys attend mediation sessions, in which he hears both sides. In separate caucus sessions with the individual disputants and their attorneys, he works to point out weaknesses in their case, the strengths in the other side's case, and reasons to settle. He works to find middle ground between the disputants, using his expertise in the workers' compensation field to give him authoritative force in his evaluations of the cases.

c. A state consumer protection agency has established a phone-in mediation clinic to handle the huge volume of grievances consumers file annually. Consumer claimants are given a list of mediators to call. A mediator takes the call, takes information from the consumer, and then tries to contact the merchant to get a settlement. Mediators are trained to be as brief as possible and to push both sides toward settlement, using threats of litigation on the merchant.

d. Social worker Inez Sykes mediates divorce and child custody disputes. Her goal in mediation, stated to the clients, is to create a setting and a structure that enable clients to negotiate effectively. She also works to educate clients about the benefits of cooperating and collaborating and to guide clients away from behaviors that create escalated conflict.

5. Ronnell, who has an R.N. degree and worked in hospital and physician settings before changing careers, has been working as a paralegal for a number of years and has developed extensive expertise in medical malpractice cases. Ronnell now wishes to change careers again. She obtains the necessary qualifications in her jurisdiction to practice medical malpractice mediation. Reviewing the facilitative and evaluative mediator strategies and tactics presented in this chapter, do you think she should practice facilitative mediation, evaluative mediation, or a mix of the two? Justify your answer.

6. Imagine that you are a paralegal working for a law firm specializing in tort cases. You have decades of experience preparing and assisting in tort litigation. You have volunteered with the local court system to mediate civil actions coming before the court. A case has been referred to you, as mediator, involving a grocery store owner and a woman who slipped and fell in the aisles, breaking a hip. The woman has sued the store for $300,000. Although the case was referred to you by the court system, each side was willing to try to use mediation to resolve the issue. Neither side has legal counsel, and both are begging you to tell how the case would come out if it were sent to court.

a. Is there any harm in your performing this evaluative function? Discuss.

b. Would your answer be different if you were an attorney? Why or why not?

7. Do you think that mediating disputants should decide what form of mediation should be applied to their interpersonal conflict, should this decision be

made by the mediator, or do you think it should be made by some other person (decided by the lawyers, perhaps)? Consider disputant self-determination and quality of consent, as well as mediator competence and temperament. Use this question as an essay topic or topic for discussion.

8. You are mediating a divorce. In caucus, the husband launches into what promises to be a long tirade against his wife, accusing her of everything from having repeated affairs to picking her nose in public. What do you do?

   a. What are the advantages of allowing the husband to vent these feelings in caucus? (After all, the wife is not there to hear them.) What are the disadvantages? (*Hint:* if you allow him to vent in this way, what would he think about what might transpire in a caucus session between the mediator and the wife?)

   b. If you felt the husband's comments should be reined in, how would you do this? What are the advantages of your approach and what are the disadvantages?

   c. Is there anything a mediator can do in a joint session to prevent this sort of quandary from arising in the caucus?

9. Choose a kind of legal dispute (e.g., medical malpractice or child custody). Write an introduction that you might give clients if you were acting as a mediator in this sort of dispute.

10. Imagine you work in a law office that handles general tort, contract, and business litigation. Prepare the text for a brochure that explains the advantages and disadvantages of mediation to clients.

11. Your client is a businessman who owns a restaurant. His partner and head chef is claiming that he is not receiving his fair share of the profits—he and your client have a difference of opinion about the ownership of revenues from a catering business run out of the restaurant premises by your client and a different chef. Your client is quite anxious to retain the restaurant, which will be vulnerable to failure if he loses the chef, so you have suggested taking the dispute to a mediator, and your client is all for it. However, the chef's attorney is balking because the chef "doesn't want to throw money down a dark hole"—in other words, he doesn't like the idea that mediation won't promise a resolution. Develop a strategy to assist this client in meeting his underlying interests and needs. Is there a way to improve the chances of reaching agreement while retaining all the relationship-protection benefits of mediation?

RECOMMENDED READINGS

Baruch-Bush, R. A. B., and J. P. Folger. 1994. *The promise of mediation.* San Francisco: Jossey-Bass.

Bennett, M. D., and M. S. G. Hermann. 1996. *The art of mediation.* Notre Dame Law School.

Bickerman, J. 1999. Great potential: The new federal law provides vehicle, if local courts want to move on ADR. *Dispute Resolution Magazine* (Fall):3–5.

Coogler, O. J. 1978. *Structured mediation in divorce settlement*. Lexington, MA: Lexington Books.

Depner, C. E., K. Cannata, and I. Ricci. 1994. Client evaluations of mediation services: The impact of case characteristics and mediation service models. *Family and Conciliation Courts Review* 32 (July):306–25.

Folberg, J., and A. Taylor. 1984. *Mediation: A comprehensive guide to resolving conflicts without litigation*. San Francisco, CA: Jossey-Bass.

Gage, D., D. Martin, and J. Gromala. 1999. Mediation during business formation or reorganization. Family Business. (Spring). *http://www.mediate.com/articles/formation.cfm* (accessed January 28, 2009).

Gaschen, D. E. 1995. Mandatory custody mediation: The debate over its usefulness continues. *Ohio State Journal on Dispute Resolution* 10:469–90.

Gauvey, S. K. 2001. ADR's integration in the federal court system. *Maryland Bar Journal* 33(2):36–43.

Grillo, T. 1991. The mediation alternative: Process dangers for women. *Yale Law Journal 100* (April):1545–1610.

Haynes, J. M. 1981. *Divorce mediation*. New York: Springer.

Heister, J. W. 1987. Appendix. Property allocation in mediation: An examination of distribution relative to equality and to gender. *Mediation Quarterly* 1987 (17, Fall):97–98.

Johnston, J. R., and L. E. G. Campbell. 1988. *Impasses of divorce: The dynamics and resolution of family conflict*. New York: The Free Press.

Kelly, J. B. 1996. A decade of divorce mediation research. *Family and Conciliation Courts Review* 34(3):373–85.

Kelly, J. B., and M. A. Duryee. 1992. Women's and men's views of mediation in voluntary and mandatory mediation settings. *Family and Conciliation Courts Review* 30(1):34–49.

Kovach, K. K., and L. P. Love. 1996. "Evaluative" mediation is an oxymoron. *Alternatives to the High Cost of Litigation* 14(3):31–32.

LaFree, G., and C. Rack. 1996. The effects of participants' ethnicity and gender on monetary outcomes in mediated and adjudicated cases. *Law and Society Review* 30(4):767–91.

Lande, J. 1997. How will lawyering and mediation practices transform each other? *Florida State University Law Review* 24 (Summer):839–901.

Love, L. 1997. The top ten reasons why mediators should not evaluate. *Florida State University Law Review* 24 (Summer):937–48.

Lowry, L. R. 2000. To evaluate or not: That is not the question! *Family and Conciliation Courts Review* 38 (January):48–58.

Marcus, M. G., W. Marcus, N. A. Stilwell, and N. Doherty. 1999. To mediate or not to mediate: Financial outcomes in mediated versus adversarial divorces. *Mediation Quarterly* 7 (Winter):143–52.

McCabe, K. 2001. A forum for women's voices: Mediation through a feminist jurisprudential lens. *Northern Illinois University Law Review* 21:459–82.

McIsaac, H. 2001. Confidentiality revisited: California style. *Family Court Review* 39(4):405–14.

Menkel-Meadow, C. J. 1985. Portia in a different voice: Speculations on a women's lawyering process. *Berkeley Women's Law Journal* 1:39–63.

Menkel-Meadow, C. J. 1991. Symposium: Pursuing settlement in an adversary culture: A tale of innovation co-opted or "the law of ADR." *Florida State University Law Review* 19 (Summer):1–46.

Mosten, F. 1997. Checklist: Eleven questions most commonly asked about mediation. *Fairshare* 17(9):5–7.

Mosten, F. S. 2003. What happens in mediation? *http://www.mediate.com/articles/mosch3.cfm.* (accessed January 29, 2009).

Pearson, J. 1991. The equity of mediated divorce agreements. *Mediation Quarterly* 9(2):179–97.

Rhode, D. L. 1999. Too much law, too little justice: Too much rhetoric, too little reform. *Georgetown Journal of Legal Ethics* 11:989–1017.

Rifkin, J. 1984. Mediation from a feminist perspective: Promise and problems. *Law and Inequality* 2:21–31.

Riskin, L. L. 1982. Mediation and lawyers. *Ohio State Law Journal* 43:29–60.

Riskin, L. L. 1996. Understanding mediators' orientations, strategies, and techniques: A grid for the perplexed. *Harvard Negotiation Law Review* 1 (Spring):7–51.

Riskin, L. L., and J. E. Westbrook (eds.). 1997. Brief takes on real mediations. In *Dispute resolution and lawyers,* 2nd ed. St. Paul, MN: West.

Shapiro, M. 1981. *Courts: A comparative and political analysis.* Chicago: University of Chicago Press.

Tondo, C.-A., R. Coronel, and B. Drucker. 2001. Mediation trends: A survey of the states. *Family Court Review* 39 (October):431–45.

Welsh, N. A. 2001. The thinning vision of self-determination in court-connected mediation: The inevitable price of institutionalization? *Harvard Negotiation Law Review* 6 (Spring):1–96.

Zumeta, Z. 2000. A facilitative mediator responds. *Journal of Dispute Resolution* 2000:335–41.

Zumeta, Z. D. 2000. Styles of mediation: Facilitative, evaluative, and transformative mediation. *http://www.mediate.com/articles/zumeta.cfm* (accessed January 29, 2009).

4

The Law and Ethics of Mediation

In civilized life, law floats in a sea of ethics.

—Earl Warren, *Chief Justice of the United States*

In this chapter, you will learn . . .

- the reasons for the regulation of mediation: to preserve the essence of mediation, to preserve the effectiveness of mediation, and to protect rights that otherwise might be compromised in mediation.
- why confidentiality is considered an important element of mediation.
- some of the ways that confidentiality is protected in mediation.
- the circumstances in which confidentiality is often waived or suspended.
- the reasons that mediation is sometimes made mandatory.
- the ways in which disputants are sometimes pressured or coerced to participate in mediation.
- the legal, constitutional, and ethical dilemmas posed by mandatory mediation.
- about the regulation of the unauthorized practice of law by nonlawyer-mediators.
- the ethical dilemmas posed by the provision of legal services by lawyer-mediators.
- about the regulation of the behavior of lawyer-advocates in mediation.
- about the need for mediator impartiality, and about some of the ways that impartiality is currently regulated.
- the kinds of mediator neutrality and their implications for the mediation process.
- about the regulation of mediator qualifications.
- about the legal standing of a mediated agreement and the complications posed by the confidentiality of the mediation process for proof and disproof of a mediated agreement.

INTRODUCTION: WHY REGULATE MEDIATION?

As many mediators often advise their new clients, mediation is a legal event. Although mediation technique is influenced by psychological considerations and sometimes resembles psychotherapy, the goal of mediation is usually a legally binding settlement. Moreover, it is necessary to protect participants from potential illegal or unconstitutional effects of mediation, especially that pushed by governmental entities such as court systems.

Early mediation pioneers operated largely in a legal vacuum. The laws of contract were virtually the only legal scaffold on which to build a viable process. But this situation is slowly changing as mediation becomes more widespread and institutionalized. An evolving regulatory structure is developing, primarily from statutory law (including regulations and rules of court and interpreted by decisional authority) and from rules of mediator ethics. Some commentators question whether the direction this evolution is taking is really in the best interests of users of mediation, or whether mediation is being inappropriately adversarialized, depleting it of its advantages in resolving conflict effectively.[1] A body of appellate case law is also beginning to develop, though trends are difficult to articulate—"[f]or now, mediators, parties, and lawyers, must swim in a relative sea of ambiguity" (Coben and Thompson 2006, 144).

The regulation of mediation can be best understood as a series of efforts designed to protect and preserve the essence of the process, to ensure its effectiveness, and to ensure that, as it is used, other legal rights and obligations are not damaged. As we have seen, however, there is much disagreement over the essence of mediation and the definition of good mediation. Moreover, there are differences of opinion over the extent to which society should promote nonadversarial forms of dispute resolution. The more radical wing of the ADR movement argues that the presence of the invisible veil keeps us from truly realizing the promise of mediation. But more traditional elements assert that pushing nonadversarial dispute resolution threatens important individual rights. Because

---

Why Is Mediation Regulated?

- ◆ To preserve the essence of mediation
- ◆ To ensure the effectiveness of mediation
- ◆ To protect other legal rights

---

[1] See, for example, Professor Carrie Menkel-Meadow's (1991) excellent discussion in "Pursuing Settlement in an Adversary Culture: A Tale of Innovation Co-opted or 'The Law of ADR,'" *Florida State University Law Review* 19: 1–46, and Professor Kimberlee Kovach's (2001) intriguing New wine requires new wineskins: Transforming lawyer ethics for effective representation in a non-adversarial approach to problem-solving: Mediation. *Fordham Urban Law Journal* 28: 935–977.

Mediation of peace treaty between China and Japan, circa 1895. Tsuchiya Koitsu, 1870–1940. Dorling Kindersley Media Library.

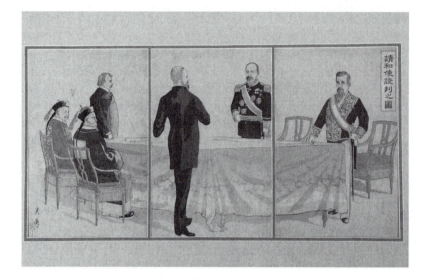

of these diverse voices affecting the mediation movement, the law and ethics of mediation are characterized by a lack of consensus, as well as by a series of tensions between conflicting goals.

PRESERVING THE ESSENCE OF MEDIATION

As already noted, mediation is such a diverse process that what one practitioner calls "mediation" can be almost unrecognizable to a colleague (Kovach and Love 1996; Riskin 1994).[2] Nonetheless, practitioners, users, and scholars of ADR have been able to agree on the following two essential characteristics of mediation, as a form of facilitated negotiation:

- ◆ A third-party mediator must be involved.
- ◆ Mediation is characterized by disputant self-determination.

It is easy to determine whether a third-party intermediary is involved in a dispute resolution process, although whether a given intermediary is correct to refer to his or her services as mediation is sometimes controversial. Little regulation exists—as yet—to control mediator "truth in advertising," although some glimmerings of this sort of regulation are beginning to appear.[3]

_____

[2] For example, the professional literature contains discussions by prominent scholars in the field over whether to call evaluative mediation "mediation" at all (Kovach and Love 1996, Riskin 1994, and Zumeta 2000a). Some processes labeled *mediation* are, in fact, nonbinding arbitration.

[3] For example, in a recent state mediator ethics case (Florida Mediator Qualifications Advisory Panel, Ethics Op. 95-007, 1995), it was stated that mediators are prohibited from advertising that clients can obtain a dispassionate case evaluation by using the mediator's service.

> ### *Essence-of-Mediation Issues*
>
> **Participation of Mediator**
>
> - Impartiality and neutrality
> - Truth in advertising and client-informed consent to the process
>
> **Client Self-determination**
>
> - Compulsion to mediate
> - Need for informed consent
> - Sources of legal advice
> - Distinguishing of mediation from evaluative ADR
>
> **Preservation of Mediation as a Nonadversarial Process**
>
> - Confidentiality in mediation

The second element of the essence of mediation—the need for self-determination—has been the topic of far more controversy among both mediation scholars and policy makers. Self-determination is the right of disputants to control the mediation and/or the outcome of the mediation. Self-determination is sometimes identified as "the fundamental principle of mediation" (ABA 2008; Welsh 2001b).

It is generally agreed that forcing an outcome on disputants is inimical to self-determination and results in a process of adjudication, not mediation. However, more controversial is whether penalizing the disputants for failing to come to a settlement violates the essence of informed consent. Still more difficult is the issue of whether, and to what extent, disputants can be compelled to participate in mediation and pressured to come to a settlement (Welsh 2001b). These incursions into self-determination are commonly justified by considerations of short-term efficacy and efficiency in resolving disputes and conserving judicial resources.

An additional problem with disputant self-determination is the extent to which it requires that disputants understand the legal consequences of their actions. The legal field interprets the concept of self-determination to mean "informed consent." Informed consent means, essentially, having all the information one needs to consent to an action. In practice, informed consent in mediation may refer to many things, including the need for the client to understand the nature of the dispute resolution process in which he or she is involved, as well as the consequences of various process and outcome choices.

There is an important difference between informed consent as understood by the legal community and self-determination as understood by the mediation community. In the domain of legal ethics, *informed consent* refers to being informed about the likely success of one's claim, should it be litigated. Although there is little argument between lawyers and mediators that disputants should understand the legal *consequences* of their agreements in order to make effective choices about their settlement, making a *prediction about the outcome* of litigation involving the legal dispute goes a step further: It is information important to knowing one's BATNA (see Chapter 2). Is knowing one's litigation ATNA essential to self-determination, or is it merely useful in negotiating effectively? Many lawyers and law professors, such as Professor Jacqueline Nolan-Haley (1999), assert that knowledge of the likely outcome of litigation is synonymous with informed consent, and, to the extent that mediation fails to provide such information, unjust results are likely. However, others argue that knowing the litigation alternative is not relevant to self-determination unless the disputants wish to adopt legal norms and practices as their index of fairness. As many mediators are aware, some disputants don't wish to use legal principles to guide them in making a fair agreement, nor are they concerned about knowing the litigation alternative to clarify their BATNA, even after these uses of the information are explained to them. Are such disputants negotiating without informed consent, or are they exercising their right to self-determination? Consider the following example:

> An unmarried couple, John and Barbara, entered mediation because they were breaking up and wished to settle issues of jointly held property. Both were articulate, sophisticated, and well-read clients in their late forties and had grown children from previous marriages. The couple decided that property held in their joint names should be divided 50 percent to Barbara and 40 percent to John, with 10 percent donated to a respected charity. This decision was a compromise between Barbara's assertion that John had wasted their money during the relationship and John's position that assets should be divided equally. The mediator, aware of the developing law in his jurisdiction regarding property held by unmarried couples, suggested that each of them get legal advice about how the property dispute might be resolved in court. To persuade the clients of the usefulness of getting legal advice, the mediator commented on the litigation alternative as useful information regarding the ideas of fairness expounded in the law. The mediator commented that the disputants were free to adopt this notion of fairness but were not required to do so. The mediator also explained the concept of the BATNA to them and posed the following hypothetical question: "How would you feel if you made the agreement you're leaning toward now but later learned that if you had gone to court you could have gotten eighty percent of the property instead?" For both John and Barbara, the response was immediate and unhesitating. "We don't care," both exclaimed. "We think our agreement is fair."

Some would argue that John and Barbara lacked the informed consent necessary to make a fair agreement, but others would respond that, although John and Barbara didn't know their BATNA, they exercised self-determination in developing shared norms and principles (Welsh 2001b) for arriving at settlement and in deciding that knowing their respective BATNAs was irrelevant to them (see Waldman 1997). Critics might also argue that disputants who lacked John and Barbara's sophistication might not appreciate the merits of knowing one's BATNA and the relationship of the BATNA to receiving legal advice.

The tension between informed consent and the larger concept of self-determination is articulated in the regulation of how legal advice is provided to mediating clients. This regulation occurs through limitations placed on evaluative mediation and the regulation of conduct considered the practice of law by mediators. More will be said about this issue later in this chapter.

Another self-determination issue relates to the provision of evaluative mediation services under the "mediation" name. It seems self-evident that the more options are provided to clients, the greater the clients' ability to exercise self-determination. On the other hand, given the prevalence of the invisible veil, a strong counterargument can be made: Unless mediation is defined in the public arena as a clear alternative to the more position-bound process that evaluative mediation represents, potential disputants will reflexively choose evaluative mediation and never reach the point of choosing the alternative. According to this argument, evaluative mediation should be recognized as the oxymoron that it is (Kovach and Love 1996), that such processes be given a name to distinguish them from "actual" mediation, and that evaluative tactics be prohibited from the practice of "actual" mediation. In the words of Kimberly Kovach,

> to allow a number of different activities to be called "mediation" only confuses the issue. If this practice is continued, lawyers will never distinguish between the processes, and mediation will lose all potential to establish a different paradigm for resolving disputes. *(Kovach 1997, 583, n. 50)*

Many other issues addressed in this chapter are tied in with the goal of preserving self-determination in mediation, such as the need for the mediator to act impartially and the extent of lawyer participation in mediation. The role of self-determination in guiding the regulation of mediation in these areas is unclear. Consider, for example, the issue of lawyer participation in mediation. A policy maker who interprets the principle of self-determination to mean that disputants should autonomously develop their own norms, principles, and agreement terms would likely advocate minimizing, or even prohibiting, the participation of lawyers in mediation sessions. A different policy maker, who equates self-determination with informed consent, might make the opposite decision and require that parties be represented by lawyers during sessions.

The issue of mediation's confidentiality, although appropriately considered relevant to ensuring effectiveness of the mediation process, may also be seen as central to the preservation of mediation's essence. Confidentiality is often seen as a precondition for open, honest, and free communication between the disputants. If mediation is viewed as a nonadversarial alternative to competitive processes of conflict resolution, then confidentiality is critical: It ensures that such communication will not be used later as part of an adversarial strategy. In addition, if mediation is viewed as a process for facilitating principled bargaining or collaboration between the disputants, confidentiality is essential to mediation's goals, since collaboration is impossible without open and honest communication about interests. If disputants feared that what they say could be used against them later, this free and open communication would likely be curtailed.

ENSURING THE EFFECTIVENESS OF MEDIATION

Mediation is also regulated to ensure its effectiveness. Here, again, controversy and uncertainty abound. One area of controversy concerns the nature of "effectiveness." You may recall the discussion of good conflict and bad conflict in Chapter 2. Assessing mediation's effectiveness in producing good conflict, and good results, depends on your point of view. One common criterion is to determine whether settlement has been reached and how much time and money it has taken to reach it. This short-term, "efficiency" approach suggests a much different set of regulations than an approach that considers the long-term impact of mediation on the overall interactions of the disputants and their overall abilities to deal with conflicts. Indeed, regulating mediation to promote short-term efficiency leads to a much different regulatory structure than regulating mediation to promote long-term social change. For example, a policy maker wishing to promote short-term efficiency goals would be tempted to promote evaluative and coercive mediation practices, which are regarded as taking less time, whereas one trying to promote a more nonadversarial approach to disputes in general (to promote its longer-term effectiveness) might outlaw evaluative mediation altogether, or at least strongly promote more facilitative practices.

Perhaps the most important regulatory issue that springs from the motivation to ensure effectiveness relates to the confidentiality of mediation. It is the consensus of most mediation scholars and practitioners that, for mediation to work well, it must be confidential, for reasons that will be discussed later in this chapter. However, to ensure that disputants are participating in mediation in good faith, to ensure that the mediator is behaving competently and ethically, to ensure that any agreements reached in mediation are being enforced appropriately and are not the result of fraud or duress, and to ensure that violations of the law are not occurring during the mediation process, various efforts have been made to limit confidentiality in mediation. For example, some jurisdictions have considered enacting rules that would require or permit sanctions against disputants who fail to mediate in good faith. To make such rules work, it would be necessary to compel or permit participants to testify about what has transpired during mediation in (see "The Duty to Participate in Good Faith"). Confidentiality is one of the most unsettled areas of mediation law.

Effectiveness in mediation is also promoted through the regulation of mediator credentialing, competence, and conduct. This effort is largely via ethical rules developed by professional ADR societies, although the ethical precepts of associated professions and a developing body of statutory law also affect the area. The behavior of others who participate in mediation, such as attorneys, is also subject to regulation, although it is primarily through preexisting professional ethical precepts, such as attorney codes of ethics, not specifically applicable to mediation. These codes are beginning to evolve to accommodate the special needs of clients involved in mediation.

Mediation Effectiveness Issues

- Perspectives on effectiveness: short term vs. long term and broad vs. narrow
- Confidentiality
- Enforceability of settlement
- Construing settlement agreement
- Good-faith participation
- Ensuring competent mediators
- Regulating credentialing, competence, behavior
- Suspending confidentiality to deal with malpractice issues

PROTECTING OTHER RIGHTS

The third major reason for the regulation of mediation is to protect the rights held by the participants in mediation and others affected by the process. For example, advocates for battered women worry that compelling them to participate in mediation with their abusers (e.g., to resolve assault cases) may create physical dangers to the victims as they confront those who may have assaulted them.

There is a tension between mediation effectiveness concerns and the desire to protect other legal rights. For example, if mediation is forced on disputants and the failure to settle is penalized, certain due process rights—most notably, the right to have one's civil claims adjudicated pursuant to an adversarial procedure—may be inappropriately compromised.

Protecting Other Rights

Due Process Considerations

- Limitations on coercion in mediation
- Informed consent
- Lifting of confidentiality to protect the right to give evidence in other proceedings

Safety Issues

- Mediation in abuse situations

Conflict with Other Rights

- Confidentiality of mediation involving the government: effects of laws rendering proceedings open to the public

LEGAL ISSUES IN MEDIATION

The goals articulated in the preceding section have led to efforts to regulate mediation confidentiality; to incorporate coercive or mandatory aspects to some mediation programs; to regulate conduct regarded as the practice of law performed by mediators; to regulate conduct of legal advocates during mediation; to adopt ethical rules governing mediator impartiality, neutrality, and competency; and to develop law governing the enforceability of mediated agreements.

CONFIDENTIALITY

Most kinds of mediation are held in a confidential setting; that is, secrets revealed or communications made in mediation can't be shared with others or used in litigation.[4] Confidentiality is invoked because it is believed that disputants won't feel as free to communicate openly with one another if they believe that what they say or reveal might be used against them. Moreover, the quality of mediation as a cooperative process could be compromised if disputants believed that communications in mediation would be the subject of discovery or trial tactics later on. In addition, confidentiality is needed to preserve the neutrality of the mediator: Disputants participating in mediation need to be reassured that the mediator will not testify against them later. Moreover, some disputants, such as large corporations with goodwill and an image to protect, choose mediation over a more public dispute resolution process so that their privacy can be protected.

Many relationships between professionals and their clients are confidential. These include the physician–patient relationship, the lawyer–client relationship, the priest–penitent relationship, and the therapist–client relationship, to name just a few. These relationships are confidential by law: Typically, a common-law rule enhanced by statutes confirming or clarifying the common law establish the confidentiality of these relationships and protect parties to the relationship from being required to reveal the substance of communications.[5] The mediator–client relationship, by contrast, has no common-law basis of confidentiality, but a body of statutory confidentiality law has been born and is growing.

Something that distinguishes the mediation situation from that of other confidential relationships is the fact that there are two clients, with divergent interests, involved. In other confidential relationships, the client is typically free to waive confidentiality (e.g., when a patient requests copies of his or her medical records and chooses to make them public). In mediation, one client's wish to end secrecy may be opposed by the other. Moreover, even if both clients consent to waiving confidentiality, many mediators assert that confidentiality should nonetheless continue. They argue that it would compromise the integrity of the

---

[4] A notable exception occurs in some governmental and administrative hearings subject to mediation. In these disputes, so-called *sunshine laws* mandate that the sessions are public. See "Conflict with Another Explicit Law."

[5] Typically, certain exceptions to confidentiality are based on the need to protect children and other possible victims from harm, such as when parents admit in confidence that they have been abusing their children.

In most types of mediation, communications shared between disputants and not otherwise made known cannot be revealed later in trial or elsewhere.
Pearson Education/PH College.

overall profession if disputants knew, upon entering mediation, that, if the clients were later involved in litigation, they could, by mutual consent, compel the mediator to serve as a weapon.

Early in the mediation movement, there were two principal sources of confidentiality in mediation: law providing for the inadmissibility of compromise negotiations and specific contracts specifying that mediation be confidential. The law of inadmissibility of settlement negotiations has both statutory and common-law sources. In legal disputes before federal court, Rule 408 of the Federal Rules of Evidence, which has been used as a model for similar statutes in many states,[6] makes evidence of conduct or statements made in the course of settlement negotiations inadmissible for the purpose of proving the validity or invalidity of the claim sought to be settled:

> Rule 408. Compromise and Offers to Compromise. (a) Prohibited uses. Evidence of the following is not admissible on behalf of any party, when offered to prove liability for, invalidity of, or amount of a claim that was disputed as to validity or amount, or to impeach through a prior inconsistent statement or contradiction: (1) furnishing or offering or promising to

---

[6] See, for example, North Dakota Rules of Evidence, Rule 408; Texas Rules of Civil Evidence 408; Pennsylvania Rules of Evidence, Rule 408.

furnish—or accepting or offering or promising to accept—a valuable consideration in compromising or attempting to compromise the claim; and (2) conduct or statements made in compromise negotiations regarding the claim, except when offered in a criminal case and the negotiations related to a claim by a public office or agency in the exercise of regulatory, investigative, or enforcement authority. (b) Permitted uses. This rule does not require exclusion if the evidence is offered for purposes not prohibited by subdivision (a). Examples of permissible purposes include proving a witness's bias or prejudice; negating a contention of undue delay; and proving an effort to obstruct a criminal investigation or prosecution.

This statute codifies the general common law rule (Federal Rules of Evidence, Notes of Advisory Committee). Since mediation is a form of assisted settlement negotiation, such rules provide some confidentiality protection for mediation. However, there are four significant limitations to this protection. First, the rule is confined to the exclusion of offers of compromise, not to all communications made during settlement discussion. Thus, other communications, such as assertions of fact and claims (which could be the basis of litigation based on fraud or duress), are not considered confidential. Second, the protection afforded by settlement discussion rules is limited to preventing admissibility in litigation and does not make the communication confidential—that is, protected against any disclosure. Third, such a rule does not specify who possesses the privilege to claim confidentiality of a communication (Rogers and McEwen 1989, §8.4). Fourth, the rule specifically allows the admission of such communications if for a purpose other than to prove or disprove a claim—such as the impeachment of a witness at trial. (See Notes of Advisory Committee on 2006 Amendments to Federal Rules of Evidence, Rule 408; *EEOC v. Gear Petroleum, Inc.,* 948 F. 2d 1542, C.A. 10, 1991).

Many jurisdictions still have absent or uncertain laws governing confidentiality in mediation. Because of this uncertainty, mediators in this situation sometimes require their clients to sign contracts making the mediation process confidential. These contracts cannot, however, bind third parties if an attorney decides to subpoena disputants or mediators to testify in court. For example, if a mediating disputant reveals evidence relevant to a nonparticipant's lawsuit, a contract binding the mediating participants to confidentiality would not prevent the nonparticipant's attorney from subpoenaing the mediator or another mediating participant to testify.

The absence of confidentiality protection of mediation is gradually being rectified: More focused efforts to codify confidentiality for mediation are underway. Kentra (1997) reported that, by the year 1997, statutes or court rules mandating some sort of confidentiality or privilege for statements made during mediation were in effect in all fifty states and all federal agencies with ADR processes.[7] Some of these statutes, however, protect communication

---

[7] The Federal Administrative Dispute Resolution Act of 1996 (5 U.S.C.A. §§571 *et seq.*) contains a provision guaranteeing confidentiality for mediation occurring under its auspices in federal agencies, and so is among these jurisdictions, but the protection is limited.

only in the mediation of certain varieties of disputes (Kentra 1997, app.), meaning that other kinds of cases are left unregulated, although the coverage of the statutory law is gradually filling in. Legal professionals and mediators must therefore research the availability and applicability of these statutes to specific cases and must work to keep abreast of a fluid and constantly evolving area of law. In addition to statutory and other regulatory sources of confidentiality rules, mediator ethical standards also provide for the confidentiality of the mediation process. Moreover, certain statutes and court rules allow courts to create a common-law privilege for certain relationships. One such rule, which has been used to develop a common-law mediation privilege, is the Federal Rules of Evidence, Rule 501. This rule has been used by the federal court to create a federal common law mediation privilege. (See *Folb v. Motion Picture Industry Pension & Health Plans*, 16 F. Supp. 2d 1164, D.C. Cal., 1998.)

Waiver of Confidentiality. Statutes and court rules, as interpreted by decisional law, provide for waiver of confidentiality in particular circumstances. Professor Carol Izumi of George Washington University Law School summarized waiver situations as follows (Feerick et al. 1995):

- Consent of the participants
- Mediator malpractice or malfeasance claim or defense
- Protection of the mediation process
- Matter to be revealed is not confidential
- Evidence of a crime or child abuse/neglect
- To uphold the administration of justice
- Confidentiality in conflict with another explicit law

Consent of the Participants. Confidentiality rules typically allow disclosure if the participants and mediator consent. However, confidentiality rules differ as to who possesses the privilege of raising a defense of confidentiality. In the federal district court case of *Olam v. Congress Mortgage Company*, 68 F. Supp. 2d 1110 (N.D. Cal., 1999),[8] both parties, but not the mediator, waived confidentiality, and the court held that the mediator was compelled to testify to mediation communications that were considered relevant to proving whether the settlement was made under duress. In contrast, in the Model Uniform Mediation Act, adopted in August 2001 (National Conference of Commissioners on Uniform State Laws 2001), a mediator is explicitly required to provide a separate waiver before he or she can be compelled to testify in such circumstances. Rules of ethics, such as the Model Standards of Conduct for Mediators (AAA/ABA/SPIDR 2005), often

---

[8] Although a trial court case, *Olam* is considered particularly important because its author, the Honorable Wayne Brazil, is a notable proponent and scholar of mediation; hence, his decision to lift confidentiality in these circumstances has been regarded as particularly noteworthy.

speak of the mediator's need to respect the other participants' expectations concerning confidentiality.

Mediator Malpractice or Malfeasance Claim or Defense. Confidentiality in mediation, and in other ADR processes that feature intervention by a third-party neutral, is generally suspended in situations in which disclosure is required either to prove or to defend against an action against the mediator for malpractice or other misconduct. This exception appears to have been widely accepted in the legal and mediation community, and, due to the lack of mediator malpractice cases (Coben and Thompson 2006, 98), it has not yet come under significant judicial scrutiny.

Protection of the Mediation Process. Disclosure of information, otherwise confidential, that is needed "to protect the mediation process" has proven to be a problematic exception to confidentiality, since many ADR professionals would contend that airtight confidentiality is, in itself, essential to the protection of the mediation process.

Disputants sometimes argue in court that confidentiality should be waived to enforce a duty of those participating in mediation do so in good faith.[9] ADR commentators note that, if disputants fail to mediate in good faith, the essence of the process is corrupted. However, confidentiality is endangered by attempts to enforce such a duty. To enforce the duty of good faith participation, the substance of the mediation must often be revealed in a subsequent adversarial proceeding to determine whether the duty was breached.

The following vignette illustrates how such an exception to confidentiality could inflict lasting damage on a mediation program:

> Fred, a federal worker, and Barry, his supervisor, enter agency-sponsored mediation to resolve their workplace dispute. Fred contends that Barry has had it in for him and is subjecting him to harassment based on his sexual preference. Barry asserts that Fred is a "hothead" and that, in addition to doing his work poorly, he has alienated everyone else in the office. It is obvious to the mediator that these disputants frame the conflict completely differently and that their mutual hostility is extreme. After three hours of mediation, no progress is made, and the mediation ends.
>
> Thereafter, Fred files an Equal Employment Opportunity Commission (EEOC) grievance proceeding. The case enters an adjudication phase. Barry seeks sanctions for Fred's failure to participate meaningfully in mediation and seeks to introduce various mediation communications into the proceeding to support his claim. Barry claims that Fred took very extreme positions, which he knew Barry could never agree to, and that, hence, his participation in mediation was a sham. The court allows the information

---

[9] Coben and Thompson (2006, 57) found that of published U.S. legal opinions posing a mediation issue, very few (eight) involved the issue of whether to lift confidentiality to deal with duty-to-mediate issues.

to enter the proceeding, commenting that Fred had a legal duty to mediate in good faith, which was violated, and awards Barry attorney's fees for the failed mediation.

Others at the agency get wind of the adjudication pending between Barry and Fred, and employment lawyers begin to counsel their clients about the option of threatening to assert failure to participate in good faith as leverage in mediation. They begin to counsel their clients to be careful about what they reveal during mediation, since what they say may be used against them in a later adjudication. Agency mediators become less facilitative since their attention is taken up more with determining which disputants are mediating in bad faith. As a result, mediation at this agency becomes less and less successful in resolving employment disputes. As the situation continues to evolve, it becomes common knowledge among employment attorneys that mediation at this agency is simply another useless bureaucratic impediment to getting to an EEOC adjudication.[10]

States have gone both ways in their attempts to resolve this issue. In *Foxgate Homeowner's Association, Inc., v. Bramalea*, 26 Cal. 4th 1 (2001), the California Supreme Court held that the mediator could not be called upon to recount communications uttered during mediation to prove, or disprove, the good faith participation of one of the parties. (The court commented that the mediator could be called upon to testify to "conduct," such as whether parties with settlement authority had attended the mediation sessions.) On the other hand, in *Olam v. Congress Mortgage Company*, confidentiality was deemed lifted in a situation in which one disputant claimed that the other had committed fraud during the mediation session in inducing her to settle. (It may have been determinative that the disputants in the *Olam* court had both consented to waiver and that the mediator was the only person opposing admission of the evidence in question.) Both decisions were purportedly based on the same confidentiality statute.

The California confidentiality statute upon which both the *Foxgate* and *Olam* decisions were based did not explicitly recognize a "protect the mediation process" exception to confidentiality, but many other state statutes do. Arizona has a statute that allows confidentiality to be waived if necessary to enforce the agreement to mediate, Wyoming allows waiver if necessary to enforce a mediated agreement, and North Dakota allows waiver to prove the validity of the settlement (Feerick et al. 1995).

Matter to Be Revealed Not Confidential to Begin With. Most mediation confidentiality rules provide that one cannot make something a secret merely by bringing it into mediation. Such an exception is universal: Virtually everyone agrees that one should not be able to render something a secret merely by bringing it into mediation. Thus, originally nonconfidential documents, provided to the other participants as part of the mediation process, are generally admissible in court.

---

[10] An excellent discussion of this issue is found in Alfini and McCabe (2001).

A Powerful Confidentiality Provision

California is considered to have one of the most powerful of the confidentiality provisions created for mediation. Here is the text of the provision (California Evidence Code, 2007, §1119):

Except as otherwise provided in this chapter:

(a) No evidence of anything said or any admission made for the purpose of, in the course of, or pursuant to, a mediation or a mediation consultation is admissible or subject to discovery, and disclosure of the evidence shall not be compelled, in any arbitration, administrative adjudication, civil action, or other noncriminal proceeding in which, pursuant to law, testimony can be compelled to be given.

(b) No writing, as defined in Section 250, that is prepared for the purpose of, in the course of, or pursuant to, a mediation or a mediation consultation, is admissible or subject to discovery, and disclosure of the writing shall not be compelled, in any arbitration, administrative adjudication, civil action, or other noncriminal proceeding in which, pursuant to law, testimony can be compelled to be given.

(c) All communications, negotiations, or settlement discussions by and between participants in the course of a mediation or a mediation consultation shall remain confidential.

Section 1120 creates very limited exceptions, and Section 1122(a)(1) provides that waiving confidentiality of mediation communications requires the consent of all participants. California's strong mediation confidentiality provision has been hailed by some for its protection of the mediation process, and criticized by others for its inflexibility.

Evidence of a Crime or Child Abuse/Neglect. Many states have statutes that explicitly require professionals in confidential relationships to suspend confidentiality when a party has indicated that he or she intends to commit a crime, or when a party has indicated a likelihood of ongoing abuse or neglect of a child, warranting intervention.

To Uphold the Administration of Justice. Occasionally, the need for confidentiality in mediation is deemed overcome by a more weighty need for its disclosure. For example, in *Rinaker v. Superior Court*, 62 Cal. App. 4th 155 (1998), a juvenile defendant wanted to admit into his trial a confidential communication made in mediation that he contended was exculpatory (i.e., it tended to prove his innocence). The appellate court ruled that the evidence could be admitted to protect the constitutional right of the accused juvenile to confront his accusers and to produce evidence of his innocence.[11] In contrast, in *Williams v. State*, 770 S. W. 2d 948 (Tex. App. 1989), the government was prevented from having inculpatory evidence from an ADR proceeding admitted to support a criminal conviction.

Confidentiality has been held to have been waived where necessary to prove or disprove the enforceability of a mediated settlement, as in *Olam*. On the other hand, a contrary result was reached under Texas law in *Smith v. Smith*, 154

---

[11] The court did rule that the defendant was required to make an in camera (out of the public eye) proffer to the court so that relevance and admissibility could be predetermined.

F.R.D. 661 (N.D. Texas, 1994). The *Olam* case concerned a mediator who claimed the privilege despite waiver by both disputants, whereas the *Smith* case concerned a dispute in which only some of the disputants wanted the privilege waived.

Considerations of justice might also be deemed to require that confidentiality be lifted if fraud occurred during the mediation session. Indeed, in their survey of recent legal decisions, Coben and Thompson (2006, 70) report that "an allegation of fraud lifted the veil of confidentiality in most of the cases where the defense was raised." Some mediation law and ethics provisions explicitly excerpt from confidentiality disclosures relevant to the proof of, or defense against, fraud or duress in the settlement of a dispute in mediation. For an example, see Maryland Rule 17-109(d)(3), which provides that:

> In addition to any disclosures required by law, a mediator and a party may disclose or report mediation communications to a potential victim or to the appropriate authorities to the extent that they believe it necessary to help: . . . assert or defend against a claim or defense that because of fraud, duress, or misrepresentation a contract arising out of a mediation should be rescinded.

Allegations of fraud in the inducement of a contract entered into during mediation can spawn difficult complexities. Consider the following example:

> Erica mediated a dispute over the dissolution of a live-in relationship between Amelia, a chief executive officer at a medium-size real estate holding company, and Jessica, a graduate student. The two women ultimately came to an agreement specifying that one-half of the couple's monetary assets would go to each of them. Later, Erica sued Jessica for failing to comply with the agreement. Jessica defended the case by claiming that Amelia stated in mediation that she put all of her wages into the couple's joint checking account, which was used for household expenses, but that Amelia secretly banked one-third of her wages in a separate account. Amelia contested this allegation of fraud, maintaining that Jessica made the allegation as a delay tactic and that she, Amelia, made no untruthful statements during mediation. Amelia further asserted that Jessica well knew about the funds going into a separate account and maintained that although paychecks were diverted to her separate account for this purpose, this was because a separate investment property was accruing earnings, which were used to replace the income in the joint account.

There's a compelling argument that, if Jessica's assertion is true, she should be able to get the agreement they reached in mediation set aside on the basis of fraud by Amelia. To prove the fraud, Jessica would have to be allowed to lift confidentiality to show how the fraud occurred. However, the argument isn't that clear-cut: Jessica's allegation of fraud has been met by a counterassertion that "I didn't lie; you just misinterpreted what I said." In the final analysis, many disputes over the meaning of comments made during negotiation can be framed as a misrepresentation by one of the disputants. Mediation advocates are concerned that allowing into court evidence about what went on in mediation in order to prove whether one of the disputants misled the other would swamp mediation as a confidential process.

Considerations similar to those attending fraud allegations make it more likely that mediation confidentiality will be lifted in cases of duress and other similar misconduct. A very difficult situation arises when a mediator presiding over an attorney-assisted mediation witnesses attorney misconduct. If a mediator reveals the behavior, confidentiality is violated and the mediator may lose neutrality in the case; however, if the mediator maintains confidentiality, the unethical behavior may wreak havoc. For example, in *In Re Waller*, 573 A .2d 780 (D.C. 1990), Waller, the attorney for a malpractice plaintiff, had filed suit against a hospital but not against the surgeon who had performed an allegedly negligent procedure. In mediation, Waller revealed to the mediator that he represented the surgeon as well as the plaintiff. Recognizing the significant disadvantage in which Waller had placed the plaintiff, the mediator tried to convince the attorney to name the surgeon in the complaint and, failing that, to self-report his conflict of interest to the court. When Waller failed to do either, the mediator revealed the communication to the judge himself, despite the fact that the revelation violated a court order in the case:

> that no statements of any party or counsel shall be disclosed to the court or admissible as evidence for any purpose at the trial of this case. . . . *Waller, supra*, 573 A.2d at 781.

If the mediator is also an attorney (as was the mediator in the *Waller* case), the duty to maintain confidentiality may clash directly with the lawyer's ethical duty to report the misconduct (Kentra, 1997). The D.C. court handling the *Waller* incident chose not to discipline the mediator, despite the absence of legal rules allowing the mediator to violate confidentiality. A few states expressly exempt such communications from confidentiality in mediation. For example, Minnesota Statutes, §595.02(n)(1a) provides the following:

> Alternative dispute resolution privilege. No person presiding at any alternative dispute resolution proceeding established pursuant to law, court rule, or by an agreement to mediate, shall be competent to testify, in any subsequent civil proceeding or administrative hearing, as to any statement, conduct, decision, or ruling, occurring at or in conjunction with the prior proceeding, except as to any statement or conduct that could:
> (1) constitute a crime;
> (2) give rise to disqualification proceedings under the rules of professional conduct for attorneys; or
> (3) constitute professional misconduct.

However, Minnesota is the exception: By and large, this situation is not dealt with directly by mediation laws. In California, a state in which no such exception is explicitly provided, the intermediate appellate court has ruled that an attorney malpractice claimant may not introduce, at trial, evidence of the allegedly negligent and wrongful behavior of the attorney in mediation in which the attorney represented the plaintiff (*Wimsatt v. Superior Court*, 152 Cal. App. 4th 137, 61 Cal. Rptr. 3d 200, 2007). Despite the statutory rules, Coben and

Thompson (2006, 59) report a fairly cavalier attitude on the part of judges as well as litigants and their attorneys, finding, to their surprise, that:

> uncontested mediation disclosures occurred in thirty percent of all decisions in the database, cutting across jurisdiction, level of court, underlying subject matter, and litigated mediation issue.

Finally, justice might compel the setting aside of confidentiality in cases where third parties not privy to mediation might be adversely affected. Coben and Thompson (2006) have reported that in cases such as class actions and actions involving the needs of children, mediation confidentiality is more likely to be set aside, either by the judge at trial or by stipulation among the litigants.

Conflict with Another Explicit Law. Mediation confidentiality sometimes conflicts with another explicit law, and in such a case, an exception to confidentiality is often carved out. This sort of exception is important in mediation involving the government as a party, as in the mediation of environmental disputes and the mediation of antitrust violations, where so-called "sunshine laws" may mandate that the proceedings be public. Such a rule may ultimately prove troublesome in cases in which there is no obvious or express intent to supersede confidentiality provisions (as in the attorney misconduct situation previously mentioned).

Implications of Regulation of Mediator Confidentiality. No thorough review of the confidentiality of the mediation process is possible in a text of this nature: This discussion is intended merely to provide an idea of the nature and scope of the law of confidentiality as it is presently evolving and how existing law is attempting to address tensions among the diverse goals of practitioners and users of mediation. Every professional involved in mediation must stay abreast of legal developments in his or her jurisdiction and field to remain current about the state of mediation confidentiality.

Overall, the role of mediation in the constructive resolution of conflict is better served by strong confidentiality protections. Because our society operates within the blinders and distortions created by the invisible veil (see Chapter 2), disputants tend to play their negotiations close to the vest. Confidentiality is needed to coax disputants into the kind of open information sharing needed for effective collaborating during mediation. Otherwise, disputants may fear that what they say in mediation might be used against them later in court. In addition, the mediator's neutrality is an important component of trust building during the mediation process. If the parties feel that the mediator is taking note of their actions for later revelation to a court or others, the relationship with the mediator may become adversarialized. On the other hand, if, regardless of what happens in mediation, the mediator has promised to refrain from being sucked into an escalation of the conflict, disputants are less likely to behave in ways that emphasize the competitive aspects of their conflict.

A Modest Confidentiality Provision

The Administrative Dispute Resolution Act of 1996, 5 U.S.C.A. §§571 *et seq.*, requires that each federal agency adopt ADR processes to resolve disputes with employees, clients, and the public. The act, which applies to *all* forms of ADR, contains a relatively modest confidentiality provision, §574. Following are subsections (a) and (b):

(a) Except as provided in subsections (d) and (e), a neutral in a dispute resolution proceeding shall not voluntarily disclose or through discovery or compulsory process be required to disclose any dispute resolution communication or any communication provided in confidence to the neutral, unless -

    (1) all parties to the dispute resolution proceeding and the neutral consent in writing, and, if the dispute resolution communication was provided by a nonparty participant, that participant also consents in writing;

    (2) the dispute resolution communication has already been made public;

    (3) the dispute resolution communication is required by statute to be made public, but a neutral should make such communication public only if no other person is reasonably available to disclose the communication; or

    (4) a court determines that such testimony or disclosure is necessary to—

        (A) prevent a manifest injustice;

        (B) help establish a violation of law; or

        (C) prevent harm to the public health or safety, of sufficient magnitude in the particular case to outweigh the integrity of dispute resolution proceedings in general by reducing the confidence of parties in future cases that their communications will remain confidential.

(b) A party to a dispute resolution proceeding shall not voluntarily disclose or through discovery or compulsory process be required to disclose any dispute resolution communication, unless—

    (1) the communication was prepared by the party seeking disclosure;

    (2) all parties to the dispute resolution proceeding consent in writing;

    (3) the dispute resolution communication has already been made public;

    (4) the dispute resolution communication is required by statute to be made public;

    (5) a court determines that such testimony or disclosure is necessary to—

        (A) prevent a manifest injustice;

        (B) help establish a violation of law; or

        (C) prevent harm to the public health and safety, of sufficient magnitude in the particular case to outweigh the integrity of dispute resolution proceedings in general by reducing the confidence of parties in future cases that their communications will remain confidential;

    (6) the dispute resolution communication is relevant to determining the existence or meaning of an agreement or award that resulted from the dispute resolution proceeding or to the enforcement of such an agreement or award;

    (7) except for dispute resolution communications generated by the neutral, the dispute resolution communication was provided to or was available to all parties to the dispute resolution proceeding.

This statute is typical of limited confidentiality rules. Note that confidentiality may be lifted for various public-policy reasons, such as the prevention of "manifest injustice" and the prevention of harm to public safety. Since such provisions allow a wide degree of judicial discretion, some might argue that they result in a chilling effect on disputants' willingness to be open and honest during mediation.

What makes this particular statute unusual is subsection (b)(7), which exempts from confidentiality any communication, except one made by the neutral, that occurs during a joint session. Essentially, in a two-party dispute, this single exception makes all disputant and advocate communications nonconfidential unless made in a caucus. Thus, unless the disputants make an agreement before the inception of mediation [§574(d)], allowing confidentiality during joint session, they would have no confidentiality there.

Vague exceptions to confidentiality, such as the interests of justice exception, may have a chilling effect on disputant communication since it is hard to predict what will and will not be protected. On the other hand, exemptions to confidentiality to protect disputants (such as reporting the attorney who represented adverse disputants in *In Re Waller*) may serve the long-term viability of mediation as a nonadversarial alternative by reassuring potential participants that mediation won't be a forum for misbehavior. Perhaps those concerned with protecting the mediation process would be most comfortable with confidentiality exemptions that relate to matters not directly associated with the conflict itself, as when confidentiality is waived to report an instance of professional misconduct.

The issue of how to raise defenses to settlements reached in mediation presents a similar dilemma for those promoting effective and constructive conflict resolution and the lifting of the invisible veil. On one hand, the viability of the mediation process requires that disputants act in good faith; hence, misconduct such as fraud during mediation shouldn't be allowed to subvert the mediation process. On the other hand, such defenses are vulnerable to tactical misuse by sharp advocates: For example, there is a fine line between puffery and fraud, and there will likely be many instances in which an adversary can make a weak but nonfrivolous claim that his or her client was misled by the other disputant or his or her legal counsel during mediation. Allowing the free use of litigation to deal with such claims could eviscerate mediation as a means of constructive conflict resolution. The mere ability of disputants to raise the contents of the mediation in an adversarial proceeding may be argued by some to poison the environment and make the mediation itself more adversarial.

Another issue is whether the mediator should have an independent privilege. On one hand, helping professionals generally don't have the independent right to withhold information if their clients want it produced. It can be argued that allowing the clients to mutually decide whether information can be made public supports the goal of disputant self-determination. On the other hand, mediators have the right and obligation to protect the profession. One argument is that in a society permeated by the invisible veil there is constant pressure on disputants to use whatever means they can (including exemptions to mediation confidentiality) to make their conflict adversarial. Those seeking to preserve mediation as a true alternative to competitive conflict resolution are likely to err in favor of a strong confidentiality rule so that the disputants are less likely to misuse the mediation process in this fashion. Allowing the mediator to retain an independent privilege to refuse to participate in the adversarialization of a mediated conflict promotes this overall goal.

MANDATING MEDIATION

Many mediation scholars believe that disputant self-determination is the essence of mediation. Thus, the mediation process is generally interpreted to require that there be a right of the disputant to refrain from settlement unless the

Mediators often must temper their enthusiasm for getting a settlement with respect for the disputants' right of self-determination. Dorling Kindersley Media Library

settlement is of his or her choosing. But can disputants be forced to try mediation, even if they can't be forced to settle? If so, how far can disputants be forced to mediate? And should disputants suffer negative consequences if they don't reach a settlement? When does such pressure violate disputant self-determination? And when does such coercion create such a deprivation of rights that it can be considered a violation of due process of law?

A preliminary question one might pose is this: Why would an element of coercion ever be considered for a voluntary process such as mediation? There are two reasons, each of which leads to a different sort of coercion. First, it has been found that, when mediation is offered, Americans don't typically choose it (the experts in ADR term this an "underuse" phenomenon). Second, policy makers comparing mediation with litigation often wish to increase the "settlement rate" of mediation.

The underuse of mediation has been well documented by researchers. There are probably five major reasons for this underuse of mediation.

First, interpersonal conflict breeds meta-conflicts. Sociologists Craig McEwen and T. Milburn (McEwen and Milburn 1993) argue that mediation is not usually considered by disputants unless they have been unable to reach settlement on their own. Disputants who negotiate unsuccessfully characteristically experience conflict escalation during the negotiation. The escalation breeds meta-conflicts that heighten anger, frustration, hostility, and vengefulness. By the time the disputants acknowledge that they need help from a third party, they are too angry to consider a cooperative intervention, such as mediation. Ironically, studies show that, when these vengeful disputants are forced to attend mediation, they are on average highly satisfied, despite not having wanted to attend in the first place, and quite pleased that they were forced to undergo mediation (Kressel and Pruitt 1989; McEwen and Maiman 1982).

Second, reactive devaluation can interfere with the decision to mediate. Voluntary mediation must start with a proposal from one of the disputants to try it. If the relationship between the disputants has entered a cycle of conflict escalation, the decision by the first disputant to suggest mediation as an option will be viewed with suspicion by the other disputant. Hence, since voluntary mediation requires consent by both disputants, often it is difficult to get the mutual consent necessary to begin mediation.

Third, disputants in an unpleasant conflict often feel overwhelmed and repulsed by the conflict and want quick finality. Since mediation can't advertise itself as guaranteeing settlement, disputants can be afraid of wasting time and money. They either don't understand the ways in which mediation can lead to more final and permanent solutions or simply fear the possibility that the dispute will still be there after mediation has been tried.

Fourth, mediation usually requires facing the other disputant across a bargaining table. Disputants involved in a conflict are upset with each other and may fear or abhor having to be in the same room with one another. They may feel better about a process, such as litigation, in which a powerful advocate acts as a buffer during the process.

Fifth, legal subculture and the invisible veil probably contribute to the underuse of mediation. Anecdotal evidence from legal and ADR professionals suggests that, as the legal community in a particular court jurisdiction becomes familiar with mediation and comes to accept it as an expected part of the process of resolving disputes, it is selected, and accepted, much more readily.[12]

The problems of mediation's underuse have been noted with concern in the scholarly mediation literature. Because of the consensus about the many advantages of using mediation as an approach to interpersonal conflict, numerous attempts have been made to persuade, or even force, disputants to participate.

In addition to underuse problems, some legal policy makers would like to reduce or eliminate the problem of mediation's lack of finality. Thus, there is pressure in some circles to make mediation more likely to result in agreement. To further this objective, some mediation programs have been the subjects of experiments with methods of making the settlement outcome of mediation more likely.

Coercion in Private Mediation.   In practice, how have the desires for greater use and greater finality of mediation played out? In addressing this question, purely private mediation should be distinguished from mediation under the auspices of a court. Private mediators often take cases of disputants who are simply trying to get help for a conflict they have not been able to resolve on their own. In most of these situations, one disputant contacts the mediator and, somehow, the

---

[12] It may also be that the invisible veil—cultural conceptions of conflict as a contest requiring adversarial solutions—contributes to the legal culture's aversion to mediation. As mediation becomes more popular among legal communities, it also tends to become more adversarial. See Menkel-Meadow (1991) and Alfini (1991).

other disputant is also convinced to try mediation. Other than the time and money invested in the mediation process, no coercion is involved.[13]

Sometimes individuals contract in advance to require that disputes be submitted to mediation before any litigation is attempted (sometimes referred to as an *executory contract to mediate*). Although both disputants may have willingly agreed to the clause originally, mediation may not be the first choice of one disputant at the time the clause is invoked by the other. Generally, requiring mediation in such circumstances is not considered a matter of coercion, provided that both disputants acted of their own free and informed will at the time they made the executory contract.

However, enforcing such a contract presents some problems. It might be inferred that the parties to such an agreement have implicitly contracted to mediate in good faith, opening the recalcitrant disputant to the possibility of legal sanctions if he or she refuses to mediate. As we have seen elsewhere in this chapter, enforcement of the duty to mediate in good faith often raises difficult confidentiality problems. Even looking beyond confidentiality considerations, defining the duty to participate in good faith in a process that is, by definition, voluntary can be problematic. To apply the perfect colloquialism to this situation, "You can lead a horse to water, but you can't make it drink." What does *good faith participation* mean in the context of a process supposedly designed with disputant self-determination in mind? Does a disputant who attends, listens, but informs the other participants that he or she does not intend to settle and thereafter remains silent meet this criterion? What about a disputant who attends and answers questions but refuses to make any proposals? What about a disputant who makes very extreme offers, which the other disputant cannot be expected to consider seriously? Should *self-determination* mean that disputants must sit in mediation and seem to listen to the proceedings so that they can make up their own minds whether to negotiate, or do disputants have a duty to negotiate affirmatively? And, if the latter, is the making of concessions required? It seems clear that the duty to participate in good faith has no simple, straightforward meaning.

An additional problem can occur if the contract has been foisted on a consumer by a large commercial entity. In certain instances, the contract may be considered one of adhesion. A **contract of adhesion** is one that is considered to be involuntary in the eyes of the law because the consumer has had no real choice in negotiating terms. Such clauses could also coerce the consumer by specifying the mediator, requiring one disputant but not the other to submit to mediation, specifying the location of mediation, and so forth. No mediation

---

Contract of adhesion
a contractual agreement between a very powerful and wealthy party, such as a major merchant or employer, and a disempowered person such as a consumer or employee. A contract is considered one of adhesion when the disparity of bargaining power between the parties presents a "take it or leave it" situation that renders the contract essentially involuntary with respect to the disempowered party.

---

[13] Mediators have a variety of techniques for encouraging full participation. Some mediators require a substantial deposit—an advance equivalent to up to ten hours of mediation, for example—to begin work. This fee is refundable only to the extent that agreement results in less time than charged. These mediators are of the opinion that the monetary investment keeps the disputants motivated to reach agreement. To the extent that the arrangement is coercive, it should be kept in mind that the parties to mediation have a choice of whether to accept the terms of mediation in the first place.

> ### *Coercive Elements in Purely Private Mediation*
>
> - Contract clauses requiring disputants to attempt mediation before taking a dispute to litigation
> - Contracts of adhesion in consumer contracts requiring the submission of disputes to mediation

clause of this sort has been contested in published litigation, although contracts of adhesion requiring dispute *arbitration* are now being subject to appellate review (see Chapter 5).[14] Commercial entities are far more likely to specify mandatory arbitration than mandatory mediation.

Coercion in Court-Connected Mediation. Court-connected mediation raises somewhat different issues. There are numerous ways that courts can, and do, coerce disputants into mediating. Some of these methods of pressure may raise important constitutional issues by burdening or impeding the right to bring an action to court.

A fully voluntary court-connected mediation program would be one offered to disputants as an alternative to litigation. To minimize fully the impact on the disputants, the mediation would be offered free of charge and would not create delays in the schedule of the disputants' pending litigation, unless both disputants consented to such delays. Court-connected "mandatory" mediation applies coercion by varying these indicia of voluntariness.

To persuade disputants to mediate, one approach that is taken by some courts is to *require some degree of participation.* The degree of coercion depends on what level of participation is required. For example, a program relatively free of coercion might require only attendance at an orientation session. [See, for example, Idaho R.C.P. 16(j).] A somewhat more coercive alternative might require attending at least one mediation session. The more participation required, the more coercive the program. At the extreme in this sort of coercion would be a program that required disputants to attend "so many sessions as the mediator directs." The state of Maryland (Md. Rule 9-205), regulating court-mandated child custody mediation, requires attendance as directed by the mediator, but not more than two sessions "unless good cause is shown and

---

[14] See *Wells v. Chevy Chase Bank,* 363 Md. 232 (2001) for an example of a possible consumer contract of adhesion involving mediation. This litigation involved a credit card agreement which specified that, at the request of the claimant, any claim arising out of the credit agreement had to be submitted to mediation, and, if mediation did not result in settlement, binding arbitration would necessarily follow (this sort of arrangement is known in the ADR industry as *med-arb-different* [see Chapter 6], meaning that mediation is followed by arbitration if no settlement results and that the arbitrator is a different person from the mediator). In the *Wells* case, the borrower contended that the ADR provision was never legally amended into the credit agreement. The court never reached the issue, ruling that, since the cardholder had never requested mediation, the issue was moot.

> ### *Coercive Elements in Court-Connected Mediation*
>
> - Extent to which attendance is required
> - Sanctioning lack of participation in good faith
> - Limits on ability to opt out of mediation
> - Regulation of payment of the mediation fee
> - Delay of litigation
> - Case evaluation by the mediator

upon the recommendation of the mediator," in which case up to two additional sessions can be ordered.[15] Further extensions are allowed only if the parties consent.

Another approach taken by courts to pressuring litigants to participate in mediation is to *sanction the failure to participate.* It's not problematic to punish a litigant for failing to attend altogether; however, if a disputant attends mediation but does not participate actively, an issue is raised as to whether he or she has attended in any *meaningful* sense. Hence, a corollary to requiring disputants to attend multiple mediation sessions is often a need to define whether a disputant "participated in good faith." The disputant failing to do so can be found in contempt of a court order and sanctioned by imposing responsibility for the other party's attorney's fees, by preventing the disputant from going forward with his or her part of the litigation, or by proceeding otherwise as provided by applicable statute.

There are compelling policy arguments both for and against the imposition of a duty to mediate in good faith. On one hand, mediation's fundamental principle of self-determination suggests a hands-off approach so that disputants aren't compelled to settle against their will. In addition, an expansive reading of a duty to participate in good faith would require the court to inquire into the process of mediation itself, compromising confidentiality. And allowing parties to engage in so-called ancillary litigation (Cole, Rogers, and McEwen 2001, §7:6) over the issue of whether each disputant negotiated in good faith during the mediation sessions undermines the special nonadversarial quality of mediation. It also compromises the mediator's special role as a neutral if he or she is required to assess whether participation was in good faith or not. On the other hand, law professor Kimberly Kovach (1997) asserts that, because the legal community and its clientele operate within the confines of the invisible veil, a duty to participate in good faith must be imposed in order to protect the process against adversarial conduct that might destroy its essence, such as adversarial posturing, misuse of the process to obtain discovery information, or use of the process to gather information for trial strategy.

---

[15] This provision raises potential confidentiality problems by requiring both "good cause"—a factual showing—and the recommendation of the mediator.

Courts and legislatures have imposed a variety of legal requirements of good-faith participation to court- and agency-connected ADR.[16] Legal rules of good-faith participation in mediation, and the court cases that interpret them, are hard to summarize because each has characteristics that make it unique. However, it may be generalized that they run from the narrow and procedural to the very broad and substantive (Cole, Rogers, and McEwen 2001, §7:6; Carter 2002). Rules of narrow scope limit the application of the good-faith participation requirement to clear conduct which prevents the possibility of the mediation's resulting in settlement—such as the failure to attend mediation, the failure to provide information or witnesses considered essential for the process to go forward, and the failure to bring a representative with the authority to settle (Weston 2001). It requires no breach of confidentiality to assess whether participants have contravened a duty to participate in good faith if limited to such conduct, and these types of litigation have been allowed to go forward in most of the few cases where it has come up (see. e.g., Carter 2002, note 61).

Other rules, however, are broader in scope, or they cover substantive behavior in mediation, such as the willingness to bargain. When litigated, these disputes are usually turned away (Carter 2002, note 63). In extreme cases, it is left to the parties to argue over whether negotiation has been in good faith or to the mediator to make such a judgment in a report to the court. These broader rules raise numerous problems. As previously discussed, these rules often require a lifting confidentiality.

Moreover, requiring the mediator to "finger" the person at fault in a process that has not made progress is inconsistent with the mediator's role as an impartial third party: It requires the mediator to, in effect, adjudicate an important issue in the case. If the disputants are not informed, at the commencement of mediation, of this adjudicatory role of the mediator, they will not be able to participate in mediation as fully informed participants, whereas if they do begin mediation with this information, they will be likely to treat the mediator as if he or she were a sort of judge or jury. As seen in Chapter 3, Deutsch's Crude Axiom provides that a disputant's perceptions of the conflict tend to create a situation consistent with the perception. If the disputants perceive the mediation process as involving the possibility of future adjudication over who has done the better job of negotiating, they are more likely to be adversarial in their conduct. Finally, abrogation of litigation rights results from determination of failure to mediate in good faith, the disputant can be effectively prevented from litigating the issue. A disputant thus obstructed may have a valid claim that he or she has been denied due process of law. Thus, a good faith rule that requires "meaningful" participation in mediation is fraught with potential problems.

Varying the ease of a disputant's ability to opt out of mediation is another action courts use to make mediation more or less mandatory. It may not take

---

[16] Many of these rules do not distinguish mediation from nonbinding evaluation processes to which courts and agencies refer disputants. Also, processes that are referred to as "mediation" are often nonbinding evaluation processes. The effects of a good-faith participation requirement on purely facilitative mediation are likely to be different from the effects on an evaluative process.

much coercion to produce participation. For example, anecdotal accounts circulating at some professional conferences on ADR suggest that participation in voluntary court-connected mediation shoots up when all litigants are automatically referred to mediation and then allowed to opt out simply by submitting a letter of request to the court. Also, studies indicate that court-connected mediation programs that allow litigants to simply opt out of the process are as well attended as those for which participation is mandatory (Bingham 2002).

A more coercive program would require additional effort to opt out. For example, in jurisdictions such as Nevada's Douglas County (Nev. N.J.D.C.R. 26), a disputant who is ordered into mediation of a child custody dispute may make a motion to opt out of mediation on the basis that mediation would be "inappropriate," and various circumstances of inappropriateness are enumerated. Coercion in these sorts of jurisdictions varies, depending on the level of proof required. Within this category of "mandatory mediation," a relatively uncoercive program might accept a letter, whereas a more coercive alternative would be to require a declaration under penalty of perjury. A still more coercive alternative would require an evidentiary hearing, at which the opting-out disputant had to satisfy the burden of providing admissible and relevant evidence on the issue of qualification to opt out. A still more coercive alternative would require the opting-out disputant to have the burden of persuasion as well as the burden of producing relevant supporting evidence.

Coercion may also be manipulated by specifying that only certain disputants and disputes are exempt from mandatory participation. For example, many court-connected child custody mediation programs allow opting out by a parent who has been physically abused by the other parent (on the theory that the balance of power required for effective negotiation probably does not exist). Most programs allow this opt-out to be automatic if the abuse victim refuses to mediate, and they allow such disputes to be ordered into mediation in certain limited circumstances. New Mexico has a typical provision:

B. When custody is contested, the court:

    (1) shall refer that issue to mediation if feasible unless a party asserts or it appears to the court that domestic violence or child abuse has occurred, in which event the court shall halt or suspend mediation unless the court specifically finds that:

        (a) the following three conditions are satisfied: 1) the mediator has substantial training concerning the effects of domestic violence or child abuse on victims; 2) a party who is or alleges to be the victim of domestic violence is capable of negotiating with the other party in mediation, either alone or with assistance, without suffering from an imbalance of power as a result of the alleged domestic violence; and 3) the mediation process contains appropriate provisions and conditions to protect against an imbalance of power between the parties resulting from the alleged domestic violence or child abuse; or

> (b) in the case of domestic violence involving parents, the parent who is or alleges to be the victim requests mediation and the mediator is informed of the alleged domestic violence. *(N.M. Stat. Ann. §40-4-8)*

Coerciveness of such an opt-out provision depends on the level of proof that the court requires in meeting the evidentiary threshold of demonstrating the history of domestic violence.

Another means by which the coerciveness of court-connected mediation is manipulated is by means of the *regulation of payment of the mediation fee*. The least coercive court-connected programs are free or require only a token fee payment. Other programs establish a set fee, typically with a sliding scale based on ability to pay. These commonly used programs often set their fees at the lower end of the market rate for private mediators. In a somewhat more coercive variation, the court takes a hands-off attitude toward fees: Disputants choose their mediators from a court-approved panel of private mediators and pay the rate the mediator specifies. Still more coercive programs split the fee if settlement is reached but assess the fee in total to the disputant who is judged to have created an impasse in mediation. As with the issue of good-faith participation, this last method of fee assessment requires lifting of confidentiality and threatens the mediator's impartial role, since it requires him or her to pass judgment on which disputant should have been more accommodating. Other forms of court-connected mediation split the fee if settlement is reached but assess the mediation fee as a court cost to the losing party if the case must be litigated. This rule serves as pressure on the disputants to settle the case for close to what they think the court would decide. Although this pressure may promote settlement, it may also promote the sort of unidimensional, zero-sum-game perspective on the dispute that mediation is used to transcend.

Other monetary penalties are sometimes assessed to pressure disputants into settling during mediation. An example sometimes cited to support this proposition is so-called Michigan Mediation, which is actually a form of nonbinding evaluation (see Chapter 3). In this process, the "mediator" holds a hearing and issues a nonbinding evaluation of the case. If the valuation is rejected and the case is brought to trial, a party rejecting the valuation must pay costs and attorney's fees if he or she does not do at least 10 percent better at trial than the valuation (Plapinger and Stienstra 1996, part II).

Court-connected mediation programs may also apply coercion by instituting *delays in the litigation process*. Some amount of delay in the process of discovery and trial preparation is often necessary to allow the mediation to proceed. When adversarial pretrial processes are proceeding apace, they can often interfere with the cooperative tone being worked toward in the mediation. Moreover, if a trial date is imminent, mediation may make no sense unless trial is put on hold for a time. However, an overly lengthy delay of litigation may put litigation so far out of reach that it effectively denies litigants the right to their trial, in which event it can be a denial of due process of law.

A final means of coercion in mediation is *evaluation of the case by the mediator*. This is a very coercive feature. Some court-connected programs have instituted processes in which the mediator either provides the court with a case evaluation (as when the mediator is a mental-health professional who provides a custody evaluation) or even issues a nonbinding decision in the dispute.[17] This sort of variation on coercion in mediation is designed not to pressure disputants into participation but, rather, to increase the likelihood of mediation's leading to settlement. Some California jurisdictions—most notably, Alameda County—have a history of using this sort of mediation program for child custody matters (McIsaac 2001).

Mediation programs that require the mediator to evaluate the dispute, or to recommend possible resolutions to the court, raise difficult and problematic issues, both of mediator role confusion and violation of confidentiality. Some commentators remark that using evaluation to pressure disputants into settling their cases is contrary to the spirit and purpose of mediation. The idea of punishing disputants who fail to settle may be seen as an adversarialization of the mediation process, which detracts from its role as a process of moving conflict into a cycle of cooperation. Indeed, one scholar, Hugh McIsaac, reviewing California's experience with nonconfidential evaluations used in court-connected child custody mediation, finds that the counties that use recommendations are actually less efficient at promoting settlement than those that retain a purely facilitative form of mediation, suggesting that the adversarialization of such dispute processes is actually counterproductive (McIsaac 2001). Moreover, court programs that prevent participation in the litigation process potentially raise constitutional problems. In particular, the availability of a nonconfidential evaluation by the mediator has been criticized by many legal scholars as opening up the system to systematic discrimination. For example, Trina Grillo, in her classic article "The Mediation Alternative: Process Dangers for Women" (Grillo 1991), asserts that, when mediators use threats of nonconfidential evaluation to pressure parties into settlement, more pressure is placed on women, whose appropriate social role is to protect relationships and to be accommodating, to make the lion's share of concessions.[18] Court systems are wrestling with these difficult issues, and the next decades promise to be eventful ones in the evolution of court-connected mediation.[19]

---

[17] Even the requirement that the mediator act as a binding arbitrator if the case does not reach agreement, known as "med-arb-same" (see Chapter 6), has been tried. In addition to raising problems of confidentiality and mediator role disruption, if the arbitration is binding and the referral to mediation is mandatory, this sort of arrangement effectively denies the disputants the right to a hearing in court and clearly raises constitutional problems.

[18] It can be argued that, regardless of the availability of nonconfidential evaluation, any mediation program that rewards mediators for short mediations and high settlement rates will result in a system that pressures lower-power litigants to make concessions in the name of getting an agreement, since such litigants are thought to be more vulnerable to pressure.

[19] McIsaac notes that, as of the year 2001, California was the only state remaining that allowed such recommendations in child custody mediation. No statistics are available on the use of nonconfidential evaluation in non–family law court-connected mediation.

Implications of Coercive Elements in Mediation Programs. Policy makers, mediators, and court personnel alike express frustration at the continuing underuse of purely voluntary mediation. As might be expected, efforts to counter this underuse problem often show the influence of the invisible veil: Mandatory mediation is characterized by coercive elements that detract from the special qualities of mediation as a paradigm departure from typical adversarial processes.

A legal professional or other participant in a conflict, after seeking to understand the dynamics of a dispute, should learn about the sort of mandatory mediation program in which the conflict participants would be required to participate. To what extent might the characteristics inherent in the available mandatory processes subvert the important interests and needs of the conflict participants? How important is creative problem solving? To what extent are long-term interests at stake? How important are emotional, as opposed to financial, considerations? To some extent, an awareness of the limitations of a mandatory process, and the education of the conflict participants, can be effective in counteracting such limitations. However, in some cases, the participants might be served more effectively by pushing for an alternative, such as voluntary private mediation, that fulfills the participants' needs better. Policy makers should carefully consider the long-term implications of adversarializing the mediation process.

PROVISION OF LEGAL SERVICES BY MEDIATORS

The cluster of issues discussed next concerns the behavior of mediation participants. Expectations about the conduct of legal professionals and clients during the course of mediation are still emergent. Coben and Thompson (2006, 90), describing their survey of mediation-related written legal opinions, offer the following summarization:

> [In contrast to the situation for other legal processes,] . . . the roles and responsibilities of the participants in the context of mediation are less developed and a bit murky. Many jurisdictions have codes of conduct for mediators . . . [h]owever, even in jurisdictions with these institutions, the regulatory process is just beginning to develop norms for expected behavior.

Many disputants enter mediation with the hope and expectation that the mediator will tell them what the law is, as well as helping them resolve their dispute. These disputants conceptualize mediation as an alternative legal service in which the lawyer acts on behalf of both disputants instead of a single disputant. It is a considerable frustration to these potential clients when they discover that mediation is not a form of "one-stop shopping," and it is tempting for a mediator to oblige by giving the clients the legal advice they seek.

How mediators deal with legal issues during the mediation process can be problematic. If a mediator activity is considered the "practice of law," and the mediator is a nonlawyer, the practitioner can be liable under civil or criminal statutes that prohibit the unauthorized practice of law (UPL). On the other hand, attorney-mediators who hold themselves out as providing legal services during mediation may be accused of representing clients whose interests are in conflict (see, for example, the ABA Code of Professional Responsibility, DR5-105).[20] If an attorney-mediator clarifies that he or she is providing mediation services, rather than legal services, then, if the services provided are determined to constitute the practice of law, he or she may be accused of advertising improprieties.

What constitutes the practice of law in the context of mediation? Generally, the trend is to focus on two major activities: the offering of legal advice and the drafting of settlement agreements (Cole, Rogers, and McEwen 2001, §10.2; Virginia Guidelines on Mediation and UPL Advisory Committee 2000). The offering of legal advice is generally considered to include either of the following activities:

- The application of legal rules to the specific facts of one's case; or
- The urging of a particular legal action (Virginia Guidelines on Mediation and UPL Advisory Committee 2000)

Some mediation scholars argue that a new set of ethical standards needs to be developed to govern the mediation process. They propose to make mediation an activity distinguished from the practice of law and subject to a different set of ethical precepts based on the notions of neutrality, client autonomy, holistic consideration of client interests, and protection of the mediation process. This work has begun in earnest: In 2002, an American Bar Association Task Force decided to include language in its final report stating flatly that mediation does not constitute the practice of law (ABA Section on Dispute Resolution, 2002). The report also concludes that when mediators draft agreements that incorporate clauses agreed to by mediation participants, it is also not the practice of law. Mediators are even advised that they may incorporate clauses not sought by clients, provided that the clients are represented by counsel who disclaims that he or she is giving legal advice. It should be noted that, whereas the ABA is highly persuasive within the legal community, its reports do not have legal impact, so there is no guarantee that a mediator following these guidelines will not be subject to ethical challenges.

BEHAVIOR OF LEGAL ADVOCATES DURING MEDIATION

Another issue that puts legal ethics in the center of controversy involves the conduct of legal advocates during the mediation process. Legal advocates are traditionally obligated by their codes of ethics to provide zealous advocacy

---

[20] In actual practice, this concern has not been borne out: it is a widespread practice to allow lawyer-mediators to provide evaluations of the strengths and weaknesses of legal cases, though some commentators recommend, and some rules require, explicit consent of the parties to do so.

for their clients. In practice, this ethical obligation translates into a duty to compete vigorously on the client's behalf, as well as to advise their clients competently and nonnegligently.[21]

The Duty to Advise Clients About Mediation and Other ADR Processes. A preliminary question is whether effective client representation includes a duty to inform a client of ADR processes, including mediation. A movement has begun to ethically require lawyers to advise their clients of the option to resolve their dispute via ADR (Breger 2000; Cochran 1999; Sander and Prigoff 1990; Warmbrod 1997). ABA Model Rules of Professional Conduct, Rule 2.1, comment 5, states that there "may" be a duty on the part of an attorney to advise the client of ADR options (American Bar Association 2008). This area of legal ethics is an evolving one. According to Marshall J. Breger of the Columbia School of Law, Catholic University (Breger 2000), an obligation to advise of, and explain, ADR can be implicitly derived from the ABA Model Rules of Professional Conduct. Model Rule 1.2(a) requires a lawyer to consult with the client about the means by which he or she will fulfill the duty of legal representation, Model Rule 1.2(b) requires that the lawyer provide enough information to the client to make informed decision possible, and Model Rule 3.2 requires the lawyer to expedite the client's matter to a reasonable extent. Considering these rules together, an argument can be made that the lawyer has an obligation to inform the client of the possible means by which his or her case can be handled (including ADR) so that the client can make an informed decision about the process he or she wishes to use. Moreover, the lawyer is particularly obligated to help the client seek an expeditious process, and ADR is noted for its time efficiency. Since ADR is now within the mainstream of the law, the duty to advise the client of ADR can be implied as part of the duty to discuss these options with the client (Breger 2000). The Virginia Rules of Professional Conduct, 1.4, Comment 1a, provides that the duty to keep a client reasonably informed about the status of a pending matter, an ethical duty ubiquitous to American legal practice, includes

> a duty to advise the client about the availability of dispute resolution processes that might be more appropriate to the client's goals than the initial process chosen. For example, information obtained during a lawyer-to-lawyer negotiation may give rise to consideration of a process, such as mediation, where the parties themselves could be more directly involved in resolving the dispute.

If other states interpret this general ethical obligation to provide informed consent in similar fashion, one could expect the duty to advise of ADR options

---

[21] For an example of lawyers who failed the duty of competence during mediation, see *Streber v. Hunter*, 221 F.3d 701, C.A. 5, 2000. In Streber, the mediation client's legal advocate failed to base tax advice on legal research, with the result that the client was required to pay substantial tax penalties. For an enumeration of alleged conduct during mediation for which lawyers have been sued by their clients, see Coben and Thompson 2006, 93–94.

to become widely recognized.[22] Beyond this implicit duty, the state bar association ethical bodies of Kansas, Michigan, and Pennsylvania have ruled explicitly that, if an ADR process has been suggested by the court or by opposing counsel, a duty arises to discuss ADR with the client. Kansas further requires that the lawyer raise the issue of ADR with the client if the lawyer deems it to be appropriate, even if no one else has raised it (Breger 2000). As of the year 2000, courts in Arkansas, Colorado, Delaware, Hawaii, Louisiana, Massachusetts, New Jersey, and New Mexico had adopted "precatory" (in other words, aspirational, nonbinding) clauses encouraging lawyers to advise clients of ADR options, whereas courts in California, Connecticut, Georgia, Minnesota, Missouri, New Hampshire, Ohio, Texas, and Virginia had adopted rules requiring lawyers to advise their clients of ADR (Breger 2000, app. A). In addition, the ADR alternative is being introduced to litigants in pretrial educational programs operating in a number of court systems or during pretrial or status conferences (Breger 2000).

Breger points out that, even if there is no ethical duty to inform the client of ADR options, the failure to do so, or the failure to suggest ADR in appropriate cases, may constitute attorney malpractice. An attorney failing to advise a client of ADR in an age in which ADR has entered the legal mainstream may be seen as failing to exercise the requisite degree of professional expertise needed to represent a client effectively. Breger warns,

> It should be pointed out that the question may no longer turn on the existence of express "ethical" language mandating ADR disclosure. The increased application of ADR as a method of dispute resolution may place an attorney at risk if he is not familiar with ADR methods, following a standard which requires him to exercise "the degree of skill, knowledge and judgment ordinarily possessed by members of the legal profession." As more state professional codes require ADR disclosure implicitly or otherwise, an attorney's failure to instruct a client regarding ADR options could therefore result in [professional malpractice] liability. *(Breger 2000, 450)*

An argument can also be made that, if there is a duty to advise clients of the availability of ADR, there is a corresponding duty of attorneys to have a deep understanding of ADR processes—what situations they work best in, and how to select from among them. Some legal scholars have also pointed out that the ethical duty to advise the client of ADR is of little value unless the legal advisor can intelligently advise the client which ADR alternative is best for that client (Sander and Goldberg 1994; Schneider 2000). Attorney and ADR practitioner Patricia Gearity, of Silver Spring, Maryland, comments that attorneys whose clients are involved in mediation must also reorient their consultations, going beyond the short-term results of the dispute under consideration and helping them focus on long-term goals and needs (Gearity 2002). In this book, the skills needed to perform these tasks is known as *conflict diagnosis* and are described in detail in Online Appendix B.

---

[22] This movement is not without its detractors: Some legal scholars—most notably, Michael L. Prigoff (1990)—worry that imposing a duty to advise clients of ADR would drive up legal fees unnecessarily.

Mediation and the Duty of Vigorous Advocacy. Presuming that clients find themselves participating in mediation, what are the strategic responsibilities of the lawyers of such clients? Lawyers are traditionally trained to use any advantage to their client, including the use of hard bargaining tactics, threats, and coercion, to achieve this zealous representation, although the duty of zealous advocacy has been tempered somewhat in recent articulations of the ethical obligations of lawyers. Judge Wayne Brazil of the United States District Court lists some of the conduct commonly associated with inappropriately adversarial strategies of some attorneys during mediation:

> Advancing arguments known or suspected to be specious, concealing significant information, obscuring weaknesses, attempting to divert the attention of other parties away from the main analytical or evidentiary chance, misleading others about the existence or persuasive power of evidence not yet formally presented, . . . resisting well-made suggestions, intentionally injecting hostility or friction into the process, remaining rigidly attached to positions not sincerely held, delaying other parties' access to information, or needlessly protracting the proceedings—simply to gain time, or to wear down the other parties or to increase their cost burdens. *(Brazil 2000, 29)*

Such behavior is recognized (e.g., Browe 1994) as antithetical to the use of mediation to overcome conflict escalation and promote collaboration, and knowledgeable conflict diagnosticians will recognize each of the actions listed by Judge Brazil as characteristic of the cycle of conflict escalation (see Figure 2-1 in Chapter 2). As you may recall from Chapter 3, Deutsch's Crude Axiom teaches that competitive behavior by a disputant's team promotes the escalation of a conflict into a destructive cycle. Thus, the lawyer's traditional adversarial role is in direct conflict with the needs of a client who wishes to take full advantage of mediation to prevent conflict escalation and promote cooperative, collaborative settlement.

In its extreme form, adversarial representation degenerates into "Rambo" litigation tactics that involve winning at all costs—such as threatening to go to trial on a case known to be frivolous. Preexisting legal ethical requirements can be used to discipline attorneys who engage in such tactics, although the need for confidentiality in mediation can often make enforcement problematic. However, many remain convinced that the skills and conduct that work well in adversarial dispute resolution, even those that are unassailable by current ethical standards, are antithetical to mediation (e.g., Love 2000). Proponents of mediation have made a variety of recommendations to modify legal ethical requirements to allow lawyers to represent clients effectively during a nonadversarial process. These range from the rather extreme suggestion that an impartial "advisory attorney," representing all disputants to the process, be hired to accommodate the needs of the clients in mediation (Coogler 1978, 85–92) to more modest proposals for the development of codes of ethics providing for "settlement attorneys," similar to British solicitors (Coyne 1999). Scholars and practitioners of mediation have also proposed (e.g., Kovach

2001) that specific ethical codes applicable to lawyers representing clients in mediation be developed.[23]

MEDIATOR BEHAVIOR

Research reported in 2006 that mediators are seldom accused of misbehavior, at least not in a court of law (Coben and Thompson 2006, 95). The reasons for this dearth are unclear. It may be that because standards of practice are only now evolving,[24] it is not clear when misconduct has occurred. It may also be that mediators are protected by the existing regulatory structure. Or it may be that the rate of settlement, positive atmosphere, and client satisfaction promoted by mediation simply do not create widespread motivation to blame mediators when things go wrong. Nevertheless, some mediator behavior that can be the subject of complaint is highlighted in the following section.

Impartiality and Neutrality of Mediators. Since one hallmark of mediation is disputant self-determination, the mediator must not pressure or coerce either disputant into accepting a particular solution to the conflict they are negotiating. Accordingly, the mediator must not be seen to favor or impose his or her will on one disputant. A mediator's reticence to favor a client or a particular result are generally known as **impartiality** and **neutrality**.[25] Mediator impartiality and neutrality are important for reasons related to effectiveness. One critical role of the mediator is to help the disputants develop trust in the mediation process so that disputants feel they can safely abandon the defensive tactics that lead to conflict escalation. If the disputants cannot trust the mediator to be even-handed, then this trust in the mediation process becomes impossible to establish. Legal scholar Paula Young comments that:

> Conduct that makes a party believe that the mediator has lost his or her impartiality is the most frequently cited reason for filing a complaint against a mediator in Virginia and Maine. It appears as the second most frequently raised allegation in Florida, Georgia, and Minnesota. *(Young 2006, 209)*

Impartiality
lack of favoritism toward a particular disputant, including the absence of a conflict of interest.

Neutrality
lack of favoritism toward a substantive dispute.

---

[23] Paulene Tesler, who has been a major proponent of collaborative law (see Chapter 3 for a description of this practice) proposes that lawyers involved in collaborative negotiation processes contract with their clients that they be held to standards of cooperativeness, good faith, open and honest communication, and openness to the other side's point of view (Tesler 2001). Similar guidelines might be considered appropriate also for lawyers assisting their clients in mediation.

[24] Model Standards of Conduct for mediators were adopted for the first time, in 1994, by the American Bar Association (ABA) in conjunction with the American Arbitration Association (AAA) and the Society of Professionals in Dispute Resolution (SPIDR), a predecessor organization of the Association for Conflict Resolution (ACR). A more fulsome set of model standards was adopted by the ABA, AAA, and ACR in 2005 (American Bar Association, 2005).

[25] Mediators are not always impartial or neutral. For example, in Imperial China, where mediation was a traditional and widely used form of dispute resolution, the mediator's role was quite coercive, and it was common for the mediator to be a widely respected, opinionated, and often pecuniarily involved elder of the community in which the dispute occurred (Shapiro 1981).

Pecuniary interests
financial or monetary interests or
concerns.

Impartiality and neutrality are not easy to define. Impartiality is generally taken to refer to the **pecuniary disinterest** of the mediator in the claim or to the lack of bias for or against any mediation participant. For example, a mediator who formerly represented a particular disputant as legal counsel might be said to lack the requisite impartiality to act as a mediator. Neutrality, on the other hand, usually denotes a mediator's *attitude toward the substantive dispute.* This definitional distinction is the one adopted by the National Conference of Commissioners on Uniform State Laws in its comments to the November 2000 draft of the Uniform Mediation Act.

Scholar Paula Young (2006, 210–220), citing mediator Greg Firestone, divides the field of impartiality/neutrality into the following categories or "quadrants":

Impartiality in the relationship between the mediator and the parties. This form of impartiality deals with whether the mediator and one or both parties are in, or previously were in, a relationship that potentially biases the mediator. One example would be a mediator who regularly plays tennis with one of the parties. Mediators who have an obvious conflict of interest with their clients often require the clients to sign a clear written acknowledgment of disclosure and consent to proceed with mediation, and as we shall see this approach comports with the applicable codes of ethics in the typical case.

Ethical mediators avoid outright conflicts of interest. For example, a mediator should never be a member of the law firm representing either client: This would be an overt conflict of interest. A California intermediate appellate decision, *Furia v. Helm* (111 Cal.App.4th 945, 2003), demonstrates some of the pitfalls that conflicts of interest can pose for mediators. In *Furia,* homeowners in dispute with their home improvement contractor asked their attorney to mediate. The attorney agreed to do so, confirming in writing that although he was remaining the homeowners' attorney, he would do his best to mediate a mutually acceptable settlement. Separately, he sent the homeowners a private letter confirming his continued advocacy on behalf of the homeowners. The mediation failed. Ultimately the contractor was sued by the homeowner and subject to professional disciplinary proceedings. The contractor sued the lawyer-mediator for malpractice. The Court of Appeal noted that a litigant in the contractor's position may have a cause of action against a mediator for failure to adequately disclose favoritism toward a client (though, in this case, the contractor failed to prove that the malpractice caused damages).

A more difficult issue arises when the mediator's firm represented both disputants in a previous controversy (e.g., the lawyer-mediator formerly represented two members of a corporate board of directors and a dispute has developed between board members). Should such an attorney take on the role of mediator between these former clients, if they have a dispute? The best answer is to avoid acting as the mediator altogether, or to act as a mediator only if the conflict of interest is carefully explained and all disputants consent to using the mediator anyway. The Model Standards of Conduct for Mediators (American Bar Association 2005) takes the approach that mediators who have a conflict of interest should avoid serving except upon the consent of the parties and upon

Mediators who have been members of the disputants' legal team face an ethical dilemma if they are asked to mediate a subsequent dispute. Pearson Education/ PH College.

full disclosure of the interest and, further, provides that the mediator may not establish a professional relationship with one of the disputants after mediation except upon the parties' consent.

The Uniform Mediation Act (National Conference 2003) does not include mandatory language requiring impartiality from the mediator. The original drafters of the act worried that such a requirement would promote unnecessary and destructive litigation over this ethics question (Ibid., Reporter's Notes). Instead, the act (at §9) requires a full disclosure of potential conflicts, followed by disclosure of potential biases by the mediator, leaving it up to the disputants whether to proceed with mediation. An optional section of the Uniform Mediation Act, §9(g), allows states to adopt a rule requiring the mediator to act impartially unless the parties agree otherwise. Optional Section 8(f) requires that the mediator act with impartiality, unless the participants consent otherwise.

Relatedly, a line of decisions beginning with *Poly Software International, Inc. v. Su*, 880 F. Supp. 1487 (D. Utah 1995) have held that, if mediation does not fully resolve a dispute, a lawyer-mediator may not be retained as counsel by one of the mediation participants in the same or a related dispute. Courts reason that, because of the likelihood of confidential information having been revealed to the mediator during mediation, the litigant retaining the former mediator would obtain an unfair advantage. If disputants entering mediation were aware of the possibility that the mediator could, in essence, abandon his or her impartial stance and use confidential communication made during mediation for an adversarial purpose, the requisite trust needed to maintain collaborative negotiation would be hard to establish.

Neutrality in the mediator's conduct toward the parties. This element includes issues of mediator-party "chemistry," bigoted attitudes on the part of the mediator, and issues of inability to work effectively with clients who have difficult personalities. Other situations that may play into this element of mediator neutrality include mediators who receive multiple case referrals from the same lawyer (thus setting up a situation in which a mediator may feel beholden to the attorney to provide positive results to their clients), as well as the acceptance of fees paid unevenly by clients. The Model Standards of Conduct (American Bar Association 2005) prohibit a mediator from providing services if neutrality is compromised and require the mediator to withdraw if such problems arise: Standard 2(c) provides that "[i]f at any time a mediator is unable to conduct a mediation in an impartial manner, the mediator shall withdraw."

Impartiality and neutrality concerning the mediator's behavior and relationship to the outcome of mediation. Mediators can have a difficult time balancing the right of client self-determination (which requires that clients refrain from making agreements they are not comfortable making) with their professional reputations as dispute resolvers. It can be tempting for mediators to apply coercive or manipulative practices if it seems possible that the result will be another settlement "notch" on the mediator's metaphorical belt. Moreover, although good and ethical mediators don't have or show favoritism toward any one disputant, mediators have feelings, values, and ethics, which don't go away just because they are involved in mediation. Young (2006) notes that some mediators are not neutral with regard to outcomes: For example, special education mediators may be, explicitly or secretively, advocates for settlements that favor the special education student and/or her parents. This element of mediator neutrality and impartiality is dealt with in the Model Standards of Conduct (American Bar Association 2005) by requiring (Standard 1) that the mediator not do anything to compromise client self-determination.

The need for client self-determination can sometimes, however, require that a mediator depart from strict impartiality: Some situations demand extra support for some disputants to allow them to negotiate effectively. It can also be argued that constituents not participating in mediation—particularly dependents, such as children—may also have interests that should be promoted directly by the mediator. The National Conference on Uniform State Laws specifically advocates against requiring mediator neutrality (National Conference 2003, comments to section 9[g]).

Mediators sometimes find themselves in the middle of a dispute that challenges their set of values, and there are variations in how a mediator handles this event. Some mediators are primarily advocates for disputant autonomy. These mediators take a completely hands-off position in the mediation process to protect the disputants' right to make any agreement, however repugnant to the mediator. The underlying ethic for such mediators is the disputants' overriding need for autonomy and freedom, using any value system with which each disputant is comfortable. When disputants apparently lack equality of bargaining power, however, this stance becomes more problematic.

Some mediators see themselves as *advocates for agreements that are workable and avoid future conflict escalation.* These mediators often use reality testing— "Let's imagine how it will play out if John's workday ends at 5:00 P.M. and he is required to pick up the children across town at 5:05"—to help guide disputants in developing agreements that will work for them.

Other mediators are *advocates for nonexploitive agreements.* These practitioners, recognizing the prevalence of power imbalances between disputants in mediation, wish to preserve the ethic of self-determination but also recognize that some disputants may not be able to hold their own in a negotiation. Often, a blatantly unfair agreement is the only clear evidence of power imbalance and overreaching (a perennial problem for such mediators is determining whether exploitation is, in fact, occurring). Such mediators conclude that complete disengagement does not serve the ethic of self-determination as well as a more active role. There are a variety of mediator responses to possible overreaching on the part of a disputant. Some mediators use reality testing to gently raise the issue of whether the less powerful disputant has considered all possible options or suggest to the disputants that other experts who can increase expert power be consulted. A more direct, but still mild, tactic is for the mediator to raise the possibility of unfairness during the mediation or to write a letter expressing his or her concern to the disputants during or at the close of mediation. A more active response is for the mediator to withdraw from a process that appears to be moving in an unfair direction.

A different interventionist stance is taken by mediators who see themselves as *advocates for unrepresented or disempowered constituents.* For example, many child custody mediators with backgrounds in child development hold themselves out as advocates for the best interests of children—and warn the parents against a clearly inappropriate plan. These mediators are concerned that disputants may not always protect vulnerable people who are relying on them.

It could be argued that *evaluative mediators* are representative of a still more interventionist position on the neutrality continuum. Evaluative mediators do not show partiality toward any disputant, but they do not hesitate to communicate what they believe to be the strengths and weaknesses of each disputant's claims—even if it means telling one disputant that his or her case is weak. Moreover, evaluative mediators, in performing an evaluation based on the legal merits of the dispute, implicitly endorse the use of the rule of law, as opposed to any other shared or compatible beliefs or values held by the disputants, as the "correct" standard to use in shaping a settlement. Young (2006, 220–21) notes that the giving of legal advice, the offering of evaluations, and other forms of impairment of client self-determination comprise the most common form of grievance filed against mediators in Florida and Georgia, and the second most common form of grievance against mediators in Virginia.

The 2005 Model Standards of Conduct take no explicit position toward the providing of evaluation in mediation. However, the standards caution (American Bar Association 2005, Standard VI[A][5] and [8]):

> The role of a mediator differs substantially from other professional roles. Mixing the role of a mediator and the role of another profession is problematic and thus, a mediator should distinguish between the roles. A mediator may provide information that the mediator is qualified by training or

experience to provide, only if the mediator can do so consistent with these Standards.

* * *

A mediator shall not undertake an additional dispute resolution role in the same matter without the consent of the parties. Before providing such service, a mediator shall inform the parties of the implications of the change in process and obtain their consent to the change. A mediator who undertakes such role assumes different duties and responsibilities that may be governed by other standards.

Young (2006) interprets this language as requiring party informed consent before a mediator slips into an evaluative role.

In the least neutral version of mediation common in Western countries, the mediator becomes a *fact finder* or *arbitrator* if the mediation does not lead to an agreement.[26] These mediators are neither impartial nor neutral in any true sense. The change of role of the mediator into an adjudicator is a clear breach of mediator ethics, unless the disputants have explicitly agreed to this type of process. If the mediation has been made mandatory by governmental statute or rule, the adjudication of a dispute by the mediator deprives the disputants of the power to engage in litigation of their dispute; in doing so, it arguably deprives the disputants of due process of law.

Given the diversity of mediator approaches to neutrality, it has proven difficult—and by some reckonings, unwise—to regulate this area of mediator conduct.

As a general rule, mediators are usually given the freedom to operate anywhere within the range of neutrality discussed in this section, provided that their stance is disclosed to the disputants before mediation begins and the disputants give their informed consent.

REGULATION OF MEDIATOR COMPETENCY

Although the skeptic might construe the regulation of mediator competency as an effort to gain advantage in a turf battle between lawyers and mental health professionals for control of the mediation field, this is probably a minority view. Mediation is a difficult profession, and there is good reason to want to ensure that the consumer of mediation services is protected from incompetent mediators. However, given the great diversity of mediation, settling on an appropriate definition of competency in mediation—and, relatedly, an appropriate set of mediator qualifications—has been problematic.

"Efficiency" proponents of ADR are most interested in inexpensive service providers and expeditious mediation, and they are more likely to support evaluative mediators with modest credentials, or lawyer-mediators with strong backgrounds and experience in the legal basis of the disputes they are mediating, who

---

[26] When a mediator switches roles and becomes an arbitrator, this is technically a hybrid form of alternative dispute resolution known as "med-arb-same." See Chapter 6 for more about this ADR form.

volunteer their time. Proponents of evaluative mediation—and this, according to the available research, includes most attorneys (Hermann, Honeyman, McAdoo, and Welsh 2001)—value substantive legal knowledge above all other competencies among mediators. On the other hand, "radical" ADR proponents most concerned with taking advantage of the many benefits of nonadversarial conflict resolution are more likely to endorse mediators with strong backgrounds and skills in conflict diagnosis, conflict management and resolution, and communication skills. Certain specialties also demand specialized training; for example, many court systems demand that court-connected child custody mediators have educational backgrounds in divorce, child development, and psychology.

Regulation of Mediator Qualifications. It should be no surprise, then, that mediator qualification has little uniformity across jurisdictions and dispute types. The Uniform Mediation Act[27] reflects the field's openness and diversity by providing (Section 9[f]) that

> [t]his [act] does not require that a mediator have a special qualification by background or profession.

Similarly, the Model Standards of Conduct for Mediators (American Bar Association 2005) provides the following:

> Any person may be selected as a mediator, provided that the parties are satisfied with the mediator's competence and qualifications. Training, experience in mediation, skills, cultural understandings and other qualities are often necessary for mediator competence. A person who offers to serve as a mediator creates the expectation that the person is competent to mediate effectively. . . . If a mediator, during the course of a mediation determines that the mediator cannot conduct the mediation competently, the mediator shall discuss that determination with the parties as soon as is practicable and take appropriate steps to address the situation, including, but not limited to, withdrawing or requesting appropriate assistance.

Private mediators (in contrast to court mediators) in most jurisdictions need not have specific qualifications except as needed to market themselves effectively to savvy potential customers (see below). Private mediators who operate in the civil and commercial litigation arena frequently also hold themselves out as experts in the substantive field of practice or as longtime litigation specialists, in keeping with the trend for these mediators to use an evaluative style of mediation. In divorce and family mediation, there is more of a trend for interdisciplinary qualification, with legal professionals acquiring mental health–related knowledge and mental-health professionals acquiring legal knowledge. In both cases, prospective mediators often take advantage of so-called "forty-hour training courses" available to people who want to become divorce mediators. These courses generally provide an overview of conflict and negotiation theory,

---

[27] As of January, 2008, the Uniform Mediation Act had been adopted by ten states. (National Conference of Commissioners on Uniform State Laws 2008)

communication theory, mediation skills, legal issues, and divorce-related psychosocial issues.[28]

Court-connected and other program-based mediators are subject to a hodgepodge of qualification requirements, such that no generalizations can be made in this textbook. An individual wishing to become a mediator must check the requirements in his or her jurisdiction for the sort of mediation he or she wishes to practice. The field is slowly becoming more unified and clear as time goes on. For example, in the state of Maryland, which has been on the vanguard of the field of regulating mediators, Maryland Rule 17-104(a), adopted in 2001, prescribes specific qualifications—a bachelor's degree, forty-hour training course, periodic monitoring, and other elements—for mediators designated for court referral. Previously, the rules allowed individual trial courts to prescribe mediator qualifications.

Marketability. It is one thing to ask whether one's qualifications to mediate comport with legal requirements and another to ask whether one's qualifications make one marketable as a mediator. In the world of commercial and tort mediation, where highly evaluative bargaining-based mediation is the norm, private mediators tend to be more marketable if they are experienced attorneys or retired judges. It is extremely difficult to obtain clients in that substantive area if one cannot hold oneself out as having handled such cases as a litigator or judge. The most marketable mediators in the area of tort and contract litigation tend to be retired judges who can perform evaluations based on their long experience on the bench.

Private organizations, such as the Association for Conflict Resolution (ACR) and the American Arbitration Association (AAA), provide certification schemes that attempt to ensure well-qualified mediators, and these may be useful marketing tools for mediation practitioners. More facilitative mediation is the norm in divorce and family mediation and in employment mediation. Divorce and family mediators often find that a dual expertise in psychology and the law, with specialized mediation training, is helpful to being marketable, whereas employment mediators typically have training in mediation and in human resources.

Membership in professional organizations devoted to mediation, such as the AAA and the ACR, add to mediator marketability, allow the practitioner access to resources that improve competency, and may even provide voluntary certification. The ACR has multiple membership levels; the highest level, Advanced Practitioner, requires the completion of specific educational requirements, plus a period of mentored practice under particular members, as well as continuing education requirements. A number of court-connected mediation programs require their court-connected mediators to be certified by such organizations. On the other hand, the codes of ethics of many mediator organizations require merely that the mediator be educated, trained, and experienced in a

---

[28] The fact that this method of training mediators is a prevalent model does not mean that it is the best method of training people to be mediators. Some argue that forty hours constitute insufficient training.

manner that is adaptive to the cases taken. Such standards provide little guidance, beyond requiring the mediator to use his or her judgment in developing competence, in providing full disclosure to potential clients, and in following whatever applicable legal requirements are in effect.

ENFORCEABILITY OF MEDIATED AGREEMENTS

The final event in mediation is often the finalization of a mediated agreement. What is the legal significance of this occurrence?

In general, since the mediation itself is an assisted negotiation, the mediated agreement is considered enforceable to the same extent as any other negotiated agreement. This simple statement belies the complexity of reconciling the confidential mediation process with the written outcome. These complexities have led to what Coben and Thompson (2006) refer to as a "disputing irony": a lot of litigation over mediation. In their survey of published cases about mediation, the authors found meta-disputes over enforcement of mediated settlements comprised 46 percent of all litigated cases.

In general, a mediated agreement may be enforced in court just as any other contract may be enforced, and it may be contested based on the same defenses (fraud, duress, incapacity of a party, statute of frauds, and so on) as those applicable to other contracts. In addition, special variants of the usual defenses to contract enforceability may occur, involving the mediator's competence, ethical behavior, or personal biases. For example, a disputant who feels the mediator was biased against him or her might claim that he or she settled under duress produced by the unethical behavior of the mediator. In addition, features of the applicable statutory framework may impact the enforceability of a mediated agreement. For example, in *Haghhighi v. Russian-American Broadcasting Co.*, 577 N.W.2d 927 (Minn. 1998), the Minnesota high court invalidated a handwritten contract made during mediation in light of an applicable state statute, which provided that to be enforceable, a mediated settlement must explicitly specify the parties' intent to make the agreement binding.

The confidentiality of the mediation process can create difficult evidentiary issues. If the mediation process is handled carefully, a clear demarcation between the mediation process itself and the mediated agreement will exist. To prevent unauthorized practice of law and conflict of interest problems, many mediators issue a written memorandum of agreement, which, by its explicit terms, is not an enforceable document until reduced to a legal writing by the disputants' attorneys. Other mediators may be more bold, offering a document that, by its terms, becomes intended for enforceability when signed. If, however, the function of the document memorializing the mediated agreement is not made clear, trouble can result.

> Smith and Jones mediated their dispute over an automobile accident in which Smith was injured. The outcome of mediation was a written document providing that Jones would pay Smith $5,000 and Smith would dismiss his complaint filed in the state court. Smith signed the document but

Jones refused. Smith contends that Jones clearly agreed to the settlement during mediation, and he wants to enforce it.

The problem is, how can Smith enforce the agreement reached in mediation without breaching confidentiality? If the unsigned agreement is deemed unenforceable, doesn't this result seem unfair to Smith? The best answer is probably to consider a mediated negotiation as similar to any other negotiation. The common law, codified in statutes such as the Federal Rules of Evidence, Rule 408, makes offers and acceptances made during compromise negotiations inadmissible to enforce a settlement agreement.

A closely related problem is the extent to which mediation confidentiality will be suspended either to prevent enforcement of the mediated agreement (due to typical contract defenses, such as fraud, duress, incompetency of a disputant, or undue influence) or to interpret the meaning of ambiguous provisions. This area of the law is unsettled at this time. Coben and Thompson (2006) report a worrisome trend toward simply ignoring confidentiality in these situations, a result that is not likely to become a permanent part of the landscape. As with other aspects of mediation law and ethics, the struggle between the desire to protect the enormous potential of mediation to pierce the invisible veil and provide nonadversarial conflict resolution, and the desire to preserve the adversarial rights of individual disputants, will make the resolution of these issues a tough challenge.

The Cartoon Bank

EXERCISES, PROJECTS, AND "THOUGHT EXPERIMENTS"

1. Refer back to exercise 5 in Chapter 3, featuring Ronnell, the paralegal who chose to become a medical malpractice mediator. In Ronnell's first case, she met in caucus with both the plaintiff, who did not have legal counsel, and the defendant physician. The plaintiff begged Ronnell to tell her how a court would decide the case. "You advertised yourself as having had twenty years of experience handling malpractice cases, and you've worked in a hospital. Just tell me how a court would deal with the case. I want to know what's fair, so that the other side doesn't steal me blind." Ronnell can't help but have opinions about what a court would do—for twenty years, she prepared cases like this one for trial and watched courts decide them. What should Ronnell do, and why?

2. Would your answer to question 1 differ if Ronnell were a qualified attorney, rather than a paralegal? Why or why not? Do any regulations or ethical standards address this situation? Is Ronnell prohibited from evaluating the case at all? If so, how do you square this conclusion with the fact that there are many mediators comfortably practicing an evaluative style of mediation?

3. Sanjay is mediating a marital breakup between Edna and Marve. As the mediation proceeds, Sanjay begins to suspect that Marve is hiding assets from Edna—he tends to be vague when asked where all the money he made has gone, and his family owns a very closely held used car business. He "has lost" all the tax returns from the past five years, and his bank account statements are very incomplete. Edna does not seem to be aware of Marve's possible deception. What should Sanjay do? How can he handle this situation in a manner that preserves the mediation process (so that if, in fact, Marve has done nothing wrong, both parties can benefit), empowers Edna, yet preserves mediator impartiality? Or is Sanjay required to terminate mediation? Is ending the mediation relationship enough to satisfy Sanjay's ethical obligations? Justify your response.

4. Choose a kind of legal dispute—medical malpractice, custody, civil litigation, tax, estates, etc. It could be the kind of legal dispute you're most interested in. For your state of residence,

   a. Perform legal research to determine whether a confidentiality statute or rule covers the mediation of this kind of dispute. If there is one, cite and summarize it.

   b. Perform legal research to determine whether there are mandatory qualifications for mediators who practice this kind of mediation. If there are mandatory qualifications, cite where they are to be found, and summarize the requirements in your own words.

   c. Repeat (a) and (b) for one or more different states, as directed by your instructor.

5. Do you believe mediation confidentiality should be suspended in cases where it is alleged that a disputant failed to mediate in good faith? Consider the following situations involving court mediators. Should the mediator be required to advise the court that one of the disputants failed to participate in good faith? What should the mediator reveal, and what should he or she advise the court? What should the mediator not reveal?

a. A judge orders the parties to mediation. One party shows up, but the other does not. The mediator calls the absent disputant, who apologizes and states that he forgot about the session. The mediator schedules a second session two weeks later and mails and telephones appointment reminders to both parties. Again, the second disputant fails to attend.

b. A judge orders the parties to mediation. One party shows up promptly. The other shows up twenty minutes late and says she was held up in heavy traffic. After the mediator's introduction, when asked whether she has any questions, the tardy disputant says "No." When asked about the situation that led her to court and mediation, she simply says that the other party sued her and that she was ordered to mediation. After the other party discusses the conflict from his point of view, the recalcitrant disputant, when asked, says she has nothing to respond to or add. After two hours, the mediator is forced to terminate mediation because it is obvious that the recalcitrant disputant is failing to participate actively.

c. A judge orders the parties to mediation. Both parties appear to participate in discussions in good faith. However, Party B refuses to make any concrete proposals for resolving the dispute, even after Party A makes several. Party B makes no constructive suggestions about the proposals made by Party A—she simply says, "That's not a good enough offer for me to accept," each time a proposal is made. The mediator feels that Party A's last proposal was extremely generous in light of the facts.

d. A judge orders the parties into mediation. One of the parties is a corporate entity. The executive vice president attends for the corporate party. After three hours of hard bargaining, the exhausted parties reach a settlement, only to have the executive vice president say, "I'll have to take this issue to the CEO and legal department. I don't have authority to sign off on any settlement."

e. A judge orders the parties into mediation. Three hours of hard work produce lots of discussion of options but no final settlement. The mediator is flabbergasted when Party B says "No" to what the mediator feels is a terrific settlement of the dispute. Later, Party A petitions the court for "sanctions"—a fine for misconduct—alleging that Party B failed to mediate in good faith. Party A asks the mediator to back him up by telling the court what a good deal Party B refused.

f. Would your reaction to fact situation e be different if the mediator were less certain about the fairness of the rejected settlement offer? What if the mediator felt that none of Party A's offers had any merit? In general, when one disputant claims the other did not mediate in good faith, should the mediator have the authority to decide whether an offer is good enough to suspend confidentiality? How would such a rule affect the strategic (mis)use of mediation for adversarial purposes during litigation?

6. Read and summarize the following appellate decisions. (If you have been trained to brief an opinion, brief rather than summarize.) How do you reconcile these decisions—or are they irreconcilable?

   a. *Olam v. Congress Mortgage Company*, 68 F. Supp. 2d 1110 (N.D. Cal., 1999)

   b. *Foxgate Homeowners' Association, Inc., v. Bramalea*, 26 Cal. 4th 1 (2001)

7. Research the state of mediator qualification law in your state.

   a. Is there one statute or regulation that covers all mediators, or are different specialties required to meet different qualification standards? Does your state describe explicit requirements or defer to a professional organization to set standards? Do court mediators have one set of qualifications and private mediators another?

   b. Choose one kind of mediator qualification law within your state and look at the standards in detail. Does the law require a particular professional background (e.g., do the mediators have to be lawyers, therapists, or social workers)? What is the nature and scope of any required mediation-specific training or education? Are prospective mediators required to apprentice to a mentor and, if so, for how long? Are qualified mediators required to fulfill mediation-specific continuing education requirements? If so, how much?

RECOMMENDED READINGS

Alfini, J. J., and C. G. McCabe. 2001. Mediating in the shadow of the courts: A survey of the emerging case law. *Arkansas Law Review* 54:171–206.

Brazil, W. D. 2000. Continuing the conversation about the current status and the future of ADR: A view from the courts. *Journal of Dispute Resolution* 2000:11–39.

Coben, J. R., and P. N. Thompson. 2006. Disputing irony: A systematic look at litigation about mediation. *Harvard Negotiation Law Review* 11 (Spring):43–145.

Cole, S. H., N. H. Rogers, and C. A. McEwen. 2001. *Mediation: Law, policy and practice,* 2nd ed. St. Paul, MN: West.

Foxgate Homeowner's Association, Inc., v. Bramalea, 26 Cal. 4th 1 (2001).

Kovach, K. K. 2001. New wine requires new wineskins: Transforming lawyer ethics for effective representation in a non-adversarial approach to problem-solving: Mediation. *Fordham Urban Law Journal* 28:935–77.

McEwen, C. A., and T. W. Milburn. 1993. Explaining a paradox of mediation. *Negotiation Journal* 9(1):23–36.

Menkel-Meadow, C. 1991. Pursuing settlement in an adversary culture: A tale of innovation co-opted or "the Law of ADR." *Florida State University Law Review* 19 (Summer):1–46.

Nolan-Haley, J. M. 1999. Informed consent in mediation: A guiding principle for truly educated decisionmaking. *Notre Dame Law Review* 74 (March):775–840.

Nolan-Haley, J. M. 2001. Mediation. In *Alternative dispute resolution in a nutshell* (2nd ed., pp. 60–137). St. Paul, MN: West.

Olam v. Congress Mortgage Company, 68 F. Supp. 2d 1110 (N.D. Cal., 1999).

Plapinger, E., and D. Stienstra. 1996. *ADR and settlement programs in the federal district courts: A sourcebook for judges and lawyers.* Federal Judicial Center and CPR Institute for Dispute Resolution. *http://.fjc.gov/public/pdf.nsf/lookup/adrsrcbk.pdf/ $file/adrsrcbk.pdf* (accessed January 29, 2009).

Weston, M. A. 2001. Checks on participant conduct in compulsory ADR: Reconciling the tension in the need for good-faith participation, autonomy, and confidentiality. *Indiana Law Journal* 76 (Summer):591–645.

5

Arbitration

*Law and settled authority is seldom resisted
when it is well employed.*

—Dr. Samuel Johnson, *The Rambler,* 1750–1752

In this chapter, you will learn …

- ◆ about arbitration, an ADR process that can closely resemble litigation.
- ◆ about the tension between providing informality and legalistic protections in arbitration.
- ◆ how the arbitration process works.
- ◆ the situations in which courts intervene to enforce, modify, or eliminate the process or outcome of arbitration.
- ◆ the many ways in which the law supports a deferential attitude toward the arbitration process.
- ◆ the principal front-end and back-end arbitration issues.
- ◆ the thorny controversies created when contracts require arbitration of civil rights claims and public-safety matters.
- ◆ the reviewability of arbitration awards.
- ◆ the problems of choice of law in interstate, international, and multinational arbitration.

Three-year-old Adam and his twin brother, Ron, are playing with Adam's football. Their rambunctious but good-natured game is threatened when Ron refuses to give Adam a turn. "I'm not finished!" shouts Ron when Adam tries to take matters into his own hands. "You had it a long time already!" counters Adam. A literal sort of "focus on positions" develops: They both grab the ball, dig in their heels, and start pulling.

Enter big sister Sonia. "Help, Sissie! He's taking my ball!" "It's my turn!" "No. it's my turn!" "You're a big doo doo head!" "No, you are!" Ron starts to cry.

Taking these remarks as a mutual request for assistance, Sonia gets involved. "Who had it first?" she asks. "He did," admits Adam. "But it's my turn now. He's had it for a year!" "Well," says Sonia, "Ron will have the ball for another five minutes. When the big hand on my watch is on the twelve, then Adam will have his turn."

Arbitration award
the binding decision issued by an arbitrator.

Adam and Ron are having perhaps their first, but not their last, experience with arbitration. By seeking Sonia's assistance to decide how to handle their dispute over who gets to play with the football, the boys implement a basic, ancient, and natural process: They are having a disagreement, and they agree to let someone else make the decision for them. Arbitration is simply a process of adjudication in which the power to decide the outcome is conferred upon a decision maker by the agreement of the disputants.[1] The binding decision made by the arbitrator is referred to as the **arbitration award.**

FROM "PEOPLE'S COURT" TO "CREEPING LEGALISM": THE DILEMMA OF MODERN ARBITRATION

For many years, arbitration was the principal form of ADR (other than negotiation) available in the United States. Arbitration fits U.S. culture particularly well: It involves a competitive process of dispute resolution, yet it allows disputants to resolve their differences outside the legal system.

Arbitration today is very different from a century or two ago. Originally a sort of "people's court," a hallmark of populism, arbitration has now evolved into something quite different, in many ways antithetical to its original purposes. This new characteristic of arbitration raises a dilemma for those who want to use it. To understand the essential dilemma of modern arbitration, it is useful to trace its history.

Informal arbitration-like behavior is common. Here, two elementary-school disputants ask their physical education teacher to decide their disagreement. Merrill Education.

---

[1] We're assuming here that the words of the two boys constituted a mutual request for Sonia to intervene and make the decision. Were we to conclude that she intervened because of her status as older sister, rather than because the boys requested her help, then this incident would be more like litigation.

A Brief History of Arbitration
in the United States

According to various commentators, arbitration can be traced back to biblical times. In pre-twentieth-century America, arbitration was largely a reaction against the restrictiveness, formality, and authoritarianism of the courtroom (Auerbach 1983). Arbitration in colonial times was a populist movement. It flourished in homogeneous communities, such as communities of faith and commerce, and in ethnic groups insulated by language or ghettoization. This form of arbitration reflected the communitarian spirit and stood in opposition to legalization and lawyers. Arbitration was an informal process conducted by respected elders of the community in which the dispute arose. For example, a dispute between families might be arbitrated by the local religious leader, whereas a dispute over a commercial transaction might be arbitrated by a prominent and respected businessman in the community. The informality of arbitration and choice of the arbitrator assured that community norms, rather than the sterile rules of prevailing law, would be applied and that the outcomes of arbitration would reflect local standards of fairness and propriety. Traditional arbitration was also marked by facilitative efforts and by compromise and integrative solutions imposed by the arbitrator, who often knew the disputants intimately and could therefore intervene in this manner.

In a sense, early arbitration law reciprocated arbitration's populist and antilegal origins, for early English law was hostile to arbitration. Although awards of an arbitrator were generally enforceable under a theory of agency, the "Ouster Doctrine" (Vynior's Case, 8 Coke Rep. 81b [1609]) provided that **executory agreements to arbitrate**—that is, agreements to submit future disputes not yet in existence to arbitration—were not enforceable because the arbitration would "oust the jurisdiction" of the courts (Cole 2001; Reuben 2000). There were also concerns that agreements to arbitrate violated the right to trial by jury (Hursh 2001) and some concerns by judges who feared loss of salary or job (Cole 2001). The rule against executory agreements to arbitrate meant that any party who entered into such an arrangement could refuse to participate in arbitration and could withdraw from the process at any time before the award was made. These rules were imported to the United States during the colonial period, where they persisted into the twentieth century. Thus, the courts left arbitration alone, and arbitrating parties left the courts alone. Because of the law hostile to arbitration, parties who willingly submitted to arbitration could gain its benefits, whereas parties who did not consent to arbitration—or who decided midstream not to continue with arbitration—did not have to do so. This legal situation left arbitration in a posture in which willing mutual consent was needed to use it. Thus, early arbitration was a flexible process that accommodated mutual disputant needs. People who did not embrace it wholeheartedly were unlikely to use it.

The early twentieth century saw a softening of attitudes toward the enforcement of arbitration agreements, both in the United States and worldwide.

**Executory agreements
to arbitrate**
agreements to submit future
disputes, not currently in
existence, to arbitration.

The most important development in the United States was the 1925 adoption of the United States Arbitration Act, the forerunner of the Federal Arbitration Act (FAA, 9 USCS § 1 *et seq.*). The purpose of the act was to place executory contracts to arbitrate in the same position as other contracts and to remove the historical judicial hostility toward the process, as specified in Section 2 of the FAA:

> *Section 2. Validity, irrevocability, and enforcement of agreements to arbitrate.* A written provision in any maritime transaction or a contract evidencing a transaction involving commerce to settle by arbitration a controversy thereafter arising out of such contract or transaction, or the refusal to per-form the whole or any part thereof, or an agreement in writing to submit to arbitration an existing controversy arising out of such a contract, trans-action, or refusal, shall be valid, irrevocable, and enforceable, save upon such grounds as exist at law or in equity for the revocation of any contract.

By the terms of this provision, an executory agreement to arbitrate is made no less enforceable than any other contractual promise to do something at a fu-ture date. Moreover, Section 3 of the Act provides that a disputant who is in-volved in the litigation of an arbitrable issue can ask that the litigation be "stayed," or suspended, to permit arbitration to be completed; and Section 4 es-tablishes a federal court procedure for compelling disputants to participate in arbitration pursuant to a preexisting arbitration agreement.

The adoption of the FAA triggered profound changes in the law of arbitra-tion in the United States. Arbitration was subsequently adopted in 1947 in the Taft-Hartley Act, 29 USCS §§141 *et seq.,* as a principal mechanism for further-ing collective bargaining negotiations and resolving unfair labor practice com-plaints. Moreover, a series of Supreme Court cases cemented a policy of deferential treatment to the arbitrator in the determination of whether an issue could be arbitrated, in how the arbitrator chose to proceed with the procedure, and in court review of an arbitration award.

Flourishing in the more favorable legal climate, arbitration, formerly a strictly voluntary process used primarily by arm's-length disputants, began to be adopted wholesale by large organizations to deal with disputes involving con-sumers, employees, and other "little guys." The National Arbitration Forum (NAF), a commercial association of arbitrators, reported at its Web site in Janu-ary 2002 that the courts have upheld contracts binding consumers to arbitrate their disputes with credit card companies, residential services providers, mail order merchants, mortgage lenders, lenders of consumer loans, auto sales merchants, and warrantors of consumer goods.[2] Such arbitration agreements

---

[2] A Google search of the Internet in January 2002 using the search terms *arbitration, cardholder,* and *agreement* returned 1,160 hits. Contained in the results were numerous credit cardholder agreements requiring consumers to submit to binding arbitration of all disputes with card issuers, requiring consumers to waive their right to a jury trial, and, in most cases, requiring cardholders to waive any right to participate in class actions against the issuers. When this search was repeated in July 2008, the search returned approximately 21,200 hits.

require the consumer to waive any right to litigate issues, should the other party elect binding arbitration. Following is a typical provision, excerpted from a Visa cardmember agreement:

> Any claim or dispute . . . by either you or us against the other, or against the employees, agents, or assigns of the other arising from or relating in any way to the Cardmember Agreement, any prior Cardmember Agreement, your credit card Account or the advertising, application or approval of your Account, will, at the election of either you or us, be resolved by binding arbitration. . . . As used in this Arbitration Agreement, the term "Claim" is to be given the broadest possible meaning. [An exception for small claims follows.] *(Chase Manhattan Bank 2002)*

In February 2003, the private-sector U.S. Payment Card Information Network reported that virtually all the major credit card issuers had incorporated mandatory, binding arbitration provisions into their cardholder agreements (CardTrak.com, 2003). By 2005, all Visa, MasterCard and American Express cardholder agreements contained mandatory arbitration agreements, according to factual determinations of a federal court.[3]

Arbitration has also become common in employment contexts: In addition to labor arbitration for unionized employees, arbitration of employment disputes has become increasingly popular, with indications that by the turn of the twenty-first century, at least one in five employers offered some sort of employment arbitration (Colvin 2007). Prospective employees are frequently required to sign promises to arbitrate, rather than litigate, any dispute arising out of employment. These agreements generally cover so-called *statutory claims,* including civil rights grievances such as claims of discrimination based on sex, race, sexual preference, and disability. Commentator Richard Bales (2007, 333), after reviewing arbitration-based litigation across the nation, believes he sees several recent trends in employment arbitration. First, he notes that employees have been surprisingly willing to engage in, rather than to legally challenge, employment arbitration. Second, many employees reap large awards in arbitration, to the evident surprise of some of the employers who enacted arbitration schemes for their employees. Finally, however, these successful employees tend to be white, male, and economically privileged, calling into question whether the current scheme really does protect those disempowered persons for whom civil rights enforcement statutes have been enacted.

Internationally, the adoption of the New York, or UNCITRAL[4], convention by participating nations made it possible for multinational disputes to be submitted to arbitration with reasonable certainty that they would be enforced

---

[3] The litigation *Ross v. American Express, et. al.*, 2005-2 Trade Cas. (CCH) P74,973 (S.D.N.Y., 2005) is an antitrust claim brought by consumers who contended, among other things, that the major credit card companies had colluded to deny them the choice of having credit cards without such provisions. As of the writing of this text, the litigation is still pending.

[4] UNCITRAL is the acronym of the United Nations Commission on International Trade Law.

by local courts and with some degree of clarity concerning the standards of enforcement that would be used.

Because of the balance shift in favor of executory agreements to arbitrate and because of the shift to imposing arbitration on disputants with inferior bargaining power, it was recognized that additional protections were needed to protect those who were being pulled along unwillingly. Moreover, because it was no longer possible simply to withdraw from an arbitration prior to completion, disputants who had initially agreed to an executory arbitration provision but regretted the decision began to use legal process to find the means to be relieved of the responsibility to arbitrate. In response, of course, the disputants wishing to enforce executory agreements litigated their claims as well. In many situations, arbitration became yet another opportunity for adversarial maneuvering. In response to, and because of, these developments, a sort of "creeping legalism" (Zirkel and Krahmal 2001) began to infuse arbitration: In many contexts, it became more formalized, more procedurally rigorous, and more vulnerable to legal attack. Although arm's-length disputants can sometimes plan for, and use, the traditional model of arbitration, they no longer can guarantee that the law of arbitration won't have some unexpected impact on the process. Moreover, traditional arbitration, which is embraced as quick, simple, and efficient, has in many settings been replaced with a legalistic morass even more baffling, expensive, and time-consuming than litigation. In addition, rules respecting the degree to which courts can become involved in disputes subject to arbitration often lead to seemingly unpredictable and illogical outcomes, undercutting the original purpose of arbitration as dispute resolution "for the people" and eliminating the original reason to use arbitration.

ARBITRATION BETWEEN A ROCK AND A HARD PLACE

In short, modern arbitration presents a dichotomy and a dilemma. The dichotomy is between the dream of arbitration as an informal people's court, in which the disputants themselves can control the adjudicatory process, and the increasing reality of a process encrusted with complex, formalized, and often counterintuitive legalisms. The dilemma is how to promote the benefits of traditional arbitration, avoiding ancient judicial hostilities toward arm's-length executory agreements to arbitrate, avoiding the intractable problems caused by overly legalistic arbitration while still protecting the rights of individuals who might be taken advantage of by another.

VARIETIES OF ARBITRATION

Beyond the dichotomy between traditional and legalistic arbitration, other variants are commonly seen in today's arbitration practice. Table 5-1 summarizes some of these varieties.

TABLE 5-1 Varieties of Arbitration

CHARACTERISTIC	VARIATIONS
Formality and rigidity of the process	**Informal:** Arbitration characterized by minimal participation by lawyers, minimal discovery, procedural rules, or rules of evidence. Arbitrator may act in a facilitative manner.
	Formal: Arbitration marked by intensive participation by lawyers and by the same sorts of formalized and rigid procedural and evidentiary rules as are characteristic of litigation. In its extreme form, this sort of arbitration is almost identical to litigation.
When a contract to arbitrate is formed	**Executory:** Agreement to arbitrate predates dispute.
	Ad-hoc: Agreement to arbitrate made after a dispute arises.
Who controls the process and provides support?	**Administered:** An arbitration organization, pursuant to agreement of the disputants.
	Nonadministered: The disputants and the individual arbitrator.
Transaction or dispute focus (labor arbitration example)	**"Interest arbitration":** Arbitration to determine terms of collective bargaining agreement.
	"Rights arbitration": Arbitration to adjudicate an unfair labor practices claim or another grievance.
Private or public sector	**Private:** Arbitration not under auspices of public sector.
	Court-connected: Nonbinding evaluation process under court auspices resulting in advisory arbitration award.
	Private judging, or rent-a-judge: Privately hired judge or referee provides arbitration with a legal impact identical to that of litigation.
Varieties that restrict the nature of the arbitrator's award	**High-low:** Arbitrator's decision is restricted to a range of possible outcomes by prior agreement of the disputants.
	Final-offer or baseball arbitration: Arbitrator must choose between the final settlement offers propounded by the disputants.
	Night baseball arbitration: Variant of final-offer arbitration in which the arbitrator renders a decision without knowing the final offers; the award is the final offer closest to the decision.
Bindingness of the arbitration award	**Binding:** Arbitration in which the outcome is binding on all disputants ("true" arbitration).
	Incentive: Nonbinding evaluation in which the disputant who rejects the evaluator's decision is subject to a penalty.
	Nonbinding or advisory: Nonbinding evaluation in which the evaluator renders a decision, which may be rejected without penalty by either disputant. (*not really arbitration in the true sense*)

Executory arbitration

arbitration based on an agreement to arbitrate that was entered into prior to the dispute arising. Often such arbitration agreements are contained in dispute resolution clauses of substantive contract.

Ad-hoc arbitration

arbitration based on an agreement to arbitrate entered into after, and in response to, the dispute arising.

EXECUTORY AND AD-HOC ARBITRATION

Executory arbitration is arbitration provided according to an executory agreement. Thus, for example, if a consumer opens a bank account with a bank that imposes a duty of arbitration on the consumer, and later a dispute arises over a bank fee, the arbitration is of the executory type. **Ad-hoc arbitration** is arbitration agreed to after the fact of a dispute. For example, if an auto accident victim agrees to arbitrate his or her claim for damages with the other driver's insurance company, the proceeding is considered ad-hoc arbitration.

ADMINISTERED AND NONADMINISTERED ARBITRATION

Another way to distinguish forms of arbitration is to consider whether the arbitration is administered or nonadministered. A number of organizations provide arbitration services to the public, the most well known of which is the American Arbitration Association (AAA, *www.adr.org*). Such organizations may be hired to provide a full range of support services, such as calendaring, hearing site, and the provision of procedural rules. Such a full-service arbitration is known as *administered arbitration.* Arbitration in which such administrative support is not provided by an arbitration organization is known as *nonadministered arbitration.* The AAA and other arbitration organizations have published model procedural rules, which can be used by disputants who wish to engage in nonadministered arbitration but who do not wish to create a set of rules from scratch.

INTEREST AND RIGHTS ARBITRATION

Labor arbitration[5] is divided into interest arbitration and rights arbitration according to the sorts of issues being arbitrated. Put simply, *interest arbitration* settles collective bargaining *transactions,* whereas *rights arbitration* deals with *disputes* such as unfair labor practices complaints.

OTHER ARBITRATION VARIETIES

De novo

latin, meaning "anew." In the law, a retrial of a previously decided dispute, in which all of the legal and factual issues may be relitigated and redecided. A trial de novo is in contrast to an appeal, in which only errors of law can be the basis for a change in the outcome.

One can distinguish between *private arbitration* and *court-based* (or court-connected) *arbitration.* However, court-based arbitration is not arbitration in the conceptual sense: It is nonbinding. In court-connected arbitration, disputants have a right to a trial **de novo.** This makes court-based arbitration a form of nonbinding evaluation: It is an assisted negotiation process, rather than an adjudicatory process, thus, court-based arbitration is discussed in Chapter 6. Another variant of arbitration, known as *incentive arbitration,* is midway between arbitration and nonbinding evaluation. In incentive arbitration, the arbitrator's decision is nonbinding but penalties are assessed against the disputant who refuses to go along. Conceptually, incentive arbitration is a hybrid ADR process, and thus is discussed in Chapter 6, which treats hybrid ADR.

Several other arbitration variants are common. In *high-low arbitration,* disputants select a range of arbitration awards and the arbitrator is allowed to select only an award within that range. A special form of high-low arbitration called *final-offer* or *baseball arbitration*—so-called because it is often used to resolve baseball player contract disputes (Neuhauser and Swezey 1999)—requires the disputants to submit their final and best offers to the arbitrator, who may only select between them. The purpose of this form of arbitration is to give the disputants incentive to negotiate in good faith and to present a less extreme case to the arbitrator. In a subvariant of this sort of arbitration, referred to colorfully as *night baseball*

---

[5] Labor conflict (in other words, union–management conflict) is itself a complex field and is not considered in this volume. However, some of the important appellate case law applicable to arbitration generally has arisen from labor disputing and is covered in this chapter. Employment arbitration—that is, arbitration in the employment arena but not involving a union as the disputant—is covered in this chapter.

arbitration, the final offers are submitted in secret, the arbitrator renders a decision without knowing them, and the final award is deemed to be the submitted offer that is closest to the arbitrator's decision. Finally, *rent-a-judge,* or *private judging,* is a form of judicial privatization in which the disputants hire a referee or an adjudicator pursuant to a statutory scheme (Kim 1994). In rent-a-judge, although the dispute is submitted by agreement to the neutral, defining the process conceptually as arbitration, the process and outcome of the proceeding are, in many respects, identical to those of litigation: The judge or referee may empanel juries, rules of evidence apply, and the result is appealable and of precedential impact.

ARBITRATION'S PLACE IN FOSTERING "GOOD CONFLICT MANAGEMENT"

How does arbitration fit into the arsenal of dispute resolution processes? The answer to this question is not a simple one because there are so many varieties of arbitration.

Whatever the variety, arbitration is an adversarial process, although some kinds of informal arbitration are less adversarial and more facilitative than other, more formal varieties. For this reason, arbitration fails to deliver many of the advantages of mediation for de-escalating conflict, protecting disputant relationships, and promoting integrative and creative solutions to conflict.[6] Arbitration tends to create position-boundedness in the disputants. As each disputant, or advocate, presents his or her side of the dispute, the human tendency is to become ego-invested in the position that is taken. Unless the arbitrator is intimately familiar with the disputants and can look beyond positions to underlying interests, the arbitrator is likely merely to choose between the positions taken or to issue some sort of compromise.[7] Arbitration may also be less useful than facilitative mediation for producing the sorts of flexible remedies that deal best with interpersonal conflict. The arbitrator's ability to conceive of innovative, creative remedies will depend on his or her appreciation of the disputants' underlying interests, but even if the arbitrator is an intimate of both disputants, his or her ability to perceive creative solutions may be blinded by the adversarial setting, and his or her ability to issue flexible solutions may be limited by the contract to arbitrate. Arbitration awards are, therefore, less likely than mediated agreements to result in a win-win outcome optimized for all concerned. Upon issuance of the award, one disputant is very likely to be unhappy with the result. This effect is important if the disputants will have any sort of continuing relationship after the conclusion of arbitration. Moreover, because the solution is unlikely to have integrative properties, it is typically less efficient in using the disputants' resources than are outcomes reached in mediation.

---

[6] The relative advantages of arbitration, compared to mediation, are discussed further in Chapter 7.

[7] An arbitrator in the United States today is unlikely to have such familiarity with the disputants because of the demand for the arbitrator to be neutral and disinterested. In other parts of the world, arbitrators sometimes sacrifice their objectivity in favor of familiarity with the dispute and the disputants.

On the other hand, the extent to which arbitration harms relationships and promotes conflict escalation depends on the attitudes of the disputants and the form of the arbitration. For example, a consumer with a credit card dispute who is forced into arbitration by an executory agreement obscured in fine print in his cardholder agreement will likely be hostile about the result if he or she doesn't win, and his or her attitude toward other aspects of the relationship with the lender is likely to deteriorate. Even if the outcome is a compromise, the cardholder may see it as a defeat because of his or her perception that the process itself was tainted. On the other hand, imagine two business partners who are unable to resolve a dispute over business profits. If they mutually and willingly enter into ad-hoc arbitration under flexible and informal rules of engagement, the process is likely to reduce hostility and promote the continuance of the relationship. This is doubly the case if having recourse to arbitration is a familiar element of industry culture. It should be borne in mind that the mediation of such a dispute might also promote the disputants' relationship and deescalate the conflict. However, if mediation has been tried and has failed to produce a settlement, informal arbitration is probably less escalating than litigating the issue. Also, if the arbitrator is an expert in the field being arbitrated (e.g., in a software intellectual property context if the arbitrator is a software developer), the disputants may emphasize the arbitrator's expert power, rather than the adversarial context: The experience may be more like receiving parental advice than like going to battle. In some informal arbitration, fairness and industry culture are emphasized over legalisms, and the outcomes of these arbitrations are likely to be less escalating than those of highly legalistic arbitrations in which the major issue is who wins.

In addition to the issues of relationship preservation and outcome creativity, another important issue is that of psychological ownership. You may recall that psychological ownership is the sense that one has chosen, and can live with, the outcome of a dispute. Any process in which the outcome is imposed on the disputants by a third party, as opposed to being agreed to voluntarily, raises the possibility that one or both disputants will not psychologically own the outcome. Lack of psychological ownership increases the likelihood of legal challenge to the outcome, sabotage of the outcome, and outright lack of compliance. So, generally, arbitration can be expected to generate less psychological ownership, in general, than a facilitative process like mediation.

However, a disputant's psychological ownership of an arbitration award depends, in part, on embracing the process. In some contexts and subcultures, arbitration is recognized as an alternative to litigation and a welcome respite from an even more adversarial process. If all disputants have this attitude, arbitration will promote psychological ownership of the process and will be less likely than litigation to generate conflict escalation. An arbitration award with which a disputant is unhappy is more likely to be psychologically owned if the disputant perceives the process itself as procedurally just—if the disputant willingly goes along with the arbitration and feels that the process is fair and just. Arbitration imposed on an unwilling consumer, for example, is much less likely to generate psychological ownership. Moreover, perceptions about procedural justice of the process also depend on the context of the dispute resolution process and the unique characteristics of the disputant. For example, in a community setting involving a neighborhood dispute, a highly formalized process involving rigid rules of evidence and other legalisms might not be understandable to the disputant and, therefore, would not be perceived as particularly fair. On the other hand, a highly informal process might be perceived as unfair and unjust to a disputant who is an experienced trial attorney or a business executive familiar with the litigation process. When arbitration between very different disputants occurs, it may be difficult to achieve a process that all parties feel is procedurally just.

You can learn more about the place of arbitration in the optimal resolution of conflict in Chapter 7, where the strengths and weaknesses of ADR processes, and methods of process selection, are discussed.

PROCESS OF ARBITRATION

Arbitration consists of eight basic steps:

1. Creating the arbitration contract
2. Demanding, choosing, or opting for arbitration
3. Selecting the arbitrator or arbitrator panel
4. Selecting a set of procedural rules
5. Preparing for arbitration
6. Participating in the arbitration hearing
7. Issuing the arbitration award
8. Enforcing the award

CREATING THE ARBITRATION CONTRACT

Arbitration always begins with a *contract to arbitrate.* The arbitration contract may be executory—that is, developed prior to the development of a dispute—or ad hoc—that is, developed in an effort to resolve an existing dispute.

1. As with any other contract, the arbitration contract should be designed to minimize the likelihood of gratuitous dispute escalation. For this reason, it should be as clear and simple as possible, should anticipate future developments, and should be appropriately fair and equitable. Gary H. Barnes (1997) of Downs Rachlin & Martin makes the following additional recommendations:

2. The matters to be arbitrated should be set out explicitly. Ambiguity in the arbitration contract as to what matters are arbitrable can open up the outcome to court challenge later. Arbitrators are generally given the benefit of the doubt in such matters, but not before the time and expense of litigation are

added to the process. (See "When Should a Dispute Be Arbitrated? Enforceability and Arbitrability" later in this chapter.)

3. The expenses of arbitration, such as the cost of the arbitrator's fee, the cost of any transcript, and the cost of renting a hearing room, should be shared equitably by the disputants.

4. Arbitrator selection and qualification should be considered carefully. It's important to have a selection process that is appropriately tailored to the dispute, that is perceived as fair by all concerned, and that minimizes the possibility of deadlock (e.g., never use an even number of arbitrators).

5. The agreement should specify whether discovery is to be permitted, and, if so, the permissible forms and extent of discovery and due dates should be specified clearly.

6. The hearing or hearings, and their duration, may be explicitly scheduled. Or this matter may be left to the arbitrator or administrating organization.

7. Privacy and confidentiality should be addressed, as should the preparation of transcripts.

8. The arbitrators' roles in the process should be clarified. For example, some disputants may want to create a hybrid process in which mediation occurs before or after an arbitration hearing. Arbitrators run the gamut from strictly judicial to informal and facilitative; if the disputants have a preference, the nature of the arbitrator's intervention should be clarified.

9. If specific rules of evidence are desired, and mutually agreed upon, they should be specified. Otherwise, the hearing will generally be informal, without rigid rules of evidence.

10. The disputants should specify whether briefs, points and authorities, and other ancillary documentation will be accepted in arbitration; if so, they should set out a schedule for their submission.

11. The agreement should specify the nature of the arbitrator's award. For example, some arbitration awards simply state the outcome, whereas others are accompanied by detailed explanatory opinions.

12. Reviewability and enforcement of the award may be spelled out. However, the prevailing law should be consulted before launching into the drafting of such a provision. There may be situations in which the arbitration contract will override prevailing law, other situations in which the prevailing law will override the contract, and situations in which the law is unsettled. (For more on this subject, a useful review is found in Curtin 2000.)

Choice of law
the determination of which jurisdiction's laws should apply.

13. Choice of law may be spelled out in the agreement if the disputants come from different states or nations, or the subject matter of the dispute may occur in a state or nation other than where one of or both of the disputants reside. However, including such a provision can open the award to attack in the courts unless the provision is very clear or explicitly vests the power to determine choice of law in the arbitrator. Choices of law sometimes lead to counterintuitive results because of local differences in procedure and substantive practice and because of the influence of the FAA and other supervening law.

14. If provisional remedies, such as preliminary or temporary injunctions, may be needed while arbitration is pending, they must be explicitly provided for in arbitration. The arbitrator's powers are limited to those specified in the arbitration contract.

15. Finally, disputants should consider including a clause providing for mediation as a first resort in any executory agreement to arbitrate. Mediation is less adversarial and can protect ongoing business relationships more effectively than can arbitration.

DEMANDING, CHOOSING, OR OPTING FOR ARBITRATION

Assuming an executory agreement to arbitrate is in effect, arbitration is triggered by a *demand* (or *notice*) *to institute arbitration.* This demand can be as informal as a telephone call, but more often it is made in writing. Professional associations such as the AAA provide forms for formally instituting arbitration. If the dispute arises in the absence of an executory agreement to arbitrate, an ad-hoc agreement to arbitrate will substitute for a demand to arbitrate.

SELECTING THE ARBITRATOR OR ARBITRATION PANEL

The third step in the arbitration process is *selecting the arbitrator.* In many cases, this will have begun with the executory agreement to arbitrate. Deciding who will serve as the arbitrator should be determined by a multitude of factors. If the dispute is highly technical, it is useful to choose an arbitrator who is an expert in the subject matter of the dispute. If emotions are running high, it may be helpful to ask a disinterested party to choose the arbitrator (e.g., a professional association such as the AAA can assign a member arbitrator to the dispute). Another common approach to a low-trust, high-conflict situation is for each of the disputants to select an arbitrator and for the two selected persons to pick a third arbitrator. Of course, a multiple-arbitrator panel is usually more costly than a single arbitrator. The arbitrator selection process is limited only by the nature of the agreement to arbitrate, the creativity of the disputants and their advocates, and the participants' shared notions of fairness.

SELECTING THE PROCEDURAL RULES

Next, the parties to arbitration should *select procedural rules* to govern the arbitration. The procedural rules are agreed to by the disputants in the contract to arbitrate; stipulated in a subsequent contract between the disputants, if there is

Some Examples of Arbitration Agreements and Demands

You can find samples of real arbitration agreements and demands for arbitration (notices of arbitration) online. Arbitration firms may, for example, establish a base of future customers by posting sample arbitration provisions in which the firm is listed as the administrator and/or source of arbitrators. For example, executory clauses for administered intellectual property arbitration are offered at the Dispute.IT! Web site, *http://www.dispute.it/sample_arbitration_clauses.htm*. Thompson & Thompson, a law firm with a history of representing nonprofits and handling intellectual property and tax matters, lists helpful executory clauses at *http://www.t-tlaw.com/bus-09.htm*, including a provision recommended by the American Arbitration Association (AAA) as a generic, broad clause for administered arbitration. This generic, and very sparse provision is duplicated far and wide by commercial entities worldwide. For another example with somewhat more detail, see United States Arbitration & Mediation's model clause at *http://www.usam.com/services/arb_clause.shtml*. For an example of a "muscular" provision that strongly curtails the right to litigate, see the sample provision offered by TheDoctors.com, a medical malpractice insurer, in an effort to funnel disputes against its insureds into arbitration (*http://www.thedoctors.com/ecm/groups/public/@tdc/@web/documents/document/agreementsample.pdf.pdf*).

The AAA itself has a large collection of agreements and other legal forms applicable to ad-hoc arbitration to be performed by AAA neutrals at *http://www.adr.org/fc_filing_forms*. The National Arbitration Forum, another large administrator of dispute resolution, has a repository of numerous forms, including forms useful for consumers who must arbitrate (*http://www.adrforum.com/main.aspx?itemID=330&hideBar=False&navID=183&news*). United States Arbitration & Mediation also offers an ad-hoc arbitration agreement form (see *http://www.usam.com/services/arb_contract.shtml*). In addition, the Independent Film & Television Alliance provides a detailed Sample Notice of Arbitration at its Web site (*http://www.ifta-online.org/IndustryServices/Publications/samplenotice.aspx*).

Increasingly, commercial entities appear to recognize the value of a stepped dispute resolution system, with arbitration required only if mediation does not settle a dispute. Numerous online executory provisions for resolution of disputes reflect this stepwise framework, such as the second and fourth sample provisions provided by Thompson & Thompson in their previously cited Web page, *http://www.t-tlaw.com/bus-09.htm;* the agreement of the Los Angeles Almanac's commercial copyright license agreement (*http://www.laalmanac.com/_main/commercial.htm, clause 12*); the sample condominium bylaw agreement offered by High Clouds, a Canadian dispute resolution service, (*http://www.high-clouds.ca/Sample%20Bylaw%20for%20arbitration%20and%20mediation%20and%20court%20in%20condo_2007.pdf*); and the sample provision offered by Maine attorney Curtis Thaxter to handle a wide range of disputes (*http://www.curtisthaxter.com/pub.php?id=12*).

As a student of alternative dispute resolution, you can benefit from studying each of these agreements and demands very carefully as well as conducting some research on your own. (One interesting approach to researching dispute resolution clauses is to look at those you have in your own consumer agreements, including bank and credit cardholder agreements.) What do they accomplish, and what do they fail to accomplish? What problems do they solve, what problems do they leave unsolved, and what problems do they create? How fair and balanced are they? How does the prevalence of these kinds of provisions affect the due process and access to justice held by common consumers in our marketplaces?

no rule specification in the original contract; or selected by the arbitrator. The general guidelines for this decision are the following:

◆ If the arbitration agreement doesn't empower the arbitrator to do something, the arbitrator won't be able to do it. For example, if the arbitration agreement doesn't specify that the arbitrator can provide provisional relief, the granting of provisional relief will be beyond the scope of the arbitration.

- In the absence of procedural rules, the arbitrator is empowered to run an informal arbitration proceeding and probably will do so.

Whether arbitration is administered or nonadministered, disputants may choose to arbitrate under the auspices of a particular professional arbitration organization's procedural rules. For example, the AAA provides rules and procedures that are intended to govern a wide range of disputes, including employment, health care, real estate, commercial, estate, intellectual property, and online disputes. (These rules and procedures are available online—see, e.g., *http://www.adr.org/sp.asp?id=22440*.) Disputants and advocates can benefit from the adoption of such model rules because it avoids the need to reinvent the wheel and helps the disputants cover all the necessary procedural issues. Disputants can agree to waive any or all of the specific rules in a set of model rules in preference for their own version. For example, disputants might agree to modify a discovery provision in a set of procedural rules to allow interrogatories, but not depositions, to streamline the process and save time and money.

It has been recognized that employment arbitration—non–collective bargaining arbitration of disputes involving individual workers and their employers—presents a special situation in which employees may be particularly vulnerable to overreaching by the employer. In 1995, a task force of employer and employee groups, as well as arbitration organizations, collaborated in the drafting of a Due Process Protocol for Employment Arbitration. This protocol has been extremely influential and has prompted the development of similar protocols for consumer disputes and health care disputes (Bales 2007). Major players in these fields—large employers, merchants, and health care providers—can protect themselves against litigation over arbitration fairness and unconscionability by relying on these protocols.

PREPARING FOR ARBITRATION

Assuming that a dispute is pending, arbitration has been demanded, and neither disputant is contesting arbitrability of the dispute, the next step is to prepare for arbitration.

The sort of preparation necessary will depend on the arbitration agreement. Preparing for an arbitration hearing is similar to preparing for litigation, except that arbitration is usually less formal. Some arbitration processes, however, are virtually indistinguishable from litigation except for the identity of the neutral and the source of the neutral's authority. As with any ADR process, effective preparation for arbitration requires maximizing one's expert power: getting up to speed on facts and law, organizing the evidence to be presented, and planning a presentation strategy that complies with the procedural rules in effect. If discovery and/or brief submission are permitted, the team should take advantage of these opportunities. In addition, the team must make strategic decisions about how to ensure that the appropriate witnesses will appear at the hearing. Many arbitration statutes confer subpoena power on the arbitrator to help the legal team ensure that witnesses attend.

As with mediation and other assisted negotiation processes, effective conflict diagnosis, including a careful interests analysis and BATNA analysis, can be critical in preparing for arbitration. Many times, arbitration will have a facilitative component, and the disputant and his or her legal team should be prepared to take advantage of such an opportunity to maximize underlying interests, values, and needs. In any event, a careful conflict diagnosis should precede the effort to prepare a case for any sort of adjudication, because it will guide the team in determining how best to present the case in view of the disputant's overall best interests. Since arbitration is more flexible than litigation in procedure and potential outcomes, it may be possible to do more in arbitration to see that underlying interests are addressed. Moreover, voluntary settlement can occur in the course of an arbitration proceeding; thus, if you are well prepared to manage a negotiation process, you or your client can be ready for such an opportunity if it comes.

PARTICIPATING IN THE ARBITRATION HEARING

The next step is to *participate in the arbitration hearing.* The character of the arbitration hearing depends on the agreement to arbitrate. In some expedited forms of arbitration, there may not be an actual hearing; instead, the arbitrator will decide the case based on documentary arguments and evidence. There are also face-to-face hearing processes that feature no witnesses, only oral argument by the lawyers. In other cases, the disputants and their attorneys attend, and the disputants and, possibly other witnesses, give evidence.

Typically, the provision of evidence is more informal in arbitration than it is in litigation. The attorneys may present opening and closing statements, and they may conduct direct and cross-examination, as with litigation. The arbitrator may also ask questions, and the disputants may be free to add their own remarks. The arbitrator may also receive (or reject, if deemed appropriate) documentary and other evidence. It is likely to be received on a less formal basis than in litigation, and the arbitrator is likely to accept a wider range of evidence than a court would. For example, the arbitrator may allow hearsay evidence, with the understanding that he or she will duly consider the possibility that it is untrustworthy. However, informality is not always a characteristic of arbitration: Some forms are virtually indistinguishable, in terms of formality and due process rules, from litigation. Some arbitration hearings are transcribed by a court reporter, if so specified in the procedural rules that the disputants have adopted.

An arbitration hearing typically has an adversarial, adjudicatory flavor, but it may also look a little like mediation. Traditionally, some arbitrators have seen their role as going beyond the rigid restrictions of legal determination and are motivated to make a decision with which all parties can live. Hence, some arbitrators facilitate negotiations between the disputants and may even encourage the disputants to settle the matter instead of waiting for the arbitration decision,

An arbitration hearing generally has an adversarial flavor but may also resemble mediation. Dorling Kindersley Media Library.

or the arbitrator may try to get a sense of what the disputants can accept, then issue a compromise decision on that basis.

ISSUING THE ARBITRATION AWARD

Following the hearing, the arbitrator, or arbitration panel, issues a decision called an *arbitration award.* The decision may be issued on the spot, or, as is more common, after a period of deliberation the outcome may be communicated by mail. (The Uniform Arbitration Act, which is a model arbitration statute adopted by a majority of the states, requires that the award be in writing.) Depending on the rules of procedure chosen, an explanatory opinion may accompany the award.

ENFORCING THE AWARD

If the arbitrator's award requires action by one of the disputants, and the disputant allegedly fails to comply, it may become necessary to engage in legal action to *enforce the arbitrator's award.* A refusal to comply with an arbitrator's award can be considered a breach of the original contract to arbitrate, so an action can be filed in an appropriate court for confirmation of and enforcement of the award. (Arbitrators are hired hands, not arms of the government, so they do not have direct power to enforce their own awards. Rent-a-judges are exceptions.) Since a breach-of-contract case can be cumbersome and time-consuming, many jurisdictions have, taking the lead of the Uniform Arbitration Act, adopted streamlined procedures that allow the confirmation and enforcement of arbitration awards.

LAW OF ARBITRATION

Arbitration would be an extremely simple process if everyone involved in every arbitration proceeding accepted it with enthusiasm. However, arbitration, being an adjudicatory process, frequently leads to at least one dissatisfied customer. And, when a disputant is dragged, kicking and screaming, into an arbitration he or she considers loathsome, the disputant is likely to search for ways to avoid the process or its outcome. From these obvious facts about human motivation, and the legal community's response to making arbitration a process that will stick, a complex, often difficult, and occasionally bizarre law of arbitration has arisen. As with mediation, the field of arbitration is rapidly evolving, and a legal or dispute professional involved in an arbitration issue must constantly update his or her understanding of arbitration law. Figure 5-1 displays the legal issues in arbitration law. "Front-end" and "back-end" issues are those specific to arbitration law, affecting when the court system will become involved with an arbitration proceeding. The law during arbitration is generally determined by the arbitrator

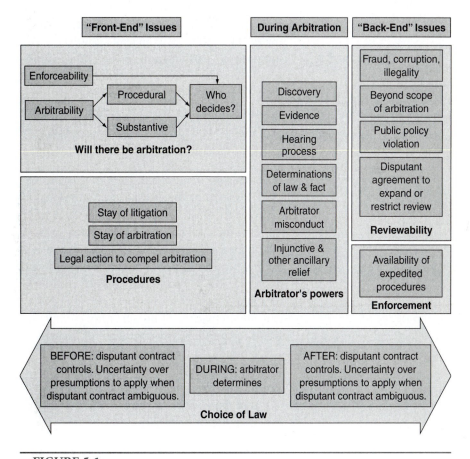

◆ **FIGURE 5-1**

Arbitration Law

and relates to the substantive and procedural law the participants will use and apply. Finally, choice-of-law issues affect the arbitration process before, during, and after the arbitration ends.

BEFORE ARBITRATION

When Should a Dispute Be Arbitrated? Enforceability and Arbitrability. If disputants make an executory agreement to arbitrate, but one disputant subsequently drags his or her feet, should the agreement be enforced? The FAA seemingly answered this question by providing (Section 2) that arbitration agreements are enforceable, as is any contract, and by providing for a federal court procedure for enforcing arbitration agreements (Section 4). This seemingly simple approach belies a level of complexity in determining the **enforceability** and **arbitrability** of disputes.

Enforceability
whether the contract to arbitrate is valid and can be enforced against the party seeking to avoid arbitration.

Arbitrability
whether a particular dispute is subject to an agreement to arbitrate.

Enforceability. Like any contract, some arbitration agreements can be successfully challenged as unenforceable. Reasons include a defect in contract formation, such as lack of notice or absence of consent to the arbitration provision (Bales 2007, 304–310); an explicit waiver of the contract; an implicit waiver resulting from participation in litigation inconsistent with the decision to arbitrate (*Morewitz v. West of England Ship Owners Mutual Protection and Indemnity Ass'n,* 62 F.3d 1356, 1366, 11th Cir. 1995); fraud in the inducement; voidness as against public policy; and illegality. For example, in *Hooters of America v. Phillips,* 173 F. 3d 933 (C.A. 4 1999)[8] , the court held that the rules of arbitration propounded by the employer-disputant in an employment arbitration were so one-sided and unfair that they merited rescission (undoing) of the arbitration agreement. In *Prima Paint Corp. v. Flood & Conklin Mfg. Corp.,* 388 U.S. 395 (1967), the claim was fraud in the inducement of one of the parties to enter into the contract of which the arbitration agreement was a part.

One increasingly controversial issue in the arbitration field is whether arbitration clauses that are imposed on consumers, or other disputants lacking bargaining power, by large commercial enterprises or other powerful entities should be enforceable. Of particular concern are arbitration agreements that are offered on a take-it-or-leave-it basis to consumers who do not have the power to negotiate an alternative. Although many commentators express a concern that such contracts are unfair to consumers (Carrington 1998; Haagen 1998; Schwartz 1997; Smith 2001; Speidel 1998), the courts have uniformly held that such contracts are valid and enforceable, even against a consumer who does not wish to arbitrate, unless something about the arbitration scheme itself is grossly unfair, as in the *Hooters* litigation. Moreover, the Supreme Court has held that state laws that attempt to restrict the abilities of commercial entities to impose such

---

[8] For details of the egregious nature of the agreement invalidated in *Hooters,* see discussion of the advantages and disadvantages of arbitration in Chapter 7.

International Perspectives on Consumer Arbitration

The favor U.S. courts confer on contracts to arbitrate that are imposed by merchants on consumers is not shared internationally, according to Phillipe Gilliéron (2008). Writing about arbitration in the online environment, he notes that the European Union essentially disallows the enforcement of merchant arbitration agreements against unwilling consumers, whereas the reverse is generally true in the United States. This discrepancy has made it difficult to establish international treaties governing online forms of arbitration. (See Chapter 6 for further discussion of online forms of ADR, also known as *ODR*.)

contracts on consumers are invalid because they conflict with the FAA. See, for instance, *Doctor's Associates, Inc. v. Casarotto,* 517 U.S. 681 (1996), which is discussed later in this chapter in the context of substantive arbitrability. Courts have generally required, under state law contract law, some additional impediment to the contract in order to deny enforcement (Smith 2001; *EEOC v. Woodmen of the World Life Ins. Soc'y,* 479 F.3d 561, C.A. 8, 2007). For example, in some arbitration agreements the costs of pursuing arbitration may unduly burden consumers and other "small players," and the Supreme Court has ruled that the courts should consider these claims on a case by case basis (e.g., *Green Tree Finance Corp. of Alabama v. Randolph,* 531 U.S. 79, 148 L. Ed. 2d 373, 121 S. Ct. 513, 2000).

Employment arbitration presents similar bargaining power imbalance concerns, in that such arbitration provisions are often imposed on prospective and current employees who have little say in the matter. As with consumer arbitration, employment arbitration provisions, even if imposed against the will of an employee, generally are upheld unless the provisions are patently one-sided. *Circuit City Stores v. Adams,* 279 F.3d 889 (C.A. 9, 2002) presents an example of the kind of contract the courts disfavor. In *Circuit City,* the U.S. Court of Appeals refused to enforce an arbitration agreement against an employee when the employer, but not the employee, had the choice of going directly to court and when the employee was disallowed from pursuing certain statutory remedies under the arbitration process. Similarly, the majority of courts refuse to impose a duty to arbitrate on an employee if the employer has one-sided authority to modify the employment agreement to require arbitration, or where the employee, but not the employer, is required to submit to waive the right to litigate claims (Bales 2007).

Courts split on whether employees can be held to an executory arbitration agreement imposed by the employer, if the employee did not knowingly and voluntarily consent to it (Bales 2007, 307–310). If a party to such an agreement, such as an employee who consents to arbitration as part of employment, formally acknowledges the agreement to arbitrate, he or she will typically be held to the terms of the agreement even if he or she later claims not to have understood its provisions (Bales 2007, 306–307).

A related issue is the enforceability of arbitration agreements that divest a (potential) disputant of the right to litigate to enforce statutorily created rights, such as the right of an employee to recover damages for discrimination by an employer. The general rule, issued in *Gilmer v. Interstate/Johnson Lane Corp.,* 500 U.S. 20 (1991) in the employment arena and *Mitsubishi v. Soler,* 473 U.S. 614 (1985) in the commercial context, is that such agreements are enforceable. The Supreme Court in *Mitsubishi* (473 U.S. at 628) explained:

> By agreeing to arbitrate a statutory claim, a party does not forgo the substantive rights afforded by the statute; it only submits to their resolution in an arbitral, rather than a judicial, forum. It trades the procedures and opportunity for review of the courtroom for the simplicity, informality, and expedition of arbitration. We must assume that if Congress intended the substantive protection afforded by a given statute to include protection against waiver of the right to a judicial forum, that intention will be deducible from text or legislative history. . . . Having made the bargain to arbitrate, the party should be held to it unless Congress itself has evinced an intention to preclude a waiver of judicial remedies for the statutory rights at issue. Nothing, in the meantime, prevents a party from excluding statutory claims from the scope of an agreement to arbitrate.

Nor does the arbitration provision have to provide a process analogous to litigation—abrogations of due process procedures, such as the right to jury trial, have been deemed so characteristic of the arbitration process that they are acceptable attributes of an agreement to arbitrate *Caley v. Gulfstream Aero. Corp.,* 428 F.3d 1359 (C.A. 11, 2005).

Courts have tended to draw the line, however, at onerous provisions that, in essence, deny statutory rights by making arbitration extremely burdensome. For example, in *Dominguez v. Finish Line, Inc.,* 439 F. Supp. 2d 688 (W.D. Tex. 2006), an employee, ill with multiple sclerosis, was forced by his employment arbitration agreement to arbitrate his discrimination claim in a distant state.[9] He successfully challenged the arbitration provision in court by arguing that the forum selection clause denied him, as a practical matter, the right to adjudicate his discrimination claim. The court enforced the arbitration agreement but "severed" (refused to enforce) the offending forum location provision. Similarly, in *Cooper v. MRM Inv. Co.* (367 F.3d 493, C.A. 6, 2004), it was held that courts may properly strike down an arbitration agreement that requires an employee earning a minimal salary to arbitrate under FAA rules that require upfront payment of substantial arbitration costs. Courts may also refuse to enforce limitations to statutory rights if the arbitration provision curtails the ability of the claimant to vindicate his or her rights, as in situations in which the arbitration provision effectively denies the claimant the right to engage in meaningful discovery of evidence, though not all courts rule this way (Bales 2007, 334).

Arbitrability. Arbitrability refers to whether the dispute in question is legally subject to arbitration under an otherwise valid arbitration agreement. Arbitrability can be of two varieties: substantive and procedural. *Substantive arbitrability*

---

[9] A provision that specifies where adjudication is to take place is known as a "forum selection" clause.

refers to whether the contract to arbitrate does, or can, cover the interpersonal conflict between the disputants. *Procedural arbitrability* refers to whether there are procedural impediments to arbitration.

Substantive arbitrability is usually thought of as including two subissues. The first is whether the language of the contract to arbitrate should be interpreted to include the dispute, as in whether an agreement to arbitrate "all disputes arising out of John Doe's employment with ABC Corporation" would cover a dispute over ABC Corporation's contracting out work to a subcontractor, thereby lessening the amount of work available for the employee. (These are substantially the facts of *United Steelworkers of America v. Warrior & Gulf Navigation Co.*, 363 U.S. 574 [1960], commonly known as *Steelworkers II.*) Although principles that apply to all contracts are used to determine whether a claim is arbitrable, agreements to arbitrate are liberally interpreted to require arbitration (see *AT&T Techs., Inc. v. Communications Workers of Am.*, 475 U.S. 643, 650, 89 L. Ed. 2d 648, 106 S. Ct. 1415, 1986, and *Highlands Wellmont Health Network v. John Deere Health Plan*, 350 F.3d 568, C.A. 6, 2003). The reason for this deferential treatment is to close a potential loophole in the scheme providing for arbitration. A disputant who wants to make an end run around arbitration may argue that the other disputant's claims for relief are so frivolous that they, in effect, are not contemplated by the arbitration agreement. By this means, the resisting disputant can bring the "merits" of the case—that is, who would win on the underlying claim—into the courtroom, short-circuiting the efficiency of the arbitration scheme. This is the sort of problem presented in *International Ass'n of Machinists, Local Number 402 v. Cutler-Hammer, Inc.*, 297 N.Y. 519 (1947). To avoid this sort of result, the Supreme Court has ruled that, in determining whether a dispute falls within an arbitration agreement, a court is confined to ascertaining whether the party seeking arbitration is making a claim which on its face is governed by the contract *(United Steelworkers of America v. American Mfg. Co.*, 363 U.S. 564, 568 [1960] *[Steelworkers I]).*

Although *Steelworkers I* involves labor law, and, thus, a different statutory scheme than nonlabor cases, this rule of presumptive arbitrability has been extended to matters of commercial arbitration governed by the FAA (Hayford 2000; *Moses H. Cone Memorial Hospital v. Mercury Construction Corp.*, 460 U.S. 1, 1983; *Hobley v. Kentucky Fried Chicken, Inc.*[10], in which an employment arbitration agreement was interpreted to cover a dispute arising after the employee was fired). In general, in determining arbitrability, a court can't go beyond looking at the plain language of the arbitration provision to determine whether the claim, on its face, could be considered within the agreement. Modern arbitration provisions in contracts are so broad that this sort of challenge to arbitrability is seldom successful.

The second issue of substantive arbitrability concerns whether a particular matter is legally excluded from arbitration. One such arbitrability question

---

[10] No. 04-7202, 2005 WL 3838163, at 1 (D.C. Cir. Dec. 22, 2005), *cert. denied*, 126 S. Ct. 2058 (2006).

arises when a statute seems to disallow arbitration of the dispute in question or provides for a process that excludes the arbitration alternative[11]. For example, in *Wilko v. Swan,* 346 U.S. 427 (1953), subsequently overruled by *Rodriguez de Quijas v. Shearson/American Express,* 490 U.S. 477 (1989), the Supreme Court held that claims by a consumer against a securities broker for fraud arising under the Securities Act of 1933 are not arbitrable because the act provided a specific adjudicatory process and prevented "stipulations" allowing waiver of the act's benefits.

Under present law, a dispute is considered arbitrable unless a statute clearly disallows arbitration. Moreover, *state* statutes, even those that clearly and explicitly require disputants to use the courts, rather than arbitration, to address disputes are typically held to be *preempted* by the FAA. In other words, such state statutes prohibiting arbitration are held to be improperly in conflict with the FAA's overriding rule favoring providing for the disputants' ability to contract for arbitration. That's substantially what happened in *Southland Corp. v. Keating,* 465 U.S. 1 (1984). In *Southland,* a group of 7-Eleven franchise owners in California claimed that Southland, the franchisor, had defrauded them and had breached their franchise agreements. The franchise agreements contained arbitration clauses, but the California Franchise Investment Law contained an explicit court procedure for deciding such issues and disallowed any effort to circumvent the judicial remedy. The U.S. Supreme Court, holding that the franchisees could not seek a remedy in court, ruled that the statute purporting to invalidate arbitration in such cases was void under the FAA.

This rule has been extended to encompass even modest statutory efforts to restrict arbitration. For example, in an effort to make arbitration agreements consumer friendly, a Montana statute provided that "notice that a contract is subject to arbitration . . . shall be typed in underlined capital letters on the first page of the contract; and unless such notice is displayed thereon, the contract may not be subject to arbitration" (Mont. Code Ann. § 27-5-114[4]). In 1996, the Supreme Court struck down this statutory provision *(Doctor's Associates, Inc. v. Casarotto),* holding that an arbitration provision that did not comply with this requirement was nonetheless valid and enforceable. The court reasoned that any restriction in arbitrability was in conflict with the liberal arbitration provisions of the FAA. It appears likely that, unless a statute limiting arbitrability is both explicit and federally promulgated, it will be deemed ineffective.

Procedural arbitrability concerns procedural matters that prevent arbitration, such as the failure to seek arbitration in a timely manner or the failure to fulfill conditions necessary before arbitration can take place. An issue of procedural arbitrability was presented to the high court of Maryland in *Wells v. Chevy Chase Bank,* 363 Md. 232 (2001). In *Wells,* a group of credit cardholders took

---

[11] If a statute specifies the situations in which arbitration agreements are considered unenforceable, then in those situations *arbitrability* is indistinguishable from *enforceability.* See, for example, *Doctor's Associates, Inc. v. Casarotto,* 517 U.S. 681 (1996).

Chevy Chase Bank to court, contending that their interest and fee charges were illegal. The cardholder agreements contained a provision providing that claimants could force mediation of a dispute covered by the agreement and that, if mediation failed to settle the dispute, mandatory binding arbitration would be triggered.

Chevy Chase Bank tried to avoid the pending litigation by moving to arbitrate. The cardholders responded that the arbitration clause had been illegally inserted into the cardholder agreement and was unenforceable, but the Court of Appeals of Maryland (Maryland's highest appellate court) instead ruled on the basis of procedural arbitrability. It held that the proper procedure to institute arbitration had not been followed in this case. By the plain language of the arbitration provision, only a "claimant" could trigger the arbitration process, by first requesting mediation. Since the "claimants" in this case were the cardholders, and since they had not requested mediation, the court ruled that the dispute was not ripe for arbitration under the agreement.

Who decides whether a case will be arbitrated? Unless the parties otherwise agree, courts decide issues of substantive arbitrability. The arbitrator is in charge of deciding procedural arbitrability, unless, as in the *Wells* case, the issue is whether to stay or dismiss pending litigation (Heinsz 2001, 39; *John Wiley & Sons v. Livingston,* 376 U.S. 543, [1964]). However, determining the enforceability of an arbitration agreement takes a middle ground. In *Prima Paint Corp. v. Flood & Conklin Mfg. Corp.,* 388 U.S. 395 (1967), the Supreme Court held that a disputant's fraud challenge to the enforceability of a contract that included an executory agreement to arbitrate was a matter to be determined by the arbitrator, not the court. This general rule—that the arbitrator decides validity if an entire contract is contended to be void—has been strongly confirmed in a line of Supreme Court cases, including (for state law disputes) *Buckeye Check Cashing, Inc. v. Cardegna,* 546 U.S. 440, 126 S. Ct. 1204, 163 L. Ed. 2d 1038 (2006) and *Preston v. Ferrer,* 169 L. Ed. 2d 917 (2008). However, **dicta** in the *Prima Paint* opinion suggest that, if the agreement to arbitrate were the only part of the contract challenged as unenforceable, determining the validity of the agreement would fall to the court. The basis for this distinction appears to be that, if the arbitration agreement itself were procured improperly, the requisite mutuality and voluntariness of the arbitration contract would itself fail; hence, the arbitrator would never have been vested with the power to make any determination at all. On the other hand, the policy of promoting executory arbitration agreements would be significantly undermined if disputants and their lawyers could, in effect, bring the substantive legal issues into court by attacking the validity of the overall contracts in which agreements to arbitrate are incorporated.

Suspending Court Proceedings and Compelling Arbitration. If one disputant has taken an interpersonal conflict to court and the conflict is subject to an arbitration agreement, another disputant may wish to suspend or terminate the litigation. Otherwise, the usefulness of the arbitration process could be sabotaged by the time and expense of litigation.

Dicta
plural of *dictum,* Latin; language in a court's opinion that is not essential to the reasoning for the court's ruling.

The FAA provides (Section 3) that a litigant can apply to a district court in which litigation is pending to stay the litigation to permit the completion of arbitration:

> If any suit or proceeding be brought in any of the courts of the United States upon any issue referable to arbitration under an agreement in writing for such arbitration, the court in which such suit is pending, upon being satisfied that the issue involved in such suit or proceeding is referable to arbitration under such an agreement, shall on application of one of the parties stay the trial of the action until such arbitration has been had in accordance with the terms of the agreement, providing the applicant for the stay is not in default in proceeding with such arbitration.

Under Section 4 of the FAA, a disputant in a dispute over which a federal court would otherwise have jurisdiction can bring an action to compel the other disputant to arbitrate, provided that enforceability and arbitrability are not successfully challenged. Similarly, Section 7 of the Uniform Arbitration Act contains provisions similar to Sections 3 and 4 of the FAA, allowing a court to stay litigation to permit arbitration to proceed and to compel a party to comply with an arbitration agreement.

Special Problems in EEOC Cases. Title VII of the Civil Rights Act, 42 United States Code, Sections 2000e *et seq.,* provides that either the EEOC or an individual can seek legal redress (such as for back pay) for a violation of civil rights in employment. In the seminal case of *Gilmer v. Interstate/Johnson Lane Corp.,* 500 U.S. 20 (1991), *the* U.S. Supreme Court ruled that an agreement to arbitrate precludes an individual employee from suing an employer for violations of civil rights under the federal statute. (The Court reasoned that the employee does not give up his or her civil rights, but only changes the forum where these rights are adjudicated, 500 U.S. at 26.) But, in the 2002 case of *EEOC v. Waffle House* (534 U.S. 279, 2002), the Supreme Court held that the EEOC itself can, through litigation, recover remedies due to individual litigants barred by an arbitration agreement from themselves bringing private litigation. Process-wise, once an action for private vindication of civil rights is brought by the EEOC, the individual claimant cannot also bring a private action; thus, the agreement to arbitrate is, essentially, of no further effect. However, until an EEOC action, the employer will not know whether it might be defending an arbitration action by the employee or litigation by the EEOC.

Law Professor Michael Green, noting that in the wake of *Waffle House* the EEOC seemingly has left the handling of such matters to private arbitration, opines that the *Waffle House* case stripped employers of the finality of arbitration of employee grievances, yet the EEOC had also abdicated its job of policing discriminatory employment practices—in other words, that the current situation is the worst of all worlds (Green 2007). The current state of EEO law in the area of employment arbitration is quite murky.

DURING ARBITRATION

The issues of enforceability, arbitrability, compelling arbitration, and stays of pending litigation are sometimes referred to as front-end issues, since they are issues that bring people into court before the arbitration gets underway. Once these issues are resolved and arbitration begins, the vast majority of legal issues that arise during the arbitration process, such as discovery problems and the admissibility of evidence, are handled by the arbitrator. Thus, courts don't typically deal with mid-arbitration problems–though the Revised Uniform Arbitration Act (RUAA) does allow for the court issuance of provisional remedies (such as preliminary injunctions) and for the enforcement of pre-award remedies issued by the arbitrator. See the RUAA, Sections 8 and 18 (National Conference of Commissioners on Uniform State Laws 2000).

Arbitrator Misconduct. Arbitrator misconduct may, rarely, result in legal action after the commencement, but before the completion, of arbitration. (Most allegations of arbitrator misconduct are raised either in disputant attempts to vacate an arbitration award [see *Vacatur*] or in efforts by disputants to defend against an action to enforce an arbitration award.) A fascinating example of what can happen is described in *Morgan Phillips, Inc. v. JAMS/Endispute, L.L.C.*, 140 Cal. App. 4th 795 (2006). An ADR neutral, Bates, member of the JAMS/Endispute firm, first acted as a mediator, helping a merchant and a manufacturer reach agreement for delivery of bedding. An ADR provision in the settlement provided that the disputants promised to use Bates and JAMS/Endispute to resolve future conflict. A dispute over conformity of the product arose, and Bates agreed to act as an arbitrator. After hearing evidence, Bates, slipping back without consent into a mediator role, engaged in a series of caucuses, evidently with the intent of producing settlement. When no settlement occurred, he withdrew unilaterally as arbitrator.

Merchant, who was teetering on the edge of insolvency at the time of the arbitration, sued Bates and JAMS/Endispute for breach of contract, negligent breach of duty, unfair competition, and false advertising. Merchant contended that Bates' behavior was intended to pressure it into settlement, in violation of Bates' contractual promise to adjudicate the matter. The appellate court held that, under the law, the case against the arbitrator could proceed to trial.[12] In addition to demonstrating the kinds of issues that can arise when an arbitrator allegedly does not fulfill his or her contractual obligations, the case also demonstrates the dangers that can result when an ADR neutral blurs his or her professional roles, or takes on multiple conflicting roles in a dispute.

Privacy and Confidentiality. Arbitration is "private" in the sense that it is established by contract (rather than by governmental mandate) and in the sense

---

[12] The ultimate disposition of the case is not known.

that observers are not free to wander into an arbitration hearing, as they are free to do in courts. Unlike negotiation and mediation, no overarching public policy reasons make arbitration a confidential process or confer a privilege of privacy on participants to arbitration; thus, typically arbitration is not deemed confidential by statute or common law. Reuben (2006) reported that only four states provided for some limitations on admissibility and discovery of arbitration proceedings, and that another thirteen states provide for some measure of confidentiality, but only for certain kinds of cases.[13] A few other states have specialized court rules regulating the admissibility of certain kinds of information arising out of arbitration proceedings, such as the fee paid to lawyers in arbitration.[14] In the absence of public policy reasons to impute confidentiality as part of the arbitration process, courts considering the issue have generally, according to Reuben, refused to protect arbitration information from disclosure.

However, arbitration participants may have personal reasons for preferring that arbitration be confidential—indeed, privacy and confidentiality may be reasons that disputants choose arbitration over litigation. Thus, arbitration agreements may establish confidentiality and may impose limitations on participants revealing the content of arbitration proceedings. Case law on the enforceability of such provisions is extremely sparse, with only one arguably relevant published case, according to Reuben (2006). The case, *BJC Health Sys. v. Group Health Plan,* 30 S.W.3d 198 (Ct.App.Mo., 2000), involved a request by an arbitration participant to obtain transcripts of a prior arbitration between the other disputant in the current arbitration and a third party who participated in only the prior arbitration. The participants in the earlier arbitration had entered into an ad-hoc confidentiality agreement while arbitration was pending, and this agreement had been ratified by the prior arbitration panel, which, said the court, gave the agreement the status of an arbitration award and therefore required deference from the court. Because of the existence of both the confidentiality agreement and the existence of the ratification, the court ruled that it was improper to allow revelation of a transcript of the first arbitration. The court also noted that Missouri law, somewhat illogically, treats arbitration as a phase of negotiation and that, thus, there are public policy reasons to protect confidentiality in arbitration. *BJC Health* does not answer the question of whether a confidentiality agreement, in and of itself (without ratification by the arbitrator), will prevent disclosure of arbitration proceedings and, in particular, whether such an agreement will prevent disclosure sought by third parties not signatories to the confidentiality agreement (as occurred in the *BJC Health* case).

---

[13] The Administrative Dispute Resolution Act of 1996, 5 U.S.C.A. §574, does provide for confidentiality of arbitration involving federal administrative agencies, but only as to caucus proceedings. However, most arbitration hearings do not involve caucusing.

[14] Relatedly, the Revised Uniform Arbitration Act, Section 14(d) is a provision rendering arbitrators not competent to testify in court proceedings except in certain limited circumstances.

"Then it's agreed. Watson, Smith, Teller, and Wilson go to Heaven; Jones, Paducci, and Horner go to Hell; and Fenton and Miller go to arbitration."

The Cartoon Bank

AFTER ARBITRATION

Litigation is more likely to begin again when the arbitration ends and the arbitrator has issued an award. Frequently seen legal proceedings include actions to enforce arbitration awards and actions to set aside arbitration awards.

Enforcement of Arbitration Awards. The FAA (Section 9) and Revised Uniform Arbitration Act (Section 22) set forth the processes for the judicial enforcement of arbitration awards. These rules provide that, upon application by a disputant, the court will issue a legal judgment based on the award of the arbitrator, thus allowing the party seeking enforcement to use judicial remedies, such as garnishment of funds and the seizure and sale of property, to pay a monetary award. Often, disputants and their legal counsel will try to attack the substance of an arbitration award by defending against such an enforcement action.

Review of Arbitration Awards. Once an arbitrator has issued an arbitration award, it is considered final. In contrast to a litigated judgment, which may be overturned on appeal if the trial court is found to have made an error of law or to have lacked evidence to support a necessary finding of fact, parties to arbitration are presumed to have bargained, as part of their agreement to arbitrate, for a non-appealable decision by the arbitrator. The rationale for this difference in treatment is that litigation is often not chosen by one of the litigants, so there must be adequate process of law for the handling of errors. In contrast, arbitration involves the presumably voluntary submission of the dispute by all disputants to the arbitrator.

Issues of arbitrator review were almost unheard of before the FAA, because disputants, having willingly submitted to arbitration, were almost always comfortable with the process. With the huge rise in the enforcement of executory

Vacatur
the overturning of an arbitration award by a court.

agreements to arbitrate against unwilling participants, challenges to arbitrators' decisions became more prevalent.

Vacatur. The FAA (Section 10) provides for the **vacatur** (overturning) of an arbitration award by a court in cases

1. Where the award was procured by corruption, fraud, or undue means.
2. Where there was evident partiality or corruption in the arbitrators, or either of them.
3. Where the arbitrators were guilty of misconduct in refusing to postpone the hearing, upon sufficient cause shown, or in refusing to hear evidence pertinent and material to the controversy; or of any other misbehavior by which the rights of any party have been prejudiced.
4. Where the arbitrators exceeded their powers, or so imperfectly executed them that a mutual, final, and definite award upon the subject matter submitted was not made.

A similar provision is contained in the Revised Uniform Arbitration Act (Section 23), and in the arena of international arbitration, the New York and Inter-American Arbitration Conventions (treaties specifying a uniform set of rules to be applied to arbitrations that cross national boundaries) specify equally restrictive grounds for vacatur. Overall, these governing laws restrict the grounds for overturning an arbitration award to situations in which an egregious error or act eviscerates the arbitrator's power to issue the award in question: Unlike court judgments, arbitration awards cannot be overturned merely because the award turned on an erroneous interpretation or application of law. Thus, it appears that, within and outside the United States, governing bodies support the finality of arbitration proceedings by making the overturning of resulting awards very difficult.

Besides vacatur, most arbitration awards reached in the United States are subject to correction or modification based on the Section 11 of the FAA:

In either of the following cases the United States court in and for the district wherein the award was made may make an order modifying or correcting the award upon the application of any party to the arbitration

a. Where there was an evident material miscalculation of figures or an evident material mistake in the description of any person, thing, or property referred to in the award.
b. Where the arbitrators have awarded upon a matter not submitted to them, unless it is a matter not affecting the merits of the decision upon the matter submitted.
c. Where the award is imperfect in matter of form not affecting the merits of the controversy.

The order may modify and correct the award, so as to effect the intent thereof and promote justice between the parties.

In addition to these somewhat narrow statutory grounds for vacating, modifying, or correcting an arbitrator's award, the courts have also overturned arbitration awards if it appears that the arbitrator decided an issue that was not substantively arbitrable under any plausible interpretation of the agreement to arbitrate. The general rule in this regard is that the arbitrator must have made a ruling that reflects the "essence of the agreement" to arbitrate. *United Steelworkers of America v. Enterprise Wheel and Car Corp.,* 363 U.S. 593 (1960) (commonly referred to as *Steelworkers III*). In practice, the courts have sometimes found it difficult to apply this standard without intruding into the arbitrator's domain of contract interpretation (Hayford 2000). This area of law is a fruitful one for adversaries who wish to use the arbitration process for strategic posturing.

Courts only very rarely vacate an arbitration award on grounds that the arbitrator exceeded his or her authority or "manifestly disregarded" applicable law: It appears that courts perceive the "manifest disregard" standard as a "slippery slope" leading inexorably to a situation in which arbitration awards would be overturned merely on the basis of legal error. Such a development would undermine the finality of arbitration by opening the floodgates for losing parties in arbitration to seek redress for legal errors of the arbitrator in court. Any contention that an arbitrator made a legal error can be plausibly reframed as a contention that the arbitrator manifestly disregarded the law applicable to the situation. Thus, the "manifest disregard" basis for vacatur is applied only very sparingly. For example, in *International, LLC. v. Hercules Steel Co.,* 441 F.3d 905, (C.A.11, 2006), a contractor–subcontractor dispute was submitted to arbitration, and the resulting award was challenged by one of the disputants, who contended that the arbitrator had misinterpreted the contract and applied the wrong completion date schedule. The U.S. Court of Appeals denied vacatur and chided the appealing party for bringing such an action for vacatur:

> The facts of this case do not come within shouting distance of [the Manifest Disregard grounds for vacatur]. This is a typical contractual dispute in which the parties disagree about the meaning of terms of their agreement. There are arguments to be made on both sides of the contractual interpretation issue, and they were made to the arbitrator before being made to the district court and then to us. Even if we were convinced that we would have decided this contractual dispute differently, that would not be nearly enough to set aside the award. *(441 F.3d at 911)*

A rare successful demand for vacatur occurred in *Montes v. Shearson Lehman Bros.,* 128 F.3d 1456 (C.A. 11, 1997). This case involved a claim by an employee for overtime pay pursuant to her rights under a federal statute. There was evidence that the arbitrator, who denied the benefits to the employee, acceded to an explicit request by the employer's counsel to ignore the applicable statutory law. Lacking any evidence that the arbitrator had applied the law, and mindful of the clear evidence that the arbitrator had been asked to disregard it, the Court of Appeals ruled that the award should be vacated. Another exception to typical court deference to arbitration awards is found in *Patten v. Signator Insurance Agency, Inc.,* 441 F.3d 230, 232 (4th Cir. 2006), *cert. denied,* 127 S. Ct. 434 (2006). An employee's employment contract contained an arbitration agreement that set forth a one-year "limitations" provision (i.e., a demand for arbitration had to be made within one year of a claim arising, else the claimant could not recover). The employee was promoted, and his new employment contract contained a new arbitration agreement that did not include any limitations provision. This new arbitration agreement contained explicit language stating that it superseded all past arbitration agreements between the employer and employee. The employee was subsequently fired. Fourteen months later he demanded arbitration. The arbitrator found for the employer, ruling that the demand for arbitration had to be made within a year. The employee went to the federal court system and asked that the court vacate that portion of the arbitration award dismissing arbitration. The U.S. Court of Appeals agreed, holding that the action of the arbitrator was in manifest disregard of both the arbitration agreement and the applicable law. Two elements make this case suitable for court intervention. First, the challenge to the arbitration agreement was brought against the employer, who had created and imposed the agreement on the employee. (Typically courts are more willing to enforce contracts against the parties who have drafted them.) Second, the court based vacatur on a misinterpretation of the explicit provisions of the arbitration agreement, whereas courts appear to be more reticent to vacate an award based solely on an error of law.

Courts will also refuse to enforce an arbitration award if the award reflects a violation of public policy. This rule comes from basic contract law: No contract that violates public policy is considered enforceable. For example, a court faced with a contract to engage in prostitution, practice income tax evasion, or defraud someone would likely refuse to enforce such an agreement.

As with other aspects of arbitration law, the public-policy exception to enforcing arbitration awards reflects a difficult balance between the strong deference shown to arbitration awards and the need to effectuate countervailing policies—here, important public policies. Such cases frequently arise in the labor field. The seminal case was *W.R. Grace & Company v. International Union of the United Rubber, Cork, Linoleum and Plastic Workers of America*, 461 U.S. 757 (1983). W.R. Grace & Company, the employer, and the union had entered into a collective bargaining agreement that contained a seniority system. Later, the Equal Employment Opportunity Commission (EEOC) determined that the company had discriminated against blacks and women in its hiring and promotional practices and that the seniority system was perpetuating the problem. While the discrimination matter was in litigation, Grace hired some female workers and promoted them over some existing male employees. The male employees filed grievances, which ultimately went to arbitration on the issue of back pay. The issue ultimately before the Court was whether an arbitrator's award of back pay violated the public policy against discrimination enunciated by the EEOC and then-existing case law. To simplify the outcome, the Supreme Court determined that the mere award of back pay to the male employees did not, in and of itself, violate public policy, since it did not require the employer to also contervene any nondiscrimination practices adopted by the employer. Thus, the Court ruled that the arbitration award could stand.

The public policy for vacatur of arbitration awards was clarified somewhat in the case of *Eastern Associated Coal Corporation v. United Mine Workers of America,* 531 U.S. 57 (2000). This case is the culmination of a line of often confusing labor litigation concerning the reinstatement, by arbitrators, of employees who have engaged in unsafe practices on the job. Employers who fire these claimants typically contend that the discharges were motivated by public safety determinations, whereas the employees argue that the public policies involved don't prevent their reinstatement. In *Eastern Associated,* the employee was fired after a random drug test provided evidence of marijuana in his system, a second such infraction. The employee opted for arbitration, and the arbitrator reinstated the employee, imposing instead a suspension and other conditions of continued employment. The Supreme Court ruled that, although the employee's behavior—being on the job while intoxicated—violated public safety policies, the arbitrator's decision should not be vacated because the award itself did not violate public policy. An arbitrator's award must be treated as an agreement between the parties to the arbitration, stated the Court. Hence,

> the question to be answered is not whether Smith's drug use itself violates public policy, but whether the agreement to reinstate him does so. *(531 U.S. at 62–63)*

The rule is that an arbitration agreement may not be vacated as against public policy unless

> such public policy [is] "explicit," "well defined," and "dominant." [Citing the *W.R. Grace* case.] It must be "ascertained by reference to the laws and legal precedents and not from general considerations of supposed public interests." *(531 U.S. at 62)*

The Court explained that the statutory scheme providing for public safety also provided for employee rehabilitation; hence, it could not be said that the arbitrator's award itself contravened explicit public policy.

The *Eastern Associated* case may, or may not, resolve uncertainty in the area of public-policy review of arbitration awards. Other, similar cases exist in which similar reinstatements have been vacated by reviewing courts, including cases decided after *Eastern Associated.*[15]

In the words of one commentator,

> Parties who have agreed to arbitrate their contractual disputes should remain aware of the ever changing and expanding body of statutes, regulations, and even common law on which public policy may be based, because awards resolving their disputes may be successfully challenged on these grounds. Like a "Hail Mary" pass such challenges will occasionally, though very infrequently, succeed. *(Glanstein 2001, 334)*

---

[15] For example, see *Chicago Fire Fighters Union Local No. 2 v. City of Chicago,* 323 Ill. App. 3d 168 (2001). A helpful review is available in Glanstein 2001.

Arbitration Agreements That Specify Reviewability. The final wrinkle in the issue of reviewability and vacatur of arbitration agreements is that occasionally parties to an arbitration agreement will try to spell out the circumstances and conditions under which an arbitration agreement may be reviewed by the court. The arbitration agreement may represent an effort to restrict reviewability, or it may represent an effort to expand it. Agreements to expand reviewability are likely to represent the more popular choice, given that the FAA reviewability rules are quite restrictive.

Before 2008, there was a split of authority regarding whether disputants may, in their arbitration agreement, agree to a broader standard of review than specified in the vacatur, correction, and modification provisions of the FAA. We start from the premise that the FAA was originally enacted both to promote disputant "freedom of contract" and to enable the inexpensive, expedient, and efficient resolution of disputes using arbitration as an adjudication device. Some courts have held that the FAA vacatur rules should represent a "default" review rule that parties to an arbitration agreement should be free to expand or limit, whereas other courts have held that disputant efforts to expand judicial review may impair the arbitration process, turn arbitration into a protracted legal battle, exceed the jurisdiction of the reviewing court, and violate the explicit review provisions of the FAA. (Curtin 2000 contains a cogent discussion of the case law at the turn of the twenty-first century.) Paul E. Mason (2007) also notes that allowing expanded judicial review could have a "chilling effect" on international commerce because parties in international commerce fear getting into protracted battles over which nation's court system has jurisdiction over their dispute. The U.S. Supreme Court has now resolved this controversy for cases occurring in the United States and involving commerce, holding that disputants have no power to provide in their arbitration agreement for expansion of judicial review beyond the grounds specified in the FAA.[16]

The rule as to whether disputants can limit reviewability to be more restrictive than the FAA provides is less certain. Curtin (2000, 367) comments that disputant agreements limiting review may promote *both* the FAA goals of promoting disputant contractual power and promoting expediency. If you are a legal professional, you should be aware that any effort to restrict judicial reviewability of an arbitrator's decision may have unanticipated effects. Agreements to restrict reviewability are more likely to be given effect than agreements to expand it.

CHOICE OF LAW

As previously noted in this chapter, choice of law refers to the problem of which state or nation's laws should apply if disputants come from differing jurisdictions, if the dispute or transaction is multijurisdictional or international, or if

---

[16] *Hall Street Assoc. v. Mattel,* 170 L. Ed. 2d 254 (2008)

for some other reason disagreement arises over whose law should apply. Choice of law can come into play at any point in the arbitration process, from the enforcement of an agreement to arbitrate and stays of pending litigation to reviewability and vacatur of an arbitration award.

Parties to arbitration can explicitly specify the jurisdiction whose law governs their dispute. However, difficult recursive issues may occur if the choice-of-law provision is ambiguous in some way (leading to the possibility of divergent interpretations depending upon which jurisdiction's choice-of-law rules are used to interpret the choice-of-law provision). If the arbitration agreement fails to specify what law applies, the applicable law can arise from several sources: the site of the arbitration, the site of the transaction from which the dispute arises (if there is such a thing), the site having the strongest connection to the subject matter of the dispute, or a treaty to which the disputants' countries of origin have signed and which specifies how a choice-of-law decision is made. International commercial disputants may allow themselves to be bound to the body of rules known as the *lex mercatoria,* a sort of etiquette of international trade. Evolving modern arbitration laws and treaties increasingly rely on the *lex mercatoria* in situations where choice of law is uncertain (Marrella and Yoo, 2007).

Choice of Law During Arbitration. Generally, choice of law during the arbitration process itself presents little difficulty. Because the arbitrator is in charge of making decisions concerning the arbitration itself, he or she is also in charge of making decisions about which law to apply, and these decisions will not be second-guessed unless they constitute the sort of action that is subject to vacatur. An example of such a vacatur-vulnerable situation is presented by an ADR neutral, who, upon being conferred the status of arbitrator under an agreement providing that "the law of California shall apply," exceeds the powers conferred by the arbitration agreement by expressly deciding to apply the law of another state. Except in this sort of extreme error, the arbitrator's application of choice of law generally prevails. Disputants, advocates, and conflict diagnosticians should become educated in the laws of the jurisdictions involved before drafting the agreement to arbitrate, so that the arbitrator applies the desired body of law. If the disputants are at odds on this point and don't specify the law, the arbitrator decides what law applies, and his or her judgment is generally given deference.

Choice of Law in Matters of Enforceability, Arbitrability, and Reviewability. Choice of law becomes a problem when the arbitration and litigation process make contact—that is, when issues of enforceability, arbitrability, and reviewability are raised. Choice-of-law issues represent an extremely difficult area in arbitration law and may impose an unfortunate lack of clarity and unpredictability into the arbitration process. The murkiness results from a lack of consensus among courts about how to choose which laws should be applicable.

In disputes arising within the United States, an arbitration agreement without a choice-of-law provision is generally interpreted with reference to the FAA. On the other hand, if the parties to an arbitration clearly spell out the law to be applied, then their intent is given effect, according to the U.S. Supreme Court in its two leading cases on the matter, *Volt Information Sciences, Inc. v. Board of Trustees*, 489 U.S. 468 (1989) and *Mastrobuono v. Shearson Lehman Hutton*, 514 U.S. 52 (1995). The problem, however, is that it is often unclear whether the contract is ambiguous as to the appropriate law. For example, the *Volt* and *Mastrobuono* cases involved executory agreements to arbitrate that were part of overall contracts between the disputants. There were clauses in both contracts clearly spelling out which state's law was to apply to the contract as a whole, but the clauses did not relate explicitly to arbitration. In this sort of circumstance, an agreement to arbitrate is considered ambiguous as to the choice of law.

In *Volt,* the dispute between the parties to arbitration was linked to a larger dispute with other disputants who were not a direct party to the arbitration agreement, and the Supreme Court held that it was appropriate to apply a state law requiring the postponement of arbitration while the linked conflict was litigated. (The FAA would have required the litigation to be stayed, pending the completion of the arbitration.) On the other hand, in *Mastrobuono,* the Court held that a state law limiting the authority of an arbitrator to award punitive damages was not applicable because the FAA applied, instead. Given the similar settings and situations of these two cases, commentators have made numerous efforts to harmonize them. For example, law professor Thomas A. Diamond suggests that the cases stand for the proposition that, if applying the state law would limit the scope of arbitration or the authority of the arbitrator, there must be a presumption against the state law's application, whereas, if applying the state law affects only arbitration procedure, no such presumption should be imposed (Diamond 1997). Professor Diamond's rationale is both common sense and based on careful and well-reasoned research; nonetheless, it does not have the status of a court decision. Confusing language in *Volt* and *Mastrobuono* has produced numerous disparities in lower-court rulings, with at least four different rationales and results (Diamond 1997, 58–60). The scene is made still muddier by the fact that different states have different choice-of-law rules; hence, one must decide not only whose substantive rules should be applied but also whose choice-of-law rules should apply to decide the choice-of-law issues.

In the international arena, choice-of-law considerations relating to arbitrability, enforceability, and reviewability depend in part on the choice of a forum for the arbitration (in other words, the nation where the arbitration is physically held) (Holland 2000). Many nations have adopted international treaties, such as the New York and Panama Conventions, to make these rules more uniform. As in wholly domestic disputes, usually disputants who explicitly and unambiguously specify the law to be applied have their intent respected. In international transactions, given the wide variety of legal and judicial systems, it is extremely important to make explicit the law to be applied. An arbitrator who is confronted with an international dispute and no guidelines for what law to apply has several choices, including applying the law of the forum; resolving the conflicts-of-law issues using the forum's conflicts rules; acting as an "amiable compositeur," which means using good conscience and a sense of equity

(Holland 2000); or applying the *lex mercatoria* in an international commercial dispute (Marrella and Yoo, 2007).

In summary, any ambiguity in the choice-of-law provisions of an arbitration agreement can produce substantial uncertainty and produce destructive meta-conflict. Since one of the major advantages of arbitration is the ability to give effect to the desires of the disputants in designing a "custom" dispute resolution process, choice-of-law problems can be ruinous, eroding disputant autonomy, perception of procedural justness, and psychological ownership of the outcome. Moreover, arbitration conducted in an atmosphere of great uncertainty is more likely to feature a high level of formality and legalism as participants try to protect themselves, driving up the cost and time investment needed. Disputants, their advocates, and others involved in conflict management and prevention should make sure that choice of law is clearly addressed in any agreement to arbitrate.

EXERCISES, PROJECTS, AND "THOUGHT EXPERIMENTS"

1. *Internet or library research.* Study the arbitration rules in the American Arbitration Association (AAA) Commercial Dispute Resolution Procedures. Also study the AAA's Supplementary Procedures for Consumer-Related Disputes. (The Association's Web site is located at *http://www.adr.org*. Click on "Rules" and follow the links to the specific procedures.) Clearly describe the differences between the two procedures. It may be useful to use a timeline or flowchart to organize the information.

2. *Find an example of an arbitration proceeding in the news media.* Describe this proceeding, and clearly explain why you conclude that this process is arbitration. Describe the nature of the interpersonal conflict, identify the arbitrator(s), and if the information is available, indicate

   a. whether the arbitration is executory or ad hoc.

   b. whether the arbitration is administered or nonadministered; and, if administered, who is administrator.

   c. whether a form of arbitration with limited outcomes, such as final-offer arbitration, is being used.

   d. any other interesting features of this arbitration proceeding.

3. Find the Web sites of at least three arbitrators who practice in different firms, whose sites include a list of their qualifications and a description of the types of cases the arbitrators accept. If you do not have access to the Internet, briefly interview at least three practicing arbitrators from three firms. Ask the arbitrators to recite their qualifications as an arbitrator and the types of cases they arbitrate. What similarities do you see in their qualifications? What differences do you see? If you do this assignment as a class project, discuss the results in class. See if you can discern patterns of qualifications among arbitrators specializing in the handling of particular kinds of cases.

4. Interview an arbitrator in depth. Some of the questions you might pose include the following:

   a. What is your professional background? If you are a lawyer, how long did you practice law before becoming an arbitrator?

   b. What, if any, specialized arbitration training or education have you completed?

   c. Are you a member of any professional arbitration or ADR associations? If so, which ones, and what benefits do you obtain from membership?

   d. What sorts of disputes do you arbitrate?

   e. How long have you been arbitrating? How many cases have you arbitrated?

   f. Do you prefer to use any particular set of procedures? Which ones, and why? Do you commonly practice in an administered or a nonadministered context?

   g. What is the most difficult aspect of the arbitration profession, and what do you do to deal with it?

   h. What is the most rewarding aspect of arbitration practice?

   i. Do you have any advice to people considering a career as an arbitrator?

5. Read and summarize (or brief, if you have been taught to brief opinions) *Hooters of America v. Phillips,* 173 F. 3d 933 (C.A. 4 1999). How can employees be protected against such egregious misuses of executory agreements to arbitrate? Consider the following examples. Try to draft a single statute that would protect Clarke, Amanda, and Bankco.

   a. Clarke applies for a job as a sanitation engineer (a position formerly termed "janitor") with an enormous petroleum company. The job site is not unionized. The employment contract specifies that any dispute arising out of Clarke's employment be submitted to mandatory arbitration. The arbitrator is to be chosen from a panel provided by the employer, and the employer, but not the employee, may opt out of arbitration. Clarke has a vague idea of what arbitration is and doesn't like it, but he feels he has no alternative for supporting his family.

   b. Amanda, the chief executive officer of a major dot-com company, is courted by a financial firm, Bankco. The potential position would pay seven figures and would be accompanied by numerous perks and benefits. Amanda retains a renowned business lawyer to assist her in developing a top-flight employment contract. After hours of tough negotiation, they reach an agreement. The negotiated contract includes a mandatory arbitration provision. If a dispute arises, each disputant is to select an arbitrator, and the two selected arbitrators are to select a third arbitrator by mutual consent. The AAA rules of commercial arbitration apply to the arbitration process.

6. The *Hooters* case shows how harmful mandatory arbitration can be. Is there any risk to individuals with limited bargaining power—consumers and

employees—of *prohibiting* mandatory arbitration provisions in employment and consumer contracts? Discuss this issue.

7. Imagine that you are a legal assistant or an attorney. All of the following
   new clients have specified that they want to use an ADR procedure to
   resolve their disputes. Would you recommend mediation or arbitration?
   If arbitration, would you recommend an informal procedure or a
   formal, litigation-like procedure? Why would you make these recommendations?

   a. The client slipped and fell in a local supermarket. She had $10,000 in
      medical expenses and lost a month of job income. Medical insurance
      covered the medical bills. The client is a secretary at a dental office and
      earns $2,000 a month. The owner of the supermarket has denied liabil-
      ity, but it is unclear why.

   b. The client purchased a golden retriever from the other disputant, pay-
      ing $500. The disputants had an oral agreement that the seller would
      forward the dog's pedigree papers to the client within three months af-
      ter sale. The seller now refuses to do so.

   c. The client is a business partner of the person with whom she is disput-
      ing. The dispute is over the interpretation of a provision in the partner-
      ship agreement that specifies who is responsible for the payment of
      accounting expenses.

   d. The client is a tenant. He claims that the landlord has failed to provide
      the signage specified in the lease for the tenant's restaurant business.
      The lease specifies that the rent be calculated as $2,000 per month plus
      a share of the profits. No mention is made of an adjustment if a party to
      the lease breaches the lease. The landlord contends that he is not re-
      quired to provide the signage because the tenant failed to open the busi-
      ness in a prompt and timely manner, thus depriving the landlord of
      expected rentals.

   e. The disputants are ex-spouses. The conflict is over the interpretation
      of a provision in the marital settlement agreement that specifies how,
      and when, the residence owned by the two ex-spouses is to be allo-
      cated between them. There is an agreement in principle that the resi-
      dence is to be refinanced in the sole name of the client, that the other
      ex-spouse is to sign over title to the client, and that an amount equal
      to one-half the value of the increase in the value of the residence over
      the original purchase price is to be paid by the client to the other
      ex-spouse. When the agreement was reached, interest rates for mort-
      gages were hovering around 6 percent. Now the due date for the
      transfer is approaching, the interest rates have doubled to around
      12 percent, and your client no longer qualifies for refinancing the
      mortgage.

RECOMMENDED READINGS

Barnes, G. H. 1997. Drafting an arbitration clause: A checklist. *Hieros Gamos—Alternative Dispute Resolution Law. http://www.hg.org/adradd1.html* (accessed February 3, 2009).

Cole, S. R. 2001. Uniform arbitration: "One size fits all" does not fit. *Ohio State Journal on Dispute Resolution* 16(3):759–789.

Curtin, K. M. 2000. An examination of contractual expansion and limitation of judicial reviews of arbitral awards. *Ohio State Journal on Dispute Resolution* 15(2):337–371.

Federal Arbitration Act, 9 USCS §1 *et seq.*

Glanstein, D. M. 2001. A Hail Mary pass: Public policy review of arbitration awards. *Ohio State Journal on Dispute Resolution* 16:297–334.

Kim, A. S. 1994. Rent-a-judges and the cost of selling justice. *Duke Law Journal* 44 (October):166–199.

National Conference of Commissioners on Uniform State Laws. 2000. *Uniform Arbitration Act. http://www.law.upenn.edu/bll/ulc/uarba/arbitrat1213.htm* (accessed February 3, 2009).

Nolan-Haley, J. M. 2001. Arbitration. In *Alternative dispute resolution in a nutshell* (2nd ed., pp. 138–196). St. Paul, MN: West.

Riskin, L. L., and J. E. Westbrook (eds.). 1997. Arbitration. In *Dispute resolution and lawyers,* 2nd ed. (pp. 502–588). St. Paul, MN: West.

Smith, S. 2001. Mandatory arbitration clauses in consumer contracts: Consumer protection and the circumvention of the judicial system. *DePaul Law Review* 50:1191–1251.

Steelworkers trilogy: *United Steelworkers of America v. American Mfg. Co.,* 363 U.S. 564, 568 (1960); *United Steelworkers of America v. Enterprise Wheel and Car Corp.,* 363 U.S. 593 (1960); *United Steelworkers of America v. Warrior & Gulf Navigation Co.,* 363 U.S. 574 (1960).

United Nations Conference on International Commercial Arbitration. 1958. Convention on the Recognition and Enforcement of Foreign Arbitral Awards: The "New York" Convention. Convention adopted by USA at 9 USCS §201. *http://www.uncitral.org/pdf/1958NYConvention.pdf* (accessed February 17, 2009).

Zirkel, P. A., and A. Krahmal. 2001. Creeping legalism in grievance arbitration: Fact or fiction? *Ohio State Journal on Dispute Resolution* 16:243–265.

6

Nonbinding Evaluation, Mixed (Hybrid), and Multimodal Dispute Resolution Processes

Necessity is the mother of invention.

—Proverb

A camel is a horse designed by a committee.

—Anonymous

In this chapter, you will learn . . .

♦ to identify and understand nonbinding evaluation: a class of dispute resolution processes that features evaluation of the merits of the dispute.

♦ some of the interesting and innovative nonbinding evaluation processes, including nonbinding arbitration, summary jury trial, minitrial, neutral evaluation, and dispute review boards.

♦ how the basic forms of dispute resolution—mediation, arbitration, and nonbinding evaluation—have been combined and modified to produce a variety of mixed (hybrid) and multimodal forms.

♦ about ombuds, a powerful means of addressing and resolving conflict within large organizations.

♦ about the uses of dispute resolution systems design for preventing escalating, destructive conflict within organizations.

♦ the history, typical features, and effects of court-connected alternative dispute resolution programs.

♦ the dizzying panoply of ADR processes available in the online environment.

Nonbinding evaluation
a form of alternative dispute resolution in which a neutral gives an opinion about or evaluation of the disputants' dispute. Alternatively, the neutral may issue an advisory, nonbinding award.

In this chapter we'll look at a number of ADR processes that are commonly referred to as "mixed" or "hybrid" dispute resolution. **Nonbinding evaluation** is the most common form of these processes and is often thought of as a hybrid process, though it is not: It is a process in which a neutral issues an evaluation or advisory decision about the disputants' conflict. True **mixed, or hybrid, dispute resolution processes** combine elements of mediation, arbitration, and/or nonbinding evaluation. Common forms that combine mediation with arbitration include med-arb, arb-med, and mediation windowing. Other mixed or hybrid processes, such as incentive arbitration, blend nonbinding evaluation with arbitration. Still others, such as ombuds, court-connected ADR programs, and dispute resolution systems, are fluid and flexible efforts to provide basic or combination ADR processes on an as-needed basis, and they might be better described as "multimodal."

NONBINDING EVALUATION

Mixed or hybrid dispute resolution
any of the forms of alternative dispute resolution that combine elements of mediation, arbitration, and nonbinding evaluation.

Nonbinding evaluation is a kind of negotiation support process used in legal disputes to evaluate the likely outcome of the dispute being taken to court. The centerpiece of nonbinding evaluation is the neutral's issuance of an evaluation, which is advisory only. The evaluation may be a specific decision, a range of likely outcomes, or an assessment of the strengths and weaknesses of each side's case. Disputants and their advocates often contemplate that the issuance of the evaluation will narrow the distance between the demands and aspirations of the disputants, promoting settlement, or indicating the need to adjudicate if one disputant seems intransigently wedded to his or her demands.

Nonbinding evaluation can take many forms. A variety of approaches to selecting the neutral are taken: The decision maker may be an expert in the merits of the case; an expert in the law, such as a retired judge, a lawyer, or a respected paralegal; a panel chosen from prospective jurors in the community; or a panel consisting of representatives of the disputants. The complexity and formality of the process is also variable: The process may be brief and informal or lengthy and detailed, and it may or may not include discovery, the taking of testimony, and the submission of other evidence. The outcome may be a single decision, a range of decisions, or a detailed assessment of strengths and weaknesses. The details of the process depend on the jurisdiction in which it is held (if it is provided by a court or another governmental entity) and on the mutual decision of the disputants and their legal teams. In any event, the hallmark of nonbinding evaluation, and the thing that makes it a process distinct from the ADR processes we have discussed so far, is that the neutral renders a decision or an opinion on the merits of the case, but the decision is not binding on the disputants. Some forms of evaluative mediation also involve the rendering of one or more opinions by the mediator about the strengths and weaknesses of the disputants' legal cases and are, in fact, difficult to distinguish from nonbinding evaluation. This conceptual problem, and the consumer confusion that it has the potential to create, have led a number of commentators to recommend giving evaluative mediation a different name to distinguish it from classic facilitative mediation. It might be most appropriate to regard evaluative mediation as a hybrid form of dispute resolution, yet this has not been the trend among ADR professionals.

Within the confines of the adversarial legal system, nonbinding evaluation can be viewed as the best of all worlds: It provides disputants and their legal teams with a preview of what might happen in litigation without going all the way to trial. Viewed from the perspective of effective conflict management, however, it might instead be seen as the worst of all worlds: It encourages an adversarial perspective on the conflict (thus promoting conflict escalation) without providing the certainty of an adjudicated outcome. Perhaps the most useful way to look at nonbinding evaluation is that it is very useful to achieve certain goals and should be considered in light of both its strengths and its weaknesses.

Because the result of nonbinding evaluation is an assessment of what would happen if the case went to court, and because court is always one way of dealing with a legal dispute, a primary function of nonbinding evaluation is BATNA clarification. You may recall from Chapter 2 that a disputant's BATNA is his or her Best Alternative to a Negotiated Agreement—a concept used to help disputants clarify when it is best to settle, when it is best to negotiate, and when to use adjudication and other nonnegotiating forms of dispute resolution. Nonbinding evaluation gives an estimate of what would happen if the case were litigated. Varieties of nonbinding evaluation are tailored to the specific kind of litigation anticipated by the advocates: Some processes use "juries" chosen from the available jury pool, whereas others use neutral adjudication professionals, such as retired judges. Still other forms of nonbinding evaluation use disputant representatives, such as chief executive officers, as the neutrals in an effort to bring the BATNA clarification process to those most likely to be in charge of the ultimate settlement decision. If the nonbinding evaluation process results in an advisory decision, the result places a case value on the legal dispute. If the nonbinding evaluation results not in an advisory decision but, rather, an assessment of the strengths and weaknesses of each side's case, then each disputant's team can use the information to increase the accuracy of its case valuation process (Connolly 1999). In either event, the additional information is used to hone each side's BATNA assessment, theoretically increasing the disputants' willingness to agree to a settlement that improves on their respective BATNAs.

Attorney-advocates who choose nonbinding evaluation also often look to it to serve two additional functions. First, they hope that the outcome will show the other side that its BATNA assessment is overblown. If nonbinding evaluation can minimize the other disputant's BATNA assessment, it can improve the other side's offers. In this way, nonbinding evaluation serves the same function that instilling doubt (Chapter 3) does in the process of evaluative mediation. Second, if, on the other hand, the nonbinding evaluation demonstrates that one's own client has a weak case, the attorney can use this result to reality test with a client who expects too much. Thus, an overly optimistic client can be sobered up without the attorney's appearing to be unenthusiastic. Generally, the neutral in a nonbinding evaluation helps support each attorney's appearance in the eyes of his or her client. This support helps the attorney demonstrate that the case itself seems to be a "loser" without compromising his or her image as a zealous and enthusiastic advocate.

You may recall from Chapter 2 that the twin metaphors of the invisible veil and the lawyer's standard philosophical map describe the societal perception of conflict as competitive and the legal profession's conceptualization of dispute resolution as adversarial. The basic skeleton of the nonbinding evaluation process is reflective of these frameworks. Nonbinding evaluation operates on the assumption that disputes are either settled through a competitive process of positional bargaining or adjudicated through an adversarial process of litigation. Within this overall framework are a number of varieties of nonbinding evaluation. Nonbinding evaluation is intended to give each disputant's legal team a preview at a litigation future, in an effort to give both sides enough information that their positions will overlap, enabling settlement to take place. The basic forms of nonbinding evaluation are summarized in Table 6-1 and discussed in the sections that follow.

Nonbinding Arbitration

Nonbinding arbitration is the most basic form of nonbinding evaluation. It consists simply of an adjudication-like process in which the outcome is not binding. Sometimes, nonbinding arbitration is a process chosen by private parties, but often, instead, it is a mandatory process ordered by the court. (Courts ordinarily cannot mandate binding arbitration without violating litigants' constitutional right to have access to trials.) In court-connected mandatory arbitration, arbitrators are often lawyers empaneled as arbitrators by the court system. The arbitrator issues a decision, which the disputants are free to disregard if they wish. In many court-connected arbitration programs, the choice is to accept the arbitrator's award or undergo a trial de novo—see, e.g., *D'Iorio v. Majestic Lanes*, 370 F.3d 354 (C.A. 3, 2004). (A few jurisdictions employ incentive arbitration.) Most jurisdictions treat the proceedings as settlement negotiations and, hence, preserve the privacy and confidentiality of the process and outcome.

Minitrial

In minitrial, the time and expense of case presentation are minimized through the presentation of a summary version of the dispute. Minitrials are usually attended by representatives of the disputants who have the authority to settle the case (such as corporate officers or board members). After case presentation, the neutral will either issue a nonbinding decision or will discuss strengths and weaknesses with disputant representatives and their advocates. Sometimes the neutral then proceeds to facilitate settlement negotiations, much as a mediator does. In a variant of minitrial, used by disputants who are typically organizations such as corporations, organizational leaders serve as the neutrals.

◆ **TABLE 6-1**   Nonbinding Evaluation Processes

PROCESS	WHO IS TYPICALLY THE NEUTRAL?	WHAT IS TYPICALLY PRESENTED?	NATURE OF OUTCOME	WHAT IS THE PROCESS USEFUL FOR?
Nonbinding arbitration	Arbitrator, who may be an attorney, a retired judge, or an ADR neutral	Oral arguments; occasionally exhibits and informal testimony (as in arbitration)	Arbitration award, advisory only; may be oral, written, or both	General BATNA clarification
Minitrial	Corporate executives with authority to settle; may also be a neutral moderator	Typically, oral arguments; may also be some evidentiary showing	Typically, no outcome *per se;* observations of hearing provide BATNA clarification to those with authority to negotiate settlement; advisory award may be issued by neutral if no settlement reached	BATNA clarification for those in a position to settle
Summary jury trial	Members of the jury pool as adjudicators; judge or retired judge as moderator	Abbreviated version of litigated case	Nonbinding verdict	Teasing out of complicated factual issues (as in class actions/products liability); BATNA if jury trial expected; "day in court" for litigants
Neutral evaluation	Experts in technical area of dispute, or lawyers with expertise in the sort of dispute being litigated	Typically, oral arguments	Assessment of the strengths and weaknesses of each side's case; may include advisory award	BATNA clarification; expert empowerment
Dispute review board	A panel of leaders or other experts in the field involved, empaneled by the owner and contractor in a construction project	A summary of a dispute that threatens to delay or derail a complex construction project	An advisory decision	Overcoming of costly impasses and delays created by disputes that occur during complex construction projects

SUMMARY JURY TRIAL

Summary jury trial is a form of nonbinding evaluation intended to promote settlement by demonstrating to the disputants and their legal teams what would be likely to happen if a jury decided the case. Invented and introduced by federal court judge Thomas Lambros in 1980 (Lambros 1984), the summary jury trial started as a court-mandated and court-supervised process intended to give disputants "their day in court" and to approximate the results of a full-blown jury trial in complex cases, such as products liability cases (Ponte 1995). Judge Lambros described the sort of dispute amenable to summary jury trial:

> There is a certain class of cases in which the only bar to settlement among parties is the difference in opinion of how a jury will perceive evidence adduced at trial. These cases involve issues, like that of "the reasonable man" in negligence litigation, where no amount of jurisprudential refinement and clarification of the applicable law can aid in the resolution of the case. *(Lambros 1984, app. A)*

In summary jury trial, an advisory jury is selected from the pool of jurors in the community and an abbreviated version (usually lasting one day or less) of the case is tried. The trial may include the calling of witnesses and the taking of testimony, and the neutral presiding over the trial may be a hired ADR professional, a lawyer, or an active judge (as in *In re Telectronics Pacing Sys.,* 137 F. Supp. 2d 985 [S.D. Ohio, 2001]). At the termination of the case, the jury deliberates and issues a decision, which is used by the parties as a basis for settlement discussions. The jury is often unaware of the nonbinding quality of their deliberations (Woodley 1997, 552). Summary jury trials are popular devices for narrowing the factual issues that bedevil complex products-liability class-action litigation and are mandated in a number of jurisdictions for complex civil litigation (Libbey 1999).

NEUTRAL EVALUATION

Neutral evaluation is a process in which an expert in the subject matter of the dispute, or a legal expert, is hired to give an assessment of the strengths and weaknesses of each side's case. Neutral evaluation has many variations and is known by a variety of terms that often are applied in inconsistent fashion. As a court-connected process, and known as *early neutral evaluation,* it is often used to circumvent the prohibitively high costs of conducting discovery prior to trial. Frequently made available under the auspices of a court system, early neutral evaluation involves the assignment of an expert, such as a retired judge or lawyer, who hears or receives oral or written statements of each disputant's case. The neutral then issues an evaluation, which may be either oral or written, detailing a likely outcome or a range of likely outcomes, as well as reasons for the evaluation. The disputants are then free to use the information to conduct settlement negotiations. The process is also known as *case evaluation* and may occur at any point prior to trial. Case evaluation can be particularly advantageous in highly technical disputes in which an expert in the substance of the dispute can do a more capable job than can a judge or other neutral of understanding and assessing the situation, providing more accurate information with which to evaluate the BATNA. In such cases, as with the arbitration of similar cases, the neutral evaluator can be selected for his or her expertise. Neutral evaluation also refers to the collection of nonbinding evaluation processes in which subject-matter experts are hired to issue evaluations of technically complex cases (e.g., intellectual property cases involving scientific or technical innovations).

In neutral evaluation and many other forms of nonbinding evaluation, the neutral issues an authoritative, but nonbinding, opinion about the likely outcome of a dispute should it be taken to court. Identikal, Getty Images, Inc., Artville LLC.

DISPUTE REVIEW BOARDS

Dispute review boards (also known as dispute resolution boards) are entities created by contract to resolve disputes as they arise during construction projects. Boards are generally composed of three members empaneled by the owner and contractor. As disputes arise during construction, they are submitted by informal hearing process to the dispute review board, which issues an advisory decision in the matter. According to the Dispute Resolution Board Foundation, only 2 percent of construction projects using dispute review boards end with outstanding disputes (Harmon 2002).

The dispute review board process is designed to facilitate the complex relationships among owners, contractors, and others involved in large construction projects. The construction of an office tower, a freeway, or a stadium is an enormously complicated process, and disputes are inevitable. If unsettled conflict is allowed to halt or slow the work, the entire project can fail. Thus, dispute review boards are designed to provide on-the-fly dispute resolution that keeps the project moving and on schedule. In this way, dispute review boards are designed to prevent conflict escalation and damage, serving a preventive function not unlike that of dispute resolution systems (described later in this chapter).

For More Information . . .

You can read more about dispute review boards at the Web site of the Dispute Resolution Board Foundation, *http://www.drb.org/index.htm.*

LEGAL ISSUES IN NONBINDING EVALUATION

Nonbinding evaluation processes are, essentially, forms of assisted negotiation. Conducted privately, nonbinding evaluation is subject to the legal principles that apply to negotiation in general (such as the inadmissibility of negotiation communications under Federal Rules of Evidence, Rule 408, and similar provisions protecting settlement negotiations).[1] In one study of construction law attorneys conducted by the ABA Forum, respondents who had participated in minitrials reported that some 63 percent were conducted pursuant to procedural rules developed by the parties and their attorneys themselves, with the remaining procedures conducted according to rules promulgated by ADR organizations such as the American Arbitration Association and the Center for Public Resources Institute (Henderson 1995). Although these agreed-to procedures constitute contracts and could theoretically be the subject of litigation if disagreements arose about how they operate, in practice very little reported litigation arises out of nonbinding evaluation in the private sector.

Public-sector nonbinding evaluation, the processes conducted under court and agency auspices, is subject to specific implementing statutes, rules, and regulations and varies widely. Matters such as eligibility, opting out, rules of procedure, pre-hearing discovery, confidentiality, costs, and duty to participate in good faith are controlled by whatever statutory law undergirds the process, and these rules are widely varying. (Some statutory schemes apply rules indiscriminately to all forms of ADR, including nonbinding evaluation.) Although flexibility in the rules that govern nonbinding evaluation are considered by some to be desirable as a way to promote innovation, at least one scholar (Woodley 1997) argues that the lack of uniformity is a threat to the long-term usefulness of public-sector nonbinding evaluation as a dispute resolution process, and it is advocated that more consistency among courts, agencies, and other public arenas would promote the long-term success of nonbinding evaluation as an effective technique. As this area of law becomes more mature, it will become easier to characterize and understand. Meanwhile, anyone who is going to become involved in nonbinding evaluation must check the law applicable to the jurisdiction, type of dispute, and court or agency under whose auspices the dispute is being processed.

MIXED AND HYBRID ADR

Mediation, arbitration, and nonbinding evaluation are basic ADR forms. Each of the "basic three" has characteristic strengths and weaknesses. What if we could go further and develop processes that combine the best of each? That's the

---

[1] For example, in *Gunter v. Ridgewood Energy Corp.*, 32 F. Supp. 2d 162 (D. NJ 1998), a district court judge ruled that early neutral evaluation proceedings were confidential and privileged under Federal Rules of Evidence, Rule 408.

idea behind mixed, or hybrid, and multimodal dispute resolution processes—they are efforts to gain the best of the attributes of each and to tailor dispute resolution more precisely to the unique situation presented. To use a metaphor, if ADR were clothing, then mediation, arbitration, and nonbinding evaluation would be off-the-rack separates, and mixed, or hybrid, processes would be expertly chosen ensembles. The concept of the multidoor courthouse introduced by law professor Frank E. A. Sander and Stephen Goldberg (Chapter 2), in which a broad variety of dispute resolution processes are available for the choosing, is the prototype multimodal ADR program. If ADR processes were clothing, multimodal processes would be an entire department store, offering a broad range of styles and sizes.

In considering a mixed (hybrid) and multimodal dispute resolution process, one should never lose sight of the fact that disputes, and their resolution, occur within a social and cultural context. In the United States, this context invariably includes the blinders of the invisible veil and its cousin, the lawyer's standard philosophical map. This context is critical when considering dispute resolution methods that combine facilitative processes, such as mediation, with processes that presume bargaining will be adversarial and positional. Culturally, we are predisposed to see the adversarial process as the best, or only, method. If a new process hybridizes a facilitative dispute resolution process with an adversarial or positional-bargaining process, disputants are likely to see the conflict, as well as the opportunities for resolution, within the cultural context of the invisible veil. Because of this focus, mixing facilitative and evaluative/adversarial processes can impair the facilitative elements.

VARIETIES OF MIXED, OR HYBRID, PROCESSES

MED-ARB

Med-arb begins with mediation, but the disputants agree beforehand that, if full settlement does not result, it will be followed by arbitration. Disputants have at least two important reasons for selecting med-arb: Some want the advantages of mediation and the certainty of an adjudication, whereas others believe the specter of arbitration acts as an incentive to push disputants to be more accommodating to one another.

Med-arb includes a number of important subvarieties. In *med-arb-same,* the arbitrator and mediator are the same person (sometimes, this person is referred to as the "med-arbitrator"), whereas in *med-arb-different,* the roles are served by different people. In *co-med-arb,* the mediator and arbitrator are different people but both attend the mediation so that time can be saved by presenting evidence only once. *Opt-out med-arb* is a variation in which med-arb-same is initially specified, but, upon the election of either disputant, the process changes into med-arb-different. Finally, *MEDALOA* is a variant in which mediation is followed by final-offer arbitration (see Chapter 5). Med-arb processes (except MEDALOA) may incorporate nonbinding evaluation instead of binding arbitration: The nonbinding version is more common in court-connected settings, where mandatory binding arbitration raises constitutional problems by curtailing the right to trial.

ARB-MED

Arb-med is a less commonly used process. It begins with the case being presented to an arbitrator, who issues a decision but keeps the decision secret. In a subsequent phase, the disputants attempt to mediate a settlement. (The arbitrator may be the same person as, or a different person than, the mediator.) The arbitration award is revealed and used if, and only if, mediation does not settle the matter. It is thought that disputants' knowledge that there is already an arbitration award and that the award may affect the disputant adversely will increase incentives to come to a reasonable, voluntary agreement in mediation.

MEDIATION WINDOWING

The concept of providing "mediation windows" (Peter 1997, 102) formalizes a practice that often occurs informally during arbitration hearings: that of informal ad-hoc facilitation by the arbitrator. Many arbitrators periodically move into a more facilitative role in an effort to get a consensual settlement instead of an arbitrated award. In a conceptual sense, it's as if the disputants make an ad-hoc agreement to mediate all or part of the conflict midstream during arbitration. Mediation windowing makes this informal practice explicit. Mediation windows may occur on an ad-hoc basis, or they may be built into the process in predetermined ways (e.g., as each new issue is raised or once every two hours). The mediator is often the arbitrator, but a purer process, and one less susceptible to impasse, is produced if the mediator is not the arbitrator.

INCENTIVE ARBITRATION

Incentive arbitration is a hybrid process falling midway between nonbinding evaluation and arbitration. The case is submitted to arbitration and an award is issued. The arbitration award is nonbinding, but there are penalties for not accepting it. For example, in one common form, a party rejecting the arbitration award must do better in litigation by a predetermined percentage or face a penalty, such as paying the other side's attorney's fees and court costs. Incentive arbitration is used in the private sector; however, in addition it is becoming a choice of court policy makers who wish to impose mandatory, binding arbitration on disputants to cut the burden on the system while retaining the finality of a binding adjudication. For example, such a process is being offered by the state courts of Idaho for cases with monetary claims of under $25,000 under the name "neutral evaluation" (Cahill 2002).

MINITRIAL

Minitrial was discussed previously in this chapter, in its incarnation as a nonbinding evaluation process. There is also a hybrid version, which does not feature an evaluation by the neutral. As you will recall, a minitrial is an abbreviated version of a litigated dispute, attended by the disputants or their officers or directors who have the authority to settle. Typically, a neutral third party is present to moderate the proceeding. A summary version of the evidence is presented so that the representatives themselves can get a sense of the strengths and weaknesses of their respective cases. Whether the presentations consist solely of statements by counsel or include some sort of witness or documentary evidence submission is up to the disputants. Following the minitrial, the disputants' representatives meet to negotiate, often without their lawyers present. There may or may not also be mediation-like settlement facilitation, sometimes by the proceeding's moderator.

MULTIMODAL ADR PROGRAMS AND PROCESSES

Mixed, or hybrid, ADR processes are specific combinations of the three basic ADR forms—mediation, arbitration, and nonbinding evaluation. Multimodal ADR programs, on the other hand, integrate multiple distinct ADR processes. Four such types of programs are presented in this section: ombuds, ADR systems, court-connected ADR, and online ADR. Of these, online ADR doesn't really fit our conceptual definition since the online environment isn't a single ADR program. However, its characteristic of offering numerous options for dispute resolution makes it most useful to include it here.

OMBUDS

An ombuds is a person, not a process.[2] The concept for this multimodal form of dispute resolution originated in Scandinavia several hundred years ago as a way to deal with governmental complaints by the populace.[3] It was recognized that, to keep government responsive to the people, the government needed a human face. The ombuds was an individual who handled the concerns of the citizenry in an informal, flexible manner. The ombuds had connections to people in power and had the authority to cut through bureaucratic red tape to resolve issues.

---

[2] Many professionals in the field recognize the original, gender-nonneutral version of the term *ombudsman* as the technically correct name of this ADR neutral. Others have adopted the term *ombudsperson*. This book uses the popular, gender-neutral *ombuds* as the term that appears to be most likely to supplant *ombudsman*.

[3] In medieval Germanic cultures, the term *ombudsman* meant "collector of the bribe." In these cultures, a neutral agent was often appointed to collect a bribe, or fine, from the family of a wrongdoer to pay to a victim. This informal adjustment of a dispute avoided the retaliatory killing of the wrongdoer by the victim or his or her family. A more modern version of the ombuds was developed by the Swedish parliament in 1809, but the concept was not adopted in large scale in the United States until the last quarter of the twentieth century (Wiegand 1996, 97–98).

Ombuds: Additional Resources

An international organization, The International Ombudsman Association (IOA), provides information, networking, training opportunities, ethical and substantive guidance, and a forum for ombuds. You can view more information about IOA and ombuds at *http://www.ombuds-ioa.org.*

The ombuds concept has gained a widespread reputation and use as a means of personalizing the dispute resolution processes of large organizations, such as corporations, municipalities, and governmental agencies. Ombuds' popularity over the past twenty to thirty years has been the result of systemic problems that accompany the formalism and bureaucracy of very large organizations. The idea of ombuds now is to provide people with the sort of individualized and flexible attention that is an attribute of well-functioning small organizations, yet in a large-organizational context. Numerous large organizations that have thoughtfully employed ombuds are thought to have realized clear gains in terms of internal morale, operating efficiency, and corporate image.

What Is an Ombuds? An ombuds is a sort of dispute-resolution jack-of-all-trades—an informal complaint and dispute manager. An ombuds (or office of ombuds) is always associated with a specific large organization, such as a particular corporation, municipality, or agency.[4] Ombuds may deal with internal, workplace issues (workplace ombuds), issues involving complaints from individuals outside an organization (client ombuds), or occasionally a combination of both.

An ombuds serves as a human factor to counterbalance all the size and formalism of a large organization—he or she is someone who can help individuals communicate their concerns and effect helpful change in a large organization. Ombuds are generally high-ranking employees of the organizations they serve but are outside the regular chain of command to ensure that they are not perceived as a tool of management or leadership. Ombuds make themselves available to hear and counsel individuals with conflicts and disputes (sometimes these individuals are referred to as "inquirers"). For example, a corporate ombuds may be available to hear concerns raised by disgruntled, demoralized employees or employees who feel harassed. Equal Employment Opportunity (EEO) departments and Employee Assistance Program (EAP) offices also handle such problems in the workplace, but ombuds can deal with such issues in a less formal, less adversarial manner and can deal with problems that lie outside the jurisdiction of these specialized offices.

Ombuds enter some conflicts because concerned persons come to them for help. Ombuds generally have lockable offices with secure telephone lines to

---

[4] Ombuds may also be sponsored by a collective of organizations. For example, Nascimento and Cousineau (2005) describe an ombuds program serving low-income users of the California health system. This program is sponsored by nine legal services organizations in collaboration.

ensure the confidentiality of communications with persons accessing the service. Effective publicity and outreach efforts by ombuds are needed to make their availability and function known to potential clients and employees. Workplace ombuds also prowl the hallways and lunchrooms of offices, and client ombuds research in front offices and public hearings to learn what is bothering people or disrupting the office or public culture.

Ombuds use a variety of techniques to address and deal with conflict. They act as a sympathetic ear for the inquirer and may serve as a confidant, as a conduit for facilitating communication between the complainant and those with whom he or she needs to make contact, and as a recommender and persuader. An ombuds may occasionally serve a mediator's role, facilitating the resolution of conflicts. He or she can also make referrals to more formalized dispute-resolution processes, such as mediation, arbitration, grievance adjudication, or nonbinding evaluation, and may refer appropriate cases to EEO and EAP offices.

Basic Features of Ombuds: Neutrality and Confidentiality. Neutrality and confidentiality are virtually universally recognized as essential characteristics of the ombuds role. A workplace ombuds does not serve management, nor does he or she advocate on behalf of inquirers, although meeting the needs of both is always a goal of a person in the ombuds role. In order to encourage people to come forward with problems and issues of concern to them, inquirers need to know that the ombuds won't turn against them, and, in order to be effective conflict resolvers, the ombuds must not appear to be acting as advocates of the inquirer. The fact that the ombuds is hired by and can be fired by management makes this neutrality fragile. Leadership must publicly lend strict and unwavering support to ombuds' neutrality to render them effective. Mistrust of this neutrality can arise easily, leading to ombuds whose client bases refuse to consult them. For this reason, organizations that have established successful ombuds programs typically take pains to protect the perceived and actual neutrality of the ombuds. Many ombuds occupy a high-level position in the corporation or agency, outside the normal chain of command. It also appears to help if the individual ombuds (or directors of the ombuds office) are well regarded by, or explicitly supported by, the representatives of various stakeholder groups, such as unions, management, and/or consumer groups (Meltzer 1998).

Confidentiality is the second cornerstone of the ombuds role. The personal and informal process of handling difficult and sometimes private or embarrassing conflicts is impossible to facilitate effectively unless inquirers feel free to share private, and sometimes unpleasant or embarrassing, information with the ombuds. The Ombudsman Association Standards of Practice require the ombuds to have a clearly delineated document-destruction policy to avoid the possibility of confidential documents' getting into the wrong hands (International Ombudsman Association, n.d., §3.3) and provide that the ombuds is to protect the anonymity of the inquirer while conducting investigations and exploring possible resolutions to conflicts (§§2.1 and 2.2).

Generally, in the workplace context, confidentiality is conferred by job description and workplace policy. However, despite the fact that ombuds who are members of The Ombudsman Association (IOA) pledge to resist any efforts to get them to testify (IOA Std. of Prac. §3), there is no statutory right to confidentiality of an ombuds in most jurisdictions. Standards of practice, such as those of IOA, rendering communications confidential and privileged will generally not protect the communications from being subpoenaed if the dispute escalates into litigation. For example, in *Carman v. McDonnell Douglas Corp.,* 114 F. 3d 790 (C.A. 8 1997), an employment dispute originally taken to the ombuds escalated into litigation. In this dispute, the employee sought to produce damaging evidence collected by the ombuds in court, and the employer contended that there should be a common-law right privilege against testimony for ombuds. The court held that no such common-law right existed in the federal system and allowed the information to come in. This ruling does not represent the universal opinion of judges: several district courts have recognized a privilege for communications made to ombuds, and several state courts have done the same. In addition, many governmental ADR statutes provide for the confidentiality of communications made during proceedings, including ombuds. For example, the Federal Administrative Dispute Resolution Act (5 U.S.C. §§571 *et seq.*), governing dispute resolution processes in federal agencies, includes the ombuds process in its definition of alternative dispute resolution (ADRA, §571[3]) and specifies the confidentiality of ADR proceedings in general (ADRA, §574).

Critical Features of Competent Ombuds. Ombuds are unique in the ADR world in that an explicit process, or set of processes, is not specified in the role of the ombuds. Rather, being an ombuds is a personal role featuring multimodal choices in dispute resolution. For this reason, the personal qualities of the ombuds are particularly important to effective functioning. A competent ombuds must be able to navigate between sometimes mistrustful sides without becoming caught up in polarizing influences and must be able to convey a sense of integrity and neutrality to all concerned. The effective ombuds should be compassionate, be an effective listener and communicator, have a high degree of integrity, have mediation skills, and have an in-depth understanding of organizational structure, culture, and politics. Because the ombuds approaches each conflict flexibly and must develop custom-designed strategies for resolving them or referring inquirers appropriately, it's also extremely important for an ombuds to be an effective conflict diagnostician and to have an in-depth understanding of how each of the strategies and processes available to bring to bear on the conflict will affect its course and outcome. Since the ombuds role is to help resolve conflict constructively and to prevent future destructive conflict, an understanding of the cycles of cooperation, competition, and conflict escalation is a must, as is an ability to engage in nonescalating, emotionally validating forms of communication.

The ombuds must also be capable of garnering respect from all sides, and this aspect of the role is particularly important at the inception of an ombuds program. When the ombuds office, program, or job description is first implemented, there must be psychological ownership of the concept by all the interested stakeholders: management, employees, unions, and so on. Otherwise, the office may be mistrusted, underused, or fail outright. When D. Leah Meltzer, ADR specialist at the Securities and Exchange Commission, investigated federal ombuds offices (Meltzer 1998), she found resistance to the appointment of ombuds from stakeholders who had been left out of the decision-making process. For example, when the U.S. Information Agency implemented an ombuds program in 1985, the employees' union had not been consulted. The union executive board members felt that the ombuds program endangered the system of grievances and remedies that had been developed in the collective bargaining process. This effort at establishing an ombuds program failed. Then, in 1988, a second effort by the agency secretary to create an ombuds program almost failed when the unions were again omitted from the decision-making process. Meltzer reports that, after an ombuds had been appointed, the union, in turn, left the ombuds out of important meetings and told members to steer clear of him. She also reports that some employees at the Smithsonian Institution have expressed fear that the ombuds there is a tool of management, whereas at the Secret Service there was initial concern that the ombuds would infringe on management's responsibilities. Meltzer found the most successful ombuds programs in agencies where all stakeholder groups were involved in program development from the outset and where the ombuds selected were trusted and respected by both union and management.

In addition, there must be adequate publicity, outreach, and education to acquaint an organization and its management, the union, EEO and EAP members, employees, and clients with the office, its neutrality, and its confidentiality and with what the ombuds can do. In a dysfunctional organization, an ombuds

Ombuds assists elderly resident at a long-term care facility. Michael Herron, Pearson Educational/PH College.

put in place without adequate prior informational outreach is likely to be mistrusted as just another gimmick and will probably go unused.

It's hard to study the impact of ombuds. Many ombuds comment that the mere fact of their availability as a listener and change agent for employees creates improvements in morale, organizational culture, and functioning (Meltzer 1998). On the other hand, a truly independent, empowered ombuds cannot exist for long in a corporate culture unless leadership is open to hearing and responding to the concerns of employees, clients, and others who may have concerns about the structure of the organization. Thus, it is difficult to assess improvements in morale, culture, and functioning and trace them causally back to an ombuds, but the explosion in the use of ombuds by organizations that must financially justify such initiatives suggests that they are perceived by many as great successes.

DISPUTE RESOLUTION SYSTEMS

Within the past decade or so, large organizations, such as private corporations and governmental agencies, have paid closer attention to ADR as it has become mainstreamed within the legal community and the courthouse. Dispute resolution systems design, like ombuds programs, is an effort to gain the benefits of alternative dispute resolution processes for organizations (Lynch and German 2002). In the past ten years, several helpful works on dispute resolution systems design have been published,[5] and the profession of dispute resolution systems design consultant has flourished. With statistics indicating that 42 percent of managerial time is being spent handling interpersonal conflicts (Hicks 2000), this new attention makes financial sense to cost-conscious organizations.

The new focus on organizational conflict management may also reflect a growing understanding that conflict within organizations, rather than simply representing an annoyance or a source of friction or damage, allows organizations to discover opportunities for reform and innovation. Consider the following example:

> Belinda Marshall works as a chief managing paralegal, and Cory Logan works as an office manager at Doms and Jason, a large and growing law firm in Anytown, USA. Belinda and Cory are at parallel levels within the firm's nonattorney hierarchy, and they frequently butt heads over a variety of issues. Right now, they are involved in a simmering dispute over the firm's efforts to adopt a new information system. Belinda is strongly in favor of adopting MicroLegal, a system that integrates a timeslip system for tracking staff billable hours with automated billing, office inventory, resource management, and other office management systems. Cory prefers LawyerTrak, a

---

[5] The best known include Costantino and Merchant (1996) and Ury, Brett, and Goldberg (1988). A fine bibliography is available online at *http://www.peacemakers.ca/bibliography/bib8design.html*, and a set of valuable full-text articles on the subject are available at *http://www.mediate.com* by selecting "Systems Design" in the topic search.

system that he feels is much better at all the management processes he has to handle. A partnership meeting is planned two months from now for making the decision. The firm does not have an established communication system for making the managing partners aware of such disputes, but, as office manager, Cory submits bimonthly reports to the partners, and he has advised them of the merits of LawyerTrak. Belinda is left out of the formal communication loop, even though the partners have reassured her that "their doors are open." She is fearful that, if LawyerTrak is adopted, it will make her job of managing her paralegal staff much more difficult. Belinda is increasingly angry that the firm seems to ignore her department's needs, and she is beginning to attribute her problems to gender discrimination.

If the firm treats Cory and Belinda's dispute as merely a problem, positive opportunities will be lost. The two have different perspectives on the problem of how to choose office management software. If the conflict is treated as an opportunity to make an effective decision about the software, the existence of the diverse perspectives will help the firm make a better choice. Moreover, dealing with the ongoing conflict between Belinda and Cory could lead to better lines of communication being established within the firm. On the other hand, if Belinda is left out of the decisional process, she is likely to feel disempowered. She is very likely to use a resource such as the EEO office to express her concerns, and this could easily result in a displaced conflict over gender discrimination. If Belinda pursues an EEO grievance, it will likely produce hostility among the male employees and partners, leading to additional meta-disputes and impairing, rather than improving, gender relations. Developing a process for allowing this conflict to be aired and discussed in a meaningful fashion may prevent destructive conflict escalation and lead to a better communication process for the firm, as well as a better decision about office management software. Thus, treating Cory and Belinda's dispute as an opportunity to improve the firm, rather than as a problem to be eliminated, can have numerous advantages for Cory, Belinda, and the firm in general.

Dispute resolution systems design requires the application of conflict diagnosis principles on a macro, organizational level, rather than on an individual level. System designers must understand not only conflict, conflict escalation, negotiation, power, and so on as presented in this text but also organizational structures, systems, processes, and functions. Dispute resolution systems designers integrate systems and organizational development knowledge with conflict diagnosis and conflict management concepts to create effective dispute systems designs. Aimee Gourlay and Jenelle Soderquist, law professors and ADR professionals, writing in the *Hamline Law Review* (Gourlay and Soderquist 1998), note that an effective dispute system resolution should encourage interest-based conflict resolution to ensure that resolution is constructive for the organization as a whole and preserves relationships within the organization. They further note that beginning a dispute resolution process after a conflict has reached the stage of a formal grievance misses a valuable opportunity to prevent the conflict from becoming destructive. Thus, Gourlay, Soderquist, and other professionals in the field argue for a preventive function for dispute resolution systems.

How do systems designers accomplish their objectives? Peter Woodrow (1998), a dispute resolution systems designer in South Africa, explains:

While every situation is unique, the typical steps involved in dispute resolution systems are the following:

- Establish a process for making decisions about new or enhanced dispute resolution processes.
- Identify and diagnose the causes of recurring organisational conflicts and the effectiveness of existing dispute handling procedures.
- Examine the range of options for additional procedures or revisions of existing procedures.
- Select or revise conflict resolution procedures, considering the corporate culture and the kinds of disputes that arise.
- Organise the selected procedures in a comprehensive conflict management system.
- Seek support from key organisational constituencies and secure approval for the proposed new system.
- Develop a plan for implementing the new system and promoting its use. Train personnel to administer the system and to provide specific services, such as mediation.
- Create a process for quality control, feedback and refinement of the system.

Systems professionals seem to agree on three areas that are vital to the effective practice of dispute resolution systems design. First, experts in the field comment on the need for the dispute resolution system to be tailored to the structure and culture unique to the organization in question. A one-size-fits-all mentality, it is believed, is doomed to failure because each organization has a unique structure and culture. The temptation to adopt someone else's version of a dispute resolution system should be resisted (Gourlay and Soderquist 1998). Thus, the experts in the field consider it vital to apply conflict diagnosis and organizational systems concepts to the specific situation in an individualized fashion. Moreover, the resultant system should be consistent with corporate values and goals, so that there is greater impetus for it to succeed (Hicks 2000). Second, experts in dispute resolution systems design comment on the need to involve stakeholders at all stages of system design and implementation, from initial planning onward. Psychological ownership of the resulting system by all potential users is essential. This is particularly true in a situation in which stakeholder groups have been at loggerheads with one another: Any effort by one group to adopt a dispute resolution system will be reactively devalued by other groups who will likely believe it to be merely a tool of "the enemy." Such suspicious stakeholders will be motivated to sabotage the new design (Gourlay and Soderquist 1998). As part of the process of stakeholder involvement, commentators further urge commitment and care in providing education, training, publicity, and outreach. Third, experts note the need for continuing evaluation of the system (Hicks 2000; Woodrow 1998). Organizations are extremely complex systems, and conflict resolution is a tricky business. A system that seems appropriate in theory may not work in practice. Moreover, the imposition of a new

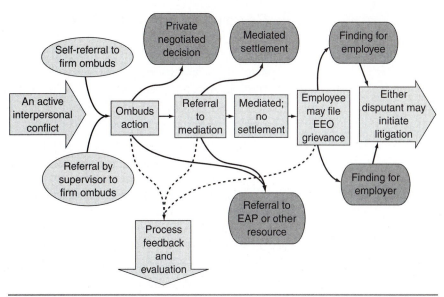

◆ **FIGURE 6-1**

A Possible Model for a Reparative Dispute Resolution System for the Doms & Jason Law Firm

dispute resolution system invariably alters organizational structure and culture so that a system that was ideally suited to the organization initially carries within itself the seeds of its own obsolescence.

In our example, what might a fully implemented dispute resolution systems design for Doms and Jason look like? Without knowing the corporate culture, recurring dispute situations, organizational structure, and stakeholder interests, it would be impossible to predict the details. However, a dispute resolution system generally combines multiple options for dispute resolution within a coherent whole. The Doms and Jason plan might have a reparative element for handling overt disputes, such as the one between Belinda and Cory, as well as a plan for preventing destructive conflict escalation by altering the organizational communication and governance system to give greater voice to stakeholders. Figure 6-1 shows one possible way of structuring a reparative dispute resolution system for Doms and Jason.

Systems Design for Federal Agencies

In 1996, the U.S. Congress passed the *Administrative Dispute Resolution Act of 1996* (PL 104–320), mandating the implementation of ADR processes to handle both client and internal disputes involving federal agencies. This mandate has prompted efforts by each agency to design and implement dispute resolution systems.

A comprehensive and periodically updated description of each federal agency's dispute resolution system is available on the Internet from the Office of Personnel Management. It is entitled "Alternative Dispute Resolution: A Resource Guide" and is available at *http://www.opm.gov/er/adrguide/toc.htm.*

COURT-CONNECTED ADR

One of the most common multimodal applications of ADR today occurs in state and federal court systems across the United States. The idea began with Frank E. A. Sander's conception of the multidoor courthouse in 1976. Sander's idea (Sander 1976, 130–133) was for courts to offer one-stop shopping to meet a variety of disputant and societal needs:

> What I am advocating is a flexible and diverse panoply of dispute resolution processes, with particular types of cases being assigned to differing processes (or combinations of processes). . . . [O]ne might envision . . . not simply a courthouse but a Dispute Resolution Center, where the grievant would first be channeled through a screening clerk who would then direct him to the process (or sequence of processes) most appropriate to his type of case. The room directory in the lobby of such a Center might look as follows:
>
> - Screening Clerk   Room 1
> - Mediation   Room 2
> - Arbitration   Room 3
> - Fact Finding   Room 4
> - Malpractice Screening Panel   Room 5
> - Superior Court   Room 6
> - Ombudsman   Room 7

History of Court-Connected ADR. By 1980, a number of courts, spurred on by visionaries such as Sander (1976) and federal judge Thomas Lambros (1984), had begun to implement experimental ADR processes as a way to divert cases from the overcrowded court system and resolve legal disputes more effectively.

Ad-hoc experimentation with ADR in the 1970s and 1980s, as well as visible and vocal support from influential leaders such as Chief Justice Warren Burger (1982) of the U.S. Supreme Court, led to increased federal congressional support for such programs. In 1988, Congress authorized twenty federal district courts to implement pilot arbitration programs: ten voluntary programs and ten mandatory programs (Judicial Improvements and Access to Justice Act, PL 100–702). This initial foray into court-connected ADR was followed by the landmark Civil Justice Reform Act of 1990 (CJRA, 28 U.S.C. §§471–482), which mandated that the federal district courts implement plans to make courts speedier and more efficient. ADR was recommended as one of the cornerstones of this process.

Section 471 of the CJRA provides

> *Requirement for a district court civil justice expense and delay reduction plan.* There shall be implemented by each United States district court, in accordance with this chapter, a civil justice expense and delay reduction plan. The plan may be a plan developed by such district court or a model plan developed by the Judicial Conference of the United States. The purposes of each plan are to facilitate deliberate adjudication of civil cases on the merits, monitor discovery, improve litigation management, and ensure just, speedy, and inexpensive resolutions of civil disputes.

Because the CJRA was intended principally to make courts more speedy, efficient, and inexpensive, it has primarily focused on diverting cases out of the trial and hearing process and making their resolution more speedy. By 1996, as a result of the CJRA and the efforts of numerous individuals committed to the development of ADR in the federal courts, 83 percent of the ninety-four district courts were engaging in, or referring litigants to, some sort of ADR, with fifty-two districts using mediation, forty-eight using summary jury trial, twenty-two using arbitration, thirteen using early neutral evaluation, three using "settlement week" proceedings (a process in which volunteer attorneys get together with litigants and their attorneys to try to hammer out settlement to pending litigation), and two using case valuation (Plapinger and Stienstra 1996).

Congress next passed the Alternative Dispute Resolution Act of 1998, mandating the provision of ADR in all federal district courts, including the bankruptcy courts. In particular, Section 652 provides in part (subsection a) that

> each district court *shall*, by local rule adopted under section 2071(a), require that litigants in all civil cases consider the use of an alternative dispute resolution process at an appropriate stage in the litigation. Each district court *shall provide* litigants in all civil cases with at least one alternative dispute resolution process, including, but not limited to, mediation, early neutral evaluation, minitrial, and arbitration as authorized in sections 654 through 658. Any district court that elects to require the use of alternative dispute resolution in certain cases may do so only with respect to mediation, early neutral evaluation, and, if the parties consent, arbitration. (emphasis added)

This provision has three important components:

1. It mandates that all district courts require litigants to consider using ADR.
2. It requires all district courts to make available to litigants at least one ADR process.
3. It authorizes, but does not require, district courts to mandate participation in either mediation or early neutral evaluation.

Individual district courts are permitted, within this broad statutory mandate, to create and implement whatever ADR program is felt to be appropriate. As of 2002, at least eleven of the federal district courts that had not reported having a court-connected program in 1996 had subsequently adopted explicit ADR rules or implemented ADR programs, leaving fewer than five without an explicit ADR program.

The trend to providing for court-connected ADR has spread to the state courts as well (Streeter-Schaefer 2001). Initially, the impetus to provide ADR on the state court level was driven by the divorce field. In the late 1970s, lawyer O.J. Coogler voiced a popular concern that the use of the adversarial system to handle divorce matters burdened family members in crisis with unnecessary financial and psychological stress. His ground-breaking book, *Structured Mediation in*

Divorce Settlement, published in 1978, recommended a less adversarial alternative, built on a carefully structured system of facilitated negotiation. Coogler's work was followed some three years later by *Divorce Mediation,* authored by social work professor and divorce mediator John M. Haynes, which proposed an alternative, and more therapeutic, model for mediating divorces (Haynes 1981). The notion of turning to mediation to create a more humane and less damaging alternative to the divorce courts was supported by developmental psychology research indicating that children exposed to destructive conflict between their parents suffered developmental setbacks, compared with their counterparts whose parents dealt with conflict constructively (Camara and Resnick, 1988, 1989). The implementation of mediation to handle divorce issues, and particularly to protect the best interests of the children of divorce, was therefore a natural step for the state court systems, which were responsible for handling family law matters. Mediation also meshed nicely with the revolution in custody law away from sole custody and toward joint custody.

Initially, a few pioneering states, such as California, Florida, and Michigan, implemented court-connected programs to mediate child custody disputes, and a scattering of pilot programs in other states began to pop up.[6] In contrast to the federal efforts, which were primarily spurred by efficiency considerations, the child custody programs were more commonly implemented because of the awareness of many legal and mental-health professionals that using an adversarial process to deal with parenting issues was likely to inflame and escalate conflict and to impair healthy child development. Despite this initial reason for implementing mediation, some of the first custody mediation programs were of the triage type, particularly in some California districts, such as Alameda County. These programs tended to be coercive, to be nonconfidential, and to focus on quick settlement rather than healthy postdivorce family functioning (McIsaac 2001). The worst travesties created by these programs were paraded very publicly in the professional journals by the scathing attacks of feminist law professors such as Trina Grillo, whose classic article "The Mediation Alternative: Process Dangers for Women" (1991) raised a considerable uproar in the legal and ADR communities. Grillo and others claimed that child custody mediation that included coercive and nonconfidential features disproportionately pressured women into giving in to their male opponents. (This contention, and the controversy it generated, is discussed in more detail in Chapter 7.) For a time, it appeared that feminist opposition to all mediation between male and female disputants would stop court-connected divorce and custody mediation dead in its tracks. However, by and large, jurisdictions adopting mediation as a way to deal with child custody and visitation disputes were able to avoid the mistakes made in California, and subsequent research, although not consistently positive, by and large suggested that women were not systematically disadvantaged by

---

[6] For example, in 1984 and 1986, the first court-connected child custody disputes in two Maryland counties were mediated as part of pilot programs developed by these jurisdictions in collaboration with the University of Maryland, College Park.

mediation (Emery, Matthews, and Wyer 1991; Gaschen 1995; Heister 1987; Kelly and Duryee 1992; Marcus, Marcus, Stilwell, and Doherty 1999; Pearson 1991; Richardson 1988). By the late 1990s, mediation was widely implemented as the court-connected ADR process of choice for family law disputes, according to Connie J. A. Beck and Bruce D. Sales of the University of Arizona (Beck and Sales 2000).

In a parallel development, ADR in state civil disputes took hold during the 1990s. Both mediation and nonbinding evaluation processes were adopted in state court-connected programs and processes to deal with commercial, contract, and tort cases. In contrast with court-connected ADR in the divorce field, which often took the form of mediation and eschewed attorney involvement in sessions, court-connected civil mediation was marked by attorney participation, often in place of the disputants themselves, and by a process that closely resembled a judicial settlement conference. These court programs began in major metropolitan areas, such as Los Angeles, achieved success in diverting cases from litigation, caught fire, and began to spread widely in the mid to latter part of the decade. In addition to mediation, nonbinding arbitration, early neutral evaluation, fact finding, and summary jury trial became popular court-connected processes.

Court-connected ADR in tort, commercial, and contract disputes is typically a highly evaluative, lawyer-controlled process. As mediation has been mainstreamed into civil litigation, it has been transformed far from its original radical roots as a facilitative, nonadversarial process into something fundamentally reflective of the adversarial system and invisible veil culture in which it operates. As previously mentioned, a number of commentators have lamented that the original promise of ADR to radically transform our somewhat pathological methods of resolving disputes has been subverted by its gaining mainstream status (Menkel-Meadow 1991; Riskin and Welsh 2008; Sabatino 1998). However, empirical research indicates that attorneys, particularly those who do *not* specialize in family law, strongly prefer evaluative ADR to more facilitative processes and believe "head-banging" neutrals who profess expertise in case valuation to be more effective than neutrals who help disputants negotiate (Deja 1999; Hermann, Honeyman, McAdoo, and Welsh 2001). And it can be presumed that some litigants (at least, a fair proportion of plaintiffs) whose cases are diverted to ADR will appreciate processes narrowly based on the rule of law and a process based on predictions of how litigation might decide the dispute (Riskin and Welsh, 2008, fn. 17, citing McAdoo and Welsh 2005 and Ackerman 2002).

Typical Features of Court-Connected ADR. Today, several varieties of court-connected ADR are common in the United States. Highly evaluative ADR processes are available to address civil disputes, such as commercial and tort cases. Mediation, early neutral evaluation, minitrial, and summary jury trial, as well as voluntary forms of arbitration and incentive arbitration, are all used by state and federal courts. In particular, summary jury trial and forms of neutral evaluation have become popular methods of dealing with very large and factually complex disputes, such as class action litigation, in which it is impractical to resolve every

Victim–Offender Mediation—Additional Resources

Additional information regarding victim-offender mediation is available on the Internet. See the Web site of the Victim Offender Mediation Association, *http://www.voma.org/index.html*; the Victim-Offender Reconciliation Program (VORP), *http://www.vorp.com;* and the U.S. Department of Justice's Directory of Victim-Offender Mediation Programs in the United States, *http://www.ojp.usdoj.gov/ovc/publications/infores/restorative_justice/96521-dir_victim-offender/welcome.html.*

issue in the formal courtroom. In addition, mediation continues to be used widely in the state courts to address child custody and visitation disputes.

ADR is also used widely to dispose of matters in small claims court—indeed, it may be most accurate to state that ADR has been adopted most consistently in very large civil cases and in very small ones.[7] In addition, criminal and juvenile courts often apply facilitative forms of mediation to the development of restitution agreements between offenders and the victims they have harmed. Although the idea of applying ADR to criminal matters seems inappropriate at first glance (guilt of a crime against society, it may be argued, should not be subject to private negotiation), victim-offender mediation is not typically used to determine guilt. Victims often comment that the experience of confronting the offender—letting him or her know the impact the offense has had and receiving an apology and restitution—can be quite healing.

Court-connected ADR of civil matters varies widely and differs by court system. It can include all or some of the following: mediation, nonbinding arbitration, voluntary binding arbitration, summary jury trial, early or other neutral evaluation, and settlement week. Apart from mediation in family courts and victim-offender mediation, court-connected ADR processes tend to be highly evaluative, with some court systems offering a single process and others more closely resembling the multidoor courthouse model envisioned by Sander (1976). Within the varieties offered by each court, the specific ADR processes used in each lawsuit are usually chosen by the settlement judge, with input from the litigants. It's typical for the ADR referral to be preceded by a series of supporting documents submitted by the attorneys, including statements of position, estimates of discovery and trial time, and other information, including recommendations for the most appropriate ADR procedure to be used.

Family law is still marked by a more facilitative form of mediation offered to deal with child custody disputes, though even in this domain, there are pending issues over how much ADR should look like an adversarial legal negotiation versus a facilitative, collaborative process. Many state courts refer all child custody disputes to mediation unless the dispute is exempt due to extraordinary circumstances, such as a history of spousal or child abuse.

---

[7] The fact that mediation has been singled out as an appropriate method of disposing of small claims, plus the fact that the mediators used in these court systems are sometimes undertrained and underpaid, prompts some commentators to identify mediation as second-class justice. See the discussion in Chapter 7.

Issues in Court-Connected ADR. For Frank Sander's (1976) vision of a multi-door courthouse to attain its full promise, two things must happen: (1) Each court system must offer a full panoply of dispute resolution processes from which disputants may select, including both facilitative and a range of evaluative processes, and (2) those in charge of deciding, or helping to decide, on the best process to use must be skilled conflict diagnosticians. Neither of these goals has been fully realized in most court systems.

For example, many court systems offer only one or two ADR processes. In many court systems, only nonbinding evaluation is offered, even though multiple forms are available. In court systems offering mediation, it often resembles nonbinding evaluation so closely that the option is merely illusory. For example, in the state of Michigan, the original mediation process offered, Michigan Mediation, is none other than early neutral evaluation. When policy makers recognized the absence of a mediation process, they added it, calling it "facilitative mediation," but even this process is highly evaluative. In jurisdictions that provide limited ADR options, there is often little for a well-informed disputant or advocate to choose from unless both sides can be convinced to voluntarily use a private practitioner whose specialty matches the needs of the disputants.

Court-connected ADR is the front line of the struggle between the radical wing of the ADR movement and our cultural institutions shaped by the invisible veil. As Bronfenbrenner's ecological theory might have predicted (see Chapter 2), ADR has transformed the overall culture, and the culture has simultaneously transformed ADR. Three decades ago, most lawyers could not have even distinguished mediation from arbitration. The few who practiced mediation outside the specialized arena of the collective-bargaining field were members of the radical wing, practicing in either the divorce or the community mediation movement. These early ADR professionals practiced a pure form of mediation. The advent of mass referrals to ADR through the court system has substantially transformed the practice of ADR from a process operating at odds with the prevailing culture into a process that in many ways resembles litigation (Alfini 1991; Guthrie 2001; Kovach and Love 1998; Riskin and Welsh 2008; Welsh 2001a). At the same time, however, the legal profession has begun to transform law school and continuing legal education to recognize and teach the principles of conflict diagnosis and the unique advantages of facilitative ADR processes. Movements in "collaborative law;" lawyers who practice holistic, interest-based client counseling; and the adoption of transformative mediation practices and ombuds by large organizations are a testament to the bidirectional influence between the radical ADR movement and the invisible veil culture.

ONLINE ADR

The electronic superhighway has made possible exciting innovations in the provision of dispute resolution services. At the same time, the Internet has created problems in interpersonal conflict that have never been encountered before.

"Never, ever, think outside the box."

The Cartoon Bank

Online dispute resolution (ODR)
ADR processes that use the
Internet as a platform.

ADR of cyber-disputes
the use of ADR to resolve disputes
that occur in the online
environment.

Thus, the Internet is responsible for both problems and promise in conflict diagnosis and alternative dispute resolution.

ADR that specifically uses the online environment as a forum, or platform, is referred to as **online dispute resolution (ODR)**. ODR processes can be used for any sort of interpersonal conflict, those occurring both online and off. The term **ADR of cyber-disputes** refers to the use of ADR to deal with disputes occurring in the online environment. Common cyber-disputes include the following:

◆ Intellectual property disputes, such as disputes over the ownership of domain names and over the fair use of material posted on the Internet

◆ Speech-related disputes, such as complaints over defamatory communication, offensive and hateful communication, and the right to free speech in the Internet environment

◆ E-commerce disputes, especially e-commerce involving business-to-consumer and consumer-to-consumer sales and barters that occur over the Internet

Tracking Down Online Dispute Resolution Providers

A good resource is *http://www.odr.info/providers.php,* a Web site maintained by the National Center for Technology and Dispute Resolution.

Cyber-disputes can be addressed using ODR or traditional ADR. In some cases, an ADR form may be mandated by a governing entity, and, in increasing numbers of cases, the vendor or service provider requires a particular form of ADR as a condition of making the sale or contract for services. This section will deal primarily with ODR, rather than with cyber-disputes, although some special conflict management aspects of cyber-disputing are considered along the way.[8]

Varieties of ODR. The Internet offers a wide variety of dispute resolution processes. The typical ADR forms are available: mediation, arbitration, and nonbinding evaluation, including case evaluation and summary jury trial. Many ODR providers also provide hybrid dispute resolution forms, such as med-arb. In addition, the Internet is home to specialized automated dispute resolution services made possible by computer technology.

Face-to-face ADR occurs in real time and involves verbal interchange, as well as the exchange and review of written documentation and supporting evidence. ODR is characterized by flexibility and variety in communication methods. Real-time interaction is possible in the ODR environment and is known as **synchronous communication.** It most commonly occurs as exchanges of text. Internet software can enable disputants and neutrals to communicate in writing using instant messaging and similar technology. A few providers also offer computer-facilitated audio- or videoconferencing, which allow the participants to hear and even see one another as they speak. The Internet, like the telephone, enables disputants to communicate over long distances.

ODR also offers disputants the opportunity to communicate at a time that is convenient to them individually. This form of communication is known as **asynchronous communication.** The most common form of Internet-based asynchronous communication platform is e-mail. Some ODR providers supply a secure threaded-discussion platform for the ODR process or provide a combination of these platforms. Asynchronous communication can also include the transmission of graphical materials, audio, or video communication. For example, an ODR process could offer streaming video of a witness's testimony, recorded earlier, or include transmission of the results of a brainstorming session conducted with a white board.

Synchronous communication
communication that occurs in real time, such as face-to-face discussion, telephone conversation, instant messaging, and videoconferencing.

Asynchronous communication
communication that occurs at the convenience of the participants rather than in real time, such as communication by letter, e-mail, or computer asynchronous conferencing.

---

[8] Some ADR professionals and scholars also include two other processes as ODR. The first are traditional complaint resolution processes in which the aggrieved party submits the claim online (Hang 2001, 848–849). The second is the so-called trustmark. Similar to the Good Housekeeping Seal of Approval, a trustmark is an approval certification provided by a watchdog agency, such as the Better Business Bureau. To obtain a trustmark, a business operating online is generally required to undergo an examination process specified by the watchdog agency, to abide by a code of ethics and fair practices, and to agree in advance to submit to a particular dispute resolution system (Teitz 2001, 995–996).

ODR is an evolving industry. The 1990s saw a proliferation of innovative efforts to adapt ADR processes to the online environment, whereas the first decade of the twenty-first century was marked by a process of winnowing down the field.[9] What remains runs the gamut of uses of the online environment.

In its simplest form, ODR can consist of ADR based on written documentation submitted online. An example is Settle Today (*http://settletoday.com*). Settle Today claimants initiate a case by submitting an informational document incorporating personal information, claim information, and argument (including legal argument, if desired). The other disputant is invited to participate and submit a rebuttal. After submissions are completed, the "mediator" (actually an arbitrator supplied by the Settle Today company) issues a binding "settlement"—guaranteed within twenty-four hours. The claimant is "on her own" to enforce the arbitration award.

Another quite simple, and quite unique, approach to ODR is so-called "blind bidding" ODR (e.g., Cybersettle, *http://www.cybersettle.com/info/products/claimresolution.aspx;* another is the Philippine Multi-Door Courthouse, *http://www.cpcap.org/odr/philippine-odr*). Very inexpensive, blind bidding—a form of binding or advisory arbitration—operates on the assumption that bargaining will be positional and that money is the only term in dispute. Blind bidding seems specifically well suited to insurance claim representatives, who may be bound by corporate policy to use positional bargaining but want to avoid the ego investment and reactive devaluation that comes from making offers directly to the other disputant's negotiating team. The process is completely automated; no human intermediator is involved; as a result, the service tends to be very rapid and inexpensive. In blind-bidding ODR, each disputant's negotiating team submits a bid, which is kept secret from the other disputant's team. If the bids are within a prescribed "distance" from each other, the computer computes a settlement, usually at the midpoint of the two bids. If the respondent's offer exceeds the claimant's demand, the claim usually is settled at the amount of the offer. Smartsettle (*http://www.smartsettle.com*) offers a "multivariate" version of blind bidding, which allows disputants to assign equivalence values to multiple concerns, allowing a blind bidding process where concerns other than money are involved. Interestingly, blind-bidding ODR sites proliferated in large numbers during the late 1990s, only to largely disappear in the first decade of the twenty-first century.

A somewhat more interpersonally rich ODR approach uses Web-based asynchronous "virtual rooms"—threaded discussion sites in which disputants

---

[9] Despite the hoopla that attended the "birth" of ODR, few ODR providers offering online mediation, arbitration, or nonbinding evaluation currently have much business, according to Philippe Gilliéron (2008). Gilliéron asserts that of online mediation providers, only SquareTrade, which has had the role of handling disputes arising on eBay, is an efficient and large-volume online mediation provider; and, notably, in May 2008, SquareTrade ceased to offer online mediation. Thus, ODR providers are now facing a level of disappointment similar to that faced by face-to-face ADR proponents. The exception is the domain-name arbitration process required by the Internet Corporation for Assigned Names and Numbers (ICANN) to resolve domain name disputes. Individuals who seek to register domain names submit to this arbitration process automatically, hence there is a captive audience for this form of ADR.

can post their communications and review the results of past exchanges and where mediators and other ADR neutrals can intervene. Entries by each participant are visible to others having access to the room but are inaccessible to members of the public. Many ODR sites will provide private spaces for disputant teams, as well as shared spaces for negotiation, mediation, nonbinding evaluation, and arbitration. This sort of ODR process is exemplified by Electronic Consumer Dispute Resolution (ECODIR, *http://www.ecodir.org*), which offers a process beginning with asynchronous negotiation, followed by mediation and then nonbinding evaluation if agreement does not result. A synchronous version, using instant messaging–style communication, is demonstrated by Resolution Forum, Inc. (*http://www.resolutionforum.org/s_demo.html*). Electronic Courthouse, (*http://www.electroniccourthouse.com*), a med-arb-same provider, also provides for synchronous text-based interactions between disputants. Electronic Courthouse provides an additional level of complexity: online "virtual spaces" within which disputants and their counsel and experts can fashion documents, perform private discussion and complex analysis, and submit supporting matter to the ADR neutral. A similar service, providing multimodal methods of communication, including shared white boards and other platforms, is provided by Mediation Arbitration Resolution Services (MARS), (*http://www.resolvemydispute. com*). This provider also offers synchronous ADR sessions by videoconference.

A more sophisticated approach is offered by SmartSettle (*http://www .smartsettle.com*) with a set of technologically sophisticated accessory tools designed to assist disputant teams in assessing their interests, fashioning appropriate proposals, and obtaining optimized outcomes. Using a facilitator and a "one text proposal" format, the parties communicate to generate a list of the terms that have to be addressed (such as price, delivery date, and so forth). Then, each side privately identifies a range of expectations for each term and an optimal resolution of the term. They also generate numbers that correspond to how important each issue is to them (e.g., time of payment may be worth 500 to the claimant but only 50 to the respondent), their expected BATNA, and so forth. Parties can even identify "even swaps" to denote how nonquantitative terms measure up (e.g., "my getting Nikes now is equally desirable to my getting Reeboks next Friday"). Thus, the disputants' interests are reduced to mathematical equations, and these are kept confidential and stored in the ODR computer. After this initial analysis, the parties issue proposals, and mediation begins online. If and when a tentative agreement is reached on all terms, the software uses the confidential information regarding interests and weights provided by each team to generate alternative proposals that improve both disputants' expressed interests as much as possible without reducing anyone's outcome. The parties may also specify a compromise solution; that is, if impasse occurs, they can ask the computational software to generate an optimized solution equidistant from the optimum levels described by the disputants.

Another unique innovation in ODR (and one which has seen a recent proliferation of providers) is the online summary jury trial. ICourthouse (*http:// www.i-courthouse.com*) harnesses the universal-access characteristic of the

Internet as a tool, by soliciting the casual Web browser to serve as a volunteer juror. (Other similar ODR processes are offered by LegalVote [*http://www. legalvote.com*] and SettleTheCase [*http://settlethecase.net/sumjury.htm*]). At iCourthouse, disputants register and then submit material to an online "trial book," which may include written text and graphics. In the online environment, jurors may browse both disputants' trial books, ask questions of disputants, and receive answers. The jurors post individual "verdicts" (and may comment as well), and these verdicts are communicated to the disputants. The verdicts are anonymous, but data are kept concerning the demographics of each juror rendering each verdict. If the verdict involves a monetary outcome, the mean of the jurors' assessments is reported. An innovation called JurySmart allows attorneys to download the information about their client's iCourthouse case, including demographic information about jurors and each juror's verdict and comments. ICourthouse has proven to be a robust player in an area characterized by ODR providers with short business lives.

Special Considerations in ODR. ODR raises interesting, and difficult, issues, as well as opportunities, for conflict diagnosticians and legal professionals. A number of psychological considerations make the ODR process different from the face-to-face process, and these differences should be considered in determining whether a given dispute should be resolved using ODR.

Advantages and Disadvantages of ODR. We naturally use spoken language and communicate face to face. The communication used in ODR is very different from face-to-face communication and raises both special opportunities and special problems.

Research concerning therapeutic interventions provided over a distance, such as by telephone, can inform us about the potential advantages of ODR. As with telephone communication (Ranan and Blodgett 1983; Springer 1991), individuals who could not otherwise get help due to geographical distance and separation can gain access to services on the Internet. This feature of ODR is particularly important in this age of borderless transactions. The asynchronous features of some Internet platforms can take disputants a step further than the telephone can: It enables communication to take place at the leisure of the participants and between participants in disparate time zones, yet at a much faster speed, and with greater ease and informality, than the exchange of letters. Imagine the problems, for example, negotiating or mediating between a disputant in Kansas City and one in Sydney, Australia. It may also be possible to facilitate communication between people who would otherwise be unable to communicate— for example, by interposing a translator for disputants who speak different languages. Translation services that would be cumbersome by telephone, or impossibly drawn out using snail-mail, could be easier to offer online and with asynchronous communication.

The asynchronous nature of some ODR platforms has other potential benefits. ODR participants can consider the statements of others in repose and contemplation, whereas in a synchronous, face-to-face interaction there is an irresistible urge to respond instantaneously to avoid long silences. An ODR participant who receives communication from another involved party can carefully review what has been said and consider the possible meanings and implications at his or her leisure, seeking further clarification if it's needed. If the participant is a knowledgeable conflict diagnostician, he or she can avoid overreacting to the other participant in the heat of the moment and can gain time to apply conflict diagnosis to the ongoing interaction. When the ODR participant does reply, he or she can write several drafts of a contemplated response and review it to ensure that it conveys the substantive, emotional, and relational content that he or she intends and that the communication will not have unintended negative side effects. Thus, an effective writer with experience and skill communicating online can masterfully overcome the perils of engaging the mouth before the brain is in gear.

Distance forms of communication can also help people who would be resistant in a traditional office setting, as when disputants are enraged by meeting face to face. Studies by Springer (1991) and Ranan and Blodgett (1983) make this point for telephone intervention, but the point is even more pertinent in text-based Internet communication, where voice inflection is absent. In addition, processes that allow participation from the disputant's home or office can make help available to individuals who are unable to attend office appointments due to physical disability (Evans, Fox, Pritzl, and Halar 1984; Springer 1991), physical illness, phobia, depression and other disabling mental problems, or inclement weather (Ranan and Blodgett 1983). Moreover, the flexibility of the Internet allows participation by all interested stakeholders, their agents and advocates, and important witnesses, as long as they have a personal computer and access to the Internet. The increased accessibility of services and service providers has been one aim of those seeking to provide ODR (Teitz 2001).

Like telephone-based intervention, the use of Internet-based dispute resolution processes can help equalize power imbalances based on the intimidation of physical proximity: An intimidated client can remain in his or her own home or office (Ranan and Blodgett 1983; Springer 1991), the object of fear is not physically present (Springer 1991), and the client can maintain a degree of privacy and anonymity (Evans, Fox, Pritzl, and Halar 1984). For example, Springer (1991) described a case in which a divorced mother and father were able to communicate effectively for the first time by teleconference because the mother was freed from seeing nonverbal cues from the father that she found intimidating. Like telephone-based therapeutic interventions (Evans, Fox, Pritzl, and Halar 1984; Springer 1991), ADR conducted in an Internet setting can save money and increase efficiency as well (Teitz 2001); as long as both disputants have access to the Internet, the cost savings can help equalize power between financial unequals. Power can be equalized in other ways as well. The anonymity of the Internet can mean that disputants may never know the race, gender, age, or physical appearance of those with whom they are dealing; thus, prejudices that might come into play in face-to-face interaction may not be activated. One commentator has noted that the anonymity of the ODR environment is often a prized commodity for disputants who have become comfortable operating in cyberspace and that this feature of ODR may be valued in its own right by cyber-disputants (Hang 2001).

ODR's flexibility and multimodality give it a substantial potential advantage over traditional distance communication, such as mail and telephone. Some platforms allow participants to choose from among synchronous and asynchronous methods and from among graphical and textual communication; as technology develops, it is quite likely that the use of audio- and videoconferencing over the Internet will become more common as well. Thus, participants with an understanding of conflict diagnosis can use the flexibility of ODR platforms to tailor the communication process to the needs of the people and the situation. Moreover, resources made possible by the technological power of Web-based resources (such as tools that allow disputants to assign relative values to multiple interests) allow disputants and their teams to refine their conflict diagnosis before and during the dispute resolution process.

The use of ODR also has some clear drawbacks compared to face-to-face ADR. Perhaps the most concern is expressed about the lack of nonverbal cues, which can block effective communication and can inhibit helpers from assessing the emotional status of clients (Ranan and Blodgett 1983). Although the use of the Internet frees the interaction from the emotional loading present in body language and tonal voice inflection, it also denies the participants access to the meanings present in these nonverbal signals. In other words, the lack of nonverbal cues adds to the ambiguity of communication. As communication becomes more ambiguous, conflict theory predicts that disputants will be more likely to project onto one another motives consistent with their beliefs about the nature of the conflict. Disputants caught up in escalating conflict or in a low-trust situation may assume the worst about the other disputant. Thus, in such situations, using a remote and nonvisual communication method might contribute to conflict escalation.

Asynchronous communication formats heighten the problem of misattribution of motive. Because there is no immediate reply to communication, mistaken impressions may fester for hours, even days or weeks. Thus, using an asynchronous remote communication method may produce meta-disputes, as each disputant defensively acts on inaccurately negative impressions about the other.

Meta-disputes can also be generated by the technology itself and by confusion over how the technology is functioning:

> Matt Randall, a Wyoming bank teller with an interest in first editions, purchased a used book through an Internet auction site from Ruth Smithe-Lovell, a woman living in Hawaii. The book arrived in very poor condition. Matt and Ruth consented to the use of the auction site's in-house ODR service, which involves e-mail–based negotiation, followed by mediation. During negotiation, an angry and suspicious Matt proposed that Ruth reduce her price by 60 percent and refund him the money right away. He demanded a response within forty-eight hours to show good faith. Matt sent the e-mail to Ruth at 3:30 P.M. on Tuesday. Unbenownst to Matt, his e-mail was held

up in transit for twenty-four hours before being sent to Ruth. It arrived in Ruth's e-mail inbox at 3:30 P.M. on Wednesday, just after she had checked her e-mail for the last time that day. By the time Ruth arrived at her computer the following morning, it had already been forty-two hours since Matt had sent his missive. Ruth immediately responded, stating with indignation that she did not send the book in bad condition. She demanded to know exactly what the problem was with the book, suspecting it had been damaged by the shipper. Actually, she planned to give him a discount, anyway, to show good faith, but she did not want to signal weakness by knuckling under right away. She mistyped Matt's e-mail address and sent the message, immediately thereafter signing off the computer and attending a day of meetings. The message was returned undelivered by the server. Ruth discovered the undelivered message, and her error, on Friday morning. By this time, Matt was furious. His mistrust in Ruth had seemingly been confirmed: In his mind, she had proven herself to be a flake and a con artist. No matter what Ruth might do at this point, there's little she can do to restore trust, and if sent to mediation the assigned mediator will face a daunting task.

Anyone who relies on e-mail will recognize this exchange as familiar in many respects. Those who do a lot of communicating online are used to technology glitches. The problem is that, in an escalated conflict, angry disputants are likely to attribute problems to evil behavior by the other disputant, rather than to malfunctioning technology.

Another problem with ODR has to do with the lack of a human face. ODR platforms reduce or eliminate disputants' abilities to see their counterpart's emotional reactions or to hear their voice inflections. Thus, the empowerment that comes from observing the nonverbal aspects of communication, and the recognition that comes from having one's emotional state validated, is lost (Hang 2001). For this reason, disputants may not experience the same emotional closure and reconciliation when settlement occurs, and the element of psychological ownership of the outcome may be compromised. In addition, because the nonverbal element is missing, suspicious disputants are likely to fill in the missing information with attributions of the other disputant's evil motives.

The lack of nonverbal information also presents difficulties for ODR providers. Facilitative neutrals, such as mediators, may be denied the nonverbal data they need to correctly evaluate clients' meanings, attitudes, and emotions. This is information the client is unlikely to provide the mediator verbally, even when asked, and, without seeing the person face to face, the neutral may have difficulty interpreting the force of emotion behind a written communication. Of course, direct verbal inquiry to confirm an emotional state (as in "I'm wondering if you felt angry as you wrote your last e-mail") may be ineffective—the disputant may be unaware of, ashamed of, or self-protective of feelings, and the question may shame the disputant if made in the presence of the other. If the ODR provider makes an incorrect assumption about a disputant's emotional state, this can spell disaster for effective dispute resolution—it can be extremely alienating to be the subject of mistaken assumptions about feelings. Therefore, it may be very difficult for the neutral to act in ways that affirm and recognize an online disputant's perspective and emotional state.

Commentators have also noted concerns with the anonymous nature of the Internet. Some believe that it is easy for disputants to disconnect from an anonymous interaction. Thus, ODR participants may be more likely to abandon the process when the negotiation gets tough. It's easy for people to overlook a pending ODR process when they are busy with other things: The computer doesn't call them on the phone or require them to keep an appointment. Thus, experienced ODR service providers find that they must make a special effort to keep participants engaged. When asynchronous methods are used, it is often necessary to include special incentives, such as schedules or deadlines, to keep the process from slowing so much that communication ceases to be effective. Moreover, there is some evidence that cyberspace anonymity is associated with loosened inhibitions on offensive or impolite communication (Bordone 1998, 180–181); however, there is no specific research to determine whether there is a greater incidence of such language, which is likely to escalate conflict, in ODR, as compared with face-to-face ADR.

Although ODR can equalize power, it can also produce power imbalances. ODR can severely disempower those who are uncomfortable using the written word or who express themselves poorly in writing. These individuals will be less able to communicate ideas, interests, concerns, proposals, and reactions. As with other written forms of communication, poor writing used in an ODR process can also disempower the writer by projecting a less intelligent, less able persona to the other participants. In addition, ODR can disempower those who rely heavily on nonverbal communication to express themselves or to read the communications of others. The advent of videoconferenced ODR should allay this problem somewhat.

ODR also disempowers those with poor or limited access to technology. For example, a disputant with outdated hardware or software or a poor Internet service provider has to work harder and spend more time engaging in ODR than someone who has up-to-date technology. In similar fashion, a disputant who must take public transportation to a public library to gain access to the Internet is impaired, relative to someone with a high-quality system at home. A lack of proficiency or comfort with using the computer and the Internet is likely to create similar impediments to empowerment. For disputants who are consumers in the Internet marketplace, these power considerations are often magnified. To use ODR in dealing with a dispute in the online marketplace, the consumer is likely a first-time user of an ODR process, whereas the merchant is likely a repeat customer, more familiar with the hardware, software, rules of the process, and ODR providers.

Although it can disempower, it should not be forgotten that ODR can empower as well. Many individuals have disempowering qualities, such as physical appearance, problems expressing themselves orally, or an inability to travel to the site of a face-to-face negotiation, that are eliminated by ODR.[10]

---

[10] For another view of the strengths and weaknesses of ODR, see Braeutigam 2006.

Legal Issues in ODR. ODR—and cyber-disputes—raise tough legal issues that are only now being faced by governments and legal policy makers. Conflict diagnosticians should become familiar with the issues facing the development of ODR so that they can follow the developments in this interesting and complex field as they happen.

Transactions conducted in cyberspace raise a basic philosophical and practical issue: Does it make sense to consider the transaction as having occurred within one or more physical territories, or should cyber-transactions be considered borderless? Consider the following example:

> Japanese citizen Kawamoto and Belgian citizen Moreau engage in a barter transaction using an online auction site. Later, they have a dispute about their transaction and agree to use an ODR service. The service markets itself as exclusively online, uses servers (the computers that hold its software) in several countries, and offers Web pages and communications platforms in English, Spanish, French, Danish, and Japanese. Mediators from anywhere may register to provide services, and the ODR service requires them to post resumés so that the participants can select the most qualified candidate.

Does it make sense to consider this potential mediation as "occurring in a specific country or jurisdiction" in any meaningful sense? When an ADR provider offers ODR services, one way of thinking about the service is that it occurs in the nonterritorial environment of cyberspace—or, as Robert C. Bordone (1998, 180–181) creatively calls it, "Cyberia." Thus, beyond the choice-of-law questions posed by the dispute itself, it is important to ask the question "Is the ODR process governed by the law of any specific territory or territories, and how can we tell which ones?" This question is important because legal considerations—such as confidentiality during ODR, the ODR provider's liability for malpractice, the enforceability of a decision to engage in ODR, and the enforceability of the outcome—may turn on the answer. Even if a particular nation's laws are referred to as being binding on the process, if legal action is brought in a different forum, that national court may not have an obligation to recognize the provision. The problem is particularly acute for consumer transactions because consumers are not sophisticated in the world of international commerce and may be unaware of the pitfalls of transacting in the absence of universally applicable consumer protection.

No one has an easy answer to this question. Some legal experts have argued that the cyberspace world should have its own law—some are advocating a "world government," others an international cyber-court, others a treaty or convention. However, without international consensus on the development of a world government, it would be impossible to ensure the adoption or enforcement of such laws. Individuals in cyberspace can voluntarily agree to abide by a set of rules, but no enforcement process is universally applicable, although international treaties and conventions developed to facilitate international commerce and the enforceability of international arbitration awards can help. One group of ODR experts points to the fact that consensual processes are more likely to be used in cyber-disputing because of the legal vacuum: Although it may be difficult to enforce an arbitration award against a recalcitrant loser, it is more likely that a mediated agreement will be followed, because both disputants consented to the settlement (Katsh, Rifkin, and Gaitenby 2000).

Voluntary and consensual mechanisms are enforced primarily by the threat of publicity that inappropriate or dishonest behavior can inflict. Some other processes make the Internet a slightly less dangerous place to transact business:

- *The trustmark process,* in which Internet providers promise to abide by a code of ethics and a dispute resolution process developed by a watchdog organization. Transgression can mean loss of the trustmark, with a consequent loss of business.

- *Escrowing or bonding,* requiring the disputants temporarily to post assets sufficient to cover anticipated future disputes with a neutral and trusted third party. Should a dispute arise and one disputant refuse to abide by the result of an ODR process, the escrowed amount can be released to the aggrieved disputant.

- *The use of credit cards in online consumer purchasing.* This technique is useful mainly in the United States, where consumer-protection laws limit monetary losses to the purchaser if he or she notifies the card issuer in writing of a problem within a certain period of time.

Until a universal convention is adopted to regulate ODR, it helps to specify choice of law and choice of forum before an online dispute resolution process is begun. Indeed, the ideal transaction will specify choice of law for the transaction itself and will have a separate provision regulating the resolution of disputes.

EXERCISES, PROJECTS, AND "THOUGHT EXPERIMENTS"

1. Research the law and rules for the United States District Court for the district in which you live. If you don't reside in the United States, choose any jurisdiction's court system. Find the rules or statutes, if any, providing for a nonbinding evaluation process to be used as ADR in litigated cases. If you cannot find any, choose a different jurisdiction. Attach a copy of the statutes or rules to your answers to the following questions:

   a. What sorts of cases can be referred to nonbinding evaluation?

   b. Is referral mandatory? If so, under what circumstances?

   c. What kind or kinds of nonbinding evaluation are available under these rules or statutes? (Remember to consider the format of the process, not just the name of the process, in answering this question.)

   d. Are the ADR neutrals private entrepreneurs, court employees, or something else?

    e. Who pays for the process, and how?

    f. Is litigation postponed to accommodate the ADR process? If so, for how long?

    g. Do you think this statutory scheme is a good one? Identify the strengths and weaknesses of the statutes or rules. What would you do to improve this system's ADR program?

2. Nonbinding evaluation (including nonbinding arbitration) is the most widely used form of ADR in civil (non–family law) court-connected programs. Why do you think this is so? Is it the best choice, or would you recommend something else for these sorts of disputes? Justify your response.

3. Should early neutral evaluators be required to be qualified attorneys or judges? Why or why not? Are there some circumstances under which evaluators should be attorneys and some not? If you think so, what are these circumstances, and why the distinction?

4. Is confidentiality more, less, or equally important in nonbinding evaluation, compared with mediation? Justify your opinion.

5. Should the outcome of a nonbinding evaluation receive greater protection from disclosure than an outcome in mediation? Why or why not?

6. Under what circumstances (if any) would it be appropriate for a judge in a litigated case referred to a nonbinding evaluation process to be informed of the outcome of the procedure? Justify your opinion.

7. In a court-connected nonbinding evaluation program, should incentives to settle be built into the program? For example, some jurisdictions provide that, if the case does not settle and if litigation does not improve a litigant's outcome over the evaluator's assessment by a specified percentage, the litigant is assessed monetary penalties, such as being required to foot the entire bill for the evaluator's services or being required to pay court costs for litigation. Is this an appropriate policy for courts to adopt? Why or why not?

8. Identify the following ADR processes offered by retired judges—as mediation, arbitration, nonbinding evaluation, or a mixed (hybrid) process:

    a. Gordon Gould is a retired judge. He offers disputants an opportunity to present their case before him. He then uses his extensive background on the bench as he gives his opinion about what the case is worth. Afterward, he sits with the disputants and tries to help them work out a settlement. If the case does not settle, he issues a binding written decision, which he promises is based on fairness as well as the law.

    b. Eileen Einhorn is a retired judge. She offers disputants the chance to present their case to her. Afterward, she meets with each disputant and his or her lawyer separately, where she uses her extensive experience on the bench to assist the teams in exploring the strengths and weaknesses of their individual cases. Einhorn also looks for any overlap in the positions of the two sides. If there is an overlap, she uses shuttle diplomacy to help the disputants reach a settlement.

c. Norton Nelson is a retired judge. He offers disputants the chance to present their case to him. Afterward, he uses his extensive experience on the bench to give the disputants an idea of what he thinks would happen if they took the case to court. He generally gives a range of likely outcomes.

d. George Garrettson is a retired judge. He offers the disputants a chance to present their case to him. Afterward, he uses his extensive experience on the bench to give the disputants a decision in the matter. The decision is considered binding. He advertises that he provides as fair and effective a decision as a court of law but at a fraction of the time and expense.

9. *Internet or library research.* Study the American Arbitration Association's Commercial Dispute Resolution Procedures (the association's Web site is located at *http://www.adr.org*). Find the provision that allows for mediation windowing. Cite the provision. Do you think this is a good provision to include in an arbitration agreement? Why or why not?

10. Frank, a buyer, and Michelle, a seller, are disputing over the sale of a baby grand piano. Frank says that Michelle misrepresented the condition of the piano when he agreed to pay $9,500 for it and that they agreed she would be responsible for transporting the piano to Frank's residence. Michelle contends that she made no misrepresentations, that she offered to allow Frank to have an appraiser inspect the piano before finalizing the sales price, and that they agreed the piano would be Frank's responsibility to move. Their written contract specifies only the transaction date, the names of the parties, and the price. Michelle has recently taken a course in ADR and wants to submit the dispute to a mediator. Frank is absolutely opposed to any process that will not result in a final settlement; however, he is receptive using med-arb. Is med-arb a good option for these individuals? Why or why not? In responding, consider what alternatives the disputants have if med-arb is not used.

11. Most court-connected and other multimodal ADR programs provide for a single confidentiality rule that applies across the board to all the processes involved. For example, look at Section 574 of the Administrative Dispute Resolution Act of 1996 (excerpted in Chapter 4). This provision applies to any ADR process, including facilitative and evaluative forms of mediation, arbitration, and any nonbinding evaluation form. Are the reasons that confidentiality is important or useful the same for all these types of ADR processes? Should the rules be different for different processes? If so, why? If not, why not? If different rules are adopted for different sorts of ADR, will the law of confidentiality become unnecessarily complicated or unpredictable? Isn't that the case, anyway, since there are exceptions to confidentiality that vest discretion to determine confidentiality in a judge?

12. *Research project.* Research the court-connected ADR program in effect in the federal district court that serves your area. Answer the following questions in a research paper:

    a. What forms of dispute resolution are used in this court system? What do they call each of these processes?

    b. Summarize the history of court-connected ADR in this district court. How long has ADR been used?

    c. Obtain statistics on the number and types of disputes sent to this program. What are the trends?

    d. Does it appear that this program is resulting in a reduction of backlog in this court? Discuss any evidence that supports your assertion.

    e. Are statistics available that track client and advocate satisfaction with this program? If so, summarize the results.

    f. Examine the rules that apply to this program. They may appear in the rules of the court, as well as in the Federal Rules of Civil Procedure. Summarize the procedural rules with respect to this program.

    g. Evaluate the program yourself. Is this a good program? Is it merely better than nothing? Could it be improved? If so, how? Is there more information the court would need to collect to make an evaluation more meaningful? Be sure to justify your answers to these questions.

13. In this chapter, dispute review boards are described as having statistically spectacular success in resolving construction disputes: Only 2 percent of disputes submitted to these entities are outstanding following the issuance of the evaluation. To what might one attribute this success? In considering this question, review the ideas in Chapter 2 and, in particular, consider the importance of underlying disputant interests. What interests of the disputants in a construction dispute might make such disputes ripe for rapid resolution?

RECOMMENDED READINGS

Alfini, J. J. 1991. Trashing, bashing and hashing it out: Is this the end of "good mediation"? *Florida State University Law Review* 19 (Summer):47–75.

Braeutigam, A.M. 2006. Fusses that fit online: Online mediation in non-commercial contexts. *Appalachian Journal of Law* 5 (Spring), 275–301.

Burger, W. W. 1982. *Isn't there a better way?* Annual Report on the State of the Judiciary, presented at the 1982 midyear meeting of the American Bar Association, Chicago, January 24. Reprinted as Burger, W. W. 1982. Isn't there a better way? *ABA Journal 68* (March):274.

Costatino, C. A., and C. S. Merchant. 1996. *Designing conflict management systems: A guide to creating productive and healthy organizations.* San Francisco: Jossey-Bass.

Hang, L. Q. 2001. Online dispute resolution systems: The future of cyberspace law. *Santa Clara Law Review* 41:837–866.

Henderson, D. A. 1995. Avoiding litigation with the mini-trial: The corporate bottom line as dispute resolution technique. *South Carolina Law Review* 46 (Winter):237–262.

Lambros, T. D. 1984. *The summary jury trial and other methods of dispute resolution.* 103 Fs.R.D. 465–477.

Meltzer, D. L. 1998. The federal workplace ombuds. *Ohio State Journal on Dispute Resolution* 13:549–609.

Nolan-Haley, J. M. 2001. Dispute resolution in the court system. In *Alternative dispute resolution in a nutshell* (pp. 197–219). St. Paul, MN: West.

Nolan-Haley, J. M. 2001. Hybrid dispute resolution procedures. In *Alternative dispute resolution in a nutshell* (pp. 220–235). St. Paul, MN: West.

Plapinger, E., and D. Stienstra. 1996. ADR and settlement programs in the federal district courts: A sourcebook for judges and lawyers. Federal Judicial Center and CPR Institute for Dispute Resolution. *http://www.fjc.gov/public/home. nsf/autoframe?openform&url_l=/public/home.nsf/inavgeneral?openpage&url_ r=/public/home.nsf/pages/119* (accessed February 4, 2009).

Posner, R. A. 1986. The summary jury trial and other methods of alternate dispute resolution: Some cautionary observations. *University of Chicago Law Review* 53 (Spring):366–393.

Riskin, L. L., and J. E. Westbrook (eds.). 1997. *Dispute resolution and lawyers,* 2nd ed. (pp. 589–657). St. Paul, MN: West.

Sabatino, J. M. 1998. ADR as "litigation lite": Procedural and evidentiary norms embedded within alternative dispute resolution. *Emory Law Journal* 47:1289–1349.

Sander, F. E. A. 1976. Varieties of dispute processing. 70 FRD 111.

Streeter-Schaefer, H. A. 2001. A look at court mandated civil mediation. *Drake Law Review* 49:367–389.

Teitz, L. E. 2001. Providing legal services for the middle class in cyberspace: The promise and challenge of on-line dispute resolution. *Fordham Law Review* 70 (December):985–1016.

Ury, W., J. M. Brett, and S. B. Goldberg. 1988. *Getting disputes resolved: Designing systems to cut the costs of conflict.* San Francisco: Jossey-Bass.

7

Putting It All Together: Selecting Optimal ADR Processes for Clients and Disputes

There is one thing stronger than all the armies in the world, and that is an idea whose time has come.

—Victor Hugo

In this chapter, you will learn . . .

- the advantages and disadvantages of mediation, arbitration, nonbinding evaluation, mixed/hybrid ADR processes, and multimodal ADR processes.
- the potential for careful selection of ADR to improve the delivery of legal services.
- a leading approach to selecting a dispute resolution process and provider, known as Fitting the Forum to the Fuss.
- an alternative approach to selecting a dispute resolution process and provider, suggested by the principles discussed in this textbook.

Many scholars date the birth of the modern ADR movement to the 1976 Pound Conference, convened at Harvard Law School to consider how to reform and improve the court system. The event was named for Roscoe Pound, former dean of Harvard Law School, who, along with business visionary Mary Parker Follett, had sought to apply some of the concepts you've learned about in Chapter 2 to the resolution of legal disputes (Hurder 2007). At the conference, Frank E. A. Sander, often regarded as the father of the modern ADR movement, proposed that the courthouse of the future would offer disputants a multidoor dispute resolution system, with a panoply of options, such as litigation, arbitration, mediation, summary jury trial, and other ADR processes. Professor Sander has been a leading proponent of the concept that disputes and disputants have unique characteristics that affect what dispute resolution process is best suited to the situation. He has called the process of matching dispute resolution processes to cases and clients "Fitting the Forum to the Fuss" (Sander and Goldberg 1994).

In Chapter 2 of this textbook, you were introduced to a theory-based set of skills (conflict diagnosis, covered in detail in Online Appendix B) that can be used to understand interpersonal conflict, particularly legal disputes. If you've tried to use these principles in your everyday conflicts, you may have found that they open your eyes to important aspects of these situations that you may not have previously recognized. These realizations can lead to more profitable, less destructive, more creative approaches to resolving conflicts. Conflict diagnosis concepts also help to explain the uses, strengths, and weaknesses of the ADR processes discussed in this textbook. In this chapter, we'll put it all together, looking directly at the advantages and disadvantages of each form of ADR, as well as at some methods of selecting ADR processes. As you review the concepts set forth in this chapter you may want to refer back to Chapter 2 or to Online Appendix B, as needed.

ADVANTAGES AND DISADVANTAGES OF ADR PROCESSES

Legal professionals increasingly find themselves in the position of recommending ADR processes to clients. Even if they do not recommend processes, legal professionals whose clients are required by a court to submit to an ADR process may be in the position of selecting an ADR provider.

A first step in attaining expertise in helping clients to select ADR processes is to understand the relative advantages and disadvantages of each process. We'll illuminate this understanding in the pages that follow.

MEDIATION

If you are a disputant, is mediation appropriate to resolve your conflict? If you are an advocate or an advocate's assistant, is mediation the best option for your client? Basic to answering these questions is the issue of what mediation can offer, compared with the alternatives.

Of all the ADR techniques considered in this textbook, mediation departs most radically from the traditional U.S. cultural version of what conflict resolution "should" look like—the "invisible veil" blueprint for resolving conflict. For this reason, comparing the advantages and disadvantages of mediation with those of litigation and other forms of ADR is a critical task for anyone trying to understand the field of dispute resolution. This comparison reveals the heart of how the theories we looked at in Chapter 2 apply to the real world of dispute resolution.

As we have seen, mediation is a highly diverse process. The advantages and disadvantages of using mediation to resolve conflict depend on which of the many types of mediation is called into play. It is possible to talk generally about some of mediation's special qualities and possibilities. In general, in the discussion that follows it will be assumed, unless otherwise noted, that a highly facilitative form of mediation is being compared with the alternatives. As you contemplate the points raised in this chapter, try to keep in mind the differences between highly facilitative mediation and the form of mediation that more closely resembles adversarial negotiation.

Advantages of Mediation. The evaluation of a process of conflict resolution depends on the perspective taken. Methods of resolving a conflict might be evaluated as very effective, for example, if a short-term perspective were taken but very ineffective if a long-term perspective were taken. Or a method of resolving a conflict might be very effective in meeting one person's financial goals yet very poor in settling an overall conflictual relationship. Or a settlement might effectively meet the disputant's needs, but at the expense of dependent constituents. There is no more important time to keep these considerations in mind than in our discussion of the advantages and disadvantages of mediation.

Efficiency Considerations. Time and money considerations—efficiency arguments—were the original impetus for the ADR movement in the United States. Early comments on the litigation explosion and the need for alternatives prominently cite the high cost of litigation, the long delays to trial, and the burden on court systems of our litigious society (e.g., Burger 1982). Thus, many early efforts to create ADR programs focused on considerations of immediate savings of time and money for clients and courts. When these programs were evaluated, researchers focused primarily on comparing the time required to mediate cases to settlement with that required to litigate to judgment, as well as on the money spent on moving the cases to their conclusion.

It is beyond refute that mediation is cheaper and quicker than litigation. Mediation is an informal process that does not require discovery, pleading, motions practice, hearings, or rules of evidence. As a result, even when lawyers are involved at every step of the mediation process, it is both much cheaper and much more rapid than litigation. If the disputants handle the mediation themselves, then they also save additional attorney's fees. Resources are conserved for the court system as well as for the individual disputants when mediation is used. It is likely that the primary reason lawyers and clients choose mediation (and other forms of ADR) is to save time and money (Meyerson 2005, 78).

The efficiency of mediation is often compared with that of litigation because it is assumed that cases that are mediated would otherwise be litigated. If mediation is compared with lawyer-assisted settlement, then the direct time and money savings of mediation are less certain. Some studies appear to indicate that mediation is still quicker and cheaper than lawyer-assisted negotiation, but others do not show such an advantage.

If mediation is compared on a short-term efficiency basis with other ADR processes, such as arbitration and nonbinding evaluation, for its ability to shorten the time to outcome, the picture becomes still more cloudy. Arbitration, as we saw in Chapter 5, ranges from a highly informal, inexpensive, and rapid process to something as expensive, slow, and complex as the most bureaucratically snarled lawsuit. Nonbinding evaluation (Chapter 6) is generally designed to be more efficient than litigation (that's partially the function of nonbinding evaluation: to get a sense of what a court would do without investing time and money for a lawsuit), but, again, the amount of time and money spent is highly variable. Arbitration has the advantage that someone will be declared the victor when the procedure is over, and the issues submitted to arbitration (if not the overall conflict) will be ended. Mediation, in contrast, will not necessarily result in a settlement.

Another way of viewing efficiency considerations is to use the conflict diagnosis perspective discussed in Chapter 2. Litigation, arbitration, and nonbinding evaluation are dispute resolution processes that approach conflict from a positional-bargaining paradigm. That is, each of these processes operates on the assumption that conflict is to be resolved through the clash of inconsistent positions, with litigation and arbitration settling the conflict through the choice of one of the positions and nonbinding evaluation depending on a softening of disputant positions based on information received in the evaluation. This is true of highly evaluative mediation as well. Purely facilitative mediation will theoretically have a different effect. Facilitative mediation generally operates on an interest-based negotiation model, whereas transformative and narrative mediation focus not on settlement but on creating personal transformation conducive to the resolution of conflict. Positional bargaining approaches to resolving conflict take less upfront time and effort than interest-based and transformative processes, because disputant interests analysis, brainstorming, searches for objective decisional standards, empowerment, recognition, and narrative reframing are not involved: Positional bargaining marches straight into the seeking of an outcome. Thus, if the time and money expenditures required to attain settlement—any settlement—are the only relevant considerations, a positional-bargaining dispute resolution process appears most efficient. Nonbinding evaluation and arbitration alternatives are likely to be even quicker and cheaper than evaluative mediation if the parties have vastly different perceptions of facts or law because they would likely reach impasse without hard evidence to refute their extreme aspirations.

On the other hand, if a longer-term view is taken, it seems likely that a dispute resolution process will be more efficient if it is facilitative and if evaluative elements are avoided. This is because these facilitative techniques are more likely than positional bargaining to lead to the efficient and effective use of joint disputant resources. Moreover, a facilitative process is likely to resolve the conflict more permanently than positional-bargaining alternatives because it is associated with a higher quality of consent and psychological ownership of the outcome than settlements produced by more adversarial alternatives (McDermott and Obar, 2004). Psychological ownership is associated with reduced levels of conflict and re-litigation after settlement, thus making a cooperative principled-bargaining process possibly more cost effective in the long run. In addition, research suggests that mediated agreements are complied with to a greater degree than are judicial awards (Kelly 1996, 377; King 1999, n. 331).

Thus, whether facilitative mediation is more efficient than informal adjudicative and nonbinding evaluative processes depends on the perspective taken.

From Overburdened Courts to Vanishing Trials: Evolving Concerns About the Judiciary

Ironically, the concerns of the legal community for overcrowded courtrooms have been supplanted by concerns over the apparent demise of evidentiary trials in the U.S. legal system. In 2003, Marc Galanter initiated a survey of adjudications, primarily in federal court, that tended to show a shift away from evidentiary trials of legal claims. For example, he notes that during the past sixty years, although case filings have shot up, the rate of civil federal lawsuits resolved by evidentiary trial fell 90 percent (Galanter 2006). This trend is in absolute numbers as well as proportional to case filings. Since Galanter's research was published, countless pages have been written by legal scholars discussing the significance of this trend, and the role of ADR in contributing to it. A number of alarm bells have been raised. Perhaps the most important concerns are for erosion of the availability of legal precedent and hence legal reform and the evolution of public values, as well as increased opportunity for oppression coming from use of private forums to resolve disputes. However, others note that the creation of legal precedent and public disposition through pretrial dispositions and appellate review have not diminished, that private dispute resolution has always been the rule, and that the historically disenfranchised have more, rather than less, access to courts today.

If a short-term, narrow perspective is taken, informal adjudication appears to be the most efficient choice, particularly when widely divergent perceptions of fact and law are involved. On the other hand, if a longer-term, broader perspective is taken, facilitative mediation appears to be the more efficient alternative.

Conflict Management and Prevention. It is in the area of reducing and preventing conflict that mediation really shines, relative not only to litigation but also to arbitration and nonbinding evaluation. To understand why, it is useful to return to the cooperation-competition theory of Morton Deutsch (see Chapter 2).

We know from our consideration of conflict theory that using cooperative, collaborative techniques tends to prevent a destructive conflict escalation cycle from occurring, to promote cooperation, to build mutual trust, and to create solutions that better meet all disputants' most deeply seated concerns and needs. We further know that the use of consensual techniques to resolve conflict, particularly collaborative conflict resolution techniques that reject the use of positional bargaining in favor of a search to meet mutual interests, tends to create psychological ownership of the resulting settlement.

Even without mediation's special qualities, just bringing a neutral third party into the discussion often improves the quality of the negotiations by changing the dynamics of the interpersonal interactions. Neither disputant wants to lose face by looking like an irrational "bad person;" hence, the mere presence of the mediator in the discussion often improves the disputants' negotiation behavior.

More than that, however, mediation presents special opportunities to address the unique problems presented by interpersonal conflict. Good mediators use the mediation process to get a deep-seated understanding of what drives the conflict, revealing the best routes to resolution—in other words, they determine the sources of the conflict and the nature of impediments and barriers to effective resolution. Good mediators also involve the disputants themselves in understanding the dynamics of their conflict so that they themselves have the roots of the conflict revealed to them and are personally able to search for and understand the available solutions. Moreover, mediation is specifically targeted to interrupt a cycle of competition and encourage formation of a cycle of cooperation. Mediators use a number of facilitative techniques to reframe perceptions, build mutual trust, create a sense of personal validation on the part of each disputant, and avoid and defuse meta-disputes. Mediators can also, by virtue of their neutral position in the negotiation, create communication opportunities where there were none. For example, a point or suggestion that, if made by the other disputant, would be reactively devalued can be more easily "heard" when made by the mediator.

Adjudicative and evaluative dispute resolution processes, on the other hand, do nothing to address the conflict cycle. Indeed, because they emphasize the merits of each disputant's case, these processes tend to nudge the disputants into viewing the conflict as a zero-sum game with a winner and a loser, increasing the probability of conflict escalation. Divorce mediators often hear this concept verbalized by new clients. A typical comment of such a client is "I want to try mediation, and I don't want lawyers to be involved. I'm afraid that, if I or the other client goes to a lawyer, we'll end up in a war. We both want to avoid letting this thing get out of hand. Please help us." Such clients sense a truth about mediation: It is more capable than other methods of reining in the natural tendency of individuals to be swept into positional bargaining and then an escalating competitive conflict cycle.

"This is where your mother and I had our first argument."

The Cartoon Bank

Relatedly, mediation can have important conflict management benefits by streamlining the conflict or dispute—even if agreement isn't reached—by clarifying the conflict, narrowing the issues, and often making communication more civil. Thus, even if other methods are needed to resolve the conflict, mediation makes these other methods more efficient. As evidence of this effect of mediation, some research indicates that disputants who fail to settle during mediation are more likely to settle prior to trial than disputants who do not attend mediation (Kelly 1996, 376).

Controversies About Mediation: Is Mediation "Second-Class Justice"?

The question here is certainly a hard one to answer because the term *second-class justice* is poorly defined. Moreover, the question requires a body of social science research that currently doesn't exist.

A number of scholars, including Owen Fiss (1984) and Laura Nader (1993), have criticized the ADR movement, contending that the diversion of so-called small cases to ADR relegates them to second-class justice. Although the argument takes varying forms, the gist is that the push to increase harmony in relations at the expense of the adversarial process is an attempt by the powerful to pacify the less powerful—in other words, an effort at social control (Nader 1993). This argument has intrinsic logic: It seems obvious that a high-power disputant will find it easier to get his or her interests addressed in a consensual process than will a low-power disputant. Moreover, many critical reforms in the treatment of the disempowered have come from the appellate litigation process.

Underlying these arguments is an assumption that court-based adversarial processes are the best way to protect the interests of the disempowered. However, empirical study to date has failed to find clear evidence that either litigation or ADR provides better outcomes for the disempowered. In addition, we are unable to measure the impact of overall culture on empowerment or disempowerment. Are the disempowered better or worse off in a culture that promotes mediation? Will the disempowered forego the pursuit of appellate litigation because mediation is available to them? If we do this research, and see certain trends, how do we know whether they were caused by ADR? As law professor Deborah Rhode has put it in her evenhanded critique of both ADR supporters and detractors:

> [C]ritics who denounce ADR as second-class justice need to consider how often first class is available, and on what terms. The deficiencies common in alternative dispute resolution are chronic in conventional adjudication as well. Private settlements are the norm, not the exception, and procedural protections that are available in theory are often missing in practice. Imbalances of wealth, power, and information skew outcomes even in cases receiving the closest judicial oversight. As the title of Professor Marc Galanter's now classic article put it, the "Haves Come Out Ahead" in most legal settings. *(Rhode 1999, 1011)*

It may make more sense to ask "What attributes of particular ADR programs and processes could result in second-class justice?" Coercive forms of mediation, mediation that imposes burdens disproportionately on disempowered disputants (as when the fees for mediation are very high), as well as mediation conducted by individuals who are insensitive to the impact of power imbalance, could be predicted to be egregious in impact. It makes sense to assume that mediation can be damaging either to disempowered disputants unable to hold their own during negotiation or if the most important source of the conflict is a structural or personal power imbalance. On the other hand, disputants sometimes comment on the empowerment gained from dealing with the other disputant in an effective consensual process. The sense of empowerment may depend on multiple factors: Some commentators note that mediation provides some disputants, particularly women, with a voice that is missing in litigation, whereas others comment that minority disputants are more comfortable in mediation and get better results if they use a mediator who shares their racial/ethnic identity. And litigation may not provide an improvement over mediation. Far more study is needed to explore the conditions under which mediation might be an improvement over litigation, and vice versa. The answers, if our current state of knowledge is any indication, are likely to be complicated. Presuming that litigation is a better option without any empirical basis for the presumption is no more logical than presuming that harmony is inherently better than contention.

Relationship Preservation. Mediation is widely regarded as the most effective dispute resolution process for preserving ongoing disputant relationships. This advantage of mediation is particularly important in situations in which disputants will be required to deal with each other after the immediate dispute is resolved. Examples of such situations include divorce conflict, disputes between neighbors, disputes between corporate shareholder groups, landlord-tenant disputes, parent-teacher conflicts, business partners disputes over partnership agreements and responsibilities, employee grievance situations, and disputes between buyers and sellers in long-term supply requirements relationships.

In these common situations, mediation can be invaluable, offering the chance to clarify misunderstandings, mend broken promises, set the stage for an apology to occur, and improve aspects of the relationship that have not functioned well in the past. Mediation typically provides the disputants with a communication structure in which they are required to relate to one another in a mutually respectful, amicable, clear, and self-assertive manner, and they are assisted in doing so. Communication lessons learned during mediation can have long-term benefits for the continued constructiveness of the relationship. In addition, mediation's flexibility—its ability to offer experimental, partial, and interim settlements—allows disputants to fine-tune contractual arrangements, maximizing the likelihood that a long-term relationship will remain functional and adapt to change. Thus, mediation can have relationship-preserving qualities not available in negotiation, adjudication, and nonbinding evaluation.

Comprehensiveness. Mediation has the capacity to deal more comprehensively with interpersonal conflict than other alternatives.

Let's begin with litigation. Litigation deals only with issues that can be stated as causes of action. If you have a dispute with another individual that cannot be set into this mold, it cannot be addressed in litigation. Consider the following anecdote, which is based on an actual lawsuit that was tried in a Maryland state trial court:

> The two litigants were neighbors who didn't get along. Their conflict had simmered along ever since litigant 2 had moved into the neighborhood nearly a decade before the trial. The conflict had started with minor affronts (such as litigant 2's children chasing balls into litigant 1's yard) and had escalated to the point that anything negative that happened to one neighbor was automatically attributed to the other neighbor. For example, if litigant 1 found dog droppings on his lawn, he attributed it to litigant 2's intentionally and out of spite allowing his dog to "do his business" on the lawn. If litigant 2 heard a car engine gunning late at night, he assumed litigant 1 had instructed his teenage son to annoy him. Obviously, a great many assumptions were made by both disputants about the role of the other in creating problems, all of them negative. Finally, one of the litigants caught the other committing what constituted an actionable tort: One litigant had scratched the paint job on the other's car. The victim sued, and the defendant was able to come up with enough legally

Controversies About Mediation:
Does Mediation Permanently Improve Relationships?

Despite anecdotal accounts of the capacity of mediation to improve relationships, and despite clear evidence of short-term improvements, empirical study has not shown consistent long-term benefit. Early research in Denver, Colorado, indicated short-term reductions in acrimony in parents undergoing mediation (Kuhn 1984, n. 71). Moreover, there is evidence of reduced rates of re-litigation among disputants who undergo mediation, suggesting that disputants who mediate learn more constructive ways to resolve future conflicts (Vestal 1999).

Law professor Carol J. King, reviewing research on divorce mediation (King 1999, 433–434), comments that one study "found that children of mediated divorce seemed better-adjusted, and that their parents were less hostile to each other," compared with a group that litigated, whereas another study found "perceived improved parental relationships among the mediation participants in the year following the divorce." However, "[t]he difference between the mediation and adjudication groups did not persist at the two-year post-divorce mark." She also notes that research on re-litigation rates seems to indicate that the rates for returning to court become more similar as the years go by, becoming indistinguishable after five years (King 1999, 435), although it is not clear whether this trend is primarily due to increases in re-litigation by mediating disputants or to the dying out of re-litigation by adversarial disputants. King comments on the brevity of mediation and the complexity of the means by which divorcing parents address their issues as reasons not to expect mediation to act as a miracle cure for escalated conflict.

These findings are consistent with Deutsch's theory (see Chapter 2), which would predict that, as the mediation process became more distant in time, the events that promote the escalation of conflict would eventually "swamp" gains made during mediation. Moreover, mediated interventions that do not feature improving negotiation skills would be predicted to have minimal, if any, effect on improving long-term relationships. Consistent with this interpretation, Joan Kelly, reviewing studies of the impact of divorce mediation on disputants, notes "small but more often short-lived" increases in cooperation and communication accompanying mediation and suggests that the inconsistencies in findings are probably due to variations in the duration of mediation, the characteristics of the clients, and the styles used by the mediators (Kelly 1996, 379). As we have learned, there are styles of mediation that focus on getting a quick settlement, not on facilitating effective negotiation. In the modern legal landscape, in which mediation of legal disputes has become increasingly "adversarialized," one would expect the impact of mediation on relationships to be minimal. Some might argue that this is a good reason to emphasize mediation and other processes that teach nonadversarial negotiation skills and conflict diagnosis.

---

nonfrivolous grievances to file a counterclaim. The case failed to settle, and eventually it went to trial. After two days of trial, the jury, obviously exasperated, found for the plaintiff and awarded him damages—a single dollar.[1] Clearly, the jury award bore little relation to the issues that brought the litigants to court. Had this case been sent to mediation, the mediator could have dealt directly with the course of the disputants' relationship, assisted the disputants in effective communication, helped the neighbors untangle and understand the course of their conflict, and helped them develop an agreement to prevent mutual harassment in the future.

---

[1] It was perhaps the perversely effective function of litigation in this case that the jury, by its obvious expression of disapproval of the disputants' choice to take their dispute to court, might have ultimately shamed the neighbors into finding alternative ways to resolve their conflict.

Another disadvantage to litigation's narrow focus on the cause of action is that it can divert participants from other important issues. For example, a patient frustrated with a physician's failure to spend enough time with her or seemingly to listen sympathetically to her concerns may be able to find (with the help of a lawyer) enough wrong with the physician's conduct to bring a malpractice case, yet this may not be what really bothers the patient. Litigation thus creates the likelihood of unnecessary legal action while diverting attention from the underlying problem, which may remain unresolved to fester.

Jonie went to the doctor with vague intestinal complaints. The doctor made her wait three hours, then examined her for about two minutes before pronouncing her as suffering from indigestion. She prescribed antacids and told Jonie to call her if she got worse. Three days later, Jonie's appendix ruptured, and she was forced to spend a week of her summer vacation in the hospital. Jonie angrily sued the doctor, and, after the usual two-year wait, the case went to trial. Because Jonie's symptoms had been ambiguous when she saw the doctor, and because Jonie had not planned to work during the summer of her illness, the jury awarded only $20,000, enough money to pay her medical insurer for the $18,500 in medical expenses, leaving Jonie a modest sum of $1,500. Her attorney took $3,000 of the total award for legal fees, leaving Jonie with nothing. Jonie is still seething about the doctor's cavalier behavior toward her. No one has benefited from the experience, except the medical insurer. Even Jonie's lawyer did not receive enough compensation to cover her time.

In addition to issues of comprehensiveness, mediation offers remedial flexibility and creativity unavailable in litigation and less likely in evaluative ADR processes. The remedies available through litigation are narrowly defined by the applicable law, and they generally involve a monetary judgment. In our example, what Jonie might really want is a sincere apology, not a lawsuit with possible money damages. In fact, even in clear cases of medical malpractice, there is evidence that taking steps to display the physician's sympathy for the patient, such as apologizing and admitting mistakes, is as important as monetary compensation. The recent experiences of one hospital indicate that, when such apologies and admissions are offered, overall malpractice expenditures are substantially reduced (Cohen 2000; but see Condlin 2008, footnote 74, speculating, without reviewing the research, that plaintiffs may want an apology without reducing monetary demands). Similarly, a study of small claims court cases in New Mexico suggested a high degree of satisfaction in (Hispanic) litigants who mediated their cases to nonmonetary settlements (LaFree and Rack 1996, 790). These more complete remedies have the merits of satisfying the victim more fully, reducing out-of-pocket expenditures by the defendants, and allowing the defendants to express their sense of responsibility for the problems, resulting in a sense of closure for all and less defensiveness on the part of those who have done wrong. It thus becomes easier for the defendants to learn from their errors. The victim obtains the precise sort of remedy he or she sought, a sense of closure, a feeling of validation, and a sense of sustained community with those against whom he or she had a grievance.

There is empirical evidence that mediation can, in fact, lead to a high number of these creative, integrative sorts of outcomes. Golann (2002, 334), studying the reported outcomes of private and court-based civil/commercial mediation by facilitative mediators, found that "almost two-thirds of all settlements in the survey were integrative," and Schepard (2000) and Kelly (1996) reported research indicating that mediated child custody plans tend to be more specific and detailed than those developed through lawyer-assisted negotiation.

Dealing Effectively with Meta-Disputes. You may recall from Chapter 2 that one cause of escalation in interpersonal conflicts is the creation of meta-disputes, which are disputes about the way a conflict is being handled. Professional mediators will comment from experience that, although it is sometimes possible for negotiators to straighten out these disputes on their own, the cycle of escalating competitive conflict can prevent the disputants from reaching and addressing these sorts of problems. Mediation is uniquely able to deal directly with these disputes, untangling how they took place and helping disputants get past them.

> In February, Martin, a free-lance carpenter, was rear-ended by an uninsured driver. He suffered a back and neck injury that required several doctor's visits and physical therapy and caused him to lose work. Martin had uninsured motorist coverage and immediately contacted his claims representative. His insurer had an automatic voice-messaging system. Martin left a message but forgot to include his policy number. Two weeks later, having not heard back, he left another message. However, the claims representative's secretary was distracted about another matter and accidentally erased the message before she got a chance to note the details. Another week later, incensed, Martin called again and left a rude message. Finally, a claims representative called Martin back, somewhat curtly (in light of the offensiveness of the voice message left by Martin) discussed the case with him, and sent him a complicated accident report form to return. It took Martin several weeks (due to a combination of a busy life and increasing but unconscious resentment toward the insurer) to get a copy of the police accident report and return the form to the insurer. Then he waited again. When September rolled around without so much as a letter, Martin got even madder, hired his brother-in-law, a new and very inexperienced attorney, and filed suit against his insurer for bad faith, seeking $2 million in punitive damages. The insurer filed a motion to have the action dismissed as frivolous.
>
> The case was referred to court-connected mediation. After reassuring the claims representative that she would be given ample time to be heard, the mediator gave Martin a lengthy opportunity to tell his story and vent his frustration at the apparent foot-dragging of his insurer. The attending claims representative apologized (after some prodding by the mediator) and also commented that it was the insurer's practice to wait twelve

months before settling personal injury claims since some injuries take time to fully manifest. The claims representative also said that it was the company's usual practice to advise insureds of the waiting period, but she also acknowledged that because communication had been rocky to say the least, she couldn't be absolutely sure Martin had received this critical piece of information. In no way, said the claims representative, was the delay "bad faith"; indeed, it was designed to ensure that the insured's total damages were known before a case was settled. In light of Martin's mistrust of the claims representative's contention that "the twelve-month waiting period is for the good of the insured," the mediator suggested that, as "homework," Martin contact some independent insurance claims representatives and/or experienced personal injury attorneys to check out the contention.

Martin did his homework and verified that some plaintiff's attorneys refuse to even discuss settling their clients' accident cases until a year has expired. At a follow-up mediation session, Martin, his brother-in-law, and the insurer agreed that Martin's complaint would be amended to a simple breach of contract action and that the claim for punitive damages would be eliminated. A date was also set (in March) for a negotiation session to settle the insurance claim. The claims representative, knowing that the insurer would eventually be paying a substantial claim, also was able to get agreement from headquarters to advance Martin the sums of $5,000 by September 30 and $5,000 by January 31. These sums would be deducted from the final settlement of the claim. The parties agreed to return to mediation if they were unable to work out an agreeable settlement on their own.

Disputant Quality of Consent. Unlike litigation and binding arbitration, mediation does not take from the disputants the power to accept or reject a possible settlement. Because of the consensual nature of mediation, there is generally (1) more satisfaction with the settlement and (2) more durability of the outcome.

As noted in Chapter 2, "quality of disputant consent" (Lande 1997) refers to how willing the disputants are to accede to a dispute resolution process and outcome. Regardless of whether the outcome itself is exactly what a disputant sought initially, he or she is more likely to buy into the outcome and own it psychologically if he or she is a willing participant in the process of developing it. Psychological ownership of a settlement is likely to promote willingness to abide by the terms of the settlement and to reduce the likelihood of future disputes.

You may recall from Chapter 2 (see "Promoting Psychological Ownership") that Lande (1997) lists seven attributes of high-quality consent in dispute resolution processes. These attributes include the disputants' articulation of underlying interests and goals, the disputants' active participation in the generation and analysis of options and solutions, and the lack of directiveness and pressure to settle from advocates and dispute resolution neutrals. Litigation and other adjudication processes provide the poorest match to these attributes because the disputants have no say in the outcome and because their interests are not identified or explored. Litigation is likely to provide the lowest quality of consent for litigants who are participating against their will. Purely facilitative mediation, by Lande's definition, is likely to provide the highest quality of consent. Facilitative mediation is aimed at giving disputants maximum self-determination in process and outcome to minimize the role of the mediator in recommending specific outcomes and to thoroughly explore and identify disputant interests, values, and needs. Collaborating or integrating negotiation processes comport with many of the elements that promote quality of consent, and if a mediator can promote this sort of negotiation, and refrain from pushing the disputants to settle or to move in a particular direction in settling, the result, according to Lande's criteria, would be extremely high in quality of consent. Because of the strong commitment to disputant autonomy, transformative and narrative mediation also share the promise of high quality of consent. (This is slightly less true of facilitative mediation into which disputants are ordered by courts against their will, but if reticence can be overcome by the "selling" of the process by the mediator, maximal quality of consent can be recaptured.) By Lande's calculation, more evaluative mediation processes would generate a lower-quality consent, since the mediator takes the lead in structuring the range of potential settlement options and may even push the disputants toward a particular outcome. One must temper this categorization with the fact that a disputant who prefers a "head-banging" mediator (someone who pushes a compromise on the disputants), and who is not convinced otherwise by the mediator, is not likely to consent in a high-quality way to facilitative mediation. Indeed, there are people who believe that the only appropriate way of resolving legal disputes is to submit them to a court for adjudication. Unless these individuals come to be convinced otherwise, mediation will never provide a high quality of consent for them.

Settlement Durability. Durability refers to the likelihood of the outcome of dispute resolution standing up over time. Thus, in a sense, a durable outcome is a more "final" outcome. Clearly, litigation (and arbitration) are more final than mediation in the sense that, once a triable issue is put before a court in a trial on the merits (or an arbitrable issue is submitted to an arbitrator), an outcome always results; whereas mediation may not achieve any settlement.

On the other hand, mediation can be viewed in several ways as more final than litigation. First, not all the issues in conflict, or even the most important issues in conflict, may come before the adjudicator. Some of the issues generating the most conflict may not state causes of action, meaning that a court cannot adjudicate them. In contrast, if the parties consent, skilled mediators will help the clients sort out, through reducing conflict escalation and exploring underlying interests, values, and needs, which issues are most important to resolve.

Second, a disgruntled or dissatisfied disputant may sabotage an outcome or make its enforcement difficult. Disgruntled losers of adjudication can do many things to make the winner miserable: For example, they can fail to make prompt damages payments, adapt a less than polite demeanor in necessary communications, follow the letter and not the spirit of a judgment or award calling for certain conduct, and so forth. Typical examples of post-litigation sabotage include a parent who is chronically a little late with child support payments, a civil defendant who refuses to pay a judgment until pushed into it by post-judgment proceedings, a loser in arbitration who challenges the award in court on "manifest disregard of the law" grounds, and a landlord whose promptness in responding to tenants' maintenance needs falls off. An agreement reached consensually through a facilitative process, such as mediation, can be expected to be less likely to be sabotaged or undermined than a judgment or award imposed on a disputant because the outcome of (well-conducted) mediation is consented to by all parties to the agreement. Thus, if mediation results in a settlement, it can be expected to be more likely than adjudication to settle the conflict permanently.

Third, a skilled mediator will also help the disputants co-opt important constituents who may also have the ability to sabotage or undermine the settlement, further reducing the likelihood that the settlement will fall apart. Fourth, many mediators deal directly with the deeply seated problems and minutiae that have caused the conflict to occur and escalate in the first place, so once settled it is fair to say that the disputants are less likely to have new problems crop up if they reached their agreement in such mediation settings.

In conclusion, if settlement does occur in a well-conducted mediation, it is likely to more finally and completely resolve the disputants' conflicts than will litigation. For these reasons, it might be argued that mediated settlements will be more durable than litigated judgments. There is some confirmation of this effect from empirical research into child custody litigation: that re-litigation rates in disputes settled by mediation tend to be lower than those for disputes litigated to conclusion, although the significance of the data is in some dispute and there seems to be some consensus that the effect does not hold up over a long-term period of several years (Beck and Sales 2000; Kelly 1996, 2002; King 1999; ver Steegh 2003).

Beyond these considerations, even mediations that do not result in a settlement may reduce, narrow, and deescalate conflict to the point that adjudication results more effectively in a permanent resolution. On the other hand, because the disputants retain the power to agree, they also retain the power to prevent mediation from leading to settlement in the first place. Disputants who are very anxious to end a dispute resolution process with some sort of final outcome, therefore, will often avoid selecting mediation in the first place. The apparent finality of litigation is often quite seductive to disputants exhausted and frightened by protracted conflict.

Mediation that actively involves the disputants is also likely to be more durable than lawyer-assisted negotiation (King 1999, 441–442). There are three reasons for this potential advantage of mediation. The first is that many versions of mediation feature the active participation of disputants. Unless a dispute involves complex or difficult legal issues, clients typically understand their own interests and concerns better than their legal counsel; thus a settlement negotiated by lawyers is less likely to be optimized to disputant interests and concerns. Second, to save time, lawyers involved in lawyer-assisted negotiations typically include so-called boilerplate clauses in their agreements, clauses that assume clients are all the same. For example, in divorce lawyering, the "custody to the mother, reasonable visitation to the father" parenting plan is frequently negotiated by the lawyers, regardless of its suitability for the individual families they are representing. Third, active involvement of the disputants directly improves the quality of disputant consent—by creating psychological ownership of the outcome. Thus, even if the ultimate settlements are identical, mediation in which disputants directly participate in negotiation could be expected to produce greater disputant satisfaction and greater compliance with settlement outcome.[2]

Individual Transformation. Some scholars assert that mediation can be "transformative" to individual disputants. They usually mean, in part, that mediation can be an empowering and enlightening process, helping participants see the issues more clearly, prompting them to do the research needed to prepare their case and understand their BATNA, and creating a safe environment in which to confront the other disputant. Here's a real-life example of how such transformation occurred in a very unexpected way:

> Private co-mediators Amy and Bob were retained to handle a divorce dispute between a wealthy husband and his stay-at-home wife. After an eight-hour marathon mediation session involving the mediators and both spouses—leading to a temporary agreement—the participants took an indefinite break. About a month later, the wife called Amy, one of the mediators, to cancel further mediation. She also thanked Amy and expressed her gratitude for the mediation experience. She stated that mediation had helped her realize, for the first time, that she had been disempowered by her husband's conduct, that it was clearly his intention to exploit her lack of experience in negotiation, and that, to negotiate with him effectively in the future over the complex financial issues raised by the divorce, she needed to hire a competent "bomber" lawyer. The fact that mediation had exposed this relationship dynamic without coercing her into signing away her rights had been instrumental in this realization.
>
> Interestingly, the two mediators themselves differed about the significance of the wife's withdrawal from mediation. Although Bob, the co-mediator, lamented the failure of the mediation, Amy viewed the empowering effects of this mediation as a positive development, despite the lack of a permanent, comprehensive settlement of the legal issues. Amy commented that any process that leads to the development of a more equal relationship between disputants is a positive step.

Mediation can sometimes also lead to a disputant's point of view being acknowledged by the other disputant for the first time. For many disputants,

---

[2] The fact that clients who actively participate in the resolution of their conflicts are more likely to get outcomes that address their interests and to "psychologically own" the outcome is important even to adversarial legal representation. The traditional paternalistic, "leave everything to me" brand of legal advocacy leaves its practitioner vulnerable to a result that, no matter how brilliant, leaves the client disgruntled and dissatisfied. Thus, adversarial legal advocates are well advised to take from the mediation movement the notion that a more active, involved client is, ultimately, a happier one.

Effective mediation can lead to individual and systemic transformation. Here, President Jimmy Carter presides over the Camp David Accord, a good example of a process that transformed the lives of many. Pearson Education/PH College.

receiving this sort of acknowledgment and recognition is a profoundly empowering event. For example, in a dispute over a personnel evaluation, both the employee and the employer may, in the course of the process, come to better understand the perspective of the other. If the employer's representative is able, with the help of the mediator, to convey the employer's interests and concerns to the employee, this information can enable the employee to be able to make career-enhancing moves in the future. The employer, on the other hand, will gain valuable information about how to improve employee feedback and training. Mediation can improve disputant perspective taking, encouraging disputants to see and understand the point of view of those with whom they disagree.

In addition, mediation can educate disputants by teaching them negotiation skills they can carry into other parts of their lives. Some scholars (prominently, Baruch-Bush and Folger 1994) view these developments as positive in a broader sense and argue that mediation that leads to personal empowerment and a sense of recognition has strong benefits for society as a whole.

Minimization of Conflicts of Interest with Legal Counsel. Mediation can be very helpful to a lawyer whose client's expectations are unreasonable. This effect is particularly obvious in evaluative mediation, although it is present in other forms as well.[3]

Lawyers must present their client's case in the best possible light when they deal with the other disputant, the other disputant's legal counsel, and the

---

[3] This effect may also operate in nonbinding evaluation, which may be one of the underlying reasons why lawyers express a preference for it. It has been noted elsewhere in this text (Chapter 3) that nonbinding evaluation is often virtually indistinguishable from evaluative mediation.

court. This need is created by the perception that the lawyer is ethically obligated to zealously represent the interests of the client. Clients whose lawyers are realistically pessimistic about the chances of their side's prevailing in litigation often doubt their lawyers' commitment to this promise of vigorous advocacy. Moreover, if a lawyer's advocacy is appropriately enthusiastic, the client often misreads the lawyer's enthusiasm as signifying that he or she has a better case than, in fact, the client really has. Thus, the duty to provide accurate advice may conflict with the duty of vigorous advocacy. To make matters worse, some lawyers get personally caught up in the rosy picture they paint publicly about their client's case and miss or underemphasize important flaws and weaknesses.[4]

Mediation allows the ADR neutral to be the bearer of bad news about the lawsuit, preserving for the lawyer the zealous advocate role. Many lawyers have found this to be an unexpected benefit of mediation. Facilitative mediation is capable of fulfilling this function as well as evaluative mediation, but in facilitative mediation the process is more indirect, relying on reality testing that allows the disputant to reach his or her own pessimistic conclusions, in effect discovering for him- or herself the unpleasant truths about the alternatives to a negotiated agreement. In either case, the lawyer is freed from the uncomfortable position of having to give the client a pessimistic prediction of the case and risking the possibility that the client will see the lawyer as uncaring or uncommitted to the client's welfare.

Advantages of Litigation Over Mediation. The preceding discussion outlines the many ways that mediation can benefit clients and their legal advocates. However, there are many aspects of legal disputes that scholars argue are better served by litigation than mediation. These include the promise of a guaranteed outcome, enforceability considerations, the availability of legal precedent and reform, the public nature of litigation, and the special needs of disempowered clients.

Guaranteed Outcome. If a cause of action can be stated, litigation always guarantees some sort of outcome, though it may not resolve the most important conflicts. In this somewhat narrow sense, litigation is more final than mediation. Because this advantage of litigation is very obvious, it causes many disputants to reject the mediation option out of hand. (See the preceding discussion of durability in mediation.)

Nature of Enforceability. It is also sometimes contended that mediated agreements have weaker enforceability than court judgments. Judgments are enforceable through the contempt process (in other words, a litigant who fails to comply with a court order can be threatened with fines and imprisonment),

---

[4] This effect can be caused by the perceptual distortion created by the cycle of conflict escalation. This topic is discussed in Chapter 2.

whereas mediated agreements are private contracts. Thus, mediated agreements are enforceable to the same extent as any out-of-court settlement: They must be taken to court and enforced in a contract action. If the other disputant contests the validity of a mediated agreement, this step may be an onerous one.

There may also be a psychological effect of a judge's pronouncing a decision, compared with disputants' reaching their own agreement in mediation. Overall, as previously noted, outcomes based on court judgments are, empirically speaking, less, rather than more, likely to be complied with than are mediated settlements. But some disputants may prefer having the authority of a judge behind the decision, and in some circumstances the gravitas of judicial pronouncement may be important in securing compliance. One problem with this approach, however, is that, if the disputant chooses to litigate the issue in court, the judge may not issue the decision the disputant wants.

Legal Precedent. As with any out-of-court settlement, mediation does not result in a legal precedent. This feature of mediation is of particular concern if a disputant has a very large number of similar cases pending and, for some reason, these cases can't be resolved in a single comprehensive mediation (e.g., when there are multiple defendants). Of course, some disputants will welcome this characteristic of mediation. The precedential impact of the chosen dispute resolution process will sometimes be a strategic issue that affects disputants' negotiation over which dispute resolution process will be used. A disputant who values precedent may simply refuse to settle in mediation or may bargain away his or her need for precedent against other valuable consideration.

A public-policy argument against mediation's lack of precedential effect is also sometimes made. There are those who argue against settlement as a general matter of public policy because legal reform often results from the rulings of appellate judges considering the appeals of judgments issued in lawsuits (see Owen Fiss's classic 1984 article, "Against Settlement"). Our legal system has a time-honored tradition of promulgating vitally important legal reforms—school integration, the right to use contraception, the right of interracial marriage, just to name a few—through this process of generating "common law," and some worry that any system that diverts cases to settlement will prevent this reform process from occurring. Mediation, as a form of facilitated settlement, is as vulnerable to this charge as any other form of settlement. However, it bears emphasizing that any legal dispute can be settled out of court; that, in fact, the vast majority of them do settle out of court, through legal negotiation; and that most legal disputes do not seem to offer significant legal questions the answers to which would reform the common law.

Of greater concern is that mediation—or any other form of ADR—could present a serious public-policy problem if large numbers of disputants were coerced or manipulated into settling. If an entire class of cases is forced into mediation and pressure is applied to these disputants to reach a settlement, it can be argued that the needed appellate litigation to create reform of the common law will not take place.

For example, in the 1980s courts began to experiment with programs that forced all child custody cases filed in particular jurisdictions into mediation. If the mediation programs had been purely consensual—in other words, if the disputants had been required to participate but not pressured into settling—the mandatory referral of cases into mediation would not have been much of a problem because the cases containing issues ripe for reform would not have been likely to settle. The problem with these experimental programs was that the mediators were poorly trained, severely overloaded with cases, and evaluated based on how many cases they could clear off the dockets. As a result, they tended to practice a form of very coercive "muscle mediation" (Folberg and Taylor 1984, 135) to move cases along, so people weren't just being required to attend mediation—they were suffering negative consequences if they didn't settle. Many scholars raised concerns that if a particular child custody issue needed to be addressed by the courts, it wasn't reaching the appellate level. In general, these coercive programs were roundly criticized. As a result, the courts have become more sophisticated about these concerns and have made court-connected mediation much less coercive (for some exceptions, see McIsaac 2001).

Privacy Issues. The intimate privacy of mediation raises disadvantages as well as advantages. In some cases, disputants may mutually prefer the privacy and consider it a benefit of mediation over litigation. However, in some cases, the lack of public forum for mediation can benefit "bad actors" because public vindication and a public reprimand do not occur. This is a problem if the "bad actor" has greater power than the "innocent victim" and is able to coercively push the other into mediating to an agreement (disputants with equal bargaining power can bargain for a public announcement of their settlement). Another problem raised by privacy in mediation is that collusion can occur, just as it can in any settlement negotiation, facilitated by ADR or not. The following example is adapted from *Rojas v. Superior Court,* 33 Cal. 4th 407 (2004):

> Frisko Corp. is a huge and highly visible homebuilder in the state of Maryland, a household name due to its intensive advertising of new housing developments. Frisko also builds high-rise and garden apartments. In 2002, Landcorp, the owner of a Frisko-built low-income apartment, sued Frisko, alleging that defects in construction had led to water leakage that had in turn caused a toxic mold problem. The court referred the matter to mediation, and during the next two years, the parties negotiated a settlement. In July 2005, the negotiations concluded, the case settled and was dismissed, and the mold was removed through remediation. All testing and other evidence pertaining to mold contamination was destroyed pursuant to the settlement. Meanwhile, during 2003 and 2004, the building's tenants had been complaining orally to the landlord about black substances on the walls, leaks in ceilings, and respiratory problems. These complaints had fallen on seemingly deaf ears. By the time the tenants brought suit against the landlord and homebuilder, all inculpatory evidence of toxic mold had been destroyed.

Mediation and Low-Power Disputants. Although effective mediators can empower and transform disputants, incompetent or biased mediators, as well as good mediators constrained by circumstances, can do the opposite. It has been commented that mediators who are insensitive to power imbalance may unwittingly help an oppressor pressure a disempowered disputant. However, some mediation detractors argue that *all* mediation, not just "bad mediation," is harmful to the disempowered. Relatedly, it has also been argued that the private nature of mediation makes prejudiced behavior against disempowered social groups, such as women and persons of color, more likely. This issue is one of the hottest, and most controversial, in the ADR field.

Research to date has been unable to document an increase in bigoted conduct in mediation as compared with litigation, and this concern applies equally to other private processes. However, the fact that mediation disputants are often encouraged to negotiate without legal counsel to speak for and protect them creates concern on the part of some commentators and scholars that the privacy of mediation, plus unwitting complicity by mediators motivated to reach settlement, may damage those who are most disempowered, as well as those vulnerable to racism and other forms of oppression.

A number of respected legal scholars, particularly some feminists and civil rights advocates, have written to attack the appropriateness of mediation, particularly for disempowered disputants, such as women and people of color. If the process of mediation is coercive—for example, when whole classes of cases are mandated to enter mediation *and* clients are pressured to reach agreement—it seems obvious to be concerned about the impact of mediation on groups whose members are often disempowered. In court-mandated "triage" mediation, in which getting an agreement quickly is more important than promoting effective negotiation by empowered participants, mediators may be subtly pressured by their employment situation into using whatever means they have at their disposal to get an agreement quickly. When mediators are working with disputants who are imbalanced in terms of personal power, one might imagine that the temptation to allow the more powerful disputant to coerce the less powerful disputant would be strong, indeed.

Women comprise the first group of concern to mediation detractors. Some commentators make the argument that, because mediation may result in overreaching by powerful male disputants against disempowered female disputants, with the insensitive complicity of the mediator, no mediation should ever take place between male and female disputants. This is one argument that has been advanced by feminists who contend that women are structurally disempowered in comparison with men and are therefore endangered by mediation. Some of these scholars cite compelling (some might instead use the term *hair-raising*) anecdotal evidence that some mediation cases have been handled this way (Bruch 1992; Bryan 1992; Fineman 1988; Lefcourt 1984; Nader 1992). The classic tract supporting this point of view, the late Trina Grillo's article (1991) "The Mediation Alternative: Process Dangers for Women," relies on examples of mediation forced on abused women who are thereby pressured to reason with and cooperate with their physical oppressor.

However, isolated anecdotes aside, these texts are largely argumentative, and many of them seem to be premised on the narrow assumptions of the lawyer's standard philosophical map. Proponents of mediation argue that eliminating mediation on this basis would be a case of "throwing the baby out with the bathwater" and that a better option would be to assess under what circumstances overreaching and oppression might occur and to reform mediation processes to address the problem.

A different arm of the feminist movement makes an argument that mediation is, instead, a gift to women, since it relies on a more "feminine" method of reaching settlement, such as the sharing of feelings and a nonhierarchical power structure (McCabe 2001; Menkel-Meadow 1985; Rifkin 1984). Empirical evidence is limited, but what is available largely supports mediation proponents (Vincent 1995, 278–282). Although the evidence is somewhat contradictory, women generally tend to express greater satisfaction than men with the mediation process. Carol J. King (1999), reviewing research results from Ohio court–mandated custody mediation programs, found that women rated mediation very positively, more positively than men on most measures. Moreover, available research indicates that there is no clear evidence that mediated agreements are either better or worse for women than litigated judgments and that, in many situations, women actually fare better than men in mediation (Gaschen 1995; Heister 1987; Kelly and Duryee 1992; LaFree and Rack 1996; Marcus, Marcus, Stilwell, and Doherty 1999; Pearson 1991; Richardson 1988). King (1999) also reports that female participants in the Ohio mediation programs reported more pressure to settle *outside* of mediation than *in* mediation. And research examining mediation between battered women and their batterers suggests that some battered women may actually experience mediation with their victimizer as an empowering event (King 1999, 443–445; Vincent 1995, 277–278).

Law professor Barbara Stark, reviewing the vigorous dialogue in the legal scholarly journals, argues that mediation is neither a disaster nor a panacea for women:

> [Among feminist scholars,] normative consensus with regard to mediation has evolved from early enthusiasm—and distrust—to a much more nuanced, contextualized, and qualified acceptance. In general, feminists view mediation as a promising alternative to the adversarial model. . . . [B]ut feminists have shown how seemingly neutral processes allow gendered norms to reassert themselves, especially in traditionally gendered contexts such as divorce. *(Stark 2000, 243–244)*

Before we leave the issue of gender and mediation, consider an interesting twist: One study produced evidence that mediation experience itself may reduce negative gender stereotyping. In a study of perceptions of undergraduates who read transcripts of a custody mediation session (Coltri 1995), the readers who reported previous personal experience with mediation displayed dramatically fewer misogynistic (antiwomen) attitudes toward the disputants than those who did not report previous mediation experience. Does mediation experience itself reduce sexist stereotyping during conflict? It is too early to tell, but this evidence is suggestive and deserves further study.

The other groups of concern to those studying the impact of mediation are people of color. The argument goes that in mediation, which is not a public setting, white, particularly male, mediators handling racially or ethnically diverse conflicts might subtly and/or unwittingly express prejudice toward disputants of color, creating a subconscious alliance between the mediator and a white disputant and increasing the likelihood of poorer outcomes for a disputant of color.

> A fair way to capsulize [the prevalent] argument goes as follows: Minorities in this country will always be the victims of oppression at one level or another. For any minority person to obtain justice, they must go to court, where the formal procedures and protections of the trial system can re-balance power. Mediation, on the other hand, will simply provide a forum for re-victimization of the minority person. Mediation services offer only second-class justice, with no safeguards for the minority victim. *(Bernard 2001, 140)*

Richard Delgado (1997) and many others further argue that persons of color are being shunted into mediation as a way to disconnect them from protective societal values that would equalize the playing field if such persons would litigate their conflicts. In response to these attacks on mediation, Michael Z. Green (2005) argues for vesting self-determination in disputants in the context of a highly facilitative form of mediation, giving full control over whether to settle, and on what terms, to the persons of color who encounter it. He asserts that a disputant who is given access to legal advice, who is able to freely refrain from consenting to mediation and to refrain from settlement if needed, who is able to choose from mediators of his or her ethnic or racial background, who has a strong say in how the mediation occurs, and whose mediator refrains from imposing judgments about the norms used by the disputants in mediation, may be empowered beyond the limitations offered by litigation in which values and goals are imposed by the courts. His argument is that individuals of color should have a choice about how they personally wish to be self-actualized, rather than being bound to norms of justice and equity demanded by progressive society.

Empirical evidence concerning the impact of mediation on racial and ethnic minority groups is, to date, sparse. The most widely cited research on the topic is the Metro Court study, which examined a small claims mediation program in New Mexico (LaFree and Rack 1996; Rack 1999). The study found that Hispanic male mediation claimants (here the term *claimants* refers to people who had brought small claims actions) received poorer monetary settlements in mediation than their Anglo male counterparts (a similar, but significantly smaller, discrepancy was found for small claims litigation). However, this discrepancy between discrimination in mediation and in litigation was not found for respondents (people who had been sued) or for females (in fact,

Anglo females did better in mediation than any other group and did better in mediation than in litigation), and monetary differences between mediation and litigation for male claimants disappeared when the mediators were also Hispanic.

The Metro Court study is often cited as proof that mediation harms minorities, but its data are difficult to interpret. LaFree and Rack based their comparisons of mediation outcomes on the sizes of monetary outcomes compared with initial claims presented in small claims complaints. For example, a settlement in which a claimant received $500 to compensate him for a defective washing machine would have been rated as a better settlement than one in which a claimant received $400, an apology, and a day of yard work in compensation for the defect. However, racial and ethnic minorities were more likely to end up with nonmonetary elements in their mediated settlements and to be pleased about it to a significantly greater extent than Anglos whose settlements had nonmonetary elements.

> Compared with Anglo claimants . . . minority claimants settled twice as often for nonmonetary outcomes . . . [and] . . . compared with cases resulting in monetary outcomes, minority claimants in mediation were significantly more satisfied with cases that included substantial nonmonetary outcomes. *(LaFree and Rack 1996, 790)*

Moreover, the authors reported that some 37 percent of the mediated claims resulted in strictly nonmonetary outcomes. These cases were not considered in the statistical assessments conducted by the researchers, calling the conclusions about outcome disparity into some question. Given the diversity and idiosyncratic nature of disputant interests, values, and needs, a monetary settlement may not fully address the best interests of disputants. Thus, relying on the monetary part of settlement to evaluate discrepancies in mediation outcomes may not tap what is really going on, yet directly comparing the adequacy of nonmonetary outcomes is virtually impossible. The mediation field is rife with such problems in how to interpret empirical data.

In considering data from research such as the Metro Court study, it should be borne in mind that assessing the quality of outcome may not tap the other benefits of mediation to ethnic and racial minority disputants. Depner, Cannata, and Ricci (1994) found that ethnic minority disputants—and members of other disempowered groups, such as the poor—actually rated mediation more helpful on several measures than did middle-class Anglo disputants. Generalizing from research conducted on a single mediation program also can be dangerous in the ADR field (Beck and Sales 2000) because mediation programs are characterized by wide variations in the characteristics of the disputants; the kinds of dispute sent to mediation; the qualifications and training of the mediators; the screening and referral protocols, if any, in place; the support of the bench and the bar; and the circumstances in which mediation is conducted (Kelly 1996). Each mediation program is unique, and a problem discovered in a single program can't be generalized to mediation in general.

It seems quite likely that gender, ethnicity, and race affect the experience of mediation in diverse ways, but much more research is needed to determine under what circumstances they appear and whether the differences warrant avoiding mediation, or other interventions. In the meantime, avoiding coercion to settle during mediation, allowing abuse victims to opt out of mediation, allowing legal counsel to participate in mediation sessions under certain circumstances, and improving mediation training and qualification are good ideas for optimizing the mediation experience for disempowered disputants. It also seems incontrovertible that benefit would be derived from recruitment and training of mediators who are members of diverse social groups, particularly members of historically disempowered groups such as females and persons of color.

Mediation Isn't the Option of Last Resort. Perhaps the most pertinent drawback of mediation is that disputants who could benefit most from the process typically don't choose it. By the time disputants find they are unable to negotiate an agreement on their own, their conflict has frequently entered an escalating phase with mutual hostility and recrimination. These litigants find the idea of cooperating with their "enemy" to be repugnant and would rather have an authority figure assigned to punish the opposition. This perspective presents two problems, of course: The first is that only the winner of the litigation obtains the sought-after vindication, and the second is that adversarial conflict resolution tends to be so costly, time consuming, and ineffective that even the vindicated litigant often loses as much as, or more than, he or she gains from a win in court. Research indicates that many of the most angry and hostile disputants, when forced to participate in mediation, often become its biggest fans (McEwen and Milburn 1993).

Advantages of Negotiation Over Mediation. The advantages of mediation over negotiation have been discussed previously. Primarily, the benefits of negotiation over mediation involve an "If it ain't broke, don't fix it" premise. Mediation is more expensive than face-to-face negotiation since a mediator must be retained. If negotiation is going very well already, there is no need to hire a mediator, and adding a third party to a well-functioning negotiation may be counterproductive.

Summary: Advantages and Disadvantages of Mediation. Table 7-1 summarizes, for your convenience, the advantages and disadvantages of mediation, compared to litigation and negotiation.

ARBITRATION

We'll now turn our focus to arbitration. What advantages and disadvantages does it have, compared with litigation? With simple and lawyer-assisted negotiation? With litigation?

ADVANTAGES OF MEDIATION, COMPARED WITH LITIGATION	DISADVANTAGES OF MEDIATION, COMPARED WITH LITIGATION
Mediation is quicker and less expensive.	Mediation does not always result in settlement.
Mediation is more likely to encourage collaboration and cooperation.	Litigation guarantees some kind of outcome.
Resolution is more efficient and makes better use of parties' resources.	Unlike litigation, mediation does not create legal precedent, which might prevent legal reform through the appellate litigation process if mediation is coercive.
Mediation can address all issues, not just those for which a cause of action can be stated.	
More creative remedies are possible.	
The *whole* conflict can be dealt with, including linkages and conflicts with nondisputants.	Incompetent mediators or mediators pressed for time may unwittingly contribute to the exploitation of a weak disputant by a strong one.
Mediation is likely to reduce meta-disputes, whereas litigation often creates more of them.	Because mediation is private, vindication and public reprimand may not be available remedies. This aspect of mediation makes it unpalatable for some disputants.
Mediation promotes greater quality of consent and psychological ownership, leading to greater satisfaction and voluntary compliance.	
Relationship advantages: "competent" mediators help defuse anger, improve communication, and specifically work on trust building.	Because mediation is private, say some scholars, bigoted disputants and mediators might be more likely to act on their prejudices than would litigants and judges.
Mediation can "transform" disputants by empowering them, teaching them negotiation skills, and helping them see the other disputant's point of view.	
Mediation that does not result in agreement can streamline the dispute, clarifying and narrowing issues and making future resolution easier, quicker, and cheaper.	

ADVANTAGES OF MEDIATION, COMPARED WITH NEGOTIATION	DISADVANTAGES OF MEDIATION, COMPARED WITH NEGOTIATION
Mediation is better able to move disputants past impasse because it is better able to handle people problems, meta-disputes, and emotional factors.	Mediation is more expensive because it includes another professional.
The presence of a third party often alters the relationship dynamics that led disputants to impasse in the first place.	If negotiation is proceeding very well, it may be counterproductive to introduce a third person (the mediator).
Mediators can say things to the disputants that the disputants would reactively devalue if they had come from one another.	
Mediation is better at teaching disputants how to negotiate effectively.	
Mediators can usually address issues of trust, anger, and communication more effectively than simple negotiation or lawyer-assisted negotiation can.	
"Good" mediators are usually more effective at diagnosing the conflict and choosing appropriate methods of addressing it than are the disputants and their lawyers.	
Compared with lawyer-assisted negotiation, mediation usually results in more creative resolutions better tailored to the interests of all disputants.	

Compared with Litigation. The advantages of arbitration over litigation depend, in part, on the type of arbitration that is used. Arbitration almost always takes less time—from the inception of a claim to the outcome—than litigation because it isn't necessary to wade through the usual backlog of court cases. The disputants simply hire an arbitrator and move directly into the process. Whether the arbitration process itself is more efficient than the litigation process depends on the kind of arbitration and on the existence of any legal challenges to arbitration. Informal, mutually chosen arbitration is much simpler, quicker, less expensive, and more efficient than litigation. Very formalized arbitration can be at least as time intensive and may be even more expensive because of the arbitrator's fees.

Informal arbitration also offers flexibility that litigation cannot. The arbitration can, with mutual consent, be structured to permit the arbitrator to make his or her ruling on fairness grounds, rather than on a strictly legal basis. Arbitrators may also be empowered to engage in a certain amount of facilitation prior to entering a ruling—which may allow the arbitrator to learn more about the disputants' underlying interests before making the award and may enable the arbitrator to increase the disputants' psychological ownership of the outcome. The arbitrator may also be given a degree of remedial flexibility that is not available in litigation because the outcome of any lawsuit is strictly limited by the applicable law. On the other hand, arbitrator flexibility, especially flexibility and informality of process, can backfire. If one of the disputants feels that the arbitrator is biased against him or her, a flexible process can undermine the sense of procedural justice of the process, and, hence, the sense of psychological ownership of the outcome, and in some cases it can even lead to a legal challenge to the award. A disinterested, rigid, and legalistic arbitration process can protect the process from the appearance or fact of bias or injustice—after all, that is the reason for procedural rigor in the litigation process.

Like mediation, another advantage to arbitration over litigation is that disputants can mutually choose whether to make the proceeding public or private. Arbitration offers a choice of private or public forum, whereas litigation is always, with limited exceptions, public. On the other hand, if public-policy considerations would favor publicizing the outcome, arbitration can be detrimental. Imagine, for example, an issue involving the validity of a common credit card provision. Arbitration's privacy can also be a problem if one disputant imposes privacy or publicity on a disputant with inferior bargaining power.

Arbitration may also offer a degree of finality that litigation cannot. As detailed in Chapter 5, arbitration awards are subject to review in only a few very extreme circumstances. This feature of arbitration can be of substantial benefit to disputants who simply need the matter settled once and for all. On the other hand, if the outcome appears to be based on an error of law, or not warranted by the evidence, this feature of arbitration can be a serious detriment because these are not grounds upon which an arbitration award can be overturned in court.

Arbitration also has advantages in situations in which, for whatever reason, adjudication is desired but litigation is impractical. For example, the litigation of a dispute between multinational disputants can raise nasty choice-of-law issues. Litigating these issues, which may require multiple hearings in multiple courts, can be time consuming, can be expensive, and can multiply the likelihood of unpredictable results. Moreover, the citizens of one nation may fear biased treatment if the matter is litigated in the court of a different nation. If the disputants are able to specify choice of law and forum in the agreement to arbitrate, these intractable issues can be avoided simply, expediently, and cheaply.

Another area in which arbitration shines, compared with litigation, is in the participants' ability to select the arbitrator. If the dispute involves a highly technical area, an expert in the field can be chosen to be arbitrator. For example, in a dispute involving the determination of responsibility of one of several contractors for the failure of a building under construction, the disputants could select a panel of arbitrators that includes an experienced construction lawyer and a structural engineer. Such selection will reduce the amount of hearing preparation required by the disputants, will help to ensure that the outcome reflects fairness in the context of industry culture, and may help to reassure the parties that the decision is based on sound wisdom. In the arbitration of a child custody matter, the disputants can select an arbitrator with a professional background in child development, ensuring that the outcome reflects a real consideration of the health and welfare of the child.

What weaknesses does arbitration have relative to litigation? When arbitration is between arm's-length disputants and is wholeheartedly embraced by all concerned, there aren't many weaknesses. But when arbitration is forced on disputants, the situation is different. Arbitration, particularly the informal variety, into which disputants are pressured or coerced, raises due process issues. The lack of procedural protections may mean that the arbitrator is not presented with an effectively balanced case to decide. The arbitration itself may be so lacking in the basic elements of fairness that the process is egregious. For example, in *Hooters of America v. Phillips,* 173 F.3d 933 (C.A. 4 1999), an employee was required by her employment contract to participate in arbitration determined by the court to be "so egregiously unfair as to constitute a complete default of [the employer's] contractual obligation to draft arbitration rules and to do so in good faith" (173 F.3d at 938). The *Hooters* agreement to arbitrate provided that the employee, but not the employer, was required to provide written notice of claim and a list of all prospective witnesses; that the employer, but not the employee, was allowed to cancel the agreement to arbitrate; that the panel of arbitrators had to be selected from a list promulgated by the employer; that the employer, but not the employee, was allowed to raise additional claims at the hearing; that the employer, but not the employee, could seek summary judgment; and that the employer, but not the employee, could seek review of the award (173 F.3d at 939).

In addition to procedural due process issues associated with the procedural details of arbitration, it has been asserted (Sternlight 2001) that executory agreements to arbitrate between disputants of unequal bargaining power impermissibly take away the weaker disputant's right to a jury trial. Even if a jury trial right is not of concern, it has been argued that executory agreements to arbitrate foisted on low-power individuals by large organizations are unfair because the large organizations are "repeat players": They have numerous such agreements, and thus far more experience with the entire process and with how to get the best possible result, and they are likely to have developed cozy relationships with the arbitrators. The low-power individuals, primarily employees and consumers, are not likely to have this sort of knowledge and experience. Commentators such as law professor Sarah Rudolph Cole (1996) assert, for these reasons, that executory agreements to arbitrate imposed on employees and consumers by employers and large commercial entities should not be enforced. The statutory structure in which arbitration is practiced within the United States does little to protect "small players" and low-power disputants from repeat players, large vendors, and employers who impose form arbitration provisions as a precondition of forming or continuing contractual relations. In *Hooters,* an agreement to arbitrate was overturned, but agreements to give up the right to litigate, imposed by large corporations on consumers and employees, are uniformly upheld by U.S. courts unless they are facially unfair in some other way, similar to the *Hooters* agreement.

Another problem with arbitration is its privacy. As with coercive forms of mediation, if large numbers of particular sorts of cases are pushed into an arbitration process, the need for legal reforms might not be communicated to the level of the appellate courts or legislatures, as they would if the matter were litigated. For example, if credit card providers require their patrons to arbitrate disputes, and if such a scheme is adopted by the entire industry (and this appears to be the case as of the writing of this text), then prevailing problems in the law of consumer credit card lending law would not reach the appellate courts. A second problem connected to privacy involves disempowerment and bigotry. As with other private ADR processes, arbitration allows for the increased possibility of oppression of weaker disputants by stronger ones. It is possible for disputants to negotiate an arbitration agreement that makes the results of arbitration public; however, this outcome is less likely if the disputant wanting publicity is relatively lacking in power. Unlike mediation, once a disempowered disputant enters arbitration, he or she cannot withdraw consent to the process.

Compared with Negotiation. Arbitration offers some major advantages when compared with negotiation not involving a neutral. Arbitration is particularly effective in overcoming a conflict whose principal source is a divergence of perception over facts or law. Nonbinding evaluation (see Chapter 6) offers similar benefits, but arbitration is also more final in that an award is definitely rendered. Often, if disputants are going to be involved in an adversarial process before a neutral, it will seem nonsensical to stop with an evaluation when a final decision can be made by the neutral, settling the entire matter.

In addition, because the arbitration decision is rendered by a third party, loss-of-face problems in making concessions can sometimes be avoided. The arbitrator can take on the possible loss of face by issuing what is clear to the disputants to be the "fair" decision, while sparing the disputant who otherwise risks loss of face. This facet of arbitration can also be desirable to attorneys who wish to retain their "gladiator" image during the proceedings. Finally, as with mediation, arbitration may be advantageous simply because it exists as an option. Often, disputants who enter arbitration have already tried negotiation, and it has failed to resolve the conflict.

Arbitration has several disadvantages, compared with negotiation without a neutral. Arbitration is likely to be more harmful to relationships because it is an adversarial process. Thus, it may settle a short-term dispute but set the stage for a long-term contentious relationship. Since it is adversarial, arbitration is more likely to result in a choice between extreme positions, rather than win-win, optimal solutions for both parties. Obviously, this is a particular problem in final-offer arbitration. Moreover, disputants in arbitration must surrender their control over the outcome of their dispute to the arbitrator, making it likely that one or both disputants will lack psychological ownership of the outcome. It is likely to be more expensive and time consuming than negotiation and, since an outcome is imposed on the disputants, it is more likely than consensual processes to be subject to legal maneuvering. (Perhaps the plethora of trial-level and appellate cases involving arbitration parties seeking to overturn or prevent arbitration awards attests to this reality.)

Compared with Mediation. Arbitration's advantages over mediation are similar to those of arbitration over other forms of negotiation. It can be useful in overcoming divergent perceptions of fact or law. Many disputants and their advocates also appreciate the binding quality of arbitration and its ability to overcome the loss-of-face issues associated with negotiation. Arbitration may simply have a more familiar feel to many attorneys, who are used to trial work and feel like fish out of water in the mediation setting. Thus, many attorneys may choose arbitration for their clients on the basis that they believe they can provide more effective representation in such a context.

Although both arbitration and mediation are noted for their efficiency, some informal varieties of arbitration are probably quicker, in the short term, than highly facilitative forms of mediation. The reason for this advantage of arbitration is that it takes less time and effort to state a position than to explore the sources of a conflict, conduct an interests analysis, invent multiple options for disputants' mutual gains, choose among the options, listen and validate the other disputant's point of view, and so on. On the other hand, facilitative mediation may be more efficient in the long run in resolving the wider conflict and supporting a more effective disputant relationship, as discussed previously in this chapter.

A relatively recent trend has been for commentators, including scholars and practitioners of arbitration, to advocate the use of mediation over arbitration as a process of "first resort" (Barnes 1997; Sander and Goldberg 1994, 59–60). The principal reason for this development is probably that the apparent usefulness of arbitration in overcoming loss of face and divergent perception may be more illusory than real: Skilled mediators have specific tools and expertise in dealing with face saving and perceptual challenges. Moreover, in many instances, a dispute that looks, at first glance, like a simple case of individual greed or divergent perception turns out to be something different and more amenable to mediation. In such cases, creative problem solving will produce much more satisfied disputants and a more optimal use of resources. Also, as discussed previously in this chapter, mediation is better able than adjudication to handle the entire landscape of an interpersonal conflict in a way that creates psychological ownership of the outcome. Without trying mediation first, however, the disputants will often be blinded to the complexities of such a conflict by the invisible veil of cultural beliefs about conflict (see Chapter 2), and the benefits of using mediation will never become evident. Moreover, since arbitration is an adversarial process, it is more likely to generate conflict escalation, whereas mediation (particularly the facilitative type) is specifically designed to de-escalate conflict. This tendency to escalate conflict will also create disputant blindness to the potential advantages of using a more facilitative process. Finally, if arbitration is in any way coercive, or imposed unwillingly on one of the disputants, issues of fairness and due process may be raised. For example, like mediation, arbitration is a private process, raising concerns about participants feeling free to engage in openly bigoted behavior. But unlike mediation and other forms of negotiation, arbitration is potentially more dangerous, because the disputant has no power to reject the outcome, and the outcome is usually even more final than a judgment reached in litigation.

Table 7-2 summarizes, for your convenience, the advantages and disadvantages of arbitration.

NONBINDING EVALUATION

Nonbinding evaluation represents an effort to obtain the benefits of both negotiation and adjudication. Does it, in fact, do so?

Compared with Litigation. The most important advantage of nonbinding evaluation over litigation is probably also its greatest disadvantage: its nonbinding quality. Nonbinding evaluation allows the disputants to retain a measure of their autonomy. A settlement reached after nonbinding evaluation is more likely to be accompanied by psychological ownership than a judgment imposed by the court because both disputants have freely chosen the outcome themselves: They've negotiated to an agreement. For this reason, nonbinding evaluation is often recommended for disputants who are engaged in a continuing relationship. An example in which such processes are considered useful is in multimillion-dollar construction projects, in which costly disputes may develop among contractors and subcontractors who must continue to deal with one another until the project is completed. Time is of the essence in such situations, and the parties are highly motivated to find rapid, practical solutions to disputes as they

◆ **TABLE 7-2**   Advantages and Disadvantages of Arbitration

COMPARISON WITH	PROS	CONS
Litigation	Informal arbitration is usually much less time consuming, less expensive, easier to handle.	Informal arbitration may create due process problems.
	Informal arbitration: Arbitrator may not be limited by "cause of action" perspective and narrow remedy options.	Arbitration imposed on consumers or others with inferior bargaining power may violate constitutional guarantees of the right to civil trial by jury.
	Some types of arbitration act as precedent.	Some arbitrators' decisions are arbitrary; limited appealability may lead to bad outcome.
	Particularly useful when there are intractable choice-of-law or choice-of-forum issues, as in international commercial conflicts.	Most arbitration does not result in the creation of legal precedent; if large numbers of particular types of cases are forced into arbitration, the need for legal reform will not be communicated to judges and legislators.
	If litigants want adjudication, hiring an arbitrator can take less time than waiting for a trial date.	
	Not reviewable to the same extent as litigation; disputants may wish to have this greater degree of finality.	Arbitrators may contribute to the exploitation of a weak disputant by a strong one; of particular concern when binding arbitration is mandated in contracts of adhesion.
	Disputants can choose an adjudicator with a specific background and expertise.	Privacy may make it easier for bigoted disputants and arbitrators to act on their prejudices than it is for litigants and judges.
	Assuming that the agreement to arbitrate is a voluntary, arm's-length transaction and perceived as procedurally "just," disputants are more likely to psychologically own the result because it is the result of their voluntary action.	Formalized arbitration designed to protect disputant due process rights can be at least as expensive, time consuming, and complex as litigation.
Negotiation	Particularly effective when the principal source of the conflict is a differing perception about facts or law.	More harmful to relationships: an adversary process; may settle a short-term dispute but set the stage for a long-term adversarial relationship.
	More final in that a final decision is definitely rendered.	Disputants must surrender control over the outcome to a third party.
	Because the decision is rendered by a third party, loss-of-face problems in making concessions are avoided.	Less likely to generate creative, optimal solutions.
		More expensive, time consuming.
		Rules of reviewability, choice of law, and arbitrability are highly complex; results are often counterintuitive and/or hard to predict; more likely to be vulnerable to legal maneuvering.
Mediation	Particularly effective when the principal source of the conflict is a differing perception about facts or law (but skilled mediators can deal effectively with this issue).	More harmful to relationships: an adversary process; may settle a short-term dispute but set the stage for a long-term adversarial relationship.
	More final in that the final decision is definitely rendered.	Disputants must surrender control over the outcome to a third party.
	"Informal arbitration" may be quicker than facilitative mediation.	Less likely to generate creative, optimal solutions.
	Because a decision is rendered by a third party, loss-of-face problems in making concessions are avoided (but mediators are often skilled at dealing with such impediments anyway).	More likely to impair due process rights because the outcome is binding.
		"Formal" arbitration is far more expensive and time consuming.
		Rules of reviewability, choice of law, and arbitrability are highly complex; results are often counterintuitive and/or hard to predict; more likely to be vulnerable to legal maneuvering.

263

arise. Although nonbinding evaluation is more adversarial than facilitative ADR processes, it is kinder on relationships than all-out litigation. And, many times, parties and their lawyers have a strong interest in avoiding court: What they really want is BATNA clarification so that they can get a better idea of the appropriate settlement range. Nonbinding evaluation is tailored to provide this information. Furthermore, nonbinding evaluation may also be a good way to give clients hell bent on litigation a taste of what they are likely to experience in court—in this way, attorneys can rein in an out-of-control client. On the other hand, nonbinding evaluation may not result in a settlement at all, in which case litigation occurs anyway, creating all the problems of litigation with an additional layer of cost and delay, though some argue that nonbinding evaluation may narrow issues, making litigation less damaging, even if settlement does not result (see Libbey 1999). Moreover, attorneys bent on adversarial behavior could misuse the process by participating, without any intention of ever settling, in order to acquire information and get a preview of the other side's planned litigation tactics (Woodley 1997).

Nonbinding evaluation is also chosen by disputants because it is potentially cheaper and faster than litigation. It can be done with less prehearing preparation than trial, and the hearings themselves are typically informal condensations of what would occur at trial. Summary jury trials are ordered by judges for class actions to achieve such time and cost savings, and those who are involved in these proceedings are beginning to see nonbinding evaluation as the rule rather than the exception.

However, nonbinding evaluation is sometimes touted as an efficiency measure without due regard for whether, in fact, the presumed cost and time savings will be realized (Posner 1986). It is not entirely clear that the wholesale referral of cases to nonbinding evaluation actually saves time and money. The Honorable John Connolly and a committee of researchers studied court-connected ADR processes in Minnesota in the mid-1990s, comparing summary jury trial with arbitration, mediation, and litigation in a scientifically controlled manner (Connolly 1999) and found little to recommend nonbinding evaluation over mediation, arbitration, or litigation, at least for legal disputes as a whole.

Judge Connolly's research committee controlled for variations in the kinds of cases that undergo various dispute resolution processes by randomly assigning approximately 100 civil cases each to non-ADR, summary jury trial, and mediation with a possibility of subsequent arbitration. He tracked the cases, collected data, and sought the opinions of both litigants and lawyers about the experiences. Although summary jury trial reduced the percentage of cases that ended in trial, the average time it took for cases to be disposed of was higher for this group than for either litigated or mediated/arbitrated cases. Moreover, an analysis of the number of court appearances that were required for each case (a measure of the court resources needed) indicated that, although summary jury trial reduced the average number of court hearings per case from .99 to .94, the cases that were referred to mediation or arbitration did far better, with an average per-case hearing rate of only .54. More mediating litigants than litigants participating in summary jury trial reported that participating in ADR saved them money, and whereas about one-third of the litigants thought that use of summary jury trial decreased the amount of time their attorneys had to spend on their case, almost 60 percent of the litigants thought that it increased the needed time. Attorneys felt that both ADR processes were more likely to save time than increase time, but there was no substantial difference between mediation and summary jury trial on this measure.

These findings call into some question the prevailing belief that nonbinding evaluation processes are time and money savers, at least when applied indiscriminately to all legal disputes. Some courts, in reviewing cases sent to nonbinding evaluation for a determination of counsel fees in subsequent litigation, have commented on the considerable time and money the process often requires. For example, in *Brotherton v. Cleveland*, 141 F. Supp. 2d 907, 911 (S.D. Ohio, 2001) the judge in charge of awarding plaintiff attorney's fees in a class action commented that

> [a]lthough the case had not yet proceeded to trial at the time of settlement, Class Counsel's participation in the Summary Jury Trial required almost as much preparation as the actual trial would have.

Another potential advantage of nonbinding evaluation is the parties' ability to choose the qualifications of the neutral. In a highly technical scientific dispute or a dispute over an arcane element of law or commerce, the choice of an expert neutral can save time and effort and can increase both disputants' expert power. When a factual question is in doubt, the summary jury trial method can provide BATNA clarification by the choice of a neutral panel that resembles a typical jury. Nonbinding evaluation is frequently used in complex products liability cases and class action litigation—it's a "natural" in factually complex situations in which a hired fact finder can efficiently and expediently deal with the principal impasses to resolution. Generally, judges do not possess this sort of expertise.

Finally, like other forms of ADR, nonbinding evaluation is typically a private process. Privacy can have both advantages and disadvantages, as previously discussed in this chapter. Some disputants may benefit from the privacy, whereas others prefer that the public be informed of the process and outcome. Moreover, public policy considerations may be affected. Although there has been a tendency to turn to nonbinding evaluation in complex products liability cases and class action litigation, these are often the very cases in which the general public has an important stake in knowing about the process and outcome of the dispute. It can be argued that they are precisely the situations that cry out for public scrutiny. As previously mentioned in the context of mediation, privacy may also increase the chances that the parties and the neutral will engage in bigoted or prejudiced behavior, though empirical support for this premise is lacking.

Compared with Arbitration. In many ways, nonbinding evaluation is similar to arbitration: In fact, it can seem indistinguishable from arbitration until the moment when one disputant decides not to accept the decision of the neutral. It should not be surprising, then, that nonbinding evaluation has many of the same advantages and disadvantages of arbitration. Like arbitration, it has a tendency to promote an adversarial, competitive perspective on the conflict and to promote positional bargaining. Unlike arbitration, the decision itself is not finalized in the outcome of the neutral's evaluation. Because the ultimate outcome depends on the disputants' reaching consensus, it may be argued that the ultimate settlement will achieve greater psychological ownership in a nonbinding evaluation and that, because the ultimate outcome is a negotiated settlement, nonbinding evaluation may be better at protecting relationships. On the other hand, settlement is less certain, and, on balance, since the conflict may not be resolved and the process tends to lead to a positional-bargaining focus, the relationship-protection aspect of nonbinding evaluation may be illusory.

Compared with Mediation. The comparison of nonbinding evaluation with facilitative varieties of mediation raises the most interesting questions for conflict diagnosticians. Nonbinding evaluation is considered effective in dealing with extreme differences of fact or law, and it is useful for BATNA clarification: It functions as a dry run at litigation, enabling attorneys and their clients to get a reasonable estimate of what would happen if the case went to trial. If BATNA clarification is important to the disputant or his or her advocates, this aspect of nonbinding evaluation may be very important. Even if a disputant would not characterize BATNA clarification as crucial for settlement, sometimes a neutral opinion that reveals the weaknesses or uncertainties of a disputant's case can break a logjam and promote settlement. Judges experienced in handling one such process, the summary jury trial, characterize it as producing very reliable estimates of what a jury would have decided had the case gone to trial, and others comment that such processes give the disputants a dose of litigation reality, giving them a taste of the nonmonetary costs of actually litigating their case and the effects of the uncertainties in their case before a fact finder (Woodley 1997). If the legal dispute is extremely complicated or difficult to understand, a neutral evaluation process that improves expert power may be very helpful in promoting an effective settlement.

Moreover, nonbinding evaluation may be a more comfortable process for some disputants and many lawyers. Trial attorneys may be more comfortable with the trial-like nonbinding evaluation process than with a facilitative mediation process (Connolly 1999). (Indeed, one possible reason advanced by some scholars for the widespread acceptance of mediation by lawyers over the past decade is that mediation has been recast and reconfigured to closely resemble nonbinding evaluation (Sabatino 1998).) Like lawyers, many disputants may be more comfortable with a process consistent with the invisible veil version of disputing. Such disputants, as well as those who wish for a "day in court" for reasons of vengeance or vindication, may prefer nonbinding evaluation as a way to provide this experience without submitting to the problems of litigation.[5]

---

[5] Some judges experienced with summary jury trial believe that the process has special qualities to offer in allowing disputants to ventilate their feelings and express their positions before a trial-like body (Libbey 1999; Woodley 1997).

Lawyer and Litigant Attitudes Toward Summary Jury Trial

As part of the Ramsey County, Minnesota, Summary Jury Trial study, Judge Connolly's research group asked attorneys and litigants questions that tapped their attitudes toward the processes they had used. Most revealing of the resulting data was the overall satisfaction each group expressed. The litigants reported about a 55 to 60 percent satisfaction rate for both SJT and mediation, with only a very slight 4 percent preference for summary jury trial (SJT). The attorneys, on the other hand, were far more likely to be satisfied with SJT, with 68 percent reporting being "satisfied" or "very satisfied," compared with only 42 percent satisfaction with mediation (Connolly 1999).

The disadvantages of nonbinding evaluation spring from its status as an adversarial process. It tends to promote the narrowed focus of positional bargaining and the lawyer's standard philosophical map, making it harder to hammer out creative, efficient, problem-solving settlements. It tends to be less protective of relationships and more likely to lead to conflict escalation. Mediation proponents often argue that good mediation can deal effectively with extreme disputes of fact anyway. In fact, there may be other, less expensive, less damaging, and equally effective methods of BATNA clarification available if the parties can think creatively about the situation.

Nonbinding evaluation and facilitative mediation need not be mutually exclusive processes. Nonbinding evaluation can be used by the disputants as an adjunct to facilitative mediation for BATNA clarification and expert empowerment. If the disputants are working collaboratively under the guidance of a good facilitative mediator, they can design a nonbinding evaluation process that addresses and promotes their needs most effectively without causing undue collateral damage.

Summary: Advantages and Disadvantages of Nonbinding Evaluation. One might appropriately generalize that nonbinding evaluation is likely to be most helpful in situations in which the disputants are highly motivated to settle and/or sophisticated and familiar with negotiation (thus minimizing the likelihood of conflict escalation), but the disputants' litigation ATNAs are difficult to determine, as in complicated fact situations and technically challenging disputes. If time is of the essence and neither outcome optimization nor relationship preservation is important, nonbinding evaluation might be the dispute resolution process of choice, though informal arbitration can save even more time in such situations. On the other hand, if the disputants can afford investing a little time in the dispute resolution process, facilitative mediation within which the disputants use nonbinding evaluation to help with BATNA clarification is a better option. Nonbinding evaluation has a tendency to produce position-boundedness: Using it within the confines of facilitative mediation can protect the disputants against falling into pure positional bargaining, ensuring that the disputants' relationship is preserved and the outcome truly meets the needs of all involved.

MIXED AND HYBRID ADR PROCESSES

In keeping with the unique qualities of mixed and hybrid dispute resolution processes, the benefits and drawbacks of mixed and hybrid ADR depend on which process is being considered. Let's look at some of the common varieties and their strengths and weaknesses.

Med-Arb. Med-arb is attractive to disputants and their lawyers for several reasons. Disputants and lawyers worried about the possibility that mediation won't produce settlement can choose med-arb, knowing that they will get some of the benefits of mediation yet will ensure an ultimate outcome. Since they are opting for arbitration as a backup, they are less likely to feel as if they are signaling weakness to an opponent. Some proponents of med-arb also believe that, because arbitration is hanging over disputants' heads, they will be more motivated to settle in mediation. Some also believe that, with med-arb-same, the disputants will make less extreme demands (they'll "behave") because they know the mediator will be adjudicating their case and the failure to cooperate and negotiate in good faith may cast them in a negative light. Anecdotal information coming to light in the 1980s suggested very high settlement rates in the mediation component of med-arb.

Despite the lure of a process that takes advantage of the unique features of mediation and arbitration, it is now considered the collective consensus of ADR scholars and professionals that combining mediation and arbitration does not create a process with desirable characteristics (Stulberg 2002).

Med-arb-same suffers from a number of fairness, neutrality, and conflict diagnosis problems (Peter 1997). During mediation, the med-arbitrator may become privy to confidential information, particularly if he or she uses the caucus heavily. He or she can't help but consider this information in making an arbitration award, which can compromise impartiality in the arbitration process. For example, information and communication relevant to the disputants in their discussion of the conflict (such as personal feelings of hostility, a sense of guilt or remorse, or a willingness to apologize) will be irrelevant and may be prejudicial to an adjudicator dealing with explicit legal issues. An additional issue of partiality arises if the mediation is evaluative: In that case, the med-arbitrator will have conducted an evaluation even before arbitration begins, further compromising partiality. In making an evaluation during evaluative mediation, the med-arbitrator is predicting how the case would come out if litigated, whereas, during the arbitration, he or she has to decide the case based on law and equitable principles. These are not necessarily the same, and it may be tough for the med-arbitrator to let go of the prediction and focus on the appropriate basis for decision. Moreover, if the med-arbitrator relies heavily on caucusing during the mediation phase, issues of fairness and due process arise. The disputants aren't able to hear and deal with comments raised by the other disputants in their mediation caucuses, yet the med-arbitrator will invariably rely on this material when wearing the hat of the arbitrator.

Trouble can also result from the incorporation of an adversarial process (arbitration) into a facilitative one, particularly in med-arb-same. The fact that the mediator may ultimately arbitrate the case creates coercion to settle (this is one of the justifications for using med-arb: to pressure disputants to settle), and this feature impairs quality of consent, decreasing psychological ownership of the outcome. A disputant who says no to a course of action explicitly recommended, or implicitly suggested, by the med-arbitrator may fear that the mediator will retaliate by ruling against him or her in arbitration, and, if the med-arbitrator makes a suggestion during the mediation phase, he or she may become ego-invested in the suggestion, which will impede independent judgment during the arbitration phase. Moreover, since the disputants must protect their positions in case arbitration occurs, interest-based, principled negotiation is likely to be curtailed: The disputants have an incentive to play things close to the belt, trading concessions from an initially extreme demand. Some commentators have also worried that mediators and arbitrators require different sorts of skills (only a problem if the med-arbitrator is not trained in both disciplines).

Med-arb-different presents fewer problems than med-arb-same. Most of the role-confusion problems of med-arb-same are absent, since the mediator and arbitrator are different people. In a sense, med-arb-different is two separate processes, except that the disputants enter mediation knowing that arbitration will definitely occur if settlement doesn't result.

There are also problems with med-arb-different, but they are more subtle. They relate to the disputants' knowledge of the ready availability of the adjudication alternative. Mediation requires the attainment of mutual consensus, which may be difficult and requires commitment and energy. In mediation without arbitration, there is no fallback to adjudication, except that litigation is a possibility. The major difference between such a situation and med-arb-different is that, in the latter, disputants commit in advance to adjudication. This knowledge that adjudication is around the corner may create a heightened awareness of the positional-bargaining aspects of the dispute that may infuse mediation and prevent creative problem solving. Moreover, since there's already an agreement to arbitrate in place, the disputants know that, if they can't reach a consensus, there will definitely be an end to their dispute. Because of this feature of med-arb-different, disputants may be less committed to putting energy into the consensus-building phase of their ADR process. The pressures to abandon mediation in favor of arbitration are likely to be especially acute when the mediation process reaches an impasse, which probably occurs in the vast majority of mediated disputes. Finally, since the egregious litigation alternative is eliminated as a possibility, the disputants can afford to be less committed to the process of mediation.[6]

---

[6] The most radical supporters of pure and transformative mediation might apply this argument to litigation as well as to med-arb. They might say that the ready availability of litigation as the "default" dispute resolution process causes disputants to short-circuit their commitment to the processes, such as mediation and negotiation, that depend on consensus. Unfortunately, although this argument has merit, our species has not yet come up with a better last resort than litigation.

Consensus

We are so accustomed to life within the invisible veil that we often don't see its effects. Does the availability of adversarial dispute resolution processes reinforce the reliance of individuals on such processes?

Some subcultures that value the rights of the individual also reject decisional processes that produce a winner and a loser. According to Richard H. Pildes and Elizabeth S. Anderson, a team consisting of a law professor and a philosophy professor, the Quaker ("Society of Friends") and Shaker societies rely solely on consensus—the agreement of all community members—before decisions are made. Why isn't voting an option in these communities? Pildes and Anderson note that it's believed that voting would harm the will of the collective, and, from a spiritual perspective, the will of the collective is believed to represent the will of God (Pildes and Anderson 1990, 2198).

Consensus can be difficult to attain, as noted by environmentalist Marc Reisner, who notes his experience with the Friends faith from his college days and exalts democratic process over consensus for many disputes (Reisner 2000, 12). A Quaker colleague of the author of this textbook has commented that Quaker meetings sometimes go on for hours, even days, while the congregation tries to persuade a single holdout to come around to the viewpoint of the other members in an effort to reach consensus. If individuals knew that they could short-circuit the often time-consuming and difficult process of consensus building by invoking majority rule, wouldn't they be likely to do it?

Does this logic apply to the analogous situation in which a facilitative dispute resolution process is paired with an adversarial process, as in med-arb? What do you think?

In addition to the more theoretical problems associated with med-arb-different, the process has the simple and practical problem of requiring two different neutrals, which costs additional time and money if mediation doesn't settle the matter. Co-med-arb, in which the arbitrator sits in on the mediation phase, saves time but can be even more expensive, and it presents some of the partiality problems of med-arb-same. In addition, since the arbitrator is observing the mediation process in co-med-arb, there is strong incentive for the disputants to couch their dispute in adversarial terms during mediation in order to maximize their chances of winning should arbitration be needed. Like med-arb-same, co-med-arb can be expected to produce adversarial posturing and positional bargaining, making it harder to achieve principled negotiation and cooperative settlement during the mediation phase.

Arb-Med. Arb-med is grounded in a positional-bargaining paradigm of conflict resolution, and it is based on incentives very similar to final-offer arbitration. Arb-med assumes that negotiation will be adversarial, with each disputant's team having an incentive to make the most extreme offers they can. It is believed that, since the disputants know that there is an arbitration award hanging over their heads, there will be counterincentives to make compromises that offset the usual motive to make extreme offers during negotiation.

Arb-med is beset with several problems. The fact that arbitration, which is an adversarial process, precedes mediation makes it more likely that disputants will be caught up in escalated conflict. Deutsch's Crude Axiom (Chapter 3) cautions that a conflict will tend to become what the disputants believe and perceive it to be: Thus, the imposition of an adversarial framework onto the conflict is likely to create the perception, and then the reality, that the dispute is competitive. Deutsch has also postulated that the more competitive the perception and reality of the conflict, the more likely the conflict is to escalate destructively, and that it is harder to move from an escalated, competitive conflict to a cooperative one than vice versa. Thus, one might expect arb-med to be associated with conflict escalation, in comparison to facilitative mediation, the paradigm of noncompetitive dispute management. This development would be especially likely if the mediator and the arbitrator were the same person—because both disputants will fear losing face and appearing to be weak in front of the neutral and the other disputant.

Arb-med also presents motivational pressures similar to those of med-arb. If the disputants reach impasse during mediation, they know that an arbitration award is available to bail them out. Given the investment of time and money in the arbitration phase and the fact that an arbitrated outcome is already ready and waiting, it's likely the disputants will simply prefer to go with the arbitration award, rather than investing great time, energy, and emotional risk in mediation.

Arb-med-same also presents a problem of arb-mediator neutrality. Once the arb-mediator has conducted the arbitration, he or she will have preconceptions about how the mediation "should" go (since he or she has already adjudicated the case) and may have an ego investment in a particular outcome. Hence, the arb-mediator may be in danger of pressuring the disputants to produce an outcome similar to the one he or she has arbitrated.

Finally, there is a practical cost-effectiveness problem with arb-med: It could be perceived as a waste of time and money (Peter 1997, 99–100). If mediation turns out to be a sufficient process, then arb-med will have imposed an unnecessary layer of time and cost.

Mediation Windowing. In the (fairly unusual) case in which arbitrating disputants are clearly receptive to principled negotiation,[7] mediation windowing can improve process and outcome by promoting a cooperation cycle, and, if the mediator is different from the arbitrator, the impartiality problems of med-arb can be minimized. On the other hand, this technique is unlikely to succeed unless both disputants fully buy into the idea: If conflict escalation is occurring, one or both disputants are likely to perceive mediation windowing as a waste of time or worse. Persons receptive to cooperative, collaborative negotiation may be candidates for facilitative mediation, and this approach may save time and money. Deutsch's Crude Axiom (Chapter 3) would predict that, once arbitration is commenced, disputants would become less and less likely to prefer a facilitative, nonadversarial dispute resolution process.

Incentive Arbitration. Disputants frequently turn to incentive arbitration in an effort to obtain the certainty of adjudication without giving up the autonomy

---

[7] Arbitrating disputants who are receptive to principled bargaining can be expected to be uncommon, because conflict theory predicts that the use of arbitration—an adversarial process—will promote a competitive orientation on the part of the disputants.

and control of a consensual process. A party is free to reject the arbitrated outcome but must be prepared to pay for it if he or she turns out to be unreasonable in his or her actions. This sort of process allows more autonomy and control than a straight adjudication—but not very much, since each disputant is vulnerable to the other disputant's decision to relitigate the dispute.

Incentive arbitration is based on a strictly adversarial model and is therefore unlikely to encourage principled bargaining, cooperation, or creative problem solving. As such, it is suitable for disputants who do not buy into a cooperative-bargaining model, as with the resolution of disputes in competitive sports compensation disputes. Whether such a process is more or less efficient than straight adjudication is unknown because it is unknown how many evaluations are rejected in favor of adjudication.

Minitrial. Minitrial is considered a very effective process for providing information about the litigation option for BATNA clarification. The disputants themselves (or the representatives of the disputants with the authority to settle) get a significant dose of reality testing. This litigation dry run can be particularly effective when there are significant uncertainties in fact or law or a human dimension that might affect outcome (such as a particularly effective or ineffective witness). In addition, some believe that the trial-like atmosphere of minitrial can provide some of the emotional catharsis and sense of vindication that a trial can. On the other hand, since the presentation is adversarial, minitrial tends to promote competition and conflict escalation to a greater degree than facilitative mediation. If the neutral avoids evaluation and sticks to moderating the process, minitrial tends to promote a higher quality of consent than purer forms of nonbinding evaluation. It can be considered for use as an adjunct process within a facilitative mediation framework for BATNA clarification.

Ombuds. It is difficult to generalize about ombuds programs because they vary so widely, and empirical study of their effects is sparse. Thus, as with many ADR processes, it is necessary to apply what we know about conflict (Chapter 2) to our understanding of the potential benefits and drawbacks of ombuds. Theoretically, ombuds can be a particularly effective tool for the constructive resolution of conflict. Because ombuds can persuade, but have no power to impose decisions and must remain neutral (and, hence, are unlikely to be in the business of giving nonbinding evaluations), a well-trained and talented ombuds can be highly effective in constructively managing conflict and in making recommendations to improve the overall functioning of an organization. Decisions reached through a well-conceived ombuds process are predicted to have a high quality of disputant consent and, therefore, to be psychologically owned and adhered to by the participants. Because the ombuds may receive confidential information from potentially numerous sources, he or she has a finger on the pulse of the organization and can be a valuable resource in diagnosing the more systemic problems within the organization that generate interpersonal conflict. As such, ombuds are an important source of information for designers of dispute resolution systems for the organizations in which they operate. On the other hand, as stated in Chapter 6, if the appropriate foundation (true and perceived neutrality, participant buy-in, and real confidentiality) is not laid, experts believe that an ombuds program is likely to be an underutilized waste of money.

Dispute Resolution Systems. The advantages and disadvantages of a particular dispute resolution system design will likely depend on how well its designers are able to understand the organization and diagnose the conflictual situations being addressed as well as how effectively the needed stakeholders are included in the design and implementation process, the organization as a whole can be educated and trained in its use, and the system is evaluated and improved. Judging by the increasing ubiquity of dispute resolution systems design in large organizations and its adoption for the federal government, it appears that these systems are achieving a degree of success in improving the operation of corporations, agencies, and others that use them.

Online Dispute Resolution. The advantages and disadvantages of online dispute resolution, compared to face-to-face forms of dispute resolution, are discussed in detail in Chapter 6. Specific strengths and weaknesses of each process depend on the nature of the process itself—whether mediation, arbitration, nonbinding evaluation, or a hybrid from.

SUMMARY: ADVANTAGES AND DISADVANTAGES OF ADR PROCESSES

It would seem from the foregoing analysis that a simple ranking of ADR processes in order of effectiveness would be a fool's errand. It would seem more accurate to say that the relative advantages and disadvantages of a given dispute resolution process depend on the unique features of the interpersonal conflict, as well as the goals of the participant considering the choice of a process. Thus, disputants, ADR neutrals, and legal professionals can better optimize the resolution of interpersonal conflicts by developing and becoming skilled at applying good methods of selecting dispute resolution processes. It is to this goal—selecting dispute resolution processes to match unique situations—that we turn next.

DISPUTE RESOLUTION PROCESS SELECTION METHODS

The use of conflict diagnosis—theories and principles for understanding interpersonal conflict—for selecting ADR processes (see Chapter 2) is a field still in its earliest infancy.[8] This lack of maturity makes the field very exciting to study

---

[8] Although the idea of diagnosing a conflict is well established, the term *diagnosis,* applied to interpersonal conflict, means different things to different people.

and practice: You might someday be one of the pioneers. In the pages that follow, we'll catch a glimpse of how principles and concepts you've learned here can be used to custom select and design an ADR process best fitting a client and his or her situation.

FITTING THE FORUM TO THE FUSS

The most well-known effort to describe how to select ADR processes was published by eminent law professors Frank E. A. Sander of Harvard Law School and Stephen B. Goldberg of Northwestern University Law School. Their groundbreaking article "Fitting the Forum to the Fuss: A User-Friendly Guide to Selecting an ADR Forum" (1994) offered a first attempt to create a systematic ADR selection process based on matching the qualities of each process to the characteristics of the clients and the conflict. Sander and Goldberg assert that the client's interests and the setting and situation of the conflict should control the choice of a dispute resolution process. They propose creating a simple grid system to represent the various strengths of the available processes. For example, using their own backgrounds and expertise, they rated mediation and early neutral evaluation best at minimizing costs and maximizing speed, whereas they rated litigation best at obtaining a binding precedent. For each dispute resolution process and each client objective, they recommend assigning a numeric score to represent, roughly, the relative utility of that process in meeting that objective. The legal professional would then assign an importance to the client of each objective. For example, a client might rate minimizing costs as very important—a "ten"—but getting a binding precedent as only moderately important—a "five." Finally, the relative utility of a given dispute resolution process for the client is determined by multiplying the utility factor by the user's importance factor and summing the products over all the client's objectives. The diagnostician then compares the scores for each dispute resolution process, with the highest score representing the best fit between the client's goals and the process. Sander and Goldberg created one grid to represent the utility of processes for meeting various client objectives and another to represent the utility of ADR processes for overcoming impediments to settlement.

Let's get a glimpse of how this process might work in a dispute.

Mark Farley, a fifty-five-year-old father of two, entered Anytown Hospital for a routine cardiac catheterization. During the procedure, something went wrong: The contrast dye used in the process led to permanent kidney impairment, and Mark was forced to go on dialysis. Although such damage is a predictable consequence in a fraction of such procedures, there was a factual issue concerning whether Mark was adequately informed of the risks and a mixed factual and legal issue concerning whether hospital protocol had allowed inadequate risk screening. As a hypertension sufferer, there was some question whether he may have had some preexisting kidney damage predisposing him to harm from the dye, a fact that might have made the procedure medically inadvisable; yet this same condition may have caused the lion's share of the damage prior to the catheterization. Moreover, the procedure uncovered an arterial blockage that was corrected with a stent, and Mark would have been at risk for heart attack had that not been done.

Mark and his family consulted a medical malpractice attorney, Bernice Jones. In her interview with the Farleys, Bernice allowed them to express their grief and anger at the event. She also explored the legal issues with them. Bernice neither encouraged nor discouraged the option of litigation but spent time in the initial interview asking the Farleys to discuss their hopes and dreams for how this matter would play out. The Farleys expressed interest in settling out of court: Mark is weak and sick much of the time, and the Farleys felt it would be in the family's best interests to avoid litigation if possible. In addition, the Farleys had few other options for medical care because they lived in a very small town. Their trust in the hospital had been severely tested but not shattered. All other things being equal, they preferred that their status as users of the hospital not be irrevocably terminated. However, they wanted visible evidence that the hospital and doctor were more trustworthy than their recent experience had indicated.

Table 7-3 shows a small excerpt from a grid created by attorney Bernice Jensen to represent her clients' typical objectives in the legal disputes (in a real dispute, there would be many more client considerations). Bernice represents the priorities her client Mark has for these objectives, as follows: minimize immediate costs, of moderate priority; get a legal precedent, low priority; preserve relationships, high priority. Thus, she assigned a "Client Priority" weight of three points (out of a possible five points) to "minimize costs," a one to "obtain precedent," and a five to "preserve or maintain relationships."

Bernice has also prepared a grid, based on her understanding of principles of conflict diagnosis, to represent how well she believes that various dispute resolution processes address each of these objectives (she calls the resultant figures Dispute Resolution Capacity weights). Her grid is shown in Table 7-4—again, we show only an excerpt from what, in the real world, would be a much larger grid reflecting many more objectives.

◆ **TABLE 7-3** Bernice Jensen's Table of Client Objectives (excerpted), with Mark Farley's Priority Weightings

Client Objective	Mark Farley's Priorities (0 = irrelevant to 5 = extremely important)
Minimize immediate costs	3
Whatever the outcome, it has precedential impact	1
Preserve or maintain relationships	5

Adapted from Sander & Goldberg (1994).

◆ **TABLE** 7-4   Bernice's Table of Dispute Resolution Capacity Weights (excerpt)

| Client Objective | Dispute Resolution Capacity Weights: How well each process addresses each possible client objective (0 = very poorly to 5 = extremely well) | | | | | | |
	Facilitative Mediation	Evaluative Mediation	Summary Jury Trial	Early Neutral Evaluation	Informal Arbitration	Formal Arbitration	Litigation
Minimize immediate costs	4	4	3	5	5	2	1
Whatever the outcome, it has precedential impact	0	0	0	0	1	2	5
Preserve or maintain relationships	5	4	3	3	2	1	1

Adapted from Sander & Goldberg (1994).

Bernice then prepares the analysis shown in Table 7-5. She multiplies the Dispute Resolution Capacity weights shown in Table 7-4 (column in black) by the Client Priority weights shown in Table 7-3. This yields the figures shown there in grey. Then she sums the results for each dispute resolution process, yielding the numbers shown in the bottom row of the table. These figures indicate that, by this analysis, facilitative mediation would be somewhat more effective than alternatives, and formal adjudication the least effective, in addressing the client priorities considered in this analysis.

Sander and Goldberg characterized their grids as merely a beginning to an ongoing discussion about fitting the forum to the fuss, and they commented that they are useful primarily in illustrating that different processes have different strengths and weaknesses in specific settings. Many ADR practitioners would probably argue that using these grids in practice would oversimplify the process of choosing a dispute resolution process and provider. Sander and Goldberg themselves offer their own grids (Sander and Goldberg 1994, 53, 55) but acknowledged that the capacity weightings they assigned were based on their own experiences and those of professionals they had worked with and not (at least, not yet) supported by empirical research (52). Utility weightings are only as good as the evidence that supports them. Although weightings can be inferred from conflict diagnosis principles, and may be an improvement over using hunches and personal experience, even this degree of precision may not be sufficiently fine grained to be the basis for making important client decisions. The usefulness of such grids also depends on the thoroughness of the interests

◆ **TABLE** 7-5   Bernice's Calculation of How Well Dispute Resolution Processes Address Client Mark Farley's Objectives (excerpt)

WHITE COLUMNS: DISPUTE RESOLUTION CAPACITY WEIGHTS (0 = VERY POORLY TO 5 = EXTREMELY WELL) FROM TABLE 7-4
GREY COLUMNS: PRIORITIES WEIGHTS MULTIPLIED BY DISPUTE RESOLUTION CAPACITY WEIGHTS

CLIENT OBJECTIVE	PRIORITIES WEIGHTS (FROM TABLE 7-3)	FACILITATIVE MEDIATION		EVALUATIVE MEDIATION		SUMMARY JURY TRIAL		EARLY NEUTRAL EVALUATION		INFORMAL ARBITRATION		FORMAL ARBITRATION		LITIGATION	
Minimize immediate costs	3	4	12*	4	12	3	9	5	15	5	15	2	6	1	3
Whatever the outcome, it has precedential impact	1	0	0	0	0	0	0	0	0	1	1	2	2	5	5
Preserve or maintain relationships	5	5	25	4	20	3	15	3	15	2	10	1	5	1	5
Capacity of process to deal with client's priorities		37		32		24		30		25		13		13	

*Figures in black column represent the priority weights from Table 7-3.
Figures in white columns represent the Dispute Resolution Capacity weights from Table 7-4.
Figures in grey columns represent the priority weights from Table 7-3 multiplied by Dispute Resolution Capacity weights from Table 7-4.
Adapted from Sander & Goldberg (1994).

analysis performed on behalf of the client because the interests analysis determines the client objectives and the priority weightings assigned to each. More troublesome, how do we account for the possibility of overlap among client goals? Is it appropriate, for example, to have "obtain vindication," "get a neutral opinion," and "maximize monetary recovery" (three client objectives identified by Sander and Goldberg) as separate client goals in the grid, if a client's sense of anger and betrayal are part of what motivates him or her to want all three? Or does this constitute triple-weighting—counting the same motive multiple times—such that the client goal is overrepresented in the analysis? Another thing that makes the grid system problematic is that the utilities of the processes are not static but vary with the situation. For example, the goal "maximize recovery" is listed by Sander and Goldberg (1994) as met optimally by litigation, but this is true only if the client has an airtight case. If the client's case is very weak or uncertain, litigation is probably the worst method of ensuring the client a good monetary outcome. Thus, dispute resolution capacity weightings, as well as client priority weightings, may be situation specific.

TOWARD A CONFLICT DIAGNOSIS APPROACH

It's unlikely that a simple grid will ever provide an appropriate substitute for the information discussed throughout this textbook. Moreover, Sander and Goldberg caution that they did not intend for the grid to serve as an all-purpose ADR selection tool. However, the basic concept illustrated by the Sander and Goldberg grids—that ADR processes should be chosen to respond to client objectives and the characteristics of the conflict—is a valid one.

THE RULE OF PRESUMPTIVE (FACILITATIVE) MEDIATION

Sander and a number of other legal and ADR scholars express a "rule of presumptive mediation"—that mediation should be tried first (Sander and Goldberg 1994, 59–60; see also Barnes 1997). Sander and Goldberg point out that mediation excels over other ADR methods in overcoming most impediments to settlement (see Chapter 2). The exceptions, they say, are the Jackpot syndrome and disparate views of fact and law—and mediators often have ways to help disputants settle that don't require the disputants to resolve disparate views of fact or law (Sander and Goldberg 1997, 59). There are a number of additional reasons to begin with mediation. First, "It can't hurt." Unless time is of the essence and one of the disputants is likely to harm the other irreparably unless immediately restrained, good mediation is, even at worst, helpful in reducing conflict escalation. Mediation may help even if agreement is not reached—if well done, it will strengthen relationships and may narrow the issues in dispute (making subsequent litigation faster and less costly), may clarify BATNAs, may help each disputant understand the other's perspective, and may help each team prepare for whatever other process they'll be involved in, including litigation and arbitration. Mediation can also result in partial agreements that can reduce the cost and trauma of any adversarial processes that may be needed later. Other processes, such as nonbinding evaluation, arbitration, and even litigation, can be used within a facilitative mediation framework to provide answers to questions that are more appropriately handled that way. In this way, the facilitative framework can help minimize conflict escalation and cope with the natural weaknesses of the other processes.

Conflict diagnosis principles suggest three important reasons to begin conflict resolution with, specifically, facilitative mediation. First, facilitative mediation is a highly consensual process. Obviously, consensual processes can provide a high quality of consent—that is, the disputants are the ones who psychologically own the decision and are more likely to make it work enthusiastically. The highest quality of consent is attained using a process in which the disputants themselves generate the settlement, rather than settling on an outcome because someone else has told them it's what they'd get if they went to court. Hence, well-done facilitative mediation, and negotiation without evaluation, can yield the highest quality of consent. Theoretically, of the facilitative mediation processes, transformative mediation—which vests in the disputants virtually complete control over the objective of the process as well as the outcome—yields the very highest quality of consent. A highly facilitative process also has the potential to do the best job of counteracting the damaging effects of conflict escalation. In contrast, evaluative processes tend to promote the competition cycle, leading to less creative problem solving and poorer settlements (as described in Chapter 2). Once this process begins, it tends to self-promote, creating a self-fulfilling prophecy: The conflict seems more and more like a zero-sum contest requiring competitive approaches to resolution. Actions taken in response tend to trigger competitive behavior in the other disputant, causing the conflict to begin to escalate, and the escalating conflict seemingly proves that it was correct to perceive the conflict from an invisible veil perspective. Theories of conflict, cooperation, competition, and negotiation style suggest that the best processes for promoting constructive, equitable, and efficacious dispute resolution are those in which the participants are persistently guided away from invisible-veil, zero-sum thinking and toward collaborative, integrative problem solving. Purely facilitative forms of mediation best fit this set of requirements. Slightly less effective are thought to be the consensual processes that avoid providing evaluations but that promote compromising. These include facilitative mediation processes that focus on compromising rather than collaborating.

Facilitative and Evaluative Mediation: The Civil Litigator's Perspective

Conflict diagnosis concepts lead to the hypothesis that facilitative mediation will, all other things being equal, lead to better conflict resolution than evaluative mediation. This is because facilitative mediation promotes a higher quality of consent—the disputants have more say in whether and how the conflict gets resolved—and the facilitative process leads to more creative problem solving and less conflict escalation.

Despite the theoretical advantages of facilitative mediation, the available empirical research indicates that lawyers involved in mediation overwhelmingly prefer evaluative mediation. In a series of studies of attitudes toward court-connected mediation (Hermann, Honeyman, McAdoo, and Welsh 2001), lawyers participating in Minnesota and Missouri civil mediation identified "provided needed reality check for my client" and "provided needed reality check for opposing counsel or party" as principal reasons for choosing mediation. Almost 70 percent of the Missouri attorneys identified "helps everyone to value the case" as an important reason they chose mediation. And, of the Missouri attorneys, 87 percent stated that "knowing how to value a case" was an important mediator qualification, more than any other criterion listed. The runner up, at 83 percent, was "mediator should be a litigator," followed by "mediator should be a lawyer," at 77 percent. In contrast, only 35 percent felt that it was important for the mediator to "know how to find creative solutions."

> ### *Advantages of Facilitative Mediation:*
> ### *The Conflict Diagnosis Perspective*
>
> ◆ It maximizes quality of consent.
>
> ◆ It avoids invisible veil thinking.
>
> ◆ It preserves relationships.
>
> ◆ It optimizes resources.
>
> ◆ It promotes voluntary compliance.
>
> ◆ It promotes cooperation.
>
> ◆ It prevents oppressive outcomes.

These purely facilitative, consensual ADR forms are followed in usefulness by consensual forms of dispute resolution that add an element of evaluation to an otherwise facilitative process. They include evaluative mediation that features large amounts of facilitation as well as minitrial without neutral evaluation. These minimally evaluative forms add a dimension of BATNA clarification, although many facilitative mediators would argue that BATNA clarification is just as attainable in facilitative mediation. The more evaluative the process, the lower the quality of consent and the more invisible-veil thinking is promoted. Thus, evaluative mediation—and minitrial without an evaluation—can be expected to be less effective in this regard than facilitative mediation in meeting these goals.

ADR featuring nonbinding evaluation as the process centerpiece—early neutral evaluation, nonbinding evaluation, minitrial with neutral evaluation, and summary jury trial—can be expected to fall below evaluative mediation and minitrial without neutral evaluation in promoting a high quality of consent and in making optimal dispute resolution possible. Although these processes falter in setting the stage for creative problem solving, and create the risk of conflict escalation if they fail to produce a settlement, they are good for situations in which rapid, low-cost determinations are needed and in which it is clear that both parties are willing to abide by the evaluation.

Nonconsensual processes bring up the rear of this hierarchy. Arbitration processes are often more consensual than litigation because the disputants have contracted that they take place. (In the case of consumer contracts of adhesion, this is usually not the case.) One can expect med-arb to be slightly more effective than straight arbitration for achieving quality of consent. Litigation is the least consensual process, unless both litigants have enthusiastically chosen it. Litigation is also generally the poorest option for reducing conflict escalation, resolving the entire landscape of the conflict, developing creative and flexible outcomes, and promoting disputant relationships. Figure 7-1 shows this relationship among dispute resolution forms, quality of consent, and ability to minimize invisible-veil thinking.

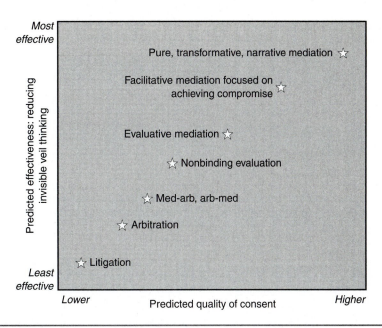

◆ **FIGURE 7-1**

Efficacy of Dispute Resolution Processes in Promoting Quality of Consent and Preventing Invisible-Veil Thinking

Thus, in considering quality of consent and ability to resolve conflict in an optimal manner—and assuming that there is a specific reason the dispute can't be resolved through collaborative, face-to-face negotiation—the highest and best form of dispute resolution is facilitative mediation that actively involves the disputants themselves and promotes collaborative, integrative forms of problem solving. Such a process is optimal in terms of quality of consent, control of conflict escalation, and capacity to optimize resources and interests creatively. Pure, transformative and narrative mediation typically satisfy this description.

WHEN THE PRESUMPTION DOESN'T APPLY

There are a number of reasons, however, that disputants and their teams don't, or shouldn't, jump directly into facilitative mediation. Some of these reasons are best dealt with by laying a more careful groundwork for using mediation. Others are better dealt with by incorporating other processes into an overall facilitative framework. Still others are best handled by jumping right to evaluative or even adjudicative processes. A summary of these reasons is presented in Figure 7-2.

Reason 1: The Other Side Won't Play. Frequently, a disputant—or his or her legal advocate—resists getting involved in a facilitative process, such as pure or

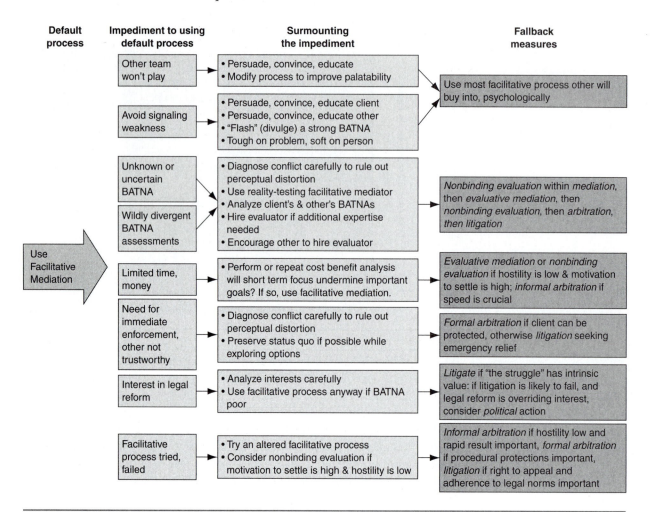

Default process	Impediment to using default process	Surmounting the impediment	Fallback measures
	Other team won't play	• Persuade, convince, educate • Modify process to improve palatability	Use most facilitative process other will buy into, psychologically
	Avoid signaling weakness	• Persuade, convince, educate client • Persuade, convince, educate other • "Flash" (divulge) a strong BATNA • Tough on problem, soft on person	
Use Facilitative Mediation	Unknown or uncertain BATNA Wildly divergent BATNA assessments	• Diagnose conflict carefully to rule out perceptual distortion • Use reality-testing facilitative mediator • Analyze client's & other's BATNAs • Hire evaluator if additional expertise needed • Encourage other to hire evaluator	*Nonbinding evaluation* within *mediation*, then *evaluative mediation*, then *nonbinding evaluation*, then *arbitration*, then *litigation*
	Limited time, money	• Perform or repeat cost benefit analysis will short term focus undermine important goals? If so, use facilitative mediation.	*Evaluative mediation* or *nonbinding evaluation* if hostility is low & motivation to settle is high; *informal arbitration* if speed is crucial
	Need for immediate enforcement, other not trustworthy	• Diagnose conflict carefully to rule out perceptual distortion • Preserve status quo if possible while exploring options	*Formal arbitration* if client can be protected, otherwise *litigation* seeking emergency relief
	Interest in legal reform	• Analyze interests carefully • Use facilitative process anyway if BATNA poor	*Litigate* if "the struggle" has intrinsic value: if litigation is likely to fail, and legal reform is overriding interest, consider *political* action
	Facilitative process tried, failed	• Try an altered facilitative process • Consider nonbinding evaluation if motivation to settle is high & hostility is low	*Informal arbitration* if hostility low and rapid result important, *formal arbitration* if procedural protections important, *litigation* if right to appeal and adherence to legal norms important

◆ **FIGURE 7-2**

A Conflict-Diagnosis Approach to Selecting a Dispute Resolution Process

transformative mediation.[9] There are many possible reasons for such a reaction. Sometimes, this reticence is due to a lack of understanding of the process; other times, it is due to the influence of the invisible veil: a belief that it can't possibly work. Sometimes, the opposition occurs as a reactive devaluation to a suggestion by the other disputant that such a process be tried, and occasionally it is because the other disputant's team feels disempowered by a facilitative process—it is unfamiliar and therefore frightening. Or the disputant's advocate, rather than the disputant, may have these reservations and therefore recommends an evaluative or adjudicative process. It is also possible that the other team has diagnosed the

---

[9] One construction lawyer, asked at a conference whether federal construction ADR would be likely to become more facilitative or remain evaluative, responded, "My clients don't want to sit in no [sic] hot tub with the enemy!"

conflict and has concluded that, for various appropriate reasons, an evaluative or a nonconsensual process would be preferable. If the other team is dragged into a facilitative process unwillingly, and cannot be sold on the process by the mediator or the other process neutral, quality of consent will be impaired.

To gain the advantages of facilitative approaches, a disputant can sometimes use persuasion. An individual who balks due to lack of knowledge can be educated. A competent mediator, for example, will always begin the mediation process by educating the participants about the nature of the process and its advantages. If the problem is reactive devaluation, sometimes the process can be ordered by a court rather than suggested by "the enemy." Sometimes, a facilitative approach can be designed to seem more familiar: For example, a mediator can structure a facilitative process to feel more like a business meeting featuring brainstorming sessions than (what many lawyers dread, usually needlessly) a psychotherapy session. Or a mediator may be chosen who will offer a free introductory session, at which he or she can sell the benefits of a collaborative process to the participants without requiring an up-front commitment.

But it may not be possible to tempt the other side into a facilitative dispute resolution process, or consent may be obtained only begrudgingly. In that case, the benefits of collaborative, integrative bargaining will have to be traded off against the quality of consent. In order to have psychological buy-in by a disputant who is uncomfortable with a facilitative process, one may need to abandon principled bargaining in favor of a more evaluative process that features a zero-sum characterization of the dispute. In other cases, the other disputant will have started litigation, and the first team will have no choice but to respond; or the other team will absolutely refuse any contact with the first team unless they file suit. If litigation does begin, it doesn't hurt to suggest settlement negotiations, with or without a mediator, at appropriate points during the pretrial process.

Reason 2: Concern About Signaling Weakness to the Other Side. Some disputants and their teams avoid suggesting mediation, or other noncompetitive approaches, because they believe it will imply they have a weak case. But, if a facilitative process would be beneficial, choosing another process to avoid seeming weak is not an optimal choice. Indeed, although disputants with weak cases can potentially benefit from a collaborative negotiation process, they are more likely to be on the losing end if they try to bang heads with a stronger opponent. Thus, this is a false consideration: The choice of mediation or another process featuring cooperation, although sometimes seen as a sign of weakness, isn't really a sign of a poor case.

What can a disputant or his or her team do to counter this problem? One option is to signal strength along with the suggestion for mediation or other facilitative or cooperative processes. One can announce one's BATNA to clearly indicate willingness to use adversarial tactics if necessary. One lawyer tells the story of attempting to negotiate collaboratively with her son's middle school for special accommodations for his learning disability. Upon encountering resistance, she wrote to the assistant principal, stating that she emphatically believed

it to be in everyone's interests to work collaboratively to support effective learning and that she felt an adversarial approach would not promote her son's interests. "On the other hand," she wrote, "you should know that I have been trained
as an attorney and am willing to use my training to advocate on behalf of my
son if it becomes necessary." This display of a powerful BATNA promptly
brought the school representative to the bargaining table for some amicable and
constructive negotiation. Once in a facilitative setting, one can directly communicate one's commitment to a fair settlement that takes advantage of no one. If
it is the other disputant who is afraid to signal weakness, it may be possible to
educate the disputant's team that acceding to a cooperative process doesn't signal
weakness and that mediation is not a cakewalk.

**Reason 3: One or Both Disputants Don't Know Their BATNAs, or BATNA
Assessments Seem Wildly Divergent.** Unless a disputant is crystal clear about
his or her deeply seated interests and knows they can't be met outside of negotiation, the lack of a clear BATNA can prevent settlement from occurring. A disputant often has difficulty deciding whether to accept a settlement if he or she is
uncertain whether there are better options. A disputant lacking knowledge of
the BATNA may back into litigation due to strategic paralysis.

For at least three important reasons legal professionals often gravitate toward
evaluative processes, which feature case valuation and BATNA clarification as the
centerpiece. First, the lawyer's standard philosophical map causes many lawyers,
and their clients, to perceive impasses in the resolution of legal disputes as a mere
matter of BATNA analysis. ("I think the case is worth only $5,000 at most, and
he won't go below $30,000. If he just realized his case is chopped liver, we could
settle it tonight.") Lawyers who believe the impasse to settlement is caused by an
opponent's unrealistic BATNA estimate will often choose a process that drives
home the reality of reduced expectations. Second, lawyers can't lose with this tactic. Sometimes, in their zeal to play the gladiator role, lawyers themselves inflate
the BATNA, or clients may develop unrealistic expectations as a result of the
thought distortions that accompany conflict escalation. If the case evaluation
seems to indicate that one's own BATNA is inflated, the client will be able to
settle at close to the case evaluation without the lawyer's appearing weak or apa-
thetic. Thus, consensual processes featuring evaluation solve a number of problems for lawyers. Third, most evaluative processes feel like processes lawyers are
familiar with—trials, motions hearings, and settlement conferences. For all these
reasons, evaluative processes have quite a lure for attorneys and clients.

Since facilitative processes have better potential than evaluative processes
for reversing conflict escalation, promoting effective and creative resource allocation, and maximizing quality of consent, the team should consider whether
there are ways to achieve BATNA clarification without moving to nonbinding
evaluation or adjudication. If the disputant and his or her team are uncertain of
the BATNA, careful case preparation can help clarify it. Skilled facilitative mediators can help guide and promote such self-evaluation. If substantial disagreement over fact or law—a discrepancy between perceived BATNAs—seems to be

occurring, a helpful approach is to use evaluative approaches within a facilitative negotiation or mediation framework—in other words, to design a multimodal process. For example, within the context of a facilitative mediation or negotiation, the disputants can agree to submit a limited question to summary jury trial, to conduct a minitrial, or even to submit the issue to arbitration. The facilitative framework helps maintain the cooperative and creative approach, control any conflict escalation that seems to be resulting from the evaluation, and ensure that the disputants' decisions are purely autonomous and voluntary.

Reason 4: Limited Time and Money. Although mediation of all sorts is usually touted as a time and money saver, in some situations evaluative processes are faster and cheaper. If, after the conflict is diagnosed, it appears that the reasons for preferring a facilitative process are relatively unimportant, using an evaluative process can sometimes be a shortcut.

There are occasions when both disputants are enthusiastic about reaching a quick settlement, see the issue as simply one of money, and are unlikely ever to see one another again. In such situations, an evaluation to clarify the BATNA can lead to prompt and efficient settlement. An online blind-bidding service (Chapter 6), either in place of binding arbitration or nonbinding evaluation, can be even more rapid and inexpensive for disputants who are highly motivated to reach a monetary settlement quickly and cheaply. However, if either side has hard feelings or an escalated conflict is involved, an evaluative process may promote positional bargaining, which can lead to lines drawn in the sand and then to impasse. If impasse occurs after any nonbinding evaluation process, the time and money savings will not take place, and each disputant may blame the other for the failure to settle, thus feeding the flames of conflict escalation. If quality of consent is truly unimportant to either side, and a quick, cheap result is paramount, informal arbitration, which offers a final outcome with minimal investment in preparation and hearing, may be the best option.

Reason 5: Need for a Rapid Enforcement Mechanism. At times immediate recourse to the court system is necessary. For example, in a marital separation a spouse may need to stop the other spouse from abusing him or her. Or, in a consumer action against a business, the court may be needed to guard against dissipation of assets. To avoid irreparable harm, such cases need to be taken to court. After interim relief is obtained, the disputant and team can think carefully about whether it is possible to build enough protections into a facilitative settlement process that advantage can be gained from using one.

> Lester, a fifty-year-old concert violinist, went to Charlie's law office to file for divorce. He and Melanie had been married twenty-five years and had no children. Lester entered the marriage with a $600,000 inheritance from an uncle; however, over the course of the marriage, the inheritance slowly dissipated and nothing was left. Melanie, a successful real estate broker, had been responsible for keeping track of the family finances during the

marriage. When he had asked her where the money was going, she had responded that home repairs had been expensive, she had needed additional money to pay a large bill, or that they had needed an extra little bit to finance a vacation. Lester now suspected that Melanie had been planning to leave him for some time and had been gradually hiding assets so that he could no longer find or get to them. He'd had his suspicions confirmed when Melanie decided to move a jointly owned $100,000 certificate of deposit to a bank in Florida, near her family of origin, in her sole name; he had learned about this when the original bank had phoned about the transaction and had spoken to him to get some identifying information. Melanie's computer records did not indicate that they owned this sort of asset or anything else other than their home and cars and a small checking account. Lester went to Charlie without first confronting Melanie; he was in terror that there were other assets and that, if Melanie became aware of his suspicions, she would systematically dispose of them.

In Lester's case, there isn't time for thorough conflict diagnosis to determine whether it is appropriate to use a facilitative process. Lester needs his legal advocate to protect the marital assets. After the immediate crisis has been taken care of, conflict diagnosis can take place, and appropriate strategies and tactics for meeting Lester's long-term interests can be developed.

Escalated conflict leads to a dramatic erosion of trust between disputants. A disputant in an escalated conflict may therefore perceive the situation as one requiring immediate interim relief, when, in fact, such is not the case. Moreover, at the outset of legal representation, because they have insufficient information to conclude otherwise, attorneys are often forced into acting as if the other disputant were maliciously motivated. Until an investigation can occur, attorneys' ethical obligation to protect the client often requires them to behave as if a worst-case scenario is occurring. Initial protective moves by just-hired attorneys often include heavy-handed, aggressive tactics such as filing lawsuits, initiating burdensome discovery, moving for protective orders, freezing or sequestering assets, and so forth. Thus, the very conduct designed to keep the client from being harmed, if it turns out to have been unnecessary, can escalate the conflict, damage the client's long-term interests, and demonize the other disputant in the eyes of the team, creating a self-fulfilling prophecy.

Thus, it behooves members of a disputant's legal team to think carefully before applying heavy-handed protective tactics. It is important for the legal professional to explain frankly to the other team why a heavy-handed tactic was used. Experienced members of the other legal team will usually understand such a protective strategy, and not hold it against him or her, but less experienced or emotionally involved legal professionals may need the additional information. Conflict diagnosis should quickly follow, to determine whether the initially defensive approach turns out to have been necessary; and, if it is safe to do so, it is important to promptly seek cooperative, collaborative negotiation with the other team. It's also important to avoid using any tactic that creates an irreparable rift with the other disputant's team unless absolutely unavoidable.

Sometimes, creative problem solving by the disputants' teams can defuse a tense situation, allowing a more facilitative approach to settlement.

> Iris went to Bernie's law office to file for divorce. She and Forrest had no children, and the couple had a house but few other valuable assets. Iris said she and Forrest had been in a couple of physical altercations within the past two months as their marriage deteriorated but that, in general, they had simply drifted apart. Forrest emphatically did not want the divorce, but Iris had thought about it for two years, had thrashed the decision out with a therapist, and was very sure this was what she wanted.
>
> Iris was frantic because, several years ago, in happier times, Forrest had taken some very sexually explicit photographs of her and, about a month earlier during a heated argument, had threatened to make them public if she left him. Bernie contacted Forrest's lawyer, who stated that Forrest had no intention of making the pictures public and would be amenable to settlement negotiations. But Forrest balked at having them destroyed—he felt they were his sole source of power over his wife. The two lawyers, after signing collaborative law contracts with one another and with their clients, worked out a deal in which the negatives and all copies of the pictures would be placed in the hands of a close and trusted friend of the family. The materials were sealed, and the friend was asked never to break the seal. Forrest and Iris signed a stipulation requesting that, if settlement negotiations had not produced an agreement after ten months, the friend was to return the sealed package to Forrest; however, if negotiations were successful, they would instruct the friend to destroy all traces of the photos. Six months later, after difficult but productive negotiations, that's what happened.

Reason 6: Uncooperative, Dishonest, or Sociopathic Disputant or Legal Advocate. A consensual process will work only if the participants can be trusted to play reasonably fairly. Participants who are so lacking in a conscience, and confident of their ability to evade discovery, that they have no difficulty committing fraud during the course of the process usually must be dealt with in litigation. Some disputants, either sociopathic or very desperate, will agree to anything, either to delay the inevitable or hoping that the other party will eventually give up and go away. (That's not to say that litigation will invariably succeed when other processes fail—it's just easier to obtain enforcement if the disputant cheats.) There may also be uncooperative clients who require continuing supervision by a court for a number of other reasons, such as the overwhelming desire for revenge.

As with the need for immediate enforcement, conflict escalation often causes disputants to come to an erroneous conclusion that the other disputant is swept up in vengeance, dishonest, sociopathic, or outright evil. (As set out in Chapter 2, the dynamics of conflict escalation tend to turn such initially erroneous assessments into self-fulfilling prophecies, unless they are addressed.) For this reason, careful conflict diagnosis, performed as soon as possible, is warranted to ensure that the perception of the other side is accurate. Although litigation is often the only option when dealing with people who have no conscience, it is a very poor remedy compared with facilitative processes in other situations. If, after careful diagnosis, this issue cannot be clarified, it may be useful to secure basic protections, using litigation if necessary, but accompanying the filing of the lawsuit with explanatory communication inviting the possibility of a facilitative, consensual process with built-in protections. If the situation permits, the disputant should go ahead with facilitative mediation and raise his or her concerns explicitly with the other disputant and the mediator. Sometimes protections that obviate the need to bring legal action can be creatively built into a mediated agreement.

Reason 7: Underlying Interest in Legal Reform. Litigation should be considered if, after careful conflict diagnosis, one concludes that an important source of the conflict is a structural or an interpersonal power imbalance that must be rectified through legal reform. Typically, only litigation, culminating in the pronouncement of an appellate court, can yield this sort of result.

It is often asserted that litigation should be used anytime a disputant suffers from disempowerment relative to the other disputant. This assertion is probably based on an assumption that the court will protect the disempowered litigant, but that's only true if the law is on his or her side. If so, then the disempowered disputant should seek out competent legal representation to maximize the effectiveness of his or her situation. The advocate may want to "flash" (divulge) the BATNA, if strong, to persuade the other side of the advantages of consensual settlement and to prepare for litigation in case the other disputant is unwilling to bend. If the law is not on the side of the disempowered person, then litigation is likely to be fruitless, unless social evolution makes overturning the existing law in the courts likely. A disputant who is disempowered because of a weak case, regardless of the morality of the situation, is unlikely to do well regardless of the setting. People usually "bargain in the shadow of the law" (Mnookin and Kornhauser, 1979)—that is, what people often get in court is reflected in what they are able to get through an alternative process. Indeed, using a competent, collaboration-focused mediator can sometimes net the disempowered disputant a better outcome than an expensive, and fruitless, court case. A disputant who goes to a legal professional's office seemingly disempowered will benefit from the power analysis phase of conflict diagnosis: There may be hidden areas of power that could be mobilized during whatever dispute resolution process is selected. The specific nature of the disputant's power will affect the selection of a dispute resolution process as well. For example, a highly articulate disputant who is a mental-health professional is likely to be able to use his or her communication skills most effectively in a process such as mediation, whereas a professional athlete's agent is more likely to be proficient in the sort of communication that takes place during an adversarial process.

Litigation may serve multiple important objectives if the social climate is ripe for legal reform. For example, consider the parents whose children were legally prevented from attending white schools in Topeka, Kansas, in the late 1940s because of their race. To change the law allowing segregation in the

Lawyers who successfully argued before the U.S. Supreme Court for abolition of segregation in public schools congratulate one another as they leave the court May 17, 1954, after announcement of the court's decision. They are (from left) George E. C. Hayes, Washington; Thurgood Marshall, New York; and James M. Nabrit. AP/Wide World Photos

public schools, these parents had to take their case to court. They eventually achieved the groundbreaking legal reform that culminated in the U.S. Supreme Court decision *Brown v. Board of Education*.[10] The families involved in the *Brown* litigation might have obtained better individual results (in a material sense) by seeking private settlements with the school board; however, it is unlikely that any amount of money or school placement could have undone the psychological damage done by living in a system in which a state law excluded one from going to school with members of the dominant race. The *Brown* plaintiffs may also have benefited psychologically and even materially by their having been so instrumental in changing the course of the history of the civil rights movement.

In considering whether to litigate a matter for its legal reform potential, one must, of course, consider the downsides. *Brown v. Board of Education* had to be taken all the way to the U.S. Supreme Court. This is not a short or an inexpensive path, although in many cases volunteer attorneys are willing to help out in pathbreaking litigation with important consequences for social reform. Moreover, there is no guarantee that the position one is advocating will prevail. In fact, such cases are usually lost—they by and large go against the prevailing law

---

[10] *Brown v. Board of Education*, 347 U.S. 483 (1954). In the *Brown* case, it was determined that having separate school systems for white and black children was inherently a denial of equal protection of the law under the Fourteenth Amendment of the Constitution, even if the facilities of such school systems were equivalent.

of the land. The disputant and legal team must balance the likelihood of losing against the intangible benefits of participating in legal pioneering, even if unsatisfying in its immediate outcome.

Reason 8: All the Alternatives Have Been Tried. Consensual processes—mediation and nonbinding evaluation—are good at achieving a high quality of consent because no disputant is forced to come to agreement. If these consensual processes fail to produce a settlement, obviously another process must be used. Quality of consent is not an issue if consent itself is unattainable.

If there is a strong interest in saving time and money, and if the parties can agree, a variant of arbitration may be useful. Informal arbitration is best if the need for efficiency outweighs the need for procedural protections, whereas a more formal version is better for situations in which achieving procedural justice is a highly valued interest. If the right to appeal is important, litigation should be considered in lieu of formal arbitration, although it will usually take longer to complete.

IN SEARCH OF MAGIC KEYS TO RESOLVING CONFLICT

Although conflict is as old as humankind itself, the scientific discipline of conflict resolution, with its implications for the selection and use of dispute resolution processes, is still in its infancy. Within this discipline, the magic keys to reaching the goals of effective conflict diagnosis, masterful ADR selection, and constructive conflict resolution may be waiting. The student of these fields may find that the paths to finding these keys seem to shimmer: Sometimes they appear clear, but at other times the ways fade into obscurity. The invisible veil of our cultural belief system is a strong and seductive influence on the handling of conflicts and disputes. Nonetheless, a cogent argument can be made that the lure of oversimplifying the messy business of human conflict into simple win-lose paradigms must no longer be surrendered to—we lose too much time, money, security, and human capital.

The advent of the twenty-first century, with its new and frightening existential challenges to peace and stability in the United States and throughout the world, creates a pressing crisis of need: We must strive to lift the veil and to understand the best ways to understand and handle conflict—in families, neighborhoods, business relationships, schools, and societies, as well as internationally. With the world becoming a smaller, more vulnerable, and more interdependent place, we have no choice but to continue to engineer an increasingly effective array of alternative tools for dealing with interpersonal conflict and to develop proficiency in choosing the right tools to handle each dispute as it occurs. Our ability to meet the challenge this crisis presents is becoming more and more critical to our survival as a species. As a student of this messy business, you are in the forefront of a critical human mission. May you gain the clarity of vision to find the magic keys we all seek.

EXERCISES, PROJECTS, AND "THOUGHT EXPERIMENTS"

1. Raymond is a senior paralegal for Jordana DeLancie PC, attorney at law. Jordana takes on a new client, Ari Kaufman, who is seeking compensation due to allegedly fraudulent behavior by a business partner, Mort McLarty. Ari is anxious to litigate the issue and take his partner to the cleaners. Raymond wonders whether litigation is the right option for Ari—Ari's feelings are clearly hurt, he seems out of control emotionally when he talks about the dispute, and he seems to have overly optimistic ideas of what will happen in court. Raymond suspects that the most important issues—in terms of what would best meet Ari's underlying goals, needs, and interests—are emotional, not monetary. Raymond feels that conflict diagnosis is important to clarify Ari's interests, values, and needs and to develop an appropriate strategy for addressing the dispute. But Ari is so angry that he will only talk about how evil and underhanded Mort has been to him and how he's going to give him what he really deserves. Raymond's time is billed to the client. What should Raymond do?

2. Suppose Raymond's firm decides to resolve issues such as that posed in question 1 by revealing upfront that the lawyers and legal assistants will use conflict diagnosis to develop effective strategies for client representation. Are there any problems with this approach?

   a. Consider the ABA's Model Rules of Professional Conduct, Rule 1.1: "A lawyer shall provide competent representation to a client. Competent representation requires the legal knowledge, skill, thoroughness and preparation reasonably necessary for the representation." What would a lawyer need to do to avoid transgressing this rule if he or she tried to diagnose a client's dispute?

   b. Is there a practical problem in marketing this lawyering approach to potential clients? If so, how could it be circumvented?

3. If you work in a law office, design a set of forms or a procedural manual that you can use to guide and streamline your use of conflict diagnosis principles in your work.

4. Emily Parrington files a grievance against her former attorney, Mike Snakeoil, in your state. She contends that Mike had a duty to advise her of ADR options and completely failed to do so. As a result, Emily chose to endure a two-year litigation trauma and paid $20,000 in legal fees, only to lose her slip-and-fall case against the assisted living facility in which she used to live. Emily has now learned about mediation and believes it would have been cheaper and quicker and might have enabled her to remain at her former home.

   a. Research the laws and legal ethics of your state. Would the legal ethics or grievance commission have a good case against Mike?

   b. Research the laws pertaining to attorney malpractice. Would Emily have a good valid cause of action against Mike? Is she likely to win? Why or why not?

c. Do you think the general law concerning the liability of attorneys who fail to meaningfully advise their clients about ADR should change or at least be clarified? What change or clarification would you recommend, and why?

d. Is punishing attorneys who fail to advise their clients about ADR the best way to encourage them to do so? Design an optimum process for meeting the goal of having the duty to advise about ADR be a necessary part of legal representation. Consider including elements that rely on the principles you learned in Chapter 2 of this text.

RECOMMENDED READINGS

Mnookin, R., and L. Kornhauser. 1979. Bargaining in the shadow of the law: The case of divorce. *Yale Law Journal* 88:950–997.

Riskin, L. L., and J. E. Westbrook. 1997. Choosing and building dispute resolution processes. In *Dispute resolution and lawyers* (2nd ed., pp. 693–800). St. Paul, MN: West.

Sander, F. E. A., and S. Goldberg. 1994. Fitting the forum to the fuss: A user-friendly guide to selecting an ADR process. *Negotiation Journal* 10 (January):49–68.

Schneider, A. K. 2000. Building a pedagogy of problem-solving: Learning to choose among ADR processes. *Harvard Negotiation Law Review* 5 (Spring):113–135.

Appendix A

Useful Web Links to ADR Resources

Administrative Dispute Resolution Act of 1996	*http://www.justice.gov/adr/pdf/adra.pdf* or *http://www.ilr.cornell.edu/alliance/resources/Legal/admin_dispute_res_act_1996.html*
ADR World	*http://www.adrworld.com*
Alternative Dispute Resolution Act of 1998	*http://www.usdoj.gov/odr/ADR%20ACT%201998.pdf* or *http://www4.law.cornell.edu/uscode/28/usc_sup_01_28_10_III_20_44.html*
American Arbitration Association	*http://www.adr.org*
Association for Conflict Resolution	*http://www.acrnet.org*
Federal Arbitration Act	*http://www4.law.cornell.edu/uscode/html/uscode09/usc_sup_01_9.html* or *http://www.adr.org/sp.asp?id=29568*
HG.org: Worldwide Legal Directories (ADR)	*http://www.hg.org/adr.html*
Mediate.com	*http://www.mediate.com*
Uniform Arbitration Act (2000 revisions)	*http://www.law.upenn.edu/bll/archives/ulc/uarba/arbitrat1213.htm*
Uniform Mediation Act	*http://www.law.upenn.edu/bll/archives/ulc/mediat/2003finaldraft.htm*

Online Appendix B

Conflict Diagnosis

A detailed description of the justification and skills of conflict diagnosis, expanding the concepts set out in Chapter 2, is provided at *http://www.prenhall. com/coltri*. This information is reprinted from a previous edition of this textbook. Here, in brief, are its contents:

References*

A Class Divided. 1987. Part of the FRONTLINE video series, available through the Public Broadcasting Service.

Ackerman, R. M. 2002. Disputing together: Conflict resolution and the search for community. *Ohio State Journal on Dispute Resolution* 18:27–91.

Alfini, J. J. 1991. Trashing, bashing and hashing it out: Is this the end of "good mediation"? *Florida State University Law Review* 19 (Summer):47–75.

Alfini, J. J., and C. G. McCabe. 2001. Mediating in the shadow of the courts: A survey of the emerging case law. *Arkansas Law Review* 54:171–206.

American Arbitration Association. 2008. AAA Filing Forms. (*http://www.adr.org/fc_filing_forms* (accessed February 3, 2009).

American Bar Association, Section of Dispute Resolution. 2002. *Resolution on mediation and the unauthorized practice of law.* *http://www.abanet.org/dispute/resolution2002.pdf* (accessed February 17, 2009).

American Bar Association 2003. *Model Rules of Professional Conduct.*

American Bar Association. 2005. *Model Standards of Conduct for Mediators.* *http://www.abanet.org/dispute/news/ModelStandardsofConductforMediatorsfinal05.pdf* (accessed January 26, 2009).

American Bar Association. 2008. What is mediation? *http://www.abanet.org/publiced/courts/mediation_whatis.html* (accessed February 1, 2008).

Antes, J. R., D. J. Della Noce, and J. Saul. 2002. *Toward intentionally theory-based instruments and approaches.* Paper presented at the 2002 symposium, Assuring Mediator Quality: What Are the Alternatives? Presented by the Institute for Conflict Transformation, Inc., and co-sponsored by the Center for Dispute Resolution at the University of Maryland Law School and the Maryland Judiciary's Mediation and Conflict Resolution Office (Maryland MACRO), December 9, at the University of Maryland School of Law, Baltimore.

Antes, J. R., J. P. Folger, and D. J. Della Noce. 2001. Transforming conflict interactions in the workplace: Documented effects of the USPS REDRESS™ program. *Hofstra Labor and Employment Law Journal* 18:429–467.

Auerbach, J. S. 1983. *Justice without law: Resolving disputes without lawyers.* New York: Oxford University Press.

*Ayres, I. 1991. Fair driving: Gender and race discrimination in retail car negotiation. *Harvard Law Review* 104:817–872.

Bales, R. A. 2007. Papers from the national academy of arbitrators conference, "Beyond The Protocol: The Future of Due Process in Workplace Dispute Resolution": Beyond the protocol: Recent trends in employment arbitration. *Employee Rights and Employment Policy Journal,* 301–344.

*Bandura, A. 1971. *Social learning theory.* Morristown, NJ: General Learning Press.

*Bandura, A. 1977. *Social learning theory.* Englewood Cliffs, NJ: Prentice-Hall.

Barker, P. 2003. Cognitive dissonance. *http://www.beyondintractability.org/essay/cognitive_dissonance* (accessed December 4, 2007).

Barnes, G. H. 1997. Drafting an arbitration clause—a checklist. *Hieros Gamos—Alternative Dispute Resolution Law.* *http://www.hg.org/adradd1.html* (accessed February 2, 2009).

Barton, T. D. 2007. The modes and tenses of legal problem solving, and what to do about them in legal education. *California Western Law Review* 43 (Spring):389–416.

Baruch-Bush, R. A. 1996. "What do we need a mediator for?" Mediator's "value-added" for negotiators. *Ohio State Journal on Dispute Resolution* 12:1–36.

Baruch-Bush, R. A., and J. P. Folger. 1994. *The promise of mediation: Responding to conflict through empowerment and recognition.* San Francisco: Jossey-Bass.

Beck, C. J. A., and B. D. Sales. 2000. A critical reappraisal of divorce mediation research and policy. *Psychology Public Policy and Law* 6 (December):989–1056.

*Bellow, G., and B. Moulton. 1978. *The lawyering process.* Mineola, NY: Foundation Press.

---

*References marked with an astrisk appear in Online Appendix B, available at *www.prenhall.com/coltri*

*Benjamin, R.W. 1975. Images of conflict resolution and social control. *Journal of Conflict Resolution* 19(1):123–137.

Bennett, M. D., and M. S. G. Hermann. 1996. *The art of mediation.* Notre Dame, IN: National Institute for Trial Advocacy.

*Berk, L. E. 1997. *Child development,* 4th ed. Needham Heights, MA: Allyn & Bacon.

Bernard, P. E. 2001. Only Nixon could go to China: Third thoughts on the Uniform Mediation Act. *Marquette Law Review* 85 (Fall):113–146.

Bickerman, J. 1999. Great potential: The new federal law provides vehicle, if local courts want to move on ADR. *Dispute Resolution Magazine* (Fall):3–5.

Bingham, L. 2002. Why suppose? Let's find out: A public policy research program on dispute resolution. *Journal of Dispute Resolution* 2002:101–126.

Bingham, L., R. Baruch-Bush, C. Hallberlin, and L. M. Napoli. 1999. *Changing workplace culture: Lessons learned from mediation of employment disputes at the United States Postal Service.* Paper presented at the 27th Annual Conference of the Society of Professionals in Dispute Resolution, September 23–25, Baltimore, MD.

*Blake, R. R., and J. S. Mouton. 1964. *The managerial grid.* Houston, TX: Gulf.

*Blake, R. R., and J. S. Mouton. 1970. The fifth achievement. *Journal of Applied Behavioral Science* 6:413–426.

*Bodenhausen, G. V., and R. S. Wyer, Jr. 1985. Effects of stereotypes on decision making and information-processing strategies. *Journal of Personality and Social Psychology* 48(2):267–282.

Bordone, R. C. 1998. Electronic online dispute resolution: A systems approach—potential, problems, and a proposal. *Harvard Negotiation Law Review* 3 (Spring):175–211.

Bordone, R. C. 2005. Fitting the ethics to the forum: A proposal for process-enabling ethical codes. *Ohio State Journal on Dispute Resolution, 21,* 1–43.

Brazil, W. D. 2000. Symposium: Continuing the conversation about the current status and the future of ADR: A view from the courts. *Journal of Dispute Resolution* 2000:11–39.

Breger, M. J. 2000. Should an attorney be required to advise a client of ADR options? *Georgetown Journal of Legal Ethics* 13 (Spring):427–476.

Braeutigam, A. M. 2006. Fusses that fit online: Online mediation in non-commercial contexts. *Appalachian Journal of Law* 5 (Spring):275–301.

Bronfenbrenner, U. 1979. *The ecology of human development.* Cambridge, MA: Harvard University Press.

*Brooks-Gunn, J., and W. S. Matthews. 1979. *He and she: How children develop their sex role identity.* Englewood Cliffs, NJ: Prentice-Hall.

Browe, K. P. 1994. A critique of the civility movement: Why Rambo will not go away. *Marquette Law Review* 77 (Summer):751–784.

Bruch, C. S. 1992. And how are the children? The effects of ideology and mediation on child custody law and children's well-being in the United States. *Family and Conciliation Courts Review* 30(1):112–134.

Bryan, P. 1992. Killing us softly: Divorce mediation and the politics of power. *Buffalo Law Review* 40:441–523.

*Bunker, B. B., J. Z. Rubin, and Associates. 1995. *Conflict, cooperation and justice: Essays inspired by the work of Morton Deutsch.* San Francisco: Jossey-Bass.

Burger, W. W. 1982. *Isn't there a better way?* Annual Report on the State of the Judiciary, presented at the 1982 midyear meeting of the American Bar Association, Chicago, January 24. Reprinted as Burger, W.W. 1982. Isn't there a better way? *ABA Journal* 68 (March):274.

Cahill, S. F. 2002. Idaho law eases dispute resolution: Measure gets backing of tort reformers and plaintiffs lawyers. *ABA Journal E-Report* (March 29). *http://web.archive.org/web/20020428073634/www.abanet.org/journal/ereport/m29arb.html* (accessed March 4, 2009).

Camara, K. A., and Resnick, G. 1988. Interparental conflict and cooperation: Factors moderating children's post-divorce adjustment. In *The impact of divorce, single parenting, and stepparenting on children,* edited by E. M. Heatherington and J. D. Arasteh. Hillsdale, NJ: Lawrence Erlbaum.

Camara, K. A., and G. Resnick, G. 1989. Styles of conflict resolution and cooperation between divorced parents: Effects on child behavior and adjustment. *American Journal of Orthopsychiatry* 59(4):560–575.

*Cantor, N., and W. Mischel. 1977. Traits as prototypes: Effects on recognition memory. *Journal of Personality and Social Psychology* 35:38–48.

CardTrak.com. 2003. "Short stick." *http://www.cardweb.com/cardtrak/pastissues/feb03.html* (accessed February 1, 2009).

Carrington, P. D. 1998. Regulating dispute resolution provisions in adhesion contracts. *Harvard Journal on Legislation* 35:225–232.

Carter, R.L. 2002. Oh, ye of little good faith: Questions, concerns and commentary on efforts to regulate participant conduct in mediations. *Journal of Dispute Resolution* 2002:367–405.

*Chaiken, S. L., D. H. Gruenfeld, and C. M. Judd. 2000. Persuasion in negotiations and conflict situations. In *The handbook of conflict resolution: Theory and practice,* edited by M. Deutsch and P.T. Coleman. San Francisco: Jossey-Bass.

Chase Manhattan Bank, USA, N.A. 2002. *Arbitration agreement and change in terms of notice.* Wilmington, DE: Chase Manhattan Bank, N.A.

*Coben, J. R. 1998. Summer musings on curricular innovations to change the lawyer's standard philosophical map. *Florida Law Review* 1998:735–751.

*Coben, J. R. 1998. Summer musing on curricular innovations to change the Lawyer's Standard Philosophical Map. *Florida Law Review,* 1998: 735–751.

Coben, J. R., and P. N. Thompson. 2006. Disputing irony: A systematic look at litigation about mediation. *Harvard Negotiation Law* Review 11 (Spring):43–145.

Cochran, R. F., Jr. 1999. ADR, the ABA, and client control: A proposal that the Model Rules require lawyers to present ADR options to clients. *South Texas Law Review* 41 (Winter):183–201.

Cohen, J. R. 2000. Apology and organizations: Exploring an example from medical practice. *Fordham Urban Law Journal* 27 (June):1447–1482.

Cole, S. R., N. H. Rogers, and C. A. McEwen. 2001. *Mediation: Law, policy and practice,* 2nd ed. St. Paul, MN: West.

Cole, S. R. 1996. Incentives and arbitration: The case against enforcement of executory arbitration agreements between employers and employees. *University of Missouri at Kansas City Law Review* 64 (spring):449–483.

Cole, S. R. 2001. Uniform arbitration: "One size fits all" does not fit. *Ohio State Journal on Dispute Resolution* 16(3):759–789.

*Coleman, P. T. 2000. Power and conflict. In *The handbook of conflict resolution: Theory and practice,* edited by M. Deutsch and P.T. Coleman. San Francisco: Jossey-Bass.

*Coltri, L. S. 1993. *Development and pilot testing of an instrument to measure conflict style in mediation disputants.* Unpublished.

Coltri, L. S. 1995. *The impact of sex stereotypes on the perception of disputant conflict style by undergraduates.* Ph.D. dissertation, University of Maryland.

Colvin, A. J. S. 2007. Papers from the national academy of arbitrators conference, "Beyond the Protocol: The Future of Due Process in Workplace Dispute Resolution": Empirical research on employment arbitration: Clarity amidst the sound and fury? *Employee Rights and Employment Policy Journal* 11:405–447.

Condlin, R. J. 2008. "Every day and in every way we are all becoming *meta* and *meta*" or how communitarian bargaining theory conquered the world (of bargaining theory). *Ohio State Journal on Dispute Resolution,* 23(2), 231–299.

Conflict: The Rules of Engagement. 1997. Videocassette featuring Pat Heim. 41 min. Buffalo Grove, IL: CorVision.

*Connolly, C., and R. Pierre. 1998. African American voters standing by Clinton. *The Washington Post* [online]. 17 September. [Cited 22 July 2002]. Available from *http://www.washingtonpost.com/wp-srv/politics/special/clinton/stories/blacks091798.htm.*

Connolly, J. S. 1999. A dose of social science: Support for the use of summary jury trials as a form of alternative dispute resolution. *William Mitchell Law Review* 25:1419–1460.

Coogler, O. J. 1978. *Structured mediation in divorce settlements.* Lexington, MA: Lexington Books.

Costantino, C. A., and C. S. Merchant. 1996. *Designing conflict management systems: A guide to creating productive and healthy organizations.* San Francisco: Jossey-Bass.

Coyne, W. F., Jr. 1999. The case for settlement counsel. *Ohio State Journal on Dispute Resolution* 14:367–413.

Curators of the University of Missouri Journal of Dispute Resolution. 2006. Symposium: The vanishing trial. *Journal of Dispute Resolution,* 2006(1).

Curtin, K. M. 2000. An examination of contractual expansion and limitation of judicial reviews of arbitral awards. *Ohio State Journal on Dispute Resolution* 15(2):337–371.

*Darley, J. M., and R. H. Fazio. 1980. Expectancy confirmation processes arising in the social interaction sequence. *American Psychologist* 35(10):867–881.

de Dreu, C. K. W., S. L. Koole, and F. L. Oldersma. 1999. On the seizing and freezing of negotiator inferences: Need for cognitive closure moderates the use of heuristics in negotiation. *Personality and Social Psychology Bulletin* 25(3):348–362.

Deja, D. R. 1999. The required submission of an ADR joint settlement plan in civil cases in the Berrien County, Michigan trial court: An evaluation of its impact on case disposition time. *Ohio State Journal on Dispute Resolution* 15(1):173–199.

Delgado, R. 1997. Conflict as pathology: An essay for Trina Grillo. *Minnesota Law Review* 81:1391–1412.

Depner, C. E., K. Cannata, and I. Ricci. 1994. Client evaluations of mediation services: The impact of case characteristics and mediation service models. *Family and Conciliation Courts Review* 32 (July):306–325.

Deutsch, M. 1973. *The resolution of conflict: Constructive and destructive processes.* New Haven, CT: Yale University Press.

*Devine, P. G. 1989. Stereotypes and prejudice: Their automatic and controlled components. *Journal of Personality and Social Psychology* 56(1):5–18.

*Dezalay, Y., and B. Garth. 1996. Fussing about the forum: Categories and definitions as stakes in a professional competition. *Law and Social Inquiry* 21:285.

Diamond, T. A. 1997. Choice of law clauses and their presumptive effect upon the Federal Arbitration Act: Reconciling the Supreme Court with itself. *Arizona Law Review* 39 (Spring):35–65.

Dispute.IT! 2003. Sample arbitration clauses. *http://www.dispute.it/sample_arbitration_clauses.htm* (accessed February 3, 2009).

District of Columbia Courts, Multi-Door Dispute Resolution Division. *http://www.dccourts.gov/dccourts/superior/multi/index.jsp* (accessed January 21, 2009).

Dunham, K. F. 2007. Is mediation the new equity? *American Journal of Trial Advocacy* 31 (Summer):87–114.

Edwards, H., & J. White (1977). *The lawyer as a negotiator.* St. Paul, MN: West.

*Eisler, R. 1988. *The chalice and the blade: Our history, our future.* San Francisco: Harper & Row.

Ehrlinger, J., T. Gilovich, and L. Ross. 2005. Peering into the blind spot: People's assessments of bias in themselves and others. *Personality and social psychology bulletin,* 31(5):680–692.

Emery, R. E., S. G. Matthews, and M. M. Wyer. 1991. Child custody mediation and litigation: Further evidence on the differing views of mothers and fathers. *Journal of Consulting and Clinical Psychology* 59(3):410–418.

*Epstein, S. 1973. The self-concept revisited or a theory of a theory. *American Psychologist,* 28:405–416.

*Erikson, E. 1950. *Childhood and society.* New York: W.W. Norton.

Evans, R. L., H. R. Fox, D. O. Pritzl, and E. M. Halar. 1984. Group treatment of physically disabled adults by telephone. *Social Work in Health Care* 9(3):77–84.

Federal Judicial Center and CPR Institute for Dispute Resolution. 1996. Eastern District of Michigan: In Brief. In *ADR and settlement in the federal district courts: A sourcebook for judges & lawyers,* 162. *http://www.fjc.gov/public/pdf.nsf/lookup/adrsrcbk.pdf/$file/adrsrcbk.pdf* (accessed January 26, 2009).

Feerick, J., C. Izumi, K. K. Kovach, L. Love, R. Moberly, L. Riskin, and E. Sherman. 1995. Symposium: Standards of professional conduct in alternative dispute resolution. *Journal of Dispute Resolution* 2005(1):95–128.

Fineman, M. 1988. Dominant discourse, professional language, and legal change in child custody decisionmaking. *Harvard Law Review* 101(4):727–774.

*Fisher, R., and W. Ury. 1981. *Getting to yes: Negotiating agreement without giving in.* New York: Penguin Books.

Fisher, R., W. Ury, and B. Patton. 1991. *Getting to yes: Negotiating agreement without giving in,* 2nd ed. New York: Penguin Books.

*Fiske, S. T., and S. L. Neuberg. 1990. A continuum model of impression formation from category-based to individuating processes: Influences of information and motivation on attention and interpretation. In Vol. 23 of *Advances in experimental social psychology,* edited by M.P. Zanna. San Diego, CA: Academic Press.

Fiss, O. 1984. Against settlement. *Yale Law Journal* 93:1073–1090.

Flowers, R. K. 1996. A code of their own: Updating the ethics codes to include the non-adversarial roles of federal prosecutors. *Boston College Law Review* 37 (September):923–974.

Folberg, J., and A. Taylor. 1984. *Mediation: A comprehensive guide to resolving conflicts without litigation.* San Francisco: Jossey-Bass.

Fuller, L. L., and J. D. Randall. 1958. Professional responsibility: Report of the Joint Conference. *ABA Journal* 44:1159–1161.

*Gadlin, H. 1994. Conflict resolution, cultural differences, and the culture of racism. *Negotiation Journal* 10 (January):33–47.

Gage, D., D. Martin, and J. Gromala. 1999. Mediation during business formation or reorganization. *Family Business* [online]. (Spring). [Cited 12 July 2002.] Available from *http://www.mediate.com/articles/formation.cfm.*

Galanter, M. 2004. The vanishing trial: An examination of trials and related matters in federal and state courts. *Journal of Empirical Legal Studies,* 1 (November), 459–570.

Galanter, M. 2006. Symposium: A world without trials? *Journal of Dispute Resolution* 2006(1):7–33.

Gaschen, D. E. 1995. Mandatory custody mediation: The debate over its usefulness continues. *Ohio State Journal on Dispute Resolution* 10:469–490.

Gauvey, S. K. 2001. ADR's integration in the federal court system. *Maryland Bar Journal* 33(2):36–43.

Gawronski, B. 2003. On difficult questions and evident answers: Dispositional inference from role-constrained behavior. *Personality & Social Psychology Bulletin,* 29(11):1459–1475.

Gearity, P. 2002. ADR and collaborative lawyering in family law. *Maryland Bar Journal* 35(3):2, 4.

Gilbert, D. T., B. W. Pelham, and D. S. Krull. 1988. On cognitive busyness: When person perceivers meet persons perceived. *Journal of Personality and Social Psychology,* 54:733–740.

Gilliéron, P. 2008. From face-to-face to screen-to-screen: Real hope or true fallacy? Ohio State *Journal on Dispute Resolution,* 23:301–342.

*Gilligan, C. 1982. *In a different voice.* Cambridge, MA: Harvard University Press.

*Gilson, R. J., and R. H. Mnookin. 1994. Disputing through agents: Cooperation and conflict between lawyers in litigation. *Columbia Law Review* 94 (March):509–566.

Glanstein, D. M. 2001. A Hail Mary pass: Public policy review of arbitration awards. *Ohio State Journal on Dispute Resolution* 16:297–334.

*Goble, F. G. 1970. *The third force: The psychology of Abraham Maslow.* New York: Pocket Books.

Golann, D. 2002. Is legal mediation a process of repair—or separation? An empirical study, and its implications. *Harvard Negotiation Law Review* 7 (Spring):301–336.

*Goldberg, S. H. 1997. Wait a minute. This is where I came in. A trial lawyer's search for alternative dispute resolution. *BrighamYoung University Law Review* 1997:653–682.

Goldfien, J. H., and J. K. Robbennol. 2007. What if the lawyers have their way? An empirical assessment of conflict strategies and attitudes toward mediation styles. *Ohio State Journal on Dispute Resolution* 23:277–319.

Goodpaster, G. 1996. A primer on competitive bargaining. *Journal of Dispute Resolution* 1996:325–377.

Gourlay, A., and J. Soderquist. 1998. Mediation in employment cases is too little too late: An organizational conflict management perspective on resolving disputes. *Hamline Law Review* 21 (Winter):261–286.

*Gray, J. 1992. *Men are from Mars, women are from Venus.* New York: HarperCollins.

Green, M. Z. 2005. Second national people of color legal scholarship conference: Tackling employment discrimination with ADR: Does mediation offer a shield for the haves or real opportunity for the have-nots? *Berkeley Journal of Employment and Labor Law* 26:321–361.

Green, M. Z. 2007. Ruminations about the EEOC's policy regarding arbitration. *Employee Rights and Employment Policy Journal,* 11:154–204.

Grillo, T. 1991. The mediation alternative: Process dangers for women. *Yale Law Journal* 100 (April):1545–1610.

*Gross, J. (ed.). *The Oxford book of aphorisms.* Oxford, England: Oxford University Press.

Guthrie, C. 2001. The lawyer's philosophical map and the disputant's perceptual map: Impediments to facilitative mediation and lawyering. *Harvard Negotiation Law Review* 6 (Spring):145–188.

Haagen, P. H. 1998. New wineskins for new wine: The need to encourage fairness in mandatory arbitration. *Arizona Law Review* 40:1039–1068.

*Hamilton, D. L., and T. K. Trolier. 1986. Stereotypes and stereotyping: An overview of the cognitive approach. In *Prejudice, discrimination, and racism*, edited by J.F. Dovidio and S. L. Gaertner. Orlando, FL: Academic Press.

*Hammock, G. S., D. R. Richardson, C. J. Pilkington, and M. Utley. 1990. Measurement of conflict in social relationships. *Personality and Individual Differences* 11(6):577–583.

Hang, L. Q. 2001. Online dispute resolution systems: The future of cyberspace law. *Santa Clara Law Review* 41:837–866.

Hansen, T. 2004. The narrative approach to mediation. *Pepperdine Dispute Resolution Law Journal* 4:297–308.

Harmon, K. M. J. 2002. The role of attorneys and dispute review boards. *ADR Currents* 2002 (March–May):6.

Hayford, S. L. 2000. Unification of the law of labor arbitration and commercial arbitration: An idea whose time has come. *Baylor Law Review* 52 (Fall):781–927.

Haynes, J. M. 1981. *Divorce mediation.* New York: Springer.

Heinsz, T. J. 2001. The Revised Uniform Arbitration Act: Modernizing, revising, and clarifying arbitration law. *Journal of Dispute Resolution* 2001:1–66.

Heister, J. W. 1987. Appendix. Property allocation in mediation: An examination of distribution relative to equality and to gender. *Mediation Quarterly* (Fall):97–98.

Henderson, D. A. 1995. Avoiding litigation with the mini-trial: The corporate bottom line as dispute resolution technique. *South Carolina Law Review* 46 (Winter):237–262.

Hensler, D. R. 1999. A research agenda: What we need to know about court-connected ADR. *Dispute Resolution Magazine* (Fall):15.

Hermann, H., C. Honeyman, B. McAdoo, and N. Welsh. 2001. *Judges, attorneys, clients, mediators: What do they want from mediation? Are they all after the same thing?* Seminar presented at the first annual international conference of the Association for Conflict Resolution, Toronto, Ontario, Canada, October 12.

Hicks, T. 2000. Steps for setting up an effective conflict management system. *http://mediate.com/articles/hickst4.cfm* (accessed March 4, 2009), citing Watson, C., and L. R. Hoffman. 1996. Managers as negotiators. *Leadership Quarterly* 7(1):63–85.

High Clouds, Inc. 2006. Sample condominium bylaw: Arbitration and mediation and court to resolve disputes. *http://www.highclouds.ca/Sample%20Bylaw%20for% 20arbitration%20and%20mediation%20and%20court%20 in%20condo_2007.pdf* (accessed February 3, 2009).

*Hochman, T. 1981. *Black and white: Styles in conflict.* Chicago: University of Chicago Press.

Holland, D. L. 2000. Drafting a dispute resolution provision in international commercial contracts. *Tulsa Journal of Comparative and International Law* 7:451–479.

*Hunt, E. J., E. J. Koopman, L. S. Coltri, and F. G. Favretto. 1989. Incorporating idiosyncratic family system characteristics in the development of agreements: Toward an expanded understanding of "success" in the mediation of child custody disputes. In *Managing conflict: An interdisciplinary approach* edited by M. A. Rahim. New York: Praeger.

Hurder, A. J. 2007. The lawyer's dilemma: To be or not to be a problem-solving negotiator. *Clinical Law Review* 14 (Fall):253–300.

Hursh, R. D. 2001. *Annotation: Constitutionality of arbitration statutes.* 55 *A.L.R.2d* 432.

*Hutchinson, E. F. 1998. GOP in south sees a war it can win. *Los Angeles Times,* 21 (pp. 231–243), December.

*Hutchinson, E. O. 1998. Impeachment is punishment for Clinton's civil rights support. *Afrocentric News. http://www. afrocentricnews.com/html/ofariclinton.html* (accessed March 4, 2009).

*Indiana Conflict Resolution Institute. 2001. *Mediation at work: The report of the National REDRESS™ evaluation project of the United States Postal Service.* Paper presented at the American Bar Association Section on Dispute Resolution Section Meeting, Washington, DC, April.

International Ombudsman Association. (n.d.). *IOA Standards of Practice. http://www.ombudsassociation.org/standards/ Stds_Practice_1-07.pdf* (accessed February 4, 2009).

Johnston, J. R., and L. E. G. Campbell. 1988. *Impasses of divorce: The dynamics and resolution of family conflict.* New York: The Free Press.

Katsh, E., J. Rifkin, and A. Gaitenby. 2000. E-commerce, e-disputes, and e-dispute resolution: In the shadow of "eBay law." *Ohio State Journal on Dispute Resolution* 15(3):705–734.

Keeva, S. 2001. What clients want. *ABA Journal,* 87 (June):48–52.

Kelly, J. B. 1996. A decade of divorce mediation research. *Family and Conciliation Courts Review* 34(3):373–385.

Kelly, J. B. 2002. Psychological and legal interventions for parents and children in custody and access disputes: Current research and practice. *Virginia Journal of Social Policy & the Law* 10:129–163.

Kelly, J. B., and M. A. Duryee. 1992. Women's and men's views of mediation in voluntary and mandatory mediation settings. *Family and Conciliation Courts Review* 30(1):34–49.

Kentra, P. A. 1997. Hear no evil, see no evil, speak no evil: The intolerable conflict for attorney-mediators between the duty to maintain mediation confidentiality and the duty to report fellow attorney misconduct. *Brigham Young University Law Review* 3:715–756.

Kentra, P. A. 2002. Personal e-mail communication (April 1).

Kichaven, J. G. 1997. The real benefit of ADR. *Los Angeles Lawyer* (September).

Kim, A. S. 1994. Rent-a-judges and the cost of selling justice. *Duke Law Journal* 44 (October):166–199.

*Kim, S. H., and R. H. Smith. 1993. Revenge and conflict escalation. *Negotiation Journal* 9(1):37–43.

*Kimmel, P. R. 2000. Culture and conflict. In *The handbook of conflict resolution: Theory and practice,* edited by M. Deutsch and P. T. Coleman. San Francisco: Jossey-Bass.

King, C. J. 1999. Burdening access to justice: The cost of divorce mediation on the cheap. *St. John's Law Review* 73 (Spring):375–475.

*Kochman, T. 1981. *Black and white: Styles in conflict.* Chicago: University of Chicago Press.

Koopman, E. J. 1983. Personal communication, College Park, Maryland.

Koopman, E. J. 1985. Personal communication, College Park, Maryland.

Kovach, K. K. 1997. Good faith in mediation—requested, recommended, or required? A new ethic. *South Texas Law Review* 38 (May):575–622.

Kovach, K. K. 2001. New wine requires new wineskins: Transforming lawyer ethics for effective representation in a non-adversarial approach to problem-solving: Mediation. *Fordham Urban Law Journal* 28:935–977.

Kovach, K. K., and L. P. Love. 1996. "Evaluative" mediation is an oxymoron. *Alternatives to the High Cost of Litigation* 14(3):31–32.

Kovach, K. K., and L. P. Love. 1998. Mapping mediation: The risks of Riskin's grid. *Harvard Negotiation Law Review* 3 (Spring):71–92.

*Krauss, R. M., and E. Morella. 2000. Communication and conflict. In *The handbook of conflict resolution: Theory and practice,* edited by M. Deutsch and P.T. Coleman. San Francisco: Jossey-Bass.

Kressel, K., and D. G. Pruitt. 1989. Conclusion: A research perspective on the mediation of social conflict. In *Mediation research: The process and effectiveness of third-party intervention,* edited by K. Kressel and D. Pruitt. San Francisco: Jossey-Bass.

Kuhn, S. C. 1984. Mandatory mediation: California Civil Code Section 4607. *Emory Law Journal* 33 (Summer):733–778.

LaFree, G., and C. Rack. 1996. The effects of participants' ethnicity and gender on monetary outcomes in mediated and adjudicated cases. *Law and Society Review* 30(4):767–791.

Lambros, T. D. 1984. The summary jury trial and other alternative methods of dispute resolution: A Report to the Judicial Conference of the United States Committee on the Operation of the Jury System. In *Federal Rules Decisions* 103:465–477. St. Paul, MN: West.

Lande, J. 1997. How will lawyering and mediation practices transform each other? *Florida State University Law Review* 24 (Summer):839–901.

*Lande, J. 1998. Failing faith in litigation? A survey of business lawyers' and executives' opinions. *Harvard Negotiation Law Review* 3 (spring):1–70.

Lande, J. 2000. Toward more sophisticated mediation theory. *Journal of Dispute Resolution* 2000:321–333.

Lande, J. 2006. How much justice can we afford? Defining the courts' roles and deciding the appropriate number of trials, settlement signals, and other elements needed to administer justice. *Journal of Dispute Resolution* 2006(1):213–252.

Lefcourt, C. 1984. Women, mediation, and family law. *Clearinghouse Review* 18(3):266–269.

*Lester, P. E., and L. K. Bishop. 2001. *Handbook of tests and measurement in education and the social sciences,* 2nd ed. Lancaster, PA: Technomic.

*Leung, K. 1988. Some determinants of conflict avoidance. *Journal of Cross-Cultural Psychology* 19(1):125–138.

Leung, K., and E. A. Lind. 1986. Procedural justice and culture: Effects of culture, gender, and investigator status on procedural preferences. *Journal of Personality and Social Psychology* 50(6):1134–1140.

Levin, M. S. 2001. The propriety of evaluative mediation. *Ohio State Journal on Dispute Resolution* 16(2):267–296.

*Lewicki, R. J., and B. B. Bunker. 1995. Trust in relationships: A model of development and decline. In *Conflict, cooperation and justice: Essays inspired by the works of Morton Deutsch,* edited by B.B. Bunker, J.Z. Rubin, and Associates. San Francisco: Jossey-Bass.

*Lewicki, R. J., and C. Wiethoff. 2000. Trust, trust development, and trust repair. In *The handbook of conflict resolution: Theory and practice* (pp. 86–107), edited by M. Deutsch and P. T. Coleman. San Francisco: Jossey-Bass.

Libbey, D. E. 1999. Avoiding a civil action: Mandatory summary jury trial in the settlement of products liability design defect cases in light of the Restatement (Third) of Torts. *Ohio State Journal on Dispute Resolution* 15:285–309.

Lord, C. G., L. Ross, and M. R. Lepper. 1979. Biased assimilation and attitude polarization: The effects of prior theories on subsequently considered evidence. *Journal of Personality and Social Psychology* 37(11):2098–2109.

Los Angeles Almanac. 2008. Commercial copyright license agreement. *http://www.laalmanac.com/_main/commercial.htm* (accessed February 3, 2009).

Love, L. P. 1997. The top ten reasons why mediators should not evaluate. *Florida State University Law Review* 24 (Summer):937–948.

Love, L. P. 2000. Teaching a new paradigm: Must knights shed their swords and armor to enter certain ADR arenas? *Cardozo Online Journal of Conflict Resolution* 1(1):3–21. *http://www.cojcr.org/vol1no1/symposia01.html* (accessed January 29, 2009).

*Love, L. P., and K. K. Kovach. 2000. ADR: An eclectic array of processes, rather than one eclectic process. *Journal of Dispute Resolution* 2000:295–307.

Lowry, L. R. 2000. To evaluate or not: That is *not* the question! *Family and Conciliation Courts Review* 38 (January): 48–58.

*Luban, D. 1998. Rediscovering Fuller's legal ethics. *Georgetown Journal of Legal Ethics* 11 (summer):801–829.

Lynch, J. 2003. Are Your Organization's Conflict Management Practices an Integrated Conflict Management System? *http://www.mediate.com/articles/systemsedit3.cfm* (accessed March 4, 2009).

Marcus, M. G., W. Marcus, N. A. Stilwell, and N. Doherty. 1999. To mediate or not to mediate: Financial outcomes in mediated versus adversarial divorces. *Mediation Quarterly* 7 (Winter):143–152.

Marks, G., and N. Miller. 1987. Ten years of research on the false-consensus effect: An empirical and theoretical review. *Psychological Bulletin,* 102(1):72–90.

Marrella, F., and C. S. Yoo. 2007. Is open source software the new lex mercatoria? *Virginia Journal of International Law* 47 (Summer):807–837.

Maryland State Bar Association. 2007. *Maryland Business Alternative Dispute Resolution Conference* (30 October). Personal communication.

Mason, P. E. 2007. *LexisNexis® Expert Commentaries: Paul E. Mason on Hall St. Assocs., L.L.C. v. Mattel, Inc., 127 S. Ct. 2875 (U.S. 2007).* Lexis-Nexis. *http://w3.lexis.com/ research2/attachment/popUpAttachWindow.do?_m=826929e fe89f500641b5d5ba68aed740&wchp=dGLzVlz- zSkAl&_md5=6f52d8ff57224af8a340e63a8fe97cc6* (accessed April 4, 2008).

Mayer, B. 2000. *The dynamics of conflict resolution.* San Francisco: Jossey-Bass.

McAdoo, B., and N. A. Welsh. 2005. Look before you leap and keep on looking: Lessons from the institutionalization of court-connected mediation. *Nevada Law Journal,* 5:399–432.

McCabe, K. 2001. A forum for women's voices: Mediation through a feminist jurisprudential lens. *Northern Illinois University Law Review* 21:459–482.

McDermott, E. P., and R. Obar. 2004. "What's going on" in mediation: An empirical analysis of the influence of a mediator's style on party satisfaction and monetary benefit. *Harvard Negotiation Law Review* 9 (Spring):75–113.

McEwen, C. A., and R. M. Maiman. 1982. Arbitration and mediation as alternatives to court. *Policy Studies Journal* 10:712–726.

McEwen, C. A., and T. W. Milburn. 1993. Explaining a paradox of mediation. *Negotiation Journal* 9(1):23–36.

McIsaac, H. 2001. Confidentiality revisited: California style. *Family Court Review* 39(4):405–414.

Meltzer, D. L. 1998. The federal workplace ombuds. *Ohio State Journal on Dispute Resolution* 13:549–609.

Menkel-Meadow, C. J. 1985. Portia in a different voice: Speculations on a women's lawyering process. *Berkeley Women's Law Journal* 1:39–63.

Menkel-Meadow, C. J. 1991. Symposium: Pursuing settlement in an adversary culture: A tale of innovation co-opted or "the law of ADR." *Florida State University Law Review* 19 (Summer):1–46.

Menkel-Meadow, C. J. 1996. The trouble with the adversary system in a post-modern, multi-cultural world. *Journal of the Institute for the Study of Legal Ethics* 1:49–77.

*Menkel-Meadow, C. J. 2000. Mothers and fathers of invention: The intellectual founders of ADR. *The Ohio State Journal on Dispute Resolution* 16(1):1–37.

Meyerson, B. E. 2005. The dispute resolution professional should not celebrate the vanishing trial. *Cardozo Journal of Dispute Resolution* 7:77–81.

Mnookin, R., and L. Kornhauser. 1979. Bargaining in the shadow of the law: The case of divorce. *Yale Law Journal* 88:950–997.

*Moore, C. 1996. *The mediation process.* San Francisco: Jossey-Bass.

*Morris, C. n.d. Dispute resolution systems and organizational conflict management. In *Conflict resolution and peacebuilding: A selected bibliography http://www.peacemakers.ca/ bibliography/bib8design.html* (accessed March 4, 2009).

Mosten, F. S. 1997. Checklist: Eleven questions most commonly asked about mediation. *Fairshare* 17(9):5–7.

Mosten, F. S. 2000. What happens in mediation? *http://www. mediate.com/articles/mosch3.cfm,* accessed March 4, 2009.

Nader, L. 1992. From legal processing to mind processing. *Family and Conciliation Courts Review* 30(4):468–473.

Nader, L. 1993. Controlling processes in the practice of law: Hierarchy and pacification in the movement to re-form dispute ideology. *Ohio State Journal on Dispute Resolution* 9(1):1–25.

Nascimento, L. M., and M. R. Cousineau. 2005. An evaluation of independent consumer assistance centers on problem resolution and user satisfaction: The consumer perspective. *Journal of Community Health 30* (April 2):89–106.

National Arbitration Forum. 2008. National Arbitration Forum: Rules and forms. *http://www.adrforum.com/main.aspx?itemID=330&hideBar=False&navID=183&news=3* (accessed February 3, 2009).

*National Federation of Paralegal Associations. 1996, updated 2001. Litigation. *http://www.paralegals.org/displaycommon.cfm?an=1&subarticlenbr=289* (accessed March 4, 2009).

Neuhauser, F., and C. L. Swezey. 1999. *Preliminary evidence on the implementation of "baseball arbitration" in workers' compensation.* Report prepared for the California Commission on Health and Safety and Workers' Compensation. *http://www.dir.ca.gov/CHSWC/Baseballarbfinal'rptcover.htm* (accessed February 2, 2009).

Nolan-Haley, J. M. 1999. Informed consent in mediation: A guiding principle for truly educated decisionmaking. *Notre Dame Law Review* 74 (March):775–840.

Nolan-Haley, J. M. 2001. *Alternative dispute resolution in a nutshell,* 2nd ed. St. Paul, MN: West.

Pearson, J. 1991. The equity of mediated divorce agreements. *Mediation Quarterly* 9(2):179–197.

Peter, J. T. 1997. Med-arb in international arbitration. *The American Review of International Arbitration* 8:83–116.

Pildes, R. H., and E. S. Anderson. 1990. Slinging arrows at democracy: Social choice theory, value pluralism, and democratic politics. *Columbia Law Review* 90 (December):2121–2214.

Plapinger, E., and D. Stienstra. 1996. *ADR and settlement programs in the federal district courts: A sourcebook for judges and lawyers.* Federal Judicial Center and CPR Institute for Dispute Resolution. *http://www.fjc.gov/public/pdf.nsf/lookup/adrsrcbk.pdf/$file/adrsrcbk.pdf* (accessed January 29, 2009).

Ponte, L. M. 1995. Putting mandatory summary jury trial back on the docket: Recommendations on the exercise of judicial authority. *Fordham Law Review* 63: 1069–1098.

Posner, R. A. 1986. The summary jury trial and other methods of alternate dispute resolution: Some cautionary observations. *University of Chicago Law Review* 53 (Spring):366–393.

Prigoff, M. L. 1990. At issue; Professional responsibility: Should there be a duty to advise of ADR options? *ABA Journal* 76 (November):50.

Pronin, E., T. Gilovich, and L. Ross. 2004. Objectivity in the eye of the beholder: Divergent perceptions of bias in the self and others. *Psychological Review,* 111(3):781–799.

*Prueher, J. 2001. *Letter from Ambassador Joseph W. Prueher to Chinese Foreign Minister Tang Jiaxuan.* [Online.] 11 April. [Cited 18 July 2002.] Available from *BBC Online, http//news.bbc.co.uk/hi/english/world/asia-pacific/newsid_1272000/1272279.stm.*

*Pruitt, D. G., and P. V. Olczak. 1995. Beyond hope: Approaches to resolving seemingly intractable conflict. In *Conflict, cooperation and justice: Essays inspired by the work of Morton Deutsch,* edited by B.B. Bunker, J.Z. Rubin, and Associates. San Francisco: Jossey-Bass.

*Psenicka, C. and M. A. Rahim. 1988. Integrative and distributive dimensions of styles of handling interpersonal conflict and bargaining outcome. In *Managing conflict: An interdisciplinary approach,* edited by M.A. Rahim. New York: Praeger.

*Putnam, L. L. (ed.). 1988. Special issue: Communication and conflict styles in organizations. *Management Communication Quarterly* 1(3):357.

Rack, C. 1999. Negotiated justice: Gender and ethnic minority bargaining patterns in the Metro Court Study. *Hamline Journal of Law and Public Policy* 20:211–298.

*Rahim, M. A.1983. A measure of styles of handling interpersonal conflict. *Academy of Management Journal* 26(2):368–376.

Ranan, W., and A. Blodgett. 1983. Using telephone therapy for "unreachable" clients. *Social Casework* 1:39–44.

Reisner, M. 2000. The new water agenda: Restoration, deconstruction, and the limits to consensus. *Journal of Land, Resources, and Environmental Law* 20:1–13.

Reuben, R. C. 2000. Constitutional gravity: A unitary theory of alternative dispute resolution and public civil justice. *UCLA Law Review* 47 (April):949–1104.

Reuben, R. C. 2006. Secrecy and transparency in dispute resolution: Confidentiality in arbitration: Beyond the myth. *University of Kansas Law Review* 54 (June):1255–1300.

Rhode, D. L. 1999. Too much law, too little justice: Too much rhetoric, too little reform. *Georgetown Journal of Legal Ethics* 11:989–1017.

*Ricci, I. 1980. *Mom's house, dad's house: Making shared custody work.* New York: Collier Books.

Richardson, J. C. 1988. *Court-based mediation in four Canadian cities: An overview of research results.* Ottowa: Department of Justice Canada.

Rifkin, J. 1984. Mediation from a feminist perspective: Promise and problems. *Law and Inequality* 2:21–31.

Riskin, L. L. 1982. Mediation and lawyers. *Ohio State Law Journal* 43:29–60.

Riskin, L. L. 1994. Mediator orientations, strategies, and techniques. *Alternatives to the High Cost of Litigation* 12(9):111–114.

Riskin, L. L. 1996. Understanding mediator orientations, strategies, and techniques: A grid for the perplexed. *Harvard Negotiation Law Review* 1(Spring):7–51.

Riskin, L. L. 2003. Decisionmaking in mediation: The new old grid and the new new grid system. *Notre Dame Law Review* 79:1–53

Riskin, L. L., and N. A. Welsh. 2008. Is that all there is? "The problem" in court-oriented mediation. *http://works. bepress.com/cgi/viewcontent.cgi?article=1000&context= nancy_welsh* (accessed January 22, 2009).

Riskin, L. L., and J. E. Westbrook. 1997. *Dispute resolution and lawyers,* 2nd ed. St. Paul, MN: West.

Rogers, N. H., and C. A. McEwen. 1989. *Mediation: Law, policy, and practice.* Deerfield, IL: Clark, Boardman, Callaghan.

*Rose, C. 1995. Bargaining and gender. *Harvard Journal of Law and Public Policy* 18:547–565.

Rothbart, M., and W. Hallmark. 1988. In-group–outgroup differences in the perceived efficacy of coercion and conciliation in resolving social conflict. *Journal of Personality and Social Psychology* 55(2):248–257.

Rothman, J. 1997. *Resolving identity-based conflict: In nations, organizations, and communities.* San Francisco: Jossey-Bass.

*Rubin, J. Z., D. G. Pruitt, and S. H. Kim. 1994. *Social conflict: Escalation, stalemate, and settlement,* 2nd ed. New York: McGraw-Hill.

Sabatino, J. M. 1998. ADR as "litigation lite": Procedural and evidentiary norms embedded within alternative dispute resolution. *Emory Law Journal* 47:1289–1349.

*Sagar, H. A., and J. W. Schofield. 1980. Racial and behavioral cues in black and white children's perceptions of ambiguously aggressive behavior. *Journal of Personality and Social Psychology* 39(4):590–598.

Sander, F. E. A. 1976. *Varieties of dispute processing.* 70 FRD 111.

Sander, F. E. A., and S. Goldberg. 1994. Fitting the forum to the fuss: A user-friendly guide to selecting an ADR process. *Negotiation Journal* 10 (January):49–68.

Sander, F. E. A., and M. Prigoff. 1990. Professional responsibility: Should there be a duty to advise of ADR options? *ABA Journal* 76 (November):50.

Schepard, A. 2000. The evolving judicial role in child custody disputes: From fault finder to conflict manager to differential case management. *University of Arkansas at Little Rock Law Review* 22 (Spring):395–428.

Schneider, A. K. 2000. Building a pedagogy of problem-solving: Learning to choose among ADR processes. *Harvard Negotiation Law Review* 5 (Spring):113–135.

Schwartz, D. S. 1997. Enforcing small print to protect big business: Employee and consumer rights claims in an age of compelled arbitration. *Wisconsin Law Review* 1997:33–132.

Schwartz, J. R. 1999. Note: laymen cannot lawyer, but is mediation the practice of law? *Cardozo Law Review* 20 (May/June):1715–1745.

*Shapiro, M. 1981. *Courts: A comparative and political analysis.* Chicago: University of Chicago Press.

*Shapiro, D. L., B. H. Sheppard, and L. Cheraskin. 1992. In Theory: Business on a handshake. *Negotiation Journal* 8(4):365–377.

*Shapiro, M. 1981. *Courts: A comparative and political analysis.* Chicago: University of Chicago Press.

*Shubik, M. 1971. The Dollar Auction Game: A paradox in noncooperative behavior and escalation. *Journal of Conflict Resolution* 15:109–111.

Smith, S. 2001. Mandatory arbitration clauses in consumer contracts: Consumer protection and the circumvention of the judicial system. *DePaul Law Review* 50:1191–1251.

Speidel, R. E. 1998. Consumer arbitration of statutory claims: Has pre-dispute mandatory arbitration outlived its welcome? *Arizona Law Review* 40:1069–1094.

Spohn, G. 1998. With no lawyers in sight, landlords and tenants talk out disputes. *http://www.mediate.com/articles/landlord. cfm* (accessed March 4, 2009).

Springer, A. K. 1991. Telephone family therapy: An untapped resource. *Family Therapy* 18(2):123–128.

Stark, B. 2000. Bottom line feminist theory: The dream of a common language. *Harvard Women's Law Journal* 23 (Spring):227–246.

Stempel, J. W. 2000. Identifying real dichotomies underlying the false dichotomy: Twenty-first century mediation in an eclectic regime. *Journal of Dispute Resolution* 2000:371–394.

Sternlight, J. R. 2001. Mandatory binding arbitration and the demise of the Seventh Amendment right to a jury trial. *Ohio State Journal on Dispute Resolution* 16(3):669–733.

Streeter-Schaefer, H. A. 2001. A look at court mandated civil mediation. *Drake Law Review* 49:367–389.

Stulberg, J. B. 2002. Symposium on the impact of mediation: 25 years after the pound conference: Questions. *Ohio State Journal on Dispute Resolution* 17(3):532–534.

*Taslitz, A. E. 1998. An African-American sense of fact: The O. J. trial and black judges on justice. *The Boston Public Interest Law Journal* 7 (spring):219–249.

Teitz, L. E. 2001. Providing legal services for the middle class in cyberspace: The promise and challenge of on-line dispute resolution. *Fordham Law Review* 70 (December): 985–1016.

*Tesler, P. H. 1999. Family law: Collaborative law: A new paradigm for divorce lawyers. *Psychology, Public Policy and Law* 5 (December):967–1000.

Tesler, P. H. 2001. *Collaborative law: Achieving effective resolution in divorce without litigation.* Chicago: American Bar Association, Section of Family Law.

Thaxter, C. 2008. Form mediation/arbitration clause. *http://www.curtisthaxter.com/pub.php?id=12* (accessed February 3, 2009).

TheDoctors.com. 2004. Physician-patient arbitration agreement (Web-based PDF file). *http://www.thedoctors.com/ecm/groups/public/@tdc/@web/documents/document/agreementsample.pdf.pdf* (accessed 25 November 2008).

Thompson & Thompson: A Professional Corporation. 2008. Sample arbitration/mediation (ADR) clauses. *http://www.t-tlaw.com/bus-09.htm* (accessed February 3, 2009).

*Tinsley, C. 1998. Models of conflict resolution in Japanese, German, and American cultures. *Journal of Applied Psychology* 83(2):316–323.

Tondo, C-A., R. Coronel, and B. Drucker. 2001. Mediation trends: A survey of the states. *Family Court Review* 39 (October):431–445.

*Trope, J. 1986. Identification and inferential processes in dispositional attribution. *Psychological Review* 93(3):239–257.

Trubisky, P., S. Ting-Toomey, and S.-L. Lin. 1991. The influence of individualism-collectivism and self-monitoring on conflict styles. *International Journal of Intercultural Relations* 15:65–84.

Ury, W., J. M. Brett, and S. B. Goldberg. 1988. *Getting disputes resolved: Designing systems to cut the costs of conflict.* San Francisco: Jossey-Bass.

*van de Vliert, E., and B. Kabanoff. 1990. Toward theory-based measures of conflict management. *Academy of Management Journal* 33(1):199–209.

van de Vliert, E., and H. C. M. Prein. 1989. The difference in the meaning of forcing in the conflict management of actors and observers. In *Managing conflict: An interdisciplinary approach.* Edited by M.A. Rahim. New York: Praeger.

ver Steegh, N. 2003. Yes, no, and maybe: Informed decision making about divorce mediation in the presence of domestic violence. *William and Mary Journal of Women and the Law* 9:145–206.

Vestal, A. 1999. Mediation and parental alienation syndrome: Considerations for an intervention model. *Family and Conciliation Courts Review* 38 (October):487–502.

*Vidmar, N., and N. M. Laird. 1983. Adversary social roles: Their effects on witnesses' communication of evidence and the assessments of adjudicators. *Journal of Personality and Social Psychology* 44(5):888–898.

Vincent, M. 1995. Mandatory mediation of custody disputes: Criticism, legislation, and support. *Vermont Law Review* 20:255–297.

Wade, J. 2001. Don't waste my time on negotiation and mediation: This dispute needs a judge. *Mediation Quarterly* 18 (Spring):259–280.

Waldman, E. A. 1997. Identifying the role of social norms in mediation: A multiple model approach. *Hastings Law Journal* 48 (April):703–769.

*Wallerstein, J. S., and J. B. Kelly. 1980. *Surviving the breakup: How children and parents cope with divorce.* New York: Basic Books.

Warmbrod, M. L. 1997. Could an attorney face disciplinary actions or even legal malpractice liability for failure to inform clients of alternative dispute resolution? *Cumberland Law Review* 27:791–819.

* *Washington Post.* 1998. *Direct access: Jesse Jackson.* Washingtonpost.com. [Online interview of Jesse Jackson.] 16 December. [Cited 22 July 2002.] Available from *http://www.washingtonpost.com/wp-srv/politics/talk/zforum/jackson121698.htm.*

*Weider-Hatfield, D. 1988. Assessing the Rahim Organizational Conflict Inventory–II (ROCI–II). *Management Communication Quarterly* 1(3):350–356.

Welsh, N. A. 2001a. Making deals in court-connected mediation: What's justice got to do with it? *Washington University Law Quarterly* 79:787–861.

Welsh, N. A. 2001b. The thinning vision of self-determination in court-connected mediation: The inevitable price of institutionalization? *Harvard Negotiation Law Review* 6 (Spring):1–96.

Weston, M. A. 2001. Checks on participant conduct in compulsory ADR: Reconciling the tension in the need for good-faith participation, autonomy, and confidentiality. *Indiana Law Journal* 76 (Summer):591–645.

Wiegand, S. A. 1996. A just and lasting peace: Supplanting mediation with the ombuds model. *Ohio State Journal on Dispute Resolution* 12:95–145.

*Wilder, D. A. 1981. Perceiving persons as a group: Categorization and intergroup relations. In *Cognitive processes and intergroup behavior*, edited by D.L. Hamilton. Hillsdale, NJ: Lawrence Erlbaum.

*Williams, G. R. 1983. *Legal negotiation and settlement.* St. Paul, MN: West.

*Williams, G. R. 1996. Negotiation as a healing process. *Journal of Dispute Resolution* 1996:1–66.

*Wolfe, J. S. 2001. Alternative dispute resolution in the twenty-first century: Across the ripple of time: The future of alternative (or, is it "appropriate?") dispute resolution. *Tulsa Law Journal* 36 (summer):785–812.

Woodley, A. E. 1997. Strengthening the summary jury trial: A proposal to increase its effectiveness and encourage uniformity in its use. *Ohio State Journal on Dispute Resolution* 12:541–620.

Woodrow, P. 1998. *Reducing the costs of conflict through dispute resolution systems design. http://www.mediate.com/workplace/woodrow.cfm* (accessed March 4, 2009). Reprinted from *Track Two* 7(2), a quarterly publication of the Centre for Conflict Resolution and the Media Peace Centre (South Africa).

*Word, C. O., M. P. Zanna, and J. Cooper. 1974. The nonverbal mediation of self-fulfilling prophecies in interracial interaction. *Journal of Experimental Social Psychology* 10:109–120.

Wright, N. 2008. Collaborative divorce practice: A revolution in family law. *Arizona Attorney* 44 (January):36–39.

Young, P. M. 2001. One-text mediation process: Clinton's Christmas 2000 proposal to the Israelis and Palestinians. First published by the *St. Louis Lawyer* (February 2001). *http://www.mediate.com/articles/young1.cfm* (accessed January 26, 2009).

Young, P. M. 2006. Rejoice! Rejoice! Rejoice, give thanks, and sing: ABA, ACR, and AAA adopt revised model standards of conduct for mediators. *Appalachian Journal of Law,* 5 (Spring):195–239.

Zirkel, P. A., and A. Krahmal. 2001. Creeping legalism in grievance arbitration: Fact or fiction? *Ohio State Journal on Dispute Resolution* 16:243–265.

Zumeta, Z. D. 2000a. A facilitative mediator responds. *Journal of Dispute Resolution* 2000:335–341.

Zumeta, Z. D. 2000b. Styles of mediation: Facilitative, evaluative, and transformative mediation. *http://www. mediate.com/articles/zumeta.cfm* (accessed March 4, 2009).

Table of Legal References*

CASES

AT&T Techs., Inc. v. Communications Workers of Am., 475 U.S. 643, 650, 89 L. Ed. 2d 648, 106 S. Ct. 1415 (1986)

BJC Health Sys. v. Group Health Plan, 30 S.W. 3d 198 (Ct.App.Mo., 2000)

Brotherton v. Cleveland, 141 F. Supp. 2d 907, 911 (S.D. Ohio, 2001)

Brown v. Board of Education, 347 U.S. 483 (1954)

Buckeye Check Cashing, Inc. v. Cardegna, 546 U.S. 440, 126 S. Ct. 1204, 163 L. Ed. 2d 1038 (2006)

Caley v. Gulfstream Aero. Corp., 428 F. 3d 1359 (C.A. 11, 2005)

Carman v. McDonnell Douglas Corp., 114 F. 3d 790 (C.A. 8 1997)

Chicago Fire Fighters Union Local No. 2 v. City of Chicago, 323 Ill. App. 3d 168 (2001)

Circuit City Stores v. Adams, 279 F. 3d 889 (C.A. 9 2002)

Cooper v. MRM Inv. Co., 367 F. 3d 493 (C.A. 6, 2004)

D'Iorio v. Majestic Lanes, 370 F. 3d 354 (C.A. 3, 2004)

Doctor's Associates, Inc. v. Casarotto, 517 U.S. 681 (1996)

Dominguez v. Finish Line, Inc., 439 F. Supp. 2d 688 (W.D. Tex. 2006)

Eastern Associated Coal Corporation v. United Mine Workers of America, 531 U.S. 57 (2000)

EEOC v. Gear Petroleum, Inc., 948 F. 2d 1542 (C.A. 10, 1991)

EEOC v. Waffle House, 534 U.S. 279 (2002)

EEOC v. Woodmen of the World Life Ins. Soc'y, 479 F. 3d 561 (C.A. 8, 2007)

Folb v. Motion Picture Industry Pension & Health Plans, 16 F. Supp. 2d 1164, D.C. Cal., 1998, aff'd 216 F. 3d 1082 (C.A. 9 2000)

Foxgate Homeowners' Association, Inc., v. Bramalea, 26 Cal. 4th 1 (2001) 621, 622

Furia v. Helm, 111 Cal.App.4th 945 (2003)

*Gardner v. Florida, 430 U.S. 349 (1977)

Gilmer v. Interstate/Johnson Lane Corp., 500 U.S. 20 (1991)

Green Tree Finance Corp. of Alabama v. Randolph, 531 U.S. 79, 148 L. Ed. 2d 373, 121 S. Ct. 513 (2000)

Gunter v. Ridgewood Energy Corp., 32 F. Supp. 2d 162 (D. NJ 1998)

Haghhighi v. Russian-American Broadcasting Co., 577 N.W. 2d 927 (Minn. 1998)

Hall Street Assoc. v. Mattel, 170 L. Ed. 2d 254 (2008).

Highlands Wellmont Health Network v. John Deere Health Plan, 350 F. 3d 568 (C.A. 6, 2003)

Hobley v. Kentucky Fried Chicken, Inc., No. 04-7202, 2005 WL 3838163, at 1 (D.C. Cir. Dec. 22, 2005), cert. denied, 126 S. Ct. 2058 (2006)

Hooters of America v. Phillips, 173 F. 3d 933 (C.A. 4 1999)

In re Telectronics Pacing Sys. 137 F. Supp. 2d 985 (S.D. Ohio, 2001)

In re Waller, 573 A. 2d 780 (D.C. 1990)

International Ass'n of Machinists, Local Number 402 v. Cutler-Hammer, Inc., 297 N.Y. 519 (1947)

International, LLC. v. Hercules Steel Co., 441 F. 3d 905 (C.A.11, 2006)

John Wiley & Sons v. Livingston, 376 U.S. 543 (1964)

* Mackey v. Montrym, 443 U.S. 1 (1979)

Mastrobuono v. Shearson Lehman Hutton, 514 U.S. 52 (1995)

Mitsubishi v. Soler, 473 U.S. 614 (1985)

Montes v. Shearson Lehman Bros., 128 F. 3d 1456 (C.A. 11, 1997)

Morewitz v. West of England Ship Owners Mutual Protection and Indemnity Ass'n, 62 F. 3d 1356, 1366 (11th Cir. 1995)

Morgan Phillips, Inc. v. JAMS/Endispute, L.L.C., 140 Cal. App. 4th 795 (2006)

Moses H. Cone Memorial Hospital v. Mercury Construction Corp., 460 U.S. 1 (1983)

Olam v. Congress Mortgage Company, 68 F. Supp. 2d 1110 (N.D. Cal., 1999)

Patten v. Signator Insurance Agency, Inc., 441 F. Supp. 2d 230, 232 (4th Cir. 2006), cert. denied, 127 S. Ct. 434 (2006)

*Polk County v. Dodson, 454 U.S. 312 (1981)

Poly Software International, Inc. v. Su, 880 F. Supp. 1487 (D. Utah 1995)

Preston v. Ferrer, 169 L. Ed. 2d 917 (2008)

Prima Paint Corp. v. Flood & Conklin Mfg. Corp., 388 U.S. 395 (1967)

Rinaker v. Superior Court, 62 Cal. App. 4th 155 (1998)

Rodriguez de Quijas v. Shearson/American Express, 490 U.S. 477 (1989)

Rojas v. Superior Court, 33 Cal. 4th 407 (2004)

Ross vs. American Express, et al., 2005-2 Trade Cas. (CCH) P74, 973 (S.D.N.Y., 2005)

Smith v. Smith, 154 F.R.D. 661 (N.D. Texas, 1994)

---

*References marked with an astrisk appear in Online Appendix B, available at www.prenhall.com/coltri

ETHICS OPINIONS

CONSTITUTIONAL PROVISIONS, STATUTES, RULES, REGULATIONS

UNIFORM ACTS

TREATIES AND CONVENTIONS

CODES OF ETHICS

---

*Pages prefaced by a "B-" refer to Online Appendix B. Italicized page numbers refer to figures, photographs, and tables.

308